Poor Banished Children of Eve

"Gale Yee has written a book that significantly advances our critical thinking about the ways in which ideology permeates scripture. The power of her analysis is that she offers a rare combination of grounded, well-articulated critical theory alongside a careful, attentive reading of texts...a rare combination in current discussions! Her book focuses on "how the biblical text legitimates such oppressive struggles in our time" concerning gender exploitation. The consequence of such a legitimization is all around us in social fallout. Yee goes behind current evidence of such oppressive struggles to consider the power of textual legitimization. Her book is compelling in requiring our steadfast rethinking on such issues."

—Walter Brueggemann
author of Theology of the Old Testament

more praise
for *Poor Banished Children of Eve*

"Poor Banished Children of Eve *is a tour de force. In this provocative and methodologically sophisticated work Gale Yee takes feminist scholarship on the Hebrew Bible to new levels. Combining traditional feminist critique with analyses of ethnicity, class, and colonial status, Yee discloses the complex forces that invisibly shape the symbolic representation of women. Even skeptics of materialist approaches will learn much from these studies. This book is essential reading for all who are interested in the future of feminist study of the Hebrew Bible."*

—Carol A. Newsom
editor of The Women's Bible Commentary

"*Using materialist-feminist analysis, Yee studies texts from the tenth century* B.C.E. *to the post-exilic period where 'female' is a signifying code for 'evil.' With keen insight and careful methodological controls, the author situates the Hebrew Bible's gender ideologies within the interlocking systems of racism, classism and colonialism in biblical Israel. This focus, wed to close textual readings, makes this work a welcome entry point into ideological criticism of texts whose ostensible subject is gender. For someone who is serious about the Bible or justice, this book is a 'must-have.'*"

—Carole Fontaine
author of Smooth Words:
Women, Proverbs, and Performance in Biblical Wisdom

"*Yee's book was satisfying and provocative in equal measure. It sets a new standard for feminist analysis of texts from the Hebrew Scriptures by reaching a new level of historical sophistication. Yee demonstrates brilliantly how ideological criticism of biblical texts can benefit from an adroit grasp of the complexities of ideology coupled with a comprehensive and nuanced social-historical perspective."*

—Robert Coote
author of Power, Politics, and the Making of the Bible

Poor Banished Children of Eve

woman as evil
in the hebrew bible

Gale A. Yee

Fortress Press
MINNEAPOLIS

POOR BANISHED CHILDREN OF EVE
Woman as Evil in the Hebrew Bible

Scripture quotations are from the NRSV unless otherwise noted.

Scripture quotations from the Revised Standard Version of the Bible are copyright © 1946, 1952, 1971 by the Division of Christian Education of the National Council of the Churches of Christ in the USA. Used by permission.

Scripture quotations from the New Revised Standard Version Bible are copyright © 1989 by the Division of Christian Education of the National Council of the Churches of Christ in the USA and used by permission.

Cover image: Sitting nude by Amadeo Modigliani (1884–1920). Pen and red wash. © Erich Lessing/Art Resource 2003. Used by permission.
Cover and book design: Ann Delgehausen
Author photo: Beverly Hall

Library of Congress Cataloging-in-Publication Data
Yee, Gale A.
ISBN: 0-8006-3457-8

The paper used in this publication meets the minimum requirements of American National Standard for Information Sciences—Permanence of Paper for Printed Library Materials, ANSI Z329.48-1984.

Manufactured in the U.S.A.
07   06   05   04   03   1   2   3   4   5   6   7   8   9   10

Contents

Abbreviations

AARASRS	American Academy of Religion Aids for the Study of Religion Series
AB	Anchor Bible
ABD	*Anchor Bible Dictionary,* ed. David Noel Freedman, 6 vols., 1992
ABRL	*Anchor Bible Reference Library*
AJSL	*American Journal of Semitic Languages and Literature*
AmAnth	*American Anthropologist*
AmEth	*American Ethnologist*
ANET	*Ancient Near Eastern Texts Relating to the Old Testament,* ed. James B. Pritchard, 3rd ed., 1969
AnthQ	*Anthropological Quarterly*
AOAT	Alter Orient und Altes Testament
BA	*Biblical Archaeologist*
BAR	*Biblical Archaeology Review*
BASOR	*Bulletin of the American Schools of Oriental Research*
B.C.E.	Before the Common Era
BETL	Bibliotheca Ephemeridum Theologicarum Lovaniensium
Bib	*Biblica*
BibInt	*Biblical Interpretation*
BibIntSer	BibInt Series
BibLitSer	Bible and Literature Series

BibOr   Biblica et orientalia
BibSem   Biblical Seminar
BJS   Brown Judaic Studies
BRev   *Bible Review*
BTB   *Biblical Theology Bulletin*
BWANT   Beiträge zur Wissenschaft vom Alten und Neuen
                  Testament
BZ   *Biblische Zeitschrift*
BZAW   Beihefte zur ZAW
CANE   *Civilizations of the Ancient Near East,* ed. Jack M.
                  Sasson, 4 vols., 1995
CBQ   *Catholic Biblical Quarterly*
CBQMS   CBQ Monograph Series
CC   Continental Commentaries
C.E.   Common Era
CRBS   *Currents in Research: Biblical Studies*
Cultu fem.   Tertullian, *De cultu feminarum* (The Apparel
                  of Women)
ETL   Ephemerides theologicae lovanienses
FCB   Feminist Companion to the Bible
FOTL   Forms of the Old Testament Literature
FRLANT   Forschungen zur Religion und Literatur des Alten
                  und Neuen Testaments
GBS   Guides to Biblical Scholarship
HAR   *Hebrew Annual Review*
HAT   Handbuch zum Alten Testament
HBT   *Horizons in Biblical Theology*
HSM   Harvard Semitic Monographs
HTR   *Harvard Theological Review*
IBC   Interpretation: A Bible Commentary for Teaching
                  and Preaching
ICC   International Critical Commentary
IDB   *Interpreter's Dictionary of the Bible,* ed. George A.
                  Buttrick, 4 vols., 1962
IDBSup   *IDB Supplementary Volume,* ed. Keith Crim, 1976
ISBL   Indiana Studies in Biblical Literature
JAAR   *Journal of the American Academy of Religion*
JANESCU   *Journal of the Ancient Near Eastern Society
                  of Columbia University*
JAOS   *Journal of the American Oriental Society*

JBL	*Journal of Biblical Literature*
JFSR	*Journal of Feminist Studies in Religion*
JNES	*Journal of Near Eastern Studies*
JNSL	*Journal of Northwest Semitic Languages*
JQR	*Jewish Quarterly Review*
JQRSup	JQR Supplements
JSJSup	Journal for the Study of Judaism Supplements
JSOT	*Journal for the Study of the Old Testament*
JSOTSup	JSOT Supplement Series
JSPSup	Journal for the Study of the Pseudepigrapha Supplements
JTS	*Journal of Theological Studies*
LAI	Library of Ancient Israel
MScRel	*Mélanges de science religieuse*
MT	Masoretic text
MTZ	*Münchener theologische Zeitschrift*
NCBC	New Century Bible Commentary
NIB	*New Interpreter's Bible*
NICOT	New International Commentary on the Old Testament
NJB	New Jerusalem Bible
NRSV	New Revised Standard Version
OBO	Orbis biblicus et orientalis
OBT	Overtures to Biblical Theology
OTE	*Old Testament Essays*
OTG	Old Testament Guides
OTL	Old Testament Library
OTM	Old Testament Message
OTR	Old Testament Readings
OtSt	*Oudtestamentische Studiën*
PEQ	*Palestine Exploration Quarterly*
PTSD	Post-traumatic stress disorder
R&T	*Religion and Theology*
RB	*Revue biblique*
RHR	*Revue de l'histoire des religions*
RNBC	Readings: A New Biblical Commentary
RSR	*Religious Studies Review*
RSV	Revised Standard Version
SBL	Society of Biblical Literature
SBLBSNA	SBL Biblical Scholarship in North America

SBLDS	SBL Dissertation Series
SBLEJL	SBL Early Judaism and Its Literature
SBLMS	SBL Monograph Series
SBLSP	*SBL Seminar Papers*
SBLSymSer	SBL Symposium Series
SemeiaSt	Semeia Studies
SFSHJ	South Florida Studies in the History of Judaism
SHANE	Studies in the History of the Ancient Near East
SHCANE	Studies in the History and Culture of the Ancient Near East
SJOT	*Scandinavian Journal of the Old Testament*
SJT	*Scottish Journal of Theology*
SO	*Symbolae Osloenses*
SWBA	Social World of Biblical Antiquity
SWJA	*Southwestern Journal of Anthropology*
TCS	Texts from Cuneiform Sources
TDOT	*Theological Dictionary of the Old Testament,* ed. G. Johannes Botterweck et al., 12 vols., 1977–
ThBü	Theologische Bücherei
Transeu	*Transeuphratène*
TS	*Theological Studies*
UF	*Ugarit-Forschungen*
USQR	*Union Seminary Quarterly Review*
VT	*Vetus Testamentum*
VTSup	VT Supplements
WBC	Word Biblical Commentary
WomBibCom	*Women's Bible Commentary,* ed. Carol A. Newsom and Sharon H. Ringe, 1992
WTJ	*Westminster Theological Journal*
ZAW	*Zeitschrift für die alttestamentliche Wissenschaft*

Preface

I am sure to forget someone in these acknowledgments, so please forgive me! I would like to thank Anthony R. Ceresko, O.S.F.S., Chris Franke, Pamela Milne, Carol Newsom, Michael Patrick O'Connor, and Naomi Steinberg, who have read some portion of this book and gave me their perceptive commentary.

I am grateful to the members of the Old Testament Colloquium, in which several of these chapters were presented and critiqued, especially Corrine Patton, Kathleen M. O'Connor, and Mark S. Smith.

Muchas gracias to Bruce J. Malina and John J. Pilch for their friendly counsel and support, particularly in the writing of chapter 3, and to Richard J. Clifford, S.J., whose great wisdom on the book of Proverbs helped the writing of chapter 7.

Merci beaucoup to my faculty colleagues at the Episcopal Divinity School, Kwok Pui Lan, Larry Wills, Angela Bauer, Joanna Dewey, Christopher Duraisingh, and Andrew McGowan, who commented on presentations of several chapters at different venues of the Boston Theological Institute.

Danke schön to Naomi Steinberg, Victor Matthews, Claudia Camp, and Daniel Smith-Christopher for prepublication manuscripts of their work.

I want to say *xie xie* to the members of the Ethnic Chinese Biblical Colloquium, where chapter 4 and chapter 6 were presented. Chapter 6 was my April 2002 Presidential Address as outgoing president of the colloquium.

I am exceedingly grateful to the University of St. Thomas sabbatical and maxi-grant program and to the Episcopal Divinity School Theological Writing Fund and sabbatical program for making it financially possible to complete this book.

Chapter 4 is an expanded version of my article "Gender, Class, and the Social-Scientific Study of Genesis 2–3," *Semeia* 87 (1999) 177–92. Chapter 5 is a modified version of "'She Is Not My Wife, and I Am Not Her Husband': A Materialist Analysis of Hosea 1–2," *Biblical Interpretation* 9 (2001) 345–83. I thank both *Semeia* and *Biblical Interpretation* for their permission to reprint these articles.

Kudos to Liza Wirtz, copy editor extraordinaire, who helped me with the infelicities of my writing.

I thank Ann Delgehausen of Fortress Press for seeing this book through the production period.

Finally, I am grateful to K. C. Hanson and Michael West for taking on this project for Fortress Press.

I have employed English versification when it differs from the Masoretic text. Readers of the Hebrew text will note that this is an issue in relatively few cases, primarily in chapter 5 on Hosea.

I am dedicating this book to my new nieces who have come into my life this year: Olivia, Miranda, and Danielle Grace. To an auntie, jaded from writing a book on the "poor banished children of Eve," they are a breath of fresh air and hope.

1 *Introduction*

The Problem

In this book I investigate the problem of the symbolization of woman as the incarnation of moral evil, sin, devastation, and death in the Hebrew Bible, and how this symbolization of a particular gender interconnects with the issues of race/ethnicity, class, and colonialism during the times of its production. Holding man in thrall by her irresistible attractions, woman embodies all that is destructive in man's experience, seducing him away from God and a life of good down paths of moral perversity and entrapment. As a foundational text in Western civilization, the Bible has been and continues to be a significant *fons et origo* of religious and social attitudes about gender, race/ethnicity, class, and colonialism. Its portrayal of woman as the embodiment of sin and corruption takes a number of forms, beginning with the one who ostensibly started it all—Eve, the very first woman, the wife of Adam, the mother of all living:

> From a woman sin had its beginning,
> and because of her we all die. (Sir 25:24)

Besides the story of Eve in Genesis 1–3, intertestamental speculation on the origin of evil also looks to Gen 6:1-8.[1] Here, the illicit sexual union between the sons of God and the daughters of men and their perverse spawn, the Nephilim, provokes God into sending the flood to destroy all of sinful humanity—all except for Noah and company.

1

The Otherness of the Nephilim, half human/half divine, becomes a signifier for evil. Racial/ethnic Otherness is particularly seen in biblical depictions of ethnically foreign women, who become incarnations of sexual danger and destruction in the piety and lives of Israelite males. The Egyptian Ms. Potiphar falsely accuses the patriarch Joseph of rape charges and lands him in jail (Gen 39:6-23). Even before the settlement of Canaan, the women of Moab seduce Israelite men to abandon their covenant with YHWH and yoke themselves to the Baal of Peor (Num 25:1-5). An Israelite man marries the Midianite noblewoman, Cozbi, and gets speared by a self-righteous priest, presumably during sexual intercourse with her (Num 25:6-15). Philistine females are Samson's peculiar vulnerability and downfall (Judges 14–16). Although he is ostensibly a "wise" man, marriages to foreign women become the ruin of the great King Solomon himself (1 Kgs 11:1-13). Ahab's Sidonian queen, Jezebel, and the religious and political havoc she creates cause both his own demise and that of his dynasty in Israel (1 Kgs 16:30-33; 18–19; 21; 2 Kgs 9:21-37). The problems of intermarriages with "foreign"[2] women especially afflict the postexilic period (Ezra 9–10; Neh 13:23-27). The book of Proverbs, written during this time, personifies the incontrovertible dangers these women present to elite Jewish men in the *'iššâ zârâ*, the Other Woman. This seductive woman is the antithesis to the object of desire sanctioned by the Jewish upper classes: Woman Wisdom.

In their own particular fashion, the prophets incarnate in female form the people's desertion of God's covenant to worship the gods of the land. In the book of Hosea, an adulterous wife Israel whores away from YHWH (Hosea 2). For Jeremiah, a wild ass in heat sniffs the wind in her lust (Jer 2:24-25). For the priest Ezekiel, Woman exemplifies a number of female relationships in their dissolute modes: wife, sister, mother, daughter. She is not only the nymphomaniacal wife Jerusalem (16:1-43), but also the corrupt daughter of a pagan mother (16:44-45). She becomes two sisters who outdo each other in lewdness and promiscuity (16:46-63; 23:1-49; cf. Jer 3:6-10).

Finally, the foreign city of Babylon becomes a symbol of disgrace and humiliation as a virgin daughter who sits in the dust (Isaiah 47; Jer 50:11-16). She is reincarnated as the ultimate symbol of fornication and corruption, the Whore of the book of Revelation, seated upon the scarlet beast, "drunk with the blood of the saints and the blood of the witnesses to Jesus" (Rev 17:1—18:24). In short, the men writing the Bible used women, particularly those who were socially, culturally, and racially Other, as tropes for evil and destruction.

Nevertheless, the symbolization of woman as evil is not a problem restricted to the biblical tradition. There is, of course, the Greek tale of Pandora, whose name ironically means "all gift." Zeus "gives" her to Prometheus as punishment for the latter's theft of divine fire. Created by a committee of several gods and goddesses, Pandora is the "evil which [men] will all delight in,"[3] with "the looks of an immortal goddess," "the mind of a bitch and the temper of a thief."[4] This feminine "booby trap"[5] opens a great jar and releases into the world every dismal evil and affliction that Zeus plans for mortals.[6]

Besides Pandora, we have the Sirens (and their German counterparts, the Lorelei), the bird-women with their sweet song, beckoning men in their ships to their deaths on the Sirens' rocky shore.[7] In legends of the *vagina dentata*, her snapping teeth ultimately personify men's obsessive anxiety about castration.[8] Witches at different points in history become the insidious nexus of evil, woman, and religion.[9] *La Belle Dame Sans Merci*, the Femme Fatale, the Treacherous Woman[10]—these are just some of the names given to Woman the Other, who, according to widespread belief, is the definitive embodiment of evil, destruction, and death itself:

> In the myths of North American Indians the first woman was the cause of all evil and brought death into the world. The northern Déné hold the same doctrine. "They have not forgotten," observes Father Petitot, "the ancient tradition which modern superior persons affect to disbelieve." The Eskimo also believe that death was brought into the world by a woman. The ancient Mexicans ascribed all the miseries of the world to the first woman, whom Father Sahagun and Don Pedro Ponce identify with Eve. The first woman is regarded as having brought death into the world by the Baila of Rhodesia, by the natives of Calabar, by the Baluka, the Kosai, and the natives of Equator Station, and by the Balola of the Congo. The tribes around Lake Tanganyika relate how a woman brought about the destruction of mankind; and the Wamyamwezi believe that men would have been immortal but for the first woman who introduced death into the world. Among the Baganda the first woman was the sister of death and the cause of human mortality. The Kabyls of the Sahara ascribe the origin of death to the first woman. Woman is likewise held responsible

for the origin of death in Melanesia. The Igorots of Luzon have a legend to the effect that the first woman instigated men to fight; previously they had lived in peace with one another. *Woman is, in fact, universally regarded as having brought death into the world and all our woe.*[11]

The Intent of This Book

It is not my intention to catalog and classify in this book the various ways in which the symbolization of woman as evil has developed in its literary shape over time. Some of this work has already been done in specialized studies.[12] My primary focus is the Hebrew Bible. Many Western attitudes toward women as a sexual threat to be avoided, exploited, suppressed, and used have their roots precisely in this ancient religious text. This work, which is foundational in more ways than one, has left its imprint on the creation of a symbol that permeates Western consciousness. As an Asian American biblical scholar coming from a lower-class background, I have become convinced in my feminist investigations of the Bible over the years that the study of gender must include race, class, and colonial status as categories of analysis. Therefore, in my study of the woman as evil, I explore any relationships between the sexism embodied in this symbol and other forms of oppression, such as racism, classism, and colonialism, in reinforcing a hegemony of domination in ancient Israel. I wish to see how ideologies of gender, race/ethnicity, economic class, and colonial status in the biblical text are interconnected with the sociopolitical structures that produced them.

The method that informs my examination, then, is ideological criticism, which incorporates a systemic analysis of interlocking oppressions. I will discuss this method at length in chapter 2. The ideological criticism I advocate in this book is a materialist-feminist investigation that correlates sexist and/or racist ideologies, such as the symbolization of foreign women as evil, with the modes of production that construct them. It takes seriously the nexus of discourse and power—namely, ideology itself, which gives meaning and coherence to material reality while concealing the fact that it is also produced in gendered, racial, economic, and/or colonial sites of struggle and competing claims. My investigation is two-pronged. Using an *ex-*

trinsic analysis, I determine the complex interrelationship between material modes of production and ideologies in the society that produces the biblical text. My *intrinsic analysis* investigates the rhetorical strategies of the text itself to ascertain the different ways in which the text inscribes and reworks ideology.

The extrinsic analysis utilizes social-scientific methods to help shed light on the sociohistorical circumstances of a text's production. I cover these methods, the questions they ask, their strengths and weaknesses, and what they have theorized regarding the social world of the Hebrew Bible in chapter 3. This chapter tries to reconstruct the nature of gender relationships during pre-state Israel and the ideologies of kinship and honor/shame that give them meaning. Two aspects of women's lives in ancient Israel have direct bearing on the symbolization of woman as evil. First, women exercised informal power by engaging in socially subversive or disruptive acts against men in authority. Their weapons of the weak included gossiping, lying, fractious behavior, sexual manipulation, and so on. This conflict-indicating behavior is encoded in biblical ideologies of woman as evil. Second, women existed in a separate world in ancient Israel, to which men had little or no access. Women exploited this segregation for their own benefit, which is the major reason why it is not described in the Hebrew Bible. The biblical text primarily narrates and legitimizes male ideologies. Its authors had no firsthand experience of women's separate world. The symbolization of woman as evil encodes this separate world as a double absence.

Chapters 4 through 7 provide extrinsic and intrinsic analyses of four specific biblical texts. Instead of dealing with narratives of "evil" female characters in the Hebrew Bible, such as Ms. Potiphar, Jezebel, or Delilah, I have chosen texts in which "woman" becomes a trope for a particular social group or nation, one embodying evil, sinfulness, and "otherness." I draw these texts from four different historical periods of Israelite history: the tenth century B.C.E., the eighth century B.C.E., the exilic period, and the postexilic period. Each is produced in societies operating under distinctive modes of production, and each utilizes different rhetorical strategies to make its ideological point.

Chapter 4 focuses on the Yahwist creation narrative (Genesis 2–3) and the person of Eve, who is reputed to have caused the downfall of "man." In this chapter, as well as in those following, I observe that gender in this (in)famous text cannot be studied in isolation from socioeconomic class. Since it *seems* to be a story primarily about male-female relations, Genesis 2–3 mystifies and conceals the class interests in the text. To legitimate royal interests and to justify the exploitation of the peasantry, Genesis 2–3 shifts the point of conflict from the public arena of class relations between men to the more private domain of household relations between men and women. Stressing the nuclear family and the marriage bond in these domestic relations, the story simultaneously subverts lineages and other local power groups that threaten the emerging state.

Chapter 5 analyzes Hosea 1–2, which portrays the northern kingdom of Israel as an adulterous wife, the unfaithful partner in the covenant between God and the nation. In this chapter, I investigate the eighth-century B.C.E. mode of production that was operative during Hosea's time. Hosea denounces this mode of production, which involved both a royal agricultural intensification and a foreign policy that exploited the peasantry. The public, state veneration of the baals comprised the cultic expression of this oppressive mode of production. Hosea directs his condemnation against the ruling elite, feminized in a metaphor of an adulterous wife who runs after her lovers (foreign nations). Through this metaphor, Hosea theologically proclaims a polemical monolatry that places him in continuity with the YHWH-alone movement that would become normative for Israel during the exilic and postexilic periods.

In chapter 6 I move to the exilic period and to the pornographic depiction in Ezekiel 23 of Israel and Judah as two nymphomaniacs. I incorporate insights from postcolonial feminists and trauma studies in order to understand the text's excessively graphic descriptions of sex and violence. Chapter 23 is Ezekiel's attempt to work through and integrate his traumatic experiences of colonization, conquest, and exile. Colluding with the androcentric ideologies he shares with his colonizer, the upper-class priest (re)presents these experiences as an extended metaphor about two rival promiscuous sisters. His text reflects the collective trauma of his class and ethnic group as symbolic, if not physical, emasculation. Encoded in his texts are a series of male racialized Others who sexually partner with the sisters in this eroticized revisionist history.

Chapter 7 takes us to the postexilic period of Yehud under Persian colonization. Here I investigate the personified adversary of Woman Wisdom in Proverbs 1–9—the *'iššâ zārâ*, which I translate as the "Other Woman." The elites return from exile as Persian functionaries to a land that has gotten along quite well without them for decades. In order to obtain the land that they lost during the exile, the returnees intermarry with ethnic Jews who remained in the land and with landowning ethnic foreignors. However, a crisis regarding these intermarriages develops generations later under Ezra and Nehemiah. Proverbs 1–9 encodes the economically driven preoccupation of the upper classes to have their sons marry the "correct" wife. Nevertheless, the apparent absence of economic class in Proverbs 1–9 symbolically resolves the ideological and material contradictions in Yehud between rich and poor, between the exiles and those who stayed in the land.

I began this work years ago, intending to study *woman* as evil in these texts. It was a great discovery for me to find that my gender-focused investigation increasingly involved an analysis of economic class, race/ethnicity, and colonial status in ancient Israel. It is hoped that readers of this book expecting a gender-centered study will also recognize the necessity of analyzing gender in the broader context of class, race, and colonialism. This is especially the case when considering the other "evil" women in the Bible whom I did not include in this book. Privileging gender blinds one to the fact that sexism interlocks with other social forms of oppression and exploitation, which are then encoded in the biblical text. Only when our exegesis incorporates this broader analysis will we be able to critique effectively how the biblical text legitimates such oppressive structures in our own time. This book stands as a modest contribution toward this end.

2 Ideological Criticism and Woman as Evil

> *What persuades men and women to mistake each other from time to time for gods or vermin is ideology.* (Eagleton, Ideology, *xiii*)

Because this book focuses on literary (biblical) texts, I devote this chapter to the method by which I will analyze these texts. I call this method "ideological criticism": a materialist-feminist reading of the text that understands literature as an ideological production of social praxis, which itself is governed by ideology.[1] While a number of materialist readings of the Bible exist,[2] there are very few materialist-*feminist* investigations of it.[3]

I find the theoretical basis for my readings in Marxist literary critics, who have, in my opinion, been the most successful critical theorists in bringing together the text and its social world. Inverting the idealist philosophies of Hegel and his followers, Marx argues that all mental (ideological) systems are the products of real social and economic relations:

> In direct contrast to German philosophy which descends from heaven to earth, here we ascend from earth to heaven. That is to say, we do not set out from what men say, imagine, conceive, nor from men as narrated, thought of, imagined, conceived, in order to arrive at men in the flesh. We set out from real, active men, and on the basis of their real life-process we demonstrate the development of the ideological reflexes and echoes of this life-process. . . . Life is not determined by consciousness, but consciousness by life.[4]

In whatever ways Marxist literary theorists modify, refine, or rede-fine Marx's relationship between *base* (socioeconomic relations) and *superstructure* (culture, ideology, politics, legal system), their core in-sight remains that literature is grounded in historical real-life rela-tions. Their models have helped me contextualize the symbolization of woman as evil in texts as an ideological production embedded in a larger drama of social practices and modes of production.

In this chapter I present a working definition of the term "ideol-ogy," particularly as it relates to the ideology of gender. Next, I outline the different strategies of ideology in its complex representations of the "reality" of gender relationships. I then turn my attention to the literary text as a production of ideology. Finally, I discuss the presup-positions of ideological criticism of texts and its two tasks: an *extrin-sic* ideological critique that takes seriously the stages of ideological production, particularly within the socioeconomic world of the bibli-cal text, and an *intrinsic* ideological critique that examines the inter-nal rhetoric of the text and how it reproduces that social world.

What Is Ideology?

The Historical Understandings

Terry Eagleton's *Ideology: An Introduction* provides a lucid examina-tion of the notoriously difficult concept of ideology. The intent of Ea-gleton's engaging and often polemical book is to reinstate ideology as a category of analysis within a properly Marxist framework. He out-lines six different ways in which ideology has been historically de-fined, ranging from the politically and epistemologically neutral to the politically partisan and epistemologically pejorative.

One can, first, characterize ideology as the general material pro-duction of ideas, beliefs, and values in social life. This impractically broad understanding of ideology accounts for its origins in the mate-rial world but neglects the important issue of partisan controversy.[5]

Second, ideology can refer to (true or false) ideas and beliefs that symbolize the circumstances and life experiences of a particular, so-cially significant group or class. This definition retains epistemologi-cal neutrality while accentuating the political positioning of the group.[6]

Third, ideology refers to those (true or false) ideas and beliefs that promote and legitimate the interests of particular social groups vis-à-vis rival factions. "Ideology can here be seen as a discursive field in which self-promoting social powers conflict and collide over questions central to the reproduction of social power as a whole."[7]

Fourth, ideology refers to those (true or false) ideas and beliefs that promote and legitimate the particular dealings of a prevailing social power. While specifying a politically dominant social power, this definition of ideology still remains epistemologically neutral.[8]

Fifth, ideology refers to those ideas and beliefs that help to legitimate the interests of a ruling group or class particularly by misrepresentation and deception.[9] Here, ideology not only specifies a dominant group, but is also epistemologically negative.

Sixth and finally, ideology can refer to false or deceptive beliefs arising from the material structure of society as a whole, and not from the interests of a dominant class. Ideology here is still epistemologically negative, but is not directed to a particular group. This understanding of ideology embraces Marx's theory of the fetishism of commodities.[10]

Eagleton does not espouse any one of these definitions over the others. For him, the matter is much more complex. He argues against those Marxist thinkers such as Lukás who reduce ideology to a disembodied class consciousness, on the one hand,[11] and those such as Althusser who reduce it to social practices, on the other.[12] He situates ideology in the realm of discourse or semiotics, which highlights its materiality (since signs are material entities) while still protecting the intuition that it is primarily concerned with *meanings*.[13] He is thus able to maintain that ideology is related intrinsically to social praxis while still having a certain autonomy from it. Insisting on this midway position, Eagleton argues that ideology neither legislates (material) situations into being nor is simply caused by them. Instead, ideology offers a set of *reasons* for these material conditions. Ideology works on the "real" situation and can thereby transform it.[14] We will see later how this understanding of ideology is at the basis of his literary criticism of texts.

Whether ideology is politically and epistemologically neutral or partisan and pejorative depends on its relational function within a particular social situation: how, when, where, and why it is used by persons or groups, and the conflicting interests among which it must ceaselessly negotiate.[15] Depending on its particular context, the ideological signifier (the belief, the practice, the text, the institution) can, on the one hand, be the site of controversy between conflicting social forces; on the other, it can simply be any significant nexus between discourse and power.[16] Eagleton summarizes his thinking on ideology:

> [Ideology] represents the points where power impacts upon certain utterances and inscribes itself tacitly within them. But it is not therefore to be equated with just any form of discursive partisanship, "interested" speech or rhetorical bias; rather, the concept of ideology aims to disclose something of the relation between an utterance and its material conditions of possibility, when those conditions of possibility are viewed in the light of certain power-struggles central to the reproduction (or also, for some theories, contestation) of a whole form of social life.[17]

The Ideology of Gender

Marxist-feminist critic Michèle Barrett provides an effective example illustrating the complexities involved in the ideological production of gender:

> Suppose I am an enterprising car manufacturer, and it occurs to me that I can tap a market of independent salaried women for my product. I advertise my car with a seductive, scantily-clad male model draped over its bonnet and an admiring, yet slightly servile, sharply-dressed man politely opening the car door for my putative client. Will my efforts be crowned with success?[18]

For Barrett, this marketing strategy, which simply replaces images of women with images of men, will most likely fail, because the representation of women is linked to a broader chain of meanings, which themselves are connected to historically grounded real relations. "To put the matter simply, we can understand why female models may be more persuasive to male customers than *vice versa* only if we take account of a prior commoditization of women's bodies."[19]

It is this "prior commodilization of women's bodies" that must be negotiated in analyzing the biblical symbolization of woman as evil. In this study I examine the relationship between the biblical discursive symbol of woman as evil and the material conditions that produce it, when those conditions are viewed in light of gender power struggles (male/female, male/male, female/female) central to the reproduction (or contestation) of the biblical world. The mere inversion, whereby men are symbolized as evil, will not succeed in that world, because the material conditions of the biblical world are internalized and inscribed in the very production of the symbolization of woman as evil. What needs clarity at this point is how ideology works, particularly an ideology of gender. What strategies bring gendered social groups together to function in cooperation, compromise, or conflict?

Ideological Strategies

As a body of meanings and values encoding certain interests germane to social power, ideology operates by means of a number of strategies. According to Eagleton, ideologies *unify, are action-oriented, rationalize, legitimate, universalize, and naturalize.*[20] We will observe in each of these strategies the potential for contradiction and dissonance in ideological formations.

Ideologies *unify* social groups, but are rarely homogeneous or pure systems, since they exist only in relation to other ideologies. A group holding a dominant ideology must constantly negotiate with the ideologies of its subordinates, thus precluding a pure self-identity. What makes a dominant ideology powerful is also what tends to make it internally heterogeneous and conflicted: its ability to engage the genuine wants, needs, and desires of those it governs, appropriating and modulating their experience. Since it must somehow recognize the "Other," ideology inscribes this Otherness as a potentially disruptive force within its own discourses.[21] For example, the ideological assertion of the Declaration of Independence that "all men are created equal" unified the early American states in a rejection of British imperialism. This statement, penned by free, white, landowning males in an eighteenth-century, androcentric slave culture, was not intended to include women and African American slaves. Nevertheless, it was appropriated and recontextualized in the struggle to emancipate slaves, give women the vote, and secure civil rights for blacks and for women, thus subverting the intentions of its originators.

Ideologies are *action-oriented*, in that to be successful they must find ways of linking the theoretical levels with the practical. Examined from the perspective of its action orientation, an ideology offers a complex set of linkages between these levels. Eagleton takes up the example of organized religion to illustrate this complexity:

> Religion consists of a hierarchy of discourses, some of them elaborately theoretical (scholasticism), some ethical and prescriptive, others exhortatory and consolatory (preaching, popular piety); and the institution of the church ensures that each of these discourses meshes constantly with the others, to create an unbroken continuum between the theoretical and the behavioural.[22]

Nevertheless, the transition from theoretical to practical does not occur smoothly. A potential for conflict exists between the overall worldview and its more concrete prescriptive elements. A variety of possible mutable relations can occur between the two levels, such as compromise, adjustment, incorporation, trade-off, and outright opposition. It is to these possible forms of cooperation and conflict that an ideological criticism attends.

We have already seen that an ideology "gives reasons" for social interests, behavior, and so on; it *rationalizes* them by providing credible explanations and justifications for social phenomena that might otherwise be the object of criticism. There exists a range in which an ideology rationalizes, from its explanatory power to account for social phenomena to its mechanisms for self-deception. For example, oppressed groups—who may rationalize just as much as their oppressors—may perceive that their situation is intolerable, but rationalize that they deserve to suffer, or that everyone is suffering, or that suffering is inescapable, or that the alternative might be even more intolerable. Oppressed groups might rationalize their condition to the point of deceiving themselves by insisting that they are not unhappy at all.[23]

The problem with rationalization involves holding conflicting beliefs simultaneously. A woman who is outwardly submissive to her husband, while engaging in subversive behavior (such as lying, gossip, infidelity) behind his back as coping mechanisms in a hierarchical situation, holds two mutually contradictory beliefs simultaneously. The submissiveness arises from the official ideology regarding gender relationships to which she assents, whereas the subversiveness origi-nates in her practical consciousness.[24] In the next chapter we will see this contradictory state of affairs in ethnographic studies of Middle Eastern gender relationships.

Strongly linked to the concept of rationalization is *legitimation*, the ideological process whereby the dominant group obtains mini-mally from its subordinates an implicit approval of its authority. "A mode of domination is generally legitimated when those subjected to it come to judge their own behaviour by the criteria of their rulers."[25] In recognizing that legitimation is an *ideological* strategy, one must also keep in mind the material nature of ideology—that ideology is grounded in complex social relations. Dominant groups have the ma-terial resources at their command for obtaining the compliance of their subordinates.[26]

One significant way in which an ideology becomes legitimate is by *universalizing* and "immortalizing" itself. Values and interests that are in fact historically and geographically specific are circulated as the only valid ideals for everyone for all time. The process of universal-ization implies the repression of oppositional voices and the claim that only one genuine voice speaks for all.[27] Conflict arises when an ideology, thought to be universal and eternal, confronts competing ideologies: "An ideology is reluctant to believe that it was ever born, since to do so is to acknowledge that it can die. Like the oedipal child, it would prefer to think of itself as without parentage, sprung parthenogenetically from its own seed. It is equally embarrassed by the presence of sibling ideologies, since these mark out its own finite frontiers and so delimit its sway."[28]

The ideological strategy of *naturalization* presents values and be-liefs as so identified with the "common sense" of a society that they become self-evident and natural. Like universalization, naturalization implicitly denies that ideas and beliefs are linked to a particular time, place, and social group—for example, the pervasive opinion that it is only natural that women stay at home and raise children. While this may have been the case for other times and places, present-day eco-nomic conditions in the United States make it the exception rather than the rule.

While all of the above strategies can be applied to an ideology of gender, four additional ones are especially pertinent for the social production of gender ideology: stereotyping, compensation, collu-sion, and recuperation.[29]

The *stereotyping* of gender is perhaps the best documented of these in feminist literature.[30] Stereotyping can be regarded as a subset of the "naturalizing" strategy of ideology, isolating particular features of a group and proclaiming them as essentially definitive of the group as a whole. Some familiar female stereotypes include the defenseless woman, daddy's girl, the dutiful daughter, the submissive housewife, the dumb blonde, the femme fatale, the ball-buster, and so forth. One can also include the biblical symbolization of woman as evil as a particular stereotype. The evaluative features of stereotypes are couched in value-laden adjectives and relate to real social groups and relationships. Nevertheless, these oversimplifications conceal the complex and contradictory structure of these groups and relations, while at the same time reinforcing the broad—often pejorative—evaluations of the groups they label. For example, aside from the fact that women can be temperamentally submissive, the submissiveness of "submissive housewives" can be due in part to many wives' economic dependence on their husbands and their reluctance to "bite the hand that feeds them," and/or partly due to the socialization of women with respect to men, reinforced by religious and legal ideologies, and so on. These complex material conditions that often give rise to the submissiveness of many wives are concealed in the stereotype, and an *effect* of these conditions becomes the "essential" feature of the group. Transformation of this stereotype can come about only with a change in the material grounds that sustain it.

As a subset of the rationalizing strategy of ideology, some ideologies of gender *compensate* for devaluations of women, which deny them opportunities within the so-called public sphere, by elevating certain socially prescribed ideals of femininity to the level of moral worth.[31] In keeping with such compensatory strategies, women are romanticized and "put on pedestals." They become "the keepers of hearth and home," where men find moral sanctuary from the corrupt outside world. The Victorian "cult of domesticity" and its overly romantic exaltation of the family home were developed during the stifling Victorian limitations on female activity. The present-day controversies regarding the suitability of women for combat in the armed services demonstrate such compensatory attitudes about gender.[32]

The ideological strategy of *collusion*—secret agreement or cooperation for a fraudulent or deceitful purpose—involves two distinct processes, depending on one's social position in a gender hierarchy. In the dominant group, collusion refers to the attempts to orchestrate and flaunt women's consent to their subordination and objectification. Collusion is related to the legitimizing strategy of ideology, when the dominant group attempts to secure a woman's complicity in her own objectification.

In the subordinate group, a second form of collusion occurs when women willingly consent to and internalize their subordination. Because it is located in the subordinate group, collusion here would be related to the rationalizing strategy of ideology. Since there exists a range in which an ideology rationalizes, one cannot simply maintain that women's collusion with the dominant group is a matter of false consciousness or a denial of the objective conditions of oppression. Women can collude with the dominant group for any number of reasons, which must be determined contextually.[33] An analysis of gender ideology in which women are always innocent, always passive victims of androcentric power, is clearly inadequate.[34]

Recuperation, the last ideological strategy of gender representation, is the process of counteracting and neutralizing challenges to the historically dominant views on gender in particular periods.[35] This strategy is particularly evident in present-day media and advertising, which redefines the gains women have achieved on their own terms. A prime example is the slogan in Virginia Slims cigarette ads, "You've come a long way, baby!" which co-opts women's economic gains for commercial purposes while simultaneously infantilizing them. Susan Faludi's book *Backlash* documents the subtle and not-so-subtle ways in which the media and popular culture try to convince women that their feelings of dissatisfaction and anxiety are the fallout of their feminism and independence, while sabotaging the little progress they have gained at home, at work, and in the political arena.[36] Recuperation is related to both the unifying and the action-oriented strategies of ideology. On the one hand, recuperation comprises an attempt by the dominant group to negotiate with competing ideologies, inscribing their otherness within its own forms, but on its own terms. On the other hand, it becomes an important bridge between the theoretical and practical levels of ideology, where compromise, adjustment, incorporation, trade-off, and downright opposition can occur.

Before moving on to investigate how ideology becomes encoded in literary texts, I would like to take stock of the discussion so far. Neither free-floating ideas on the one hand nor social practices on the other, ideology is a discourse, a symbolic/linguistic system used in human communication. As discourse, it is produced in a particular situation, and thus solidly anchored in the social world. Nevertheless, because ideology concerns the production of meaning, it cannot merely be reduced to social praxis. It retains a certain autonomy from the world in which it is produced.

If a common thread exists in the ideological strategies discussed above and their corollaries, it is the endeavor to explain and give some meaning to how we experience ourselves in relation to each other and to the social structures in which we live. Real people operating under diverse material conditions produce ideologies to give reasons for their social world. Nevertheless, when they interface with social power wielded by people in many different ways, these explanations become partial and partisan. By its very nature and autonomy, ideology is incomplete and wedded to particular struggles for power that make it possible. As the nexus between discourse and power, it explains the "real" but cannot account for it totally, even though, as we have seen, it sometimes offers its explanation as totalizing and absolute. Contradictions and potentials for conflict are inscribed in the elaborate connections between ideology and power. While helping us to make sense of the world, it also conceals or represses our "real" relationship to it.

By advancing its explanation, ideology necessarily leaves some things unsaid, particularly those material things that would contradict or contest it. According to Marxist critic Fredric Jameson, ideologies are "strategies of containment" in that they prematurely close off critical inquiry into what is really occurring in the historical situation and repress its contradictions and any evidence of power struggles. In its explanation of "the way things are," ideology articulates through various strategies the imaginary or formal "solutions" to these irresolvable social contradictions or resistances.[37] The unspoken historical situation becomes an absence that Jameson calls "the political unconscious."[38]

The Ideological Production of the Literary Text

The play's the thing, wherein I'll catch the conscience of the king!
(Shakespeare, *Hamlet*, act II, scene 2)

In *Criticism and Ideology*, Eagleton explains how a literary text is a certain *production* of ideology by comparing it to a dramatic production. "A dramatic production does not 'express,' 'reflect' or 'reproduce' the dramatic text on which it is based; it 'produces' the text, transforming it into a unique and irreducible entity."[39] A dramatic performance does not simply "mediate" the dramatic script, but produces it. The staging of a particular play manipulates the play's script and performs it interpretively; it generates a unique production that operates under its own internal logic.[40]

Just as a dramatic performance is a historically variable production, so too is a literary text. Written during a particular history, the literary text produces an ideology that reveals something about its relationship to that history. The text in its production becomes an ideological act in its own right, with its own internal logic as a socially symbolic act.[41] It is significant that Eagleton's comparison of a literary text to a dramatic production rejects metaphors of literary representation, where the text is thought to be a window through which the historical world is seen, or a mirror that reflects it, or a crystal that refracts it.[42]

Extending the analogy of the dramatic production further, Eagleton notes that the dramatic text, on which the staging of the play is based, is itself a product of a particular history, articulating its own understanding of that history. Hence the dramatic performance of the text becomes *a production of a production*. By reinterpreting the dramatic text's construal of history, the dramatic production becomes *an ideology of an ideology*. Similarly, the literary text becomes an ideology of an ideology; it becomes a complex reworking of already existing ideological discourses. Ideology, like the dramatic script, is a production of sociohistorical realities; the literary text, like the dramatic production, orchestrates and reworks this ideology to "re-produce" it in its own way. Eagleton diagrams the parallels he sees between a literary production and a dramatic production in the following table:[43]

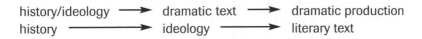

Table 1: Parallels between a literary production and a dramatic production.

Ideology offers a set of *reasons* for the material conditions of the historical situation by working on this situation in transformative ways.

These "reasons," while not identical to material conditions but still very much grounded in them, are produced in the literary text.

A strategy of containment, ideology represses the truth about the power struggles in which it is produced. This concealed history is an absence. In the production of the literary text, this unspoken history is "present" in the form of a double absence.[44] This double absence of history has implications for the textual production of the biblical symbolization of woman as evil. Ideologies of gender offer reasons for the historical relationships and power struggles among the genders. They try to make sense of the complexities of these real relationships. Moreover, when these relationships become sites of struggle or contradiction, they try to resolve these gender relations through various strategies and with varying degrees of success. In the biblical text, one does not encounter "real" gender relationships firsthand. Rather, one encounters them as a double absence: as already encoded in particular socially determined significations, in ideological formations that real situations of gender relations in the biblical world have actually produced.

Categories for a Materialist Theory of Literary Production

In the investigation into the biblical symbolization of woman as evil, the text cannot be the sole basis for the analysis. The investigation must be pursued within the larger framework of the text's production. The historical situation of the text cannot merely be rallied to provide "background" material, as biblical scholars have customarily described it. In this case, the historical situation is secondary to the text, which still remains the primary point of departure. The historical situation, however, in all its material and ideological complexity, actually *produces* the textual symbolization of woman as evil. What the literary text can offer is an *indication* of the limits within which this symbolization is constructed and negotiated in a given social formation. Any exegesis of the text must be able to take this wider historical production into account.

In an endeavor to provide such a theoretical framework, Eagleton lays out the major categories of a materialist theory of literature, in which the text is understood as the product of "complex historical *articulations*" of the following:

1. General Mode of Production
2. Literary Mode of Production
3. General Ideology
4. Authorial Ideology
5. Aesthetic Ideology
6. The Text[45]

Eagleton differentiates between modes of production and ideologies
in the production of the text. Nevertheless, these distinctions do not
imply completely autonomous operations. Rather, they are primarily
heuristic. Since I will be taking up Norman Gottwald's understanding
of ancient Israelite modes of production in the next chapter, I offer
his definition of "mode of production":

> In a narrower sense, mode of production . . . refers to the way human
> capacities and technology are socially organized for the labor neces-
> sary to meet basic human needs and to allocate what is produced. In
> a broader sense, mode of production includes the social ramifications
> of the labor process in class and status divisions, in political process,
> in family organization, and in juridical procedures.[46]

A mode of production, therefore, comprises the whole operation of
the social relations (family organization, status, class, etc.) and forces
(technological, political, juridical, etc.) of material production. The
general mode of production is the one that is dominant in a particular
society.[47]

The *literary mode of production* is the combination of the forces
and social relations in literate societies that produce texts within the
bounds of the general mode of production. Several distinct modes of
literary production can exist together in a society in varying degrees
of cooperation or conflict. One of these will usually dominate. Literary production and consumption presume certain levels of literacy,
physical and mental well-being, leisure, and the material conditions
for writing and reading—for example, economic assets, shelter, lighting, and privacy. As we will see, the literary production and consumption of texts symbolizing woman as evil are primarily restricted to the
upper classes of ancient Israel. Eagleton notes that in conditions of
poverty, physical and mental impediments due to prolonged and intensive labor, illiteracy or partial literacy, insufficient housing, privacy, and lighting, the general mode of production will impinge on

the literary mode of production to exclude or partially exclude certain social groups and classes from literary production and consumption—a factor that is also of ideological significance.[48] These conditions characterize to a degree the majority of those living in the labor-intensive, subsistence culture of ancient Israel. Israel's particular literary mode of production of biblical texts, focused primarily in the upper classes, will have a decisive bearing on the symbolization of woman as evil.

The general mode of production produces a *general ideology*: the dominant ideological formation composed of a relatively coherent set of discourses of values, representations, and beliefs. These discourses are embedded in certain material apparatuses (e.g., the family; religious, political, and educational systems) and are related to the structures of material production.[49] They duplicate the relations of individual subjects to their social conditions in such a way "as to guarantee those misperceptions of the 'real' which contribute to the reproduction of the dominant social relations."[50]

The general ideology exists, therefore, with the general mode of production in a mutually (re)productive relationship. The literary mode of production, already a specialized vehicle within the general mode of production, is likewise an important conveyor of the general ideology, but in sometimes dialectical ways. As mentioned above,[51] the literary text that is produced becomes an ideology of an ideology, a complex reworking of already existing ideological discourses. The literary text may (re)produce the dominant ideological formation or (re)produce mutually antagonistic ideological formations.[52] However, when specific groups are excluded from the literary mode of production (as in ancient Israel), because of their extended labor, poverty, illiteracy, and so on, the dominant and antagonistic ideologies in the literary texts are primarily the articulations of the upper classes.

Authorial ideology is determined by the author's specific mode of biographical insertion into the hegemonic ideology, governed by considerations such as social class, sex, nationality, religion, geographical region, and so on. The authorial ideology can relate in various ways to the general ideology, ranging from effective correspondence or partial separation to serious contradiction. It should neither be collapsed into the general ideology, on the one hand, nor equated with the ideology of the text, on the other.[53]

Aesthetic ideology is a specific aspect of the general ideology, functioning in varying degrees with other ideologies, such as the ethical, religious, and so on, but ultimately governed by the general mode of production. An internally complex discursive formation, the aesthetic ideology contains a number of subdivisions, of which the *literary* is one. This subdivision is also internally complex and comprises a number of layers, such as theories of literature, critical practice, literary traditions, genres, conventions, and the like.[54] In ancient Israel the use of prophetic and wisdom genres would fall under aesthetic ideology.

Finally, the *text* is a product of the specific, complex, mutual interactions among the general and literary modes of production and the ideologies that they produce. Nevertheless, while a result of these conjunctures, the text is not simply a passive product. The text itself is also an *active production* as a complex reworking of the ideologies that produce it, an ideology of ideology.[55] Any analysis of the text needs to consider how the text rhetorically duplicates, legitimates, modifies, or conflicts with the ideologies that produce it. It is to the parameters of this analysis that I now turn.

Ideological Criticism: Presuppositions and Tasks

At first glance Eagleton's categories for a materialist theory of literary production may seem to be unduly deterministic. However, the great merit of his schematization is that it demonstrates the complexities involved in the production of the text. If anything, his categories highlight the dangers in other literary theories—even more deterministic—that assume an unproblematic identification between the text and the author or between the text and its historical background, as well as those theories (e.g., New Criticism) that make no connection at all between the text and its social world.

Presuppositions

An ideological criticism of the text presumes that the text constitutes an ideological production of an already established ideology that universalizes, legitimates, and naturalizes the world that produces it. Although the relationship between the ideology of the text and the ideology upon which it works may not necessarily be a homologous one, the literary text still internalizes in some way the material conditions of its production: "every text intimates by its very conventions the way it is to be consumed, encodes within itself its own ideology of how, by whom and for whom it was produced."[56]

Since the text is an ideological reworking of a prior chain of signification, an ideological criticism presumes a double absence of history in the text. According to Marxist critic Pierre Macherey, "in order to say anything, there are other things *which must not be said*."[57] Absent is the history that pretextual ideology must marginalize in order to give itself voice; absent also is the history that the text itself excludes in its (re)production of ideology. It is in these silences at the margins of the text, in its gaps and absences, that the presence of literary ideology is most tangibly perceived:

> We should question the work as to what it does not and cannot say, in those silences for which it has been made. The concealed order of the work is thus less significant than its real *determinant* disorder (its disarray). The order which it professes is merely an imagined order, projected onto disorder, the fictive resolution of ideological conflicts, a resolution so precarious that it is obvious in the very letter of the text where incoherence and incompleteness burst forth.[58]

An ideological criticism presumes, therefore, that the text is a symbolic resolution of real contradictions, inventing imaginary or formal "solutions" to unresolved ideological dilemmas.[59] We have already observed that a potential for conflict and contradiction among social groups exists when ideologies attempt to unify, legitimate, rationalize, and so on, the society that produces them. These dilemmas themselves are produced by such things as unequal social relations in modes of production, the resulting inequities of class and status, and the marginalization and exploitation of some social groups. The conflicts and contradictions concealed by this fictive resolution are the silences that an ideological criticism must interrogate and try to make articulate. Firmly encoded with gaps and silences, the text is incomplete. The critic's task is not, however, to fill in the work; it is to seek out the sources of its conflict of meanings, and to show how this conflict is produced by the work's relation to ideology.[60]

Extrinsic and Intrinsic Analysis of the Text

An ideological criticism thus involves an attempt to read the text backwards, so to speak, by examining the nature of its pretextual "problems" in the light of their textual "solutions."[61] Presuming the intrusion of ideology between text and history, one determines inversely from the text both the ideology, which produced the text and which the text reworks, and the sociohistorical circumstances of its production. An ideological criticism is "not so much an interpretation of content as it is a *revealing* of it, a laying bare, a restoration of the original message, the original experience, beneath the distortions of the censor."[62]

In the case of the biblical symbolization of woman as evil, for instance, one does not automatically assume a homologous relationship between this symbolization and real women, or simply assert that the "patriarchal world" creates the symbol in its misogyny. Both assumptions are inadequate. Instead, one examines the prior ideology of gender that this symbolization reworks. This examination necessarily entails determining the material conditions affecting real gender relations and the contradictions and conflicts that result, all of which encourage the production of this ideology. It investigates the particular strategies of this ideology to (re)produce the social conditions of its production. On the one hand, it avoids simply reiterating the text's ideology, say, in the book of Hosea, where men are good and faithful and women unfaithful and deserving of punishment. On the other hand, it circumvents depicting a monolithic patriarchy that simplifies gender relations to the point that men are always oppressive and women always victims. At different points in history, women have been both oppressed and oppressive, submissive and subversive, victim and agent, allies and enemies both of men and of one another. An ideological criticism situates the text in a wider, more complex context of ideological and material social struggles, examining both the mechanisms of dominance and subordination and the resources available to women as agents of social change.

The ideological criticism that informs my work requires a twofold task: both an extrinsic and an intrinsic analysis of the text.[63] An *extrinsic analysis* recovers the concrete social and historical conditions of the text's production. What are the modes of general and literary production and the general, authorial, and aesthetic ideologies that (re)produce them? What are the strategies of these ideologies in effecting social control and reproducing the dominant system? What contradictions and possible conflicts arise from these strategies? On whose behalf do these ideologies speak? Whose voices, what groups, do they exclude? In chapter 3 I lay out the social world of ancient Israel, its different modes of general and literary production at various points in its history, particularly as they affect family relationships and the ideologies of gender that reinforce them. This general introduction to the sociohistorical world of ancient Israel provides the basis for my materialist reading of specific texts dealing with the symbolization of woman as evil in the subsequent chapters.

An *intrinsic analysis* of the text inductively determines how the text reworks the ideologies that produce it. The text encodes and internalizes the often conflicting forces and relations of its material and ideological production. It presents imaginary "solutions" to the ideological perplexities that produce it. First, an intrinsic analysis pays heed to the particular genre of the text that reveals its literary-aesthetic ideology. The choice of genre over and against other conventional literary discourses is already an ideological act.[64] How does the text conform to the conventions of the genre, and how does it depart from them? It is in these departures that the text reworks the ideology that intrudes between it and its history.

Second, an intrinsic analysis requires an in-depth investigation of the structural and rhetorical features of a text. I understand rhetoric here in the classical sense, in which rhetorical skills and features were regarded as forms of power exerted upon the world.[65] These features disclose the reinscription of general, authorial, and aesthetic ideologies into the text. While the text may relate to these ideologies through varying degrees of cooperation or conflict, it is firmly embedded in them as a result of their production. Furthermore, these features also betray the ideological strategies of the text itself as it reworks these ideologies for its own purposes.

Third, an intrinsic analysis attends to the particular absences in the text. Since history is present in the text in the form of a double absence, how are the absent voices suppressed by ideology inscribed in the very production of the text? Whose voices does the text doubly conceal and repress? This aspect of an intrinsic analysis locates itself "in the very incompleteness of the work in order to *theorize* it—to explain the ideological necessity of those 'not-saids' that constitute the very principle of its identity. Its object is the *unconsciousness* of the work—that of which it is not, and cannot be, aware."[66]

Summary

In this chapter I have surveyed the different historical understandings of ideology as they have been worked out by Marxist theorists. Following Eagleton, I understand ideology as a discourse of meaning, both embedded in social practice and autonomous from it. The study of gender ideology, in particular, reveals the complex relationships between the discourse on gender and the material conditions that make it possible, when those conditions are seen in light of the gender power struggles central to the reproduction of society.

Ideology operates through strategies that perform different sets of effects germane to social power and reproduction. Ideology unifies, is action-oriented, rationalizes, legitimates, universalizes, and naturalizes. Four corollaries to these strategies are especially pertinent to an ideology of gender: stereotyping, compensation, collusion, and recuperation.

By its very nature ideology is incomplete and often fixed in power struggles that make it possible. By giving reasons for the social world, it also conceals or represses one's real relationship to it, a relationship that is frequently marked by contradiction and conflict.

A literary text becomes a production of ideology in two senses. A text is a complex product of a society's general and literary modes of production and the general, authorial, and aesthetic ideologies that they produce. Moreover, a text (re)produces ideology by reworking the ideologies on which it is based in a way analogous to the operations of a dramatic production on a dramatic text. Like a dramatic production, a literary text becomes an ideology of an ideology. The text is neither a mirror of nor a window on the sociohistorical world that produced it. This world enters the text only as ideology—an already established complex and contradictory discourse on this world. The text takes as its object not real history, but certain chains of meaning by which the real social world lives. Thus, history is only present in the text in the form of a double absence: an absence due to the camouflaging and repressive mechanisms of ideology that produce the text and to those of ideology that the text itself produces.

An ideological criticism takes into account both of these senses of the text as a production of ideology. Its extrinsic analysis examines the text inductively as a product of certain modes of production and ideologies. Its intrinsic analysis investigates how the text reworks and (re)produces ideology through the specific genre in which it is written, through its structural and rhetorical features, and through its various absences.

In order to understand the ideological symbolization of woman as evil, I turn in the next chapter to the first task of my ideological criticism: an extrinsic analysis of the modes of production and ideologies of ancient Israel.

3 The Social Sciences and the Biblical Woman as Evil

Ideological criticism's extrinsic analysis of literary texts necessarily involves the social sciences in reconstructing the social world of gender relationships in the biblical period.[1] Since the majority of texts that I examine come from the Hebrew Bible, my frame of reference at this point is the reconstruction of gender relationships in ancient Israel. The pertinent questions for this study in employing the social sciences include: What is the nature of gender interaction in the ancient Israelite world that gives rise to symbolizations of the female gender as evil in the biblical text? What are the modes of production upon which these gender relations are based?

Because of the paucity of literary sources and their distinct negative valuation or even complete exclusion of women, we cannot depend on using them to reconstruct gender relationships and recover women's lives in ancient Israel.[2] This reconstruction and recovery must draw on interdisciplinary resources already engaged in the study of human social interaction to help interpret what little data we have in a more intelligible way. These resources can provide analogies and models to help recover the structural contours of Israelite society in general and of gender relations in particular. Since our biblical texts originated in cultures different from our own, their interpretation will always be a process of cross-cultural analysis.[3] It is here that the social sciences become important theoretical tools to help fill in the lacunae in the data. The research of feminist cultural anthropologists—especially their ethnographic studies on gender

relationships in non-Western, preindustrial societies—is singularly
useful for my investigation.[4]

Utilizing this cross-cultural and ethnographic data to help reconstruct Israelite society[5] is not without its dangers and limitations.[6]
The analogies and models derived from this data are primarily useful
in finding commonalities among individual societies by bracketing
differences, inconsistencies, and irregularities. This usefulness is
negated when the data are forced to conform to the model. The analogy or model exists to clarify the data, not shape the data into its
image. In a methodologically rigorous fashion, an interpreter must attend not only to the parallels that exist between comparative materials but also to the divergences. Because of the great historical
distance between ancient Israelite and modern societies, differences
between the two will be inevitable and should be appreciated and ex-
plained.[7] More importantly, these dissimilarities are revelatory of ideology, to which an ideological critic must pay heed.

In this chapter, recognizing the strengths and limitations of the social sciences, I first discuss the *general modes of production* in ancient
Israel during the course of its history. I then focus on the ramifications of the familial mode of production for the *social structure* of pre-
state Israel and the place of the "family" within this social structure
as the major site at which males and females interact and struggle.
Intrinsically related to the social importance of the "family" are the
kinship ideologies of Israelite society, in which gender plays a critical
role. Descent, marriage relations, family residence, and inheritance
are all decided along kinship lines. After studying the structural configurations of gender, I turn to the ideological value system of *honor
and shame* that seems to be at work in Israelite society, and how it legitimates the privileging of the male in a patrilineal system. I then examine the *power relations* between the genders as they are expressed
in the so-called domestic and jural-political spheres. One important
element of this discussion of where power is exhibited concerns the
relationship between formal power (usually associated with men) and
informal power (usually associated with women). Women's informal
strategies for coping and exerting power reveal the ideological contradictions and conflicts within the social system and will be encoded
in distinctly literary symbolizations of woman as evil. Also significant
for this literary symbolization is the investigation of how a separate
woman's world, created by the segregation of the genders, offers
women opportunities for empowerment, as well as limitations. Men's

restricted access into this separate world will be an important factor in the double absence[8] of women in the literary text. All of these material elements of Israelite society converge in producing the biblical symbolization of woman as evil.

Modes of Production

In the previous chapter I contended that any analysis of a literary text must take into account the material and ideological complexity of the historical situation that produced the text. The literary mode of production is embedded within a society's general mode of production, or dominant system of social relations and forces of material production developed to meet basic human needs and allocate what is produced.[9] Norman Gottwald distinguishes three general modes of production operative in ancient Israel: a pre-state *communitarian* mode, a *tributary* mode from the monarchy into the Hellenistic period, and a *slave* mode in the late Hellenistic-Roman period.[10] Residues of prior modes and prototypes of future modes existed simultaneously and often in conflict with the current dominant mode of production.

David Jobling has argued that problems exist with describing Israel's pre-state period as a "communitarian" mode of production. He prefers Sahlins's proposal of a "familial" mode of production, in which "families are *constituted* for production primarily by the sexual division of labor."[11] Not only does this label more accurately describe the mode of production in premonarchic Israel, it also opens up the discussion to integrate the critical roles that women play in the Israelite family household. Hence, following Jobling, I prefer to designate the mode of production characteristic of pre-state Israel as "familial."

Tribal Israel: A Familial Mode of Production

Emerging primarily from the indigenous peoples of Canaan in the thirteenth to twelfth centuries B.C.E., tribal Israel was composed of an agrarian populace that moved into the highland region during the decline of the Egyptian empire and the Canaanite city-states.[12] The economy of this new society continued the cultivation of "grain,

wine, and oil,"[13] supplemented by animal husbandry. In spite of technological developments such as terracing and cistern construction,
productivity was still challenged by the difficult typography of the
land and the arid climate, which limited resources. Nevertheless, in
contrast to their immediate neighbors, the population enjoyed a tributary-free economy, in which no class of ruling elite demanded a tax
or tribute from them and channeled their human resources for its
own economic and military purposes.

Under a familial mode of production, pre-state Israel was characterized by a minimal division of labor, a tendency toward class leveling, contractual or kin social relations, and the direct consumption of
wealth.[14] Pre-state Israel had a strong self-supporting family- and village-based mode of life in which customary law mandated mutual
aid.[15] Women held crucial positions in food production and preparation, as well as in the general supervision of the family household.[16]
Yahwism was the dominant religious ideology, which unified the
tribes under a familial idiom of mutuality and kinship that expressed
itself in the economic and social interests of the people.

Independent Monarchy:
A Native-Tributary Mode of Production

A combination of external and internal factors steered tribal Israel toward statehood. On the one hand, the Philistine encroachment into
the land compelled the tribes to centralize military power and political leadership. On the other hand, certain successful landowners in
Israel supported a permanent state as a way to advance their interests. A native-tributary mode of production, in which an Israelite elite
taxed and indebted their own people, thus developed.[17] The transition from the familial to the native-tributary mode of production was
completed under the rule of Solomon, who increased the taxation
and forced labor of the peasants to support his ambitious building
projects in Jerusalem and his status in the region.[18]

The state exploited and impoverished the peasant class through
two programs of revenue. A tax cycle demanding goods and resources
as well as forced labor siphoned off the peasants' surplus production.
When they could not meet their tax payment because of crop failure
or war, a debt cycle in the form of credit held at high interest rates was
imposed, resulting in an endless circle of debt. Protests by prophets

against this tax-debt system bankrupting the peasants emerged from the social quarters that suffered most from this shift in mode of production, as well as from those from the upper classes who affiliated themselves with the peasants. The ideological foundations for these protests were the communitarian ideals generated by the pre-state familial mode of production, which, although supplanted by the native-tributary mode, still survived in some rural areas.

Colonial Israel under a Foreign-Tributary Mode of Production

During foreign occupation, both the peasant underclasses and the deposed ruling classes of the former state of Israel appropriated the familial values and practices of the tribal period in order to endure the loss of national status and devastation of the people. These values and practices secured religious encoding in the editing of the Pentateuch and in the exilic prophets. The lower classes remained in the land, while their ruling elite were deported to Babylonia. The conditions of the lower classes in Palestine during this period are uncertain.[19] On the one hand, we have evidence that some were able to take over the estates of the deported elite and thus have their economic status raised. On the other hand, they still had to pay tribute from their agricultural production, this time to colonial, rather than native, elites. After the traumas of deportation and resettlement, the deported elite evidently prospered in exile, some of them serving in the royal courts of the Babylonians and Persians, others in agricultural settlements for the empire. Some cherished high hopes of returning to the land and regaining their administrative positions.

Many of the frictions that characterized the postexilic period were due to the conflicts between those who had remained in Judah and the returning exiles.[20] A two-layered system of taxation was imposed on the peasant classes operating under a foreign-tributary mode of production. "By allowing home rule among Palestinian Jews, the Persian tribute-takers granted the operation of a native-tributary mode of production headed by a Jewish elite."[21] Hence the lower classes were forced to render tribute to both native and foreign ruling aristocracies. This double tax-debt burden became exacerbated under the Ptolemies and especially under the Romans. Although an alliance of communitarian and tributary Jewish sectors overthrew the Seleucid

form of the tributary mode of production, Hasmonean royals suppressed the communitarian aspects of the Maccabean revolt, while
preserving an oppressive native-tributary economy.

Colonial Israel under a Slave-Based Mode of Production

Rome's slave-based mode of production in agriculture, industry, and
commerce empowered it to accumulate greater stores of wealth,
which it used to extend its vast kingdoms and exert tighter control
over occupied nations. Due to the enormous productivity of its slave-
based economy, Rome was able to suppress two significant Jewish re-
bellions during the first two centuries C.E. Under the Romans, the
tax-debt system of surplus extraction attained its highest levels in
Palestine. Much of the revenue was channeled through the temple
economy, where Sadducean priests and their lay associates collected
taxes for themselves and the Romans. The peasants and the wage la-
borers carried the heaviest load of this economic system.[22]

As one can see, the mode of production in its economic, political, and
social dimensions shifted over the course of Israelite history. Conflicts and contradictions existed in each of these modes, particularly
as they overlapped in the transition from one to the other. A particular mode of production and the social relations that sustained it had
a determinative effect on the literary production of text. More importantly, as Israel's dominant mode of production changed, so did the
nature of its gender relations. It is in this context that the literary
symbolization of woman as evil should be placed.

The Social Structure of Tribal Israel

The "Father's House," Lineage, and Tribe

In describing the social structure of ancient Israel in this chapter, I
focus primarily on the formative premonarchic period, with its familial mode of production. The specific biblical texts examined in the

subsequent chapters are products of other modes of production. Using this chapter as a springboard, I will show how the particular text reinscribes modifications in gender relations due to the change in the mode of production.

Studies on the social structure of pre-state Israel concentrate on the meaning of the Hebrew terms *bêt 'āb* (lit. "father's house"), *mišpāḥâ*, and *šēbeṭ* (customarily translated as "clan" and "tribe," respectively).[23] The *bêt 'āb* is a comprehensive term referring to nuclear and extended families and to lineages. The *nuclear family* consists of parents and their dependent children and seems to describe the predominant residential family unit in pre-state Israel.[24] The *extended family* comprises two or more nuclear families linked together by a patrilineal kinship ideology, in which descent is traced through the male line. Like the nuclear family, the extended family is a residential group whose members live together, sometimes including three generations in one household. *Lineage* in ancient Israel primarily refers to a patrilineal descent group, whose members (agnates) trace their ancestry to a founding forefather (the apical ancestor) by known genealogical links. It consists of more than fifty persons who live as separate family groups. Israelite nuclear and extended families did live together in larger kin-group lineages forming the population of small towns or villages.[25] The *bêt 'āb* can therefore refer to one's immediate family, one's extended family, and one's descent group or lineage.[26]

The term *mišpāḥâ* is often (wrongly) considered to denote the most important social and political group in pre-state Israel. Like the term "father's house," *mišpāḥâ* seems to cover different social levels. It can refer to one's lineage, a social level that "father's house" also designates, or to one's "maximal lineage," the level between the lineage and the tribe.[27] The boundaries between the *mišpāḥâ* and the *bêt 'āb* are therefore fluid, because they both refer to the lineage. *Mišpāḥâ* tends to be used for the higher levels of Israelite society, while *bêt 'āb* is employed for the lower. Nevertheless, it would be incorrect to argue, as some do, that the *mišpāḥâ* is the most important level of pre-state Israel's social structure. Whether it signified the family or the lineage, the "father's house" was the socioeconomic unit of greatest significance by far.[28] In everyday affairs, the family (either nuclear or extended) took precedence. The lineage came to the fore when economic or political events disrupted the community or a conflict occurred within the family itself.[29]

The biblical texts commonly refer to the twelve "tribes" (*šēbeṭ*) of Israel. Nevertheless, how the tribe was organized and governed is difficult to determine on the basis of these texts, which are later than the pre-state period and have been considerably reworked by editors. It would seem that a tribe was identified with a particular geographical area. It would also seem that it was comprised of nuclear families at the bottom and maximal lineages at the top. However, it also appears that the family/lineage was independent of tribal organization, since it survived the establishment of the monarchy.[30]

Because the family/lineage was such a crucial unit in the larger pre-state social structure and mode of production, and even afterward, I direct my discussion to the dynamics of gender relationships within the *bêt 'āb*. I first examine the patrilineal kinship ideology of the lineage system, with its concomitant residence and inheritance arrangements. I then turn to the family and its distribution of power and authority based on this kinship ideology, which privileged the male gender.

Patrilineality, Patrilocality, and Patrimony

Kinship refers to the patterns of social relations based on the culturally recognized connection between parents and children, between siblings, and through parents to more distant relatives.[31] Kinship is an ideology, in that it determines the ways in which humans live out their relationships in society, giving them a coherent purpose and identity vis-à-vis other groups. One can particularly observe in a kinship structure the unifying, rationalizing, and legitimizing strategies of ideology.[32] Crucial for this study is the fact that kinship ideology is inextricably bound up with an embedded system of gender categories: "Gender and kinship are not merely two independent structures that happen to be functionally enmeshed in the ethnographic record. Rather, gender is inherent in the very nature of kinship, which could not exist without it—kinship's historical precondition, not temporary bedfellow."[33]

In greater or lesser ways, kinship decides a man's or woman's access (or lack thereof) to economic means of production, rank in the social order, descent and ability to inherit, status in religion and cult,[34] and marriage partners. In short, kinship ideology is embedded in a society's general mode of production. Although foundational for the interdependence, collective identity, and group cohesion that characterize this society,[35] kinship ideology is nevertheless permeated with contradiction and contains the potential for conflict.

The patrilineal kinship ideology practiced in ancient Israel was supported by a number of social practices that privileged the male.[36] The locus of power and authority over a particular family household was the oldest living male. Ownership of goods and resources lay with this paterfamilias, who passed his assets as patrimony on to his eldest son according to customs of primogeniture. Endogamous marriages—marriages with one's closest kin—were the preferred forms of conjugal unions.[37] Endogamy could mitigate any conflict between one's affines (in-laws or relatives by marriage) and one's own family by subsuming the conjugal bond under the prior and more legitimate kinship bond. This in-group marriage was thought to preserve and strengthen a lineage, guaranteeing the greatest number of males available for conflict situations. It was also believed that endogamy kept goods and resources within the family by isolating the lineage. The ideal wife for a particular son in this endogamous system was the father's brother's daughter, or a man's female cousin on his father's side.[38] After the father negotiated for a particular wife for his son, she was brought to live in the father's residence or multifamily compound, according to patrilocal customs.

In spite of its collaborative family-oriented ideology, however, contradictions and conflicts exist in a segmentary patrilineal society under a familial mode of production. For an ethnographic analogue, one may look at the Awlad 'Ali bedouin studied by Lila Abu-Lughod, a village-based patrilineal segmented society (like pre-state Israel) that prizes its egalitarianism, although it does not live it out in its social relations.[39] Among the Awlad 'Ali, a hierarchical distinction exists between the elder men and the junior men that is tied directly to the control of economic resources. The lineage elders supervise the tribally owned wells and land. The family within this patrilineal system becomes the paradigm of hierarchical relationships within the lineage. The paterfamilias totally controls a particular household's resources for all his dependents.[40] Older siblings take precedence over younger siblings, the oldest son ranking above his other brothers and obtaining the largest share of the patrimony. Unequal family relationships are particularly evident with respect to gender. A husband has authority over his wife, older brothers have authority over their younger sisters, and, as adults, younger brothers have authority over their older sisters. A mother who exerts her authority over her son in his younger years will eventually find herself dependent on her son when her husband dies.

Such relations of gender inequity have already been documented for ancient Israel.[41] By its patrilineal descent, patrimonial inheritance, and patrilocal residence customs, ancient Israel privileged the male and disenfranchised the female in a hierarchy of gender.[42] Patrilocal marriage arrangements involved female mobility and male stability.[43] The young woman had to leave her natal household and enter into the unfamiliar and often contentious domicile of her husband. Love and romance were not major factors in the joining of a couple in wedlock.[44] A father often used the marriages of daughters to forge or strengthen alliances with other family households and lineages. Even though in an endogamous marriage a wife was probably an agnate (a member of the patriline) of her husband, his household was still unfamiliar, having already tightly established sets of relations, which had to be realigned with the appearance of the bride. A new wife occupied an ambiguous position when she entered her husband's household. She retained ties to her own family, who had to support her if she ever left her husband's house.[45] But, having left her family to join her husband, she belonged neither to her natal house nor to her husband's house entirely. She became a full member of her husband's household only when she bore a son. Her new household could sometimes be a hostile environment, particularly if co-wives were present. Co-wives often vied for their husband's attention and the resultant status it could bring, the most important of which, in a society organized around the principles of patrilineality and agnatic solidarity, was being the mother of a man's sons.[46]

In pre-state Israel's labor-intensive agrarian society, the birth of children was necessary for survival. Sons were especially valued because they continued the patriline, were the beneficiaries of the father, and did not leave the household. In fact, they brought into the household additional human resources in the persons of wives and the potential children they would bear. The wife's primary contribution to the household was her sexual fertility, bearing legitimate sons to carry on the family name and keep limited commodities such as land and other resources within the household.[47] We will see shortly that the sexuality of wives, daughters, and sisters was therefore carefully guarded and controlled, because it constituted the material basis for an ideology of honor and shame, which legitimized this androcentric hierarchy.

Another contradiction and potential source of conflict that had an impact on women's status within a segmentary patrilineage was the endogamous marriage itself. Endogamy was supposed to preserve patrilineal descent in the lineage and keep limited material resources within it, because a man married his closest female kin on his father's side. Nevertheless, it became difficult to keep one's descent through the male line consistent when both wife and husband, mother and father, were from the same patriline. Endogamy can obscure male descent lines because maternal and paternal ties meld together two or more generations back, placing descent-group members in ambivalent relations to one another. The potential to trace one's ancestry through both father and mother (otherwise known as bilateral kinship) "is the very antithesis of the patrilineal ideology."[48] This contradictory situation is evident in the ancestral narratives of Genesis.[49]

One ideological strategy to counteract the threat to patrilineal descent posed by women marrying back into their lineages is to ignore or manipulate maternal links in the genealogies. Several anthropological studies of the bedouin confirm that female names are intentionally concealed so that the maternal connections do not lead back to the endogamous descent group.[50] In order to maintain patrilineal descent, the very fact of marriage and the female partner has to be effaced: "Measured against the network of social roles, the patrilineality of endogamous descent groups is an untruth that can perdure only through a suppression of truth."[51]

Besides the obfuscation of genealogies, the conflict between marriage and patrilineality in these endogamous groups gives rise to other attempts to hide, disguise, or deny the importance of women through veiling, seclusion, and similar controls over their sexuality.[52] Analyzing the Genesis theme of the barrenness of the matriarchs, Nathaniel Wander claims that the procreativity of the matriarchs has to be treated ambiguously because of their importance as wives and mothers in order to resolve the conflict between marriage and descent.[53]

How does one reconcile an ostensibly communitarian ideology and the social fact of hierarchical arrangements, particularly with regard to gender relationships, not only within the family but within the lineage itself? According to Abu-Lughod, the potential for conflict between communitarian ideals and the realities of hierarchy among the Awlad 'Ali is resolved through a family idiom in which relations of inequity are regarded as complementary rather than antagonistic. Notions of unity and love bonding family members are emphasized. Moreover, those in power and exerting power have obligations and responsibilities to protect and care for the weak: "This responsibility of the strong is, in the familial idiom, motivated not only by a sense of duty but also by concern and affection. Thus inherent in the division between weak and strong is a unity of affection and mutual concern. The key terms of this rationale legitimizing inequality are dependency and responsibility, embedded within a moral order."[54]

Abu-Lughod brings to this discussion the insight that this social system was sustained not by tyranny but by such values as affection, responsibility, deference, and choice. An ideology of honor and shame embodying these values intersects with patrilineal kinship ideology to help rationalize the social inequity and control some have over others in a society that prizes familial ideals. The conjunction of these two ideologies tries to resolve the social contradiction that things are not, in fact, completely communal. In order to understand gender relationships in ancient Israel more fully in context, we need to examine this honor/shame ideology in greater depth.

The Ideological Value System of Honor and Shame

Anthropologists have devoted considerable attention to the values of honor and shame, which seem to characterize the Mediterranean Basin as a cultural unity.[55] Biblical scholars have likewise noted that this value system is operative in both Old and New Testament societies.[56] According to Julian Pitt-Rivers, "Honour is the value of a person in his own eyes, but also in the eyes of his society. It is his estimation of his own worth, his *claim* to pride, but it is also the acknowledgement of that claim, his excellence recognized by society, his *right* to pride."[57] Consequently, an interdependency exists between an individual and the society that confers or withholds honor. The honor of a person—one's reputation or status—is embedded within the social group.

One can become honorable in two ways. Honor can be *ascribed* to a person on the basis of qualities or attributes such as age, wealth, gender, class, or kinship ties. Honor can also be *acquired* by acts of a person that are socially deemed to be honorable, such as one's moral behavior, military prowess, or showing in social games, such as challenge and riposte, that seem to characterize the agonistic (competitive) societies of the circum-Mediterranean.[58]

Unlike our modern-day negative concept of shame,[59] shame in the circum-Mediterranean is a positive concern for one's reputation. And, like honor, it is socially recognized: "[Shame] is what makes a person sensitive to the pressure exerted by public opinion."[60] Some form of both honor and shame exists in any society in which public behavior is subject to social evaluation. What is distinctive about the Mediterranean context is the particular connection of honor and shame to the material conditions of sexuality, economics, and gender behavior.[61] According to Pitt-Rivers, the Andalusian male embodies the positive value of honor in his manliness, his courage, his ability to provide economically for his family and defend their honor, and his assertion of sexual masculinity. The female embodies the positive value of shame in her concern for her reputation. This concern manifests itself in her meekness and timidity, her deference and submission to male authority, her passivity, and her sexual purity.[62] A man failing to support his family and defend the family honor, or a woman failing to remain sexually pure, would equally be rendered *shameless* and therefore *get shamed* by the community. Both genders would have failed to consider their personal reputations and that of their families; they would not *have shame*.[63] However, the individual causes of their *shamelessness* would differ according to their gender. Abou Zeid has described a similar honor/shame dynamic among the Awlad 'Ali bedouin, particularly in the context of kinship honor.[64]

Some anthropologists have objected to the seemingly narrow focus on or distortion of sexuality in studies of honor and shame in the Mediterranean.[65] Michael Herzfeld would prefer to define honor in terms more of hospitality than of sexuality.[66] Unni Wikan protests the binary opposition of honor and shame that particularly identifies shame exclusively with women, as if they can never obtain honor.[67] While David Gilmore is correct in noting that an "organic connection [exists] between sexuality and economic criteria in the evaluation of moral character,"[68] these anthropologists issue serious caveats about appropriating the honor/shame model for ancient Israel uncritically. As we will see shortly, women and men of lower status can aspire to honor that can be described as modesty or deference, but not as shame. This modesty or deference is linked to the hierarchy of socioeconomic relationships within a patrilineal society espousing a communitarian ideology. Moreover, both women *and* men can forfeit their honor because of sexual misbehavior, among other things.

The Hebrew Bible employs several words that occur frequently to designate "honor": *kābôd* (usually translated as glory), *kābēd* (weighty, impressive), *hādār* (honor, glory, splendor), *hôd* (majesty, splendor, authority), *tip'eret* (beauty, glory, honor, respect), and *yĕqār* (honor, esteem, preciousness). Wealth and riches are associated with honor.[69] The gray hairs of elders and long life are marks of respect.[70] Parents are worthy of their children's honor.[71] A man's strength and military prowess is deemed honorable.[72] Those of royal[73] and religious[74] rank, as well as the wise,[75] garner respect. Women are expected to honor their husbands.[76] Nevertheless, wives and mothers are worthy of respect themselves.[77] The Hebrew Bible makes no gender distinction in the vocabulary of honor. It is not the case that honor is exclusively associated with the male and shame with the female.

Shame is the very opposite of honor. The vocabulary of shame in the Hebrew Bible includes the verbs *bôš* (to be ashamed) and *hārap* (to reproach, dishonor, taunt) and the nouns *bōšet*, *qālôn*, *kĕlimmâ*, *nĕbālâ*, *herpâ*, and *hesed* (variously translated as shame, disgrace, dishonor, insult, etc.). The negative feelings evoked by these terms are those of inadequacy, inferiority, and worthlessness. Dishonor can be incurred through military disgrace or defeat,[78] national disgrace or sinfulness,[79] loss of civic morale,[80] personal humiliation,[81] personal embarrassment,[82] and idolatry.[83] In contrast to the wise, fools are without honor and are thus reproached.[84] Those who are shamed include drunkards,[85] rebellious sons,[86] thieves,[87] and the proud.[88] Women are disgraced in their lack of a man's name[89] and in their barrenness.[90] A good wife contrasts with one who brings her husband shame.[91]

Because anthropological studies place considerable emphasis on the socioeconomic connections between honor, shame, and sexuality, I now explore in greater depth the gender dimensions of these concepts in the Hebrew Bible. Biblical notions of honor and shame are (re)productions of an established *male* ideology. They do *not* indicate how women evaluate themselves or their men. Embodying many of the above characteristics, the character of Job described in Job 29–30 provides an excellent springboard for understanding honor and shame in Israel from a male perspective.

In Job 29 Job longs nostalgically for the past, when God watched over him (v 1) and when his "honor"[92] was fresh (v 20). He was an elder in his prime with his many children surrounding him, a wealthy man whose steps "were washed with milk" and "streams of oil" (vv 4-5). His status and reputation were evidenced by the respectful behavior of his community toward him:

> When I went out to the gate of the city,
>   when I took my seat in the square,
> the young men saw me and withdrew,
>   and the aged rose up and stood;
> the nobles refrained from talking,
>   and laid their hands on their mouths;
> the voices of princes were hushed,
>   and their tongues stuck to the roof of their mouths.
> When the ear heard, it commended me,
>   and when the eye saw, it approved. (29:7-11)

Verses 12-17 give the reasons for Job's elevated station: his concern for and responsibility to the weak and helpless:

> Because I delivered the poor who cried,
>   and the orphan who had no helper.
> The blessing of the wretched came upon me,
>   and I caused the widow's heart to sing for joy.
> I put on righteousness, and it clothed me;
>   my justice was like a robe and a turban.
> I was eyes to the blind,
>   and feet to the lame.
> I was a father to the needy,
>   and I championed the cause of the stranger.
> I broke the fangs of the unrighteous,
>   and made them drop their prey from their teeth. (29:12-17)

We see here a hierarchy of male relationships within this community, in which Job has a preeminent rank, even among nobles, princes, and aged men. Job's lofty honor resides not only in his wealth, children, and age—which some of the other men presumably also have—but particularly in his concern for the weak.[93] Earlier, I quoted Abu-Lughod pointing out that the inequalities among the Awlad 'Ali are legitimated by a family idiom that places the dependency of the weak upon the responsibility of the strong toward them.[94]

By virtue of his wealth, sexual virility, and age, Job is an autonomous person, free from dependency on others.[95] Nevertheless, he is not free to exploit or oppress those beneath him. The ideology of honor simultaneously demands Job's obligations to the weak and justifies his control over them. Job would be shamed if he abused this control. Zeid, who also studied the Awlad 'Ali, describes the nature of this hierarchy concisely: "Thus it is a man's responsibility to help the needy, to defend the weak and to protect and support the oppressed within his own lineage and to a lesser degree his clan. Failing to comply with these binding duties brings shame on him and on his immediate *beit* [family household]."[96] Within the male hierarchy described in Job 29, those men "under" Job resolve their lesser honor with respect to him through voluntary acts of deference, acknowledging Job's patronage of the weak.

Job 30 describes a completely opposite state of affairs. Here Job bemoans his present state of disgrace, in which his "honor is pursued as by the wind" and his "prosperity has passed away like a cloud" (30:15):

> But now they make sport of me,
> >   those who are younger than I,
> whose fathers I would have disdained
> >   to set with the dogs of my flock. (30:1-2)

> And now they mock me in song:
> >   I am a byword to them.
> They abhor me, they keep aloof from me;
> >   they do not hesitate to spit at the sight of me.
> Because God has loosed my bowstring and humbled me,
> >   they have cast off restraint in my presence. (30:9-11)

By casting off restraint before Job, these men shame him by their lack of deference.

In contrast, deference, meekness, and propriety comprise the posture of one before a more honorable person. Men exemplify deference in a number of ways in the Hebrew Bible. Besides the acts of withdrawing from, rising before, and refraining from speaking in the presence of a man of honor—all described in Job 29—the Hebrew Bible contains frequent expressions of falling on one's face, bowing down, and doing obeisance before a more exalted person.[97] Sirach 4:21 distinguishes between a "shame that leads to sin" and a "shame that merits honor [lit. 'glory'] and favor." It is in the second sense that shame carries the positive connotation of deference and modesty. In the Hebrew Bible, however, the usage of shame terminology highlights the negative connotations of shame as disgrace and dishonor. Rather than describe the concern for reputation as *shame*, I follow Abu-Lughod in preferring to consider deference and modesty as the *honor* of the weak.[98]

The modesty and deference of lower-status men furnish clues in understanding women's place in the hierarchy of male honor. If honor is exemplified through one's personal independence and autonomy, based on wealth, status, patrilineal kinship, *and* care for the weak, then women have the lowest rank within this honor system, being peripheral to the patriline and inheriting no material resources. As a result, they are dependent on men. However, they are not without honor in this system. As with lower-status men, women resolve the contradictions between their lower social positions and the communitarian ideology of their lineage through voluntary acts of deference and modesty. Manifesting a sensitivity for their own reputations, women gain honorable recognition through these actions.[99] Their men will be shamed and disgraced if their submission is procured through tyranny or coercion. In the ideology of honor, their compliance has to be perceived by men as freely granted, which helps to explain why women would choose to submit to this androcentric system. Since a man must deserve honor through his moral worthiness in caring for the weak, "the free consent of dependents is essential to the superior's legitimacy. What is voluntary is by nature free and is thus also *a sign of independence*. Voluntary deference is therefore the honorable mode of dependency."[100] At work here is the legitimizing strategy of ideology that requires "an at least tacit consent to its authority."[101] Through this deference women acquire some form of honor, if not the higher levels of honor that men can attain.

Although both women and lower-status men engage in honorable acts of deference and modesty, undeniable differences based on gender nevertheless exist. By virtue of their gender, men have access to the avenues of honor, where honor in good part rests on patrilineal descent, male inheritance, and so on. Women do not. Lower-status men have the potential to become more socially recognized as honorable as they age or acquire more wealth and status. Women do not. Moreover, lower-class men will always have more status than women, except in the case of upper-class women. Women are therefore socialized into a constant state of deference and modesty before the more powerful. They are trained from the beginning to withdraw before men, to be meek and refrain from speaking, and to be obedient and cooperative.

In anthropological studies, women have been described as the "weak link" in the chain of male honor.[102] Our glimpse of Job points out that any biblical man of honor is vulnerable to being shamed by the withdrawal of acts of deference and modesty by his subordinates, who include both women *and* lower-status men. However, female sexual shame exacerbates male shame because of the society's exclusive stress on patrilineality and its economics. Here the ideology of honor and shame intersects with the ideology of patrilineal kinship to make women, paradoxically, the chink in the coat of male honor.

In pre-state Israel, a society organized by patrilineal honor/shame ideologies, a wife's primary contribution to the family household was her sexual fertility, bearing legitimate sons to carry on the family name and keep limited assets such as land and property in the household. In this labor-intensive society, maternity was an adaptive response to harsh ecological conditions, as the Israelites took possession of the highlands.[103] Both husband and wife were shamed when the wife was barren and unable to perpetuate the lineage.[104] A man was also shamed if he chose the wrong wife, as in the case of Esau, who married a woman outside the lineage (Gen 27:46; 28:8-9). In order to ensure patrilineality and guarantee a husband's paternity (and thus his honor), the sexual behavior of women had to be carefully supervised and controlled.[105] Women's chastity became a limited commodity that had to be protected like any other scarce resource.[106] Since female sexual purity symbolized a family's ability to protect its material resources,[107] a large measure of a man's honor rested on the sexual behavior of women, whether his wife's, daughter's, sister's, or mother's. If a woman was sexually shameless in any way, it would be revealed publicly that her husband, father, brother, or son, as the stronger of the two genders, had failed in his responsibility to preserve the family honor by this inability to protect or control her. The man and his family would consequently forfeit honor in the community. Sirach depicts the plight of fathers regarding their daughters nicely:

A daughter is a secret anxiety to her father,
    and worry over her robs him of sleep;
when she is young, for fear she may not marry,
    or if married, for fear she may be disliked;
while a virgin, for fear she may be seduced
    and become pregnant in her father's house;
or having a husband, for fear she may go astray,
    or though married, for fear she may be barren.
Keep strict watch over a headstrong daughter,
    or she may make you a laughingstock to your enemies,
a byword in the city and the assembly of the people,
    and put you to shame in public gatherings. (42:9-11, italics mine)

Moreover, the extent of a man's disgrace correlated inversely with the status of the one who shamed him: the lower the status, the greater the shame. Job, for example, laments that younger men of inferior lineage ridicule him, thus compounding his humiliation (30:1). Likewise, the sexual transgressions of or against a man's woman resulted in greater dishonor and warranted extreme condemnation and punishment. Hence Shechem's rape of Dinah brings disgrace to her brothers, which compels them to take retributive action against the perpetrator and his family (Genesis 34; cf. 2 Samuel 13). Moreover, Dinah's rape and dishonor preclude any possibility of a more honorable endogamous marriage (and resulting benefits) arranged for her by her patrikin. A woman who was not a virgin at the time of her marriage dishonored her father's house and was condemned to stoning (Deut 22:21). According to Jon Levenson, David seduces Saul's wife and Jonathan's mother, Ahinoam of Jezreel, and later marries her.[108] Saul accuses Jonathan of being infected by the shame of his mother's nakedness (1 Sam 20:30; cf. Hos 2:4-5).

In a society operating under patrilineal and honor/shame-based ideologies, adultery is a first-class offense.[109] It violates a man's absolute right to the sexuality of his wife and places his paternity in question—very threatening and disruptive in a society governed by a patrilineal kinship structure. Adultery results in a considerable loss of honor not only for the husband but also for all those reciprocally involved in his honor: his family and his lineage.

While the adulterer himself incurs disgrace and condemnation in an affair (Jer 29:22-23; Prov 6:32-33), an implicit double standard exists in the biblical evaluation of a man who breaks wedlock. Extramarital activity, which would be inexcusable for the wife, is tolerated for the husband in many cases. From an honor/shame perspective, a lack of chastity in women places the family honor accumulated in the patriline in jeopardy, whereas in men it destroys the honor of *other* families.[110] A man is not punished for having sex unless an engaged or a married woman is involved *and* he is caught in the act (Deut 22:22-29). Furthermore, engaging the services of prostitutes is acceptable (Gen 38:12-26; Josh 2:1-7; 1 Kgs 3:16-27). This double standard underscores the issues of honor and legal paternity that characterize the ideological structure of Israelite society, making the woman the primary offender in adulterous acts.

Weapons of the Weak: Women's Informal Power

Carol Meyers argues convincingly that modern categories of domestic and public are flawed when applied to pre-state Israel, where the lines between the two domains are blurred. Because of the importance of the family household in Israelite social structure, women's strong role in the management of the household had wider social implications. For Meyers, "female power will be as significant as male power and perhaps even greater."[111] In line with feminist anthropologists, she differentiates power from authority (the legally sanctioned right to make decisions), defining it as the ability to influence and effect control despite or independent of official authority. The type of power women usually exercise is informal, rather than formal: "Female power typically involves informal and unofficial modes of behavior that may never receive male acknowledgment but through which females may exert considerable and systematic direction over a range of circumstances."[112] I would qualify Meyers's claim that expressions of women's informal power may never be acknowledged by men. They do receive recognition (and critique) when inscribed in men's literary symbolization of woman as evil. I now explore in detail something that Meyers recognizes but does not discuss: the manipulative, disruptive, and covert exercises of women's informal power.[113]

Women can exploit the contradictions of patrilineal honor/shame ideologies for their own purposes. Contradictions inhere in Israel's familial mode of production, in which women can have decisive roles in the supervision of the family household and yet are formally excluded from the material sources of honor and prestige—that is, descent and inheritance. Being thus denied access to formal avenues of power, women often revert to conflict-indicating behavior to get what they want.[114] It is this behavior that is ideologically encoded in the biblical text.

In a class analysis, James Scott analyzes the exercise of power among Malaysian peasants, finding that they resist daily oppression, not by collective organized effort, but by individual acts of passive aggression, manipulation, foot-dragging, gossip, petty thievery, arson, and so on. He calls these actions "weapons of the weak," which avoid direct protest against the authority and norms of dominant/elite groups.[115] Scott's notion of "weapons of the weak" can be applied to women's conflict-indicating behavior. In gender analyses feminist anthropologists raise crucial issues of how we recognize and regard everyday forms of female resistance to male authority.[116] Reversing Foucault's famous declaration that "where there is power, there is resistance," Abu-Lughod argues that "where there is resistance, there is power." Instead of romanticizing resistance as a sign of weakness in dominant power structures or as the creative refusal of the human spirit to be dominated, she thinks we should use resistance as a *diagnostic* of power.[117] Resistance then becomes an exercise of power, rather than a reaction to it.

The "weapons of the weak" used by females—their strategies of resistance/power to male authority and control—can take an endless number of forms. Within their sexually segregated world, women can use secrets and silences to their advantage, colluding to keep knowledge of socially unacceptable behavior from their spouses.[118] Conversely, they can gossip about their husbands and spread stories about them, bringing shame to the patriline.[119] They can skillfully manipulate their husbands verbally.[120] They can steal from their husbands.[121] They can oppose and stonewall marriages arranged by their male relatives.[122] They can crudely poke fun at masculine shortcomings with sexually irreverent discourse.[123] They can socialize their children about the fickleness of their fathers and use their sons covertly to achieve their aims.[124] They can practice sorcery upon their husbands to influence their attitudes or keep them faithful to their marriage vows.[125] They can nag incessantly or become shrewish and quarrelsome.[126] They can refuse to cook or have anything to do with domestic or agricultural tasks.[127] Finally, they can exploit their men sexually, by refusing sexual intercourse with them or by threatening and actually pursuing sexually unacceptable behavior with other men.[128] Thus: "While acknowledging male authority, women may direct it to their own interests, and in terms of actual choices and decisions, of who influences whom and how, the power exercised by women may have considerable and systematic effect."[129]

Feminist biblical scholars have already noted many of these tactics used by women in the biblical text. Naomi Steinberg examines the contentious and quarrelsome women figuring in Prov 19:13; 21:19; 25:24; 27:15, and in the matriarchal stories of Genesis.[130] In a section describing women's strategies in pursuit of goals, Tikva Frymer-Kensky records how biblical women worked through men in power, petitioning, convincing, and influencing them to do their bidding.[131] Sarah, Rachel, Achsah, and the widow of Zarephath use several "guilt-producing rhetorical tactics" that work very effectively on men. The lovers and wives of Samson take up nagging as a weapon to influence him. Women, like Jael, use food and nurture (symbols of the so-called private domain) to their advantage. A number of scholars have analyzed the numerous instances in the Bible in which women deceive.[132]

If one looks beyond the Hebrew Bible to related Jewish literature, one can observe other revealing examples of women wielding "weapons of the weak." The book of Judith narrates the story of a widow who uses both her sexually charged beauty and her exceptional rhetorical skills to kill an enemy:[133]

> She anointed her face with perfume:
>   she fastened her hair with a tiara
>   and put on a linen gown to beguile him.
> Her sandal ravished his eyes,
>   her beauty captivated his mind,
>   and the sword severed his neck! (Jdt 16:7-9)

Sirach has a number of negative opinions on the "wickedness" and "evil" of wives and daughters, particularly in Sirach 25–26. Sirach prefers "any wickedness, but not the wickedness of a woman" (25:13), and "would rather live with a lion and a dragon than live with an evil woman" (25:16). Alluding to the primordial Eve in Genesis 3, he declares: "From a woman sin had its beginning, and because of her we all die" (25:24). Sirach is quite specific about the "evils" that women inflict on their husbands, revealing significant clues to the informal ways in which women control their men: through their wrath and contentiousness (25:15), their violent quarrels with co-wives (26:6), their drunken behavior (26:8), their garrulousness (25:20; cf. 26:27), their bold words (25:25), their beauty and wealth (25:21-22), their willfulness (26:25), and their sexual infidelity (26:9).

Much of the language in Sirach 25–26 is expressed in the vocabulary of honor and shame.[134] A man's personal honor is vulnerable to the behavior of his women—their deference to his authority or lack thereof. Sirach's grossly explicit exhortation that fathers exercise stringent control over their daughters exemplifies how susceptible a man's honor actually is:

> Keep strict watch over a headstrong daughter,
>   or else, when she finds liberty, she will make use of it.
> Be on guard against her impudent eye,
>   and do not be surprised if she sins against you.
> As a thirsty traveler opens his mouth
>   and drinks from any water near him,
> so she will sit in front of every tent peg
>   and open her quiver to the arrow. (26:10-12)

The nexus between the idea of women as evil and their various manipulative sexual behaviors can be found in another second-century B.C.E. Jewish work, the *Testament of Reuben*:[135]

> *For women are evil, my children, and by reason of their lacking authority or power over man*, they scheme treacherously how they might entice him to themselves by means of their looks. *And whomever they cannot enchant by their appearance they conquer by a stratagem.* Indeed, the angel of the Lord told me and instructed me that women are more easily overcome by the spirit of promiscuity than are men. They contrive in their hearts against men, then by decking themselves out they lead men's minds astray, by a look they implant their poison, and finally in the act itself they take them captive. *For a woman is not able to coerce a man overtly, but by a harlot's manner she accomplishes her villainy.* Accordingly, my children, flee from sexual promiscuity, and order your wives and your daughters not to adorn their heads and their appearances so as to deceive men's sound minds. For every woman who schemes in these ways is destined for eternal punishment. (T. Reu. 5:1-5, italics mine)

Despite its clear androcentric ideology, what is significant about this text is its perceptive analysis of power relations. Because women lack authority or power over men (5:1), they resort to schemes and sexual strategies in particular to manipulate them. They are not able to coerce their men overtly (5:4), as men customarily coerce one another. Instead, they use their sexual seductiveness—"a harlot's manner"—to accomplish their "villainy." Men are therefore enjoined to "order" their wives and daughters to dress and act modestly, so as not "to deceive men's sound minds" (5:5). Offensive and biased as these sentiments are according to contemporary values, they still give us indicators of gender power relationships and their complexities in an androcentric society. Feminist anthropological research supports the idea that women adopted these strategies. Rather than viewing these tactics simply as the machinations of women who are "victims" of an androcentric society, one should regard them as "diagnostics of power." The conflict-indicating behavior of women reveals them as actors within an androcentric society, exercising power and manipulating and subverting its structures.[136]

It is noteworthy that many of the tactics described above maximize and exploit the vulnerable areas of the patrilineal code of honor. Marginalized from it, women often threaten to bring shame to the patriline to get what they want, even at the risk of losing access to sources of their economic well-being.[137] Although they are regarded as unnecessary or superfluous in a patrilineal ideology, they are nevertheless crucial to men as wives, sisters to be exchanged for wives, and mothers who produce a labor force and heirs for the lineage. "Because they are important, they are powerful, yet theirs is a power opposed to formal norms."[138] Contradictions in patrilineal and honor/shame ideologies become apparent when women consciously exploit these ideologies for their own purposes. Their subversive actions are not shameful in their eyes; rather, such actions are seen as exercises of power that disclose countercoherences in the ideologies that regulate women's world.

———————————————

Women's control over food preparation, allocation of resources, and other subsistence-level activities, their major roles in the socialization and education of children, and their influence in major decisions of the family household all contribute to their informal power within pre-state Israelite society.[139] Nevertheless, men have a dominant position in the general mode of production, as elders who control economic resources, as the recipients of the family name and patrimony, as the paterfamilias, and so on. Whatever power women have is subsumed in male power and authority. The dominance of men in pre-state Israel is a material and ideological fact. Women may not experience themselves as subordinate, but they are in a structurally subordinate position with respect to men.[140]

In conflict situations in which ideological contradictions become apparent, gender relations become sites of power struggles between dominant and subordinate groups. In spite of their lesser social position, women may enact a number of strategies that strike at the very heart of the patrilineal, honor-based system, threatening the status quo. These strategies are both a function of and an adaptation to women's subordinate and dependent position with regard to control over resources.[141] Because of the interpenetration of the public and domestic domains in ancient Israel, women's activities and concerns are therefore not isolated, privatized issues, but rather thoroughly political ones. Men inscribe these politics of gender in the production of the literary symbolization of woman as evil.

A Conspiracy of Silence: Women's Separate World

One final area of Israelite society remains to be discussed, one that also affects the male symbolization of woman as evil: the separate world of women. The biblical text does not provide detailed descriptions of women's world in ancient Israel—their personal stories, emotional experiences, and interpersonal relationships. Feminist ethnographies can help us reconstruct what this separate world might have been like.

Was there a separate women's world in ancient Israel? Based on archaeological and ethnographic evidence, Meyers has documented a clearly defined gender division of labor and the important role of women within the subsistence economy of pre-state Israel.[142] Moreover, the biblical text does contain clues that some forms of physical segregation of the genders were customary in ancient Israel. Although clearly eavesdropping at the tent door, Sarah remained inside the tent while Abraham showed hospitality to his three male guests

(Gen 18:9-10). Wells seem to have been a common place at which
the genders encountered each other (Gen 24:11-14; 29:6-11; Exod
2:16-17). Nevertheless, women appear to have gone out in groups to
the wells (Exod 2:16; 1 Sam 9:11), particularly in the evening, which
seems to have been a special time when women came to draw water
(Gen 24:11-13). Men and women lived in separate tents (Gen 31:33;
Judg 4:17). Women engaged in separate harvesting activities (Ruth
2:8), harvesting rituals (Judg 21:20-21), and victory celebrations
(Exod 15:20-21; 1 Sam 18:6-7; 21:11; 29:5; cf. Judg 11:34; 2 Sam
1:20). Women took solace in each other's company, like Jephthah's
daughter, who with her companions "bewailed" her virginity for two
months in the mountains. Her story is remembered in a four-day ritual celebrated by women (Judg 11:37-40).

Descriptions of female interaction in the Hebrew Bible are rare
and refracted through the eyes of its male authors. The most notable
instances in which females relate with each other are those of conflict, as in the stories of Hagar and Sarah (Genesis 16 and 21), Leah
and Rachel (Genesis 30), and Hannah and Peninnah (1 Samuel 1).
Nevertheless, the stories of Lot's daughters (Gen 16:30-38) and Ruth
and Naomi (Ruth 1–4) describe cooperation between women and intrigue in their dealings with their male relatives.

Feminist ethnographies of Middle Eastern societies can help us to
imagine the female world, about which the biblical text is mostly
silent. If analogies between the social world of women in pre-state Israel and these ethnographies are correct, women themselves most
likely restricted men from having unlimited access to their private
world. This would partially explain the absence of this female world
in the biblical text.

Abu-Lughod describes the separate women's community of the
Awlad 'Ali bedouin as a subsociety, not defined by physical spaces rel-
egating women and children to the home and men to more public
places, as it is in other areas of the Middle East. Instead, segregation
is maintained by the separation of activities that results from the gender division of labor, and especially by mutual avoidance. This gender
separation of activities has parallels with that of ancient Israel, which
also had some forms of physical segregation of the genders.

As we have seen, the Awlad 'Ali patrilineal social structure accords
authority and prestige to the male, to agnates (members of the patriline), and to senior kinsmen. This structure is upheld by strict codes
of honor and modesty that discourage the expression of sexuality,

which conflicts with them. "The denial of sexuality is best expressed by avoiding members of the opposite sex with whom one might have a sexual relationship, and deferring, through modest avoidance, to those senior kinsmen who embody and represent the social ideals of independence and the triumph of agnation."[143] Interaction between the genders is therefore circumscribed by the factors of age, kinship relation, and social status. Younger kinsmen, household members, and low-status men—those who are not regarded as sexual threats or authority figures—have easier access to women's separate world. Given the code of modesty and deference, however, loquacious women will fall silent, disperse, or change their conversation with the appearance of fathers, paternal uncles, or fathers-in-law. Furthermore, men who are not kin, particularly those of high status, would not even approach an area where a group of women was gathered.[144]

Instead of judging segregated social worlds as a liability for women, ethnographic evidence indicates that "the segregation of women can alternatively be seen as an exclusion of men from a range of contacts which women have among themselves."[145] Hence, while women are nonparticipating observers of the male world that cross-cuts their lives, men have even *less access* to the female subculture.

> Bedouin women collude to erect a barrier of silence about their world. Information flows unidirectionally from the men's arena into the women's and not vice versa. Since women become deferentially silent in the presence of most adult men, men generally do not overhear the natural conversations of women. Young and low-status men have easy access to the women's community, and they bring information to the women about what goes on in the male world. But such men, because they are circumspect in their own community and must be deferential to senior males, do not report back about what goes on among women.[146]

Daisy Dwyer observes that Moroccan women advocate the segregation of the genders because it provides their activities with considerable camouflage and shelter. Since men are frequently separated from women in many contexts and during many activities, they can supervise and regulate their women only with a certain difficulty. Gender segregation can afford women opportunities for veiled acts of autonomy from and defiance of male authority. Each gender rationalizes gender segregation differently. For men, women should be kept

separate because they are inferior. Other men are men's preferred social companions. For women, however, gender separation moves men
out of their daily life space and provides occasions for subversive activities.[147]

Besides providing a screen for acts of defiance, the separation of
the genders allows women to become arbiters of their own morality.
Older women guide the moral development of girls through teasing,
gossip, and other forms of indirect criticism.[148] Although women are
socialized in the moral ideals of a male-dominated society, in their
own world they can judge moral infractions from a different perspective than that of men. For example, Wikan records a case in which
condemnation of a woman's adultery was circumvented among her
female neighbors because she had become a more hospitable person
because of it. In this female domain, the value of hospitality and
solidarity among women took precedence over the value of sexual
fidelity.[149]

Instead of viewing women's social control as reproducing the androcentric values of the society that keeps them subordinate, Abu-
Lughod argues that by managing their own affairs rather than letting
men do so, women avoid direct experiences of their own subordination and dependency. Women can come to realize that they are responsible moral beings, not impotent victims whose only advantage
lies in covert intrigue and subversion.[150]

Summary

Foundational for an extrinsic analysis of biblical texts symbolizing
woman as evil, this chapter utilizes the social sciences to help reconstruct the social world of premonarchic Israel operating under a familial mode of production. Since an interrelationship exists between
the text and the society that produces it, gender relations should be
situated in the wider context of the most important socioeconomic
unit in Israelite tribal structure: the family household, or bêt 'āb.
Governing the family household are a patrilineal descent ideology,
patrilocal marriage residence customs, endogamy, and patrimonial
inheritance rights, all of which privilege the male and subordinate
the female in an asymmetrical hierarchy.

A moral ideology of honor and shame interfaces with the ideology
of patrilineal descent and helps to justify the social inequity and con-

trol possessed by senior kinsmen in a society that prizes familial ideals. Men accorded honor are those who, by virtue of their lineage, wealth, age, status, and so on, are autonomous and free from dependency on others. Their patronage and protection of the weak legitimates their authority over them. The weak, which includes lower-status men and all women, operate under a code of modesty in deference to men of honor. While lower-status men have the potential to claims of honor and higher status, women are socialized into a fixed situation of deference and modesty before men.

Nevertheless, men's honor is particularly vulnerable to the actions of women. Although this social system runs harmoniously on the *voluntary* deference of its weaker members, women can adopt various strategies to exploit the vulnerabilities of male honor and patrilineality. Particularly threatening to both male honor and patrilineality are women's sexual transgressions or the threat thereof. The various strategies that women employ can be construed as "weapons of the weak" and should be regarded as diagnostics of power. As diagnostics of power, they must be analyzed from the perspective of women who are not only resisting male authority but also exerting control over their lives in an androcentric situation.

Finally, women's private world in ancient Israel may be reconstructed by analogy with Middle Eastern ethnographies. This world is not described in the biblical text, because, if the analogies are correct, adult men had no immediate access to it. On the one hand, the ideology of honor and shame precluded informal interchange between adult men and women. On the other hand, women welcomed this segregation, preventing men from having unlimited passage into their separate world. This world provided camouflage and shelter for women's subversive acts of defiance. It was characterized by intense personal relationships and solidarity among women, even though conflict did occur. It also provided a place where women's moral breaches could be judged on a different scale than in the men's world.

Two gendered worlds would thus have existed in ancient Israel: the female world encapsulated by the male world, but for the most part invisible and inaccessible to it. Both domains would be sites of power struggle during times of intergender conflict. Nevertheless, what appears predominantly in the biblical text is the male world. The biblical text narrates and legitimizes male ideologies of lineage, descent, and honor as they are lived out in obedience to the biblical God YHWH. It is silent about the female world because this world exists in the text as a double absence. One does not encounter "real" gender relationships firsthand. Instead, one confronts them as already encoded in ideological formations that real situations of gender relations have actually produced. The biblical perception of the female world and the informal power women exert is skewed in its symbolization of woman as evil.

4 Eve in Genesis:
The Mother of All Living
and We Her Children

In Western tradition, the symbolization of woman as evil is usually traced back to the primeval person of Eve.[1] In the words of the ancient sage Sirach, "From a woman sin had its beginning, and because of her we all die" (Sir 25:24).[2] The all-too-familiar injunction of 1 Tim 2:11-15 directs the silencing and submission of women to men because "Adam was formed first, then Eve; and Adam was not deceived, but the woman was deceived and became a transgressor. Yet she will be saved through childbearing, provided they continue in faith and love and holiness, with modesty." Nevertheless, according to Tertullian, Eve, the mother of all living, is not saved by childbearing. As the devil's gateway (*Cultu fem.* 1.1), Eve's first child becomes a demon's offspring: "Let no one say that Eve conceived nothing in her womb at the devil's word. The devil's word was the seed for her so that afterward she should give birth as an outcast and bring forth in sorrow. In fact she gave birth to a devil who murdered his brother; while Mary bore one who with time would bring salvation to Israel" (*De Carne Christ* 17).

Except for Genesis, the Hebrew Bible contains no other speculation on Eve.[3] In this chapter I focus on the Yahwist's portrayal of Eve in Genesis 2–3, since it is chiefly the Yahwist's narrative that triggers subsequent symbolizations of Eve as the origin of evil.[4] In my extrinsic analysis of Genesis 2–3, I first discuss the dating of the Yahwist (or J) during the monarchical period of Israelite history, with its change in mode of production. I then show that a slow but conscious effort

native
tributary

to control sexuality and gender relationships occurred during this time. This increased supervision of gender relations would be encoded in the textual production of Genesis 2–3. In the intrinsic analysis that follows, I reveal the various ideological depictions of hierarchy constructed by the Yahwist: human beings to YHWH, of the tribes to their king, and of woman to her man.

Extrinsic Analysis of Genesis 2–3

The fact that pentateuchal studies are still in a considerable state of flux can be seen in the different datings for the Yahwist's work.[5] His creation and fall narratives have been variously assigned to the tribal period,[6] Davidic monarchy,[7] the Solomonic monarchy,[8] the exilic and postexilic periods,[9] or to a redactional composite of datings from the monarchy to the exilic or postexilic eras.[10]

I will broach the problem of J's dating not by pinpointing his work within a specific historical context, but by situating it as a literary product within a particular mode of production. I will show that, if myths of origins are symbolic resolutions by the dominant class of real social contradictions,[11] the ideology of Genesis 2–3 reflects contradictions that occurred when Israel moved from the familial mode of production typical of its tribal period to the native-tributary mode of production typical of the preexilic monarchy.[12] As I will argue, this ideology encodes the struggle between the social and economic interests of the Judahite royal elite and the peasant class and provides the theological justification for the division between these classes.[13] I touched on the native-tributary mode of production in chapter 3;[14] here I discuss this mode of production in greater detail, particularly as it affects gender relationships.

From Tributary to Familial Mode of Production: Premonarchic Israel

Biblical and archaeological evidence suggests that, rather than occurring through invasion or immigration from the outside, the emergence of Israel in Canaan during the thirteenth to twelfth centuries B.C.E. was an indigenous phenomenon.[15] The rise of Israel can be correlated with an interlocking complex of ecological, economic, and political factors that were evident in Late Bronze Age Canaan. During this time, major settlements were concentrated in urban centers in the coastal plain and the northern valleys. These city-states were ruled by kings and military families, who themselves were under Egyptian hegemony. The basic economy depended on the agrarian cultivation (under adverse conditions) of grains, fruits, and vegetables, augmented by animal products. Only a very sparse village culture existed, since the cultivators of the land—the peasants—tended to live around the urban centers and sought the protection their city walls afforded.[16]

Under this tributary mode of production, the peasant bore the heaviest tax burden of the state vis-à-vis other social groups. A considerable percentage of the peasant population escaped their oppressive situation by fleeing to the highland areas and becoming nomads, refugees, or outlaws, outside the jurisdiction of the urban centers and Egyptian authority.[17] This withdrawal of the peasant population had a negative impact on the city-states, which lost a significant portion of their tax base and were confronted with populations beyond their control that threatened trade relations with surrounding nations.

The Early Iron Age in Canaan (ca. 1200–1000 B.C.E.) witnessed a dramatic growth and cultivation in the highland areas and the rise of village life. Settlement in the "frontier" regions of the land was made possible by the technology in cistern building and terracing that the peasants brought with them. Scholars correlate the emergence of Israel with this push into the hill country and the development of a new mode of production: "In the course of time, it became possible for this 'outlaw' population group to consolidate their toehold in the highlands and, through socio-political integration, to achieve such a degree of independence that they were able, as tribes, to administer their own territories, settle in them, clear new land for a growing population, and defend them against outside interference."[18]

The organization of this new society was strongly kinship-based, consisting of "the father's house," "lineage," and "tribe" (described in detail in chap. 3 above). Operating under a familial mode of production, the family household was the basic socioeconomic unit. As self-sufficient, mutually supporting, and protecting entities, the households, lineages, and tribes were tributary-free, having no state mechanisms to appropriate their surpluses.

From Familial Back to Tributary:
Monarchic Israel

The tribes remained in a familial mode of production as free agrarians for about two centuries. The transition to a monarchy and tributary mode of production resulted from complex external and internal pressures affecting Israel. The biblical texts describe Philistine military incursions into Israelite territories as the chief impetus for the tribes' demand for a king. For one thing, Israel's growth and prosperity in the highland areas posed a political threat to Philistine strongholds along the coast, and to the Amalekites in the south and the Ammonites in the east. In addition, the highland tribes cultivated agricultural products less available in the lands belonging to these peoples, providing an economic attraction for Philistine, Amalekite, and Ammonite expansion.[19]

Besides these external factors, internal forces not readily apparent in the biblical texts were at work in the change to a monarchy. Robert Coote and Keith Whitelam delineate three areas in the shift in highland infrastructure that facilitated state formation. First, the expansion of horticulture and the population increase in highland regions were crucial for the emergence of Israel. Nevertheless, once the frontier was "tamed," there was no more room for further economic expansion, and population growth put considerable stress on limited natural resources. Moreover, agriculture was subject to the vagaries of the arid climate, exacerbating the problem of feeding the growing population. "Under these conditions, the rise of kingship may have been largely a self-generating process."[20]

The second factor that expedited state formation was the increasing socioeconomic stratification in the Israelite population.[21] The limits put on available land for cultivation, the increased population growth, and the depletion of resources created a disproportionate degree of inequity among Israelite social groups.[22] "Its consequence would have been that the more fortunate Israelites were in a position to bind their poorer kinsmen to them by means of contracts which transformed what were originally independent peasants into indentured peasants in the service of their fellow countrymen. Over the course of time the latter took on the character of local petty nobles or wealthy farmers."[23]

Finally, increasing political centralization promoted the rise of the monarchy. While most free agrarians supported the move toward a monarchy to defend themselves against Philistine hegemony, prosperous landholders within Israel saw in the monarchy a way to advance their own economic and political interests. The monarchy represented the "means by which a subgroup of emergent landed elite in Israel imposed greater costs of national defence upon village smallholders and retained political control over their participation in trade among themselves."[24]

Through foreign conquests and the taxation of non-Israelite land in Canaan, King David was able to forestall the extraction of tribute from free agrarians. However, he initiated an array of political and economic structures that, under the rule of his son Solomon, assimilated the tribes back into a tributary economy and exacerbated the social stratification among free agrarians.[25] Those among the landed elite became part of the ruling class or otherwise profited from tax concessions and latifundiary arrangements. For the majority of Israel's free agrarians, however, this was not the case. The king and the ruling elite began to demand their surpluses, in both human and natural resources, to pay for the centralized bureaucracy, ambitious building projects, and luxurious court lifestyle.[26] Thus these farmers became progressively more impoverished. Over time, they fell to peasant status as they were increasingly taxed. Often, this taxation resulted in the loss of their ancestral lands to the state in order to pay their debts.[27] Norman Gottwald's comments on Israel's relation to the state from the time of its inception are insightful: "Although Israel arose in opposition to the state system, and in time survived apart from any particular state structure, its history and ethos were fashioned in intimate response to the commanding position of the state. In both native and foreign guises, the state intruded insistently upon the economy and ideology of the villages which constituted the heartland of Israel."[28]

Genesis 2–3 was a product of this traumatic time, encoding the inconsistencies and ruptures of this period. It responded to a particular socioeconomic contradiction: to maintain national unity and security against the threats of invaders, the confederated tribes of Israel reverted back to an oppressive political system and mode of production that they rejected when they became a confederacy.[29] What began as a loose confederation of family groups, lineages, and tribes in reaction to state hegemony—a federation committed to mutual aid and defense—now reverted back to a hierarchical, socially stratified, and centralized territorial state governed by a dynastic monarchy.

Effects on Family and Gender Relationships

Niels Lemche points out that one decisive difference between state
and tribe is that the former controlled its citizens through *political
force*, possessing any number of state apparatuses to get what it
wanted, while members of the latter were united by ties of *social solidarity* based on kinship connections, at least on the ideological level.[30]
Patrilineal kinship ideology was present among the populace throughout this shift toward the state, and it became an important trope to describe relationships between God and the king and between the king
and his people. As the paterfamilias had governed his family, so now
the king (God's human representative) governed his people.[31]

Changes in political system and mode of production had a sub-
stantial effect on family and gender relations. Under the familial
mode of production, the family kin group was the basic socioeconomic unit. In cutting across tribal boundaries to divide the territory
into twelve administrative districts, Solomon undermined tribal organization and kin-group loyalties by redirecting them to the centralized government in Jerusalem (1 Kgs 4:7-19). The family household
gradually lost its power and authority as the primary socioeconomic
unit. Moreover, impoverishment of households had damaging effects
on all members, as the state siphoned off their products and human
resources.[32]

The effects of state formation on the position of women in the society have been analyzed extensively by feminist anthropologists and
historians.[33] Investigations into women's status in ancient Near Eastern civilizations are particularly pertinent for this study. Ruby
Rohrlich correlates women's loss of status in ancient Sumer with the
destruction of egalitarian kinship relations as a result of the military
and political consolidation of the state.[34] For Barbara Lesko, the consequences of a permanent kingship in Sumer—for example, the con-
centration of land among the aristocracy, heavy taxation, and social
stratification—eroded women's position and limited their rights.[35]

We saw in chapter 3 that during the tribal confederacy and under
a familial mode of production, Israelite women were still materially
subordinate to men within ideological structures of patrilineality, patrilocality, and patrimony. This material subordination was articulated in an ideological value system of honor and shame.
Nevertheless, when the mode of production was based in the family
household, women did exercise considerable power and authority in

the allocation of resources and productive domestic tasks. As power shifted from the family household to the state—with its male king and male political and religious bureaucracies—this female power and prestige receded.[36] When the family household became progressively more impoverished by the state, women bore the greater burden. As society itself became more economically and politically stratified by the state, hierarchical relations among male and female family members intensified.

The formation of the state particularly affects women and their men in the area of sexuality. Anthropologist Yehudi Cohen cross-culturally explores one of the ways in which some national rulers exercise political authority by regulating sexual behavior. What is particularly relevant about Cohen's study is that part of his database comprises the nascent monarchy in Israel. Cohen discovered that legislations regulating sexuality are characteristic of a certain type of state: the inchoate incorporative state, an emerging state that has not yet completely subverted local sources of solidarity, allegiance, and authority—for example, kinship ties and political and economic autonomy. In such a state, dominant and subordinate groups are culturally similar, speak the same language, share similar notions of cause and effect, and hold similar idioms regarding kinship and social organization. Since the symbolic gap between rulers and ruled is very narrow from the outset, rulers must adopt measures that foster social distance between strata.[37] In legal matters, an individual has a dual loyalty: one to the state and the other to the individual's local corporate group, such as their lineage.[38]

Because it competes with local sources of authority for the allegiance of its citizens, an emerging state must proceed slowly in subverting local nexuses. A radical destruction of the traditional ways would provoke resistance and rebellion. Moreover, the rulers themselves are products of the lineages and other social organizations that they seek to undermine. Hence, to legitimate its authority, the state must effect changes in the daily lives of the people subtly and gradually, before anyone realizes what is happening.[39]

Cohen argues that one of the ways the emerging state imperceptibly displaces and eventually replaces local authorities is by enacting tighter controls over sexual behavior. Laws demanding the death penalty for adultery, for example, have four consequences that are advantageous for the state. Laws that prescribe death for adulterous acts encourage and intensify the marital bond at the expense of the kinship bond. Moreover, strengthening the marriage bond does not conflict with the objectives of the emerging state. In fact, besides minimizing the kinship connection, it strengthens a bond that, in contrast to that of a lineage, cannot be a source of potential conspiracy and rebellion. Weakened kinship bonds can support a couple's mobility. This mobility reduces the potential for revolt, since rulers often try to disperse members of local corporate groups, in the most extreme cases by forced resettlement. Finally, because rulers in inchoate incorporative states must adopt strategies to widen the symbolic gap between ruler and ruled, adultery between a commoner and a ruler's wife is regarded as a very serious transgression.[40]

With respect to ancient Israel, Solomon's administration set into motion the breakdown of kinship authority through the redistricting of his kingdom. Moreover, several studies on sex and family laws in the Deuteronomic Code confirm Cohen's hypothesis that emerging states tend to adopt more restrictive jurisdiction over sexuality (including the death penalty), gradually subverting regional social bonds. These laws cover the premeditated murder of a community member (Deut 19:1-13), filial disrespect (21:18-21), accusations of female unchastity (22:13-21), adultery (22:22), adultery with a betrothed women in a town (22:23-24), the rape of a betrothed woman in an open area (22:25-27), and the rape of a virgin (22:28-29). In separate articles, Naomi Steinberg, Louis Stuhlman, and Tikva Frymer-Kensky demonstrate how these sex and family laws slowly eroded the power of the paterfamilias in favor of the state.[41] What could have been resolved by the male head of the household is brought into the wider public arena:

> D [the Deuteronomic Code] apparently intends to restrict the absolute power of the paterfamilias by (1) placing the state under obligation to take action against the wrongdoer, (2) involving the elders of the city (*zqny h'yr*) in the legal process, and by (3) punishing the guilty at the city gates (*h'yr š'r*)—the municipal court. As a result, the paterfamilias in D can no longer act extra-judicially and serve as the ultimate source of authority over his household.[42]

Steinberg also shows how the legislation of Deuteronomy 19–25 strengthens the nuclear family and the marital bond at the expense of the wider lineage, besides breaking down the dispute-settling authority of kin-group heads in favor of extrafamilial entities.[43] Bolstering the nuclear family and the marital bond intensifies ties that cannot become possible sources for insurrection. The increased mobility of the nuclear family also minimizes the potential for rebellion. Although it may appear that women benefit under the Deuteronomic Code by becoming less subject to the absolute jurisdiction of the paterfamilias, they actually become more subject to control in the politics of state centralization, along with their men.[44] "Once authority moved away from the family to the public tribunal and law, women actually had less influence on those under whose authority they came than they did in the household. Moreover, since the public hierarchy of ancient Israel was composed of men, the shift of authority over the woman moved from the concentrated authority of *one* man to the diffuse authority of many."[45]

An extrinsic analysis of Genesis 2–3 reveals that the circumstances of its production should be correlated with the transition in Israel from a familial mode of production to a native-tributary mode of production. The Yahwist's text is an ideological artifact that arises from and refers back to a tributary mode of production. As a myth of origins transmitted by a sector of the dominant class,[46] it attempts to resolve the essential contradiction of the tribes returning to a political economy they had previously rejected in their formation as a confederacy. The politics of gender relations encoded in Genesis 2–3 should be placed within the overall politics of state centralization. In what follows, I show that Genesis 2–3 articulates a gender ideology that (1) privileges the marital bond over the kinship bond in the interests of state control over the population; and (2) legitimizes an increased subordination of the wife to her husband, who himself becomes subordinate to a wider social hierarchy.

Intrinsic Analysis of Genesis 2–3

Because the story of Eve and Adam has been pivotal in legitimating a long history of woman's subordinate status and symbolization as evil, it has been an important focus of contemporary feminist biblical scholarship.[47] Phyllis Trible's significant contributions during the 1970s tried to recover the story as an egalitarian text, one that presents a more positive picture of woman than had been previously thought.[48] More recent studies, however, strongly question the notion that Genesis 2–3 is as liberating for women as Trible thinks it is. They prefer to admit the androcentricism of the Bible and to deconstruct its conceptually vulnerable system of logic.[49]

The materialist approach advocated in this study concurs that an androcentric society (investigated in an extrinsic analysis) encodes an androcentric ideology in its literary production (studied in an intrinsic analysis). My interpretive strategy in examining Genesis 2–3 is to determine the internal logic of its complex ideologies: how the general ideology (reflective of the dominant mode of production) becomes encoded in the text's literary ideology.[50] I place special emphasis on the ideology of gender.

Distinct royal ideologies are discernible in the Genesis 2–3 creation story, those both of the Yahwist and of other ancient Near Eastern myths that affected and were modified by J in light of his Yahwism.[51] Mesopotamian mythologies describe the creation of human beings for the purpose of serving the gods, freeing the gods from the menial labor associated with the land.[52] They reflect and legitimize social stratification between the ruling elite and the peasants who work the land in their particular societies. Although the Yahwist represents a specifically Judean "theology of resistance" in his critique of the apparent self-deification of Jerusalemite kings,[53] he did not intend the abolition of the monarchy. On the contrary, his creation story is permeated with royal ideology in the way it structures relations among the dramatis personae.

Θ: creation :: king : Israel

Adam and God/The People and Their King: Hierarchical Relations

The ideological design of Genesis 2 creates parallels between God's role in creation and the king's role in Israel. Correspondences exist between the activity of "YHWH, a god," in ordering chaos and the king's endeavors to restructure the autonomous and acephalous tribes into a unified state.[54] J's infrequent expression, "YHWH, a god," highlights the difference between the divine and human realms and the prerogatives inherent in each.[55] This divine/human separation corresponds to the symbolic gulf between the king and his people that must be established in an inchoate incorporative state. The rest of the Genesis story, in which the human farmer and his wife arrogate divine privilege and are banished from this God's presence, will make this gulf very clear.

The Yahwist situates the story in an arid land, where no wild or cultivated plants have yet sprung up. No wild plants exist, because "YHWH, a god, had not caused rain to fall upon the land." Nor are there cultivated plants, since "there was no male human being ('ādām) to till the ground ('ādāmâ)" (2:6).[56] God proceeds to rectify the absence of cultivated plants by fashioning a man from the ground (2:7). Although several feminists have accepted Trible's explication of 'ādām as generic for "human being,"[57] it seems clear from the analyses of others that the first human is envisioned in this text as a male peasant, responsible for tilling the ground in the production of cultivated plants.[58] As the primordial man fashioned from the ground is utterly dependent on YHWH, a god, for his very life, so the Israelite peasant who works the ground is reliant on the king as his provider.[59]

In the Yahwist's narrative, the man does not immediately begin the work of tilling the ground and growing crops, because YHWH, a god, plants a royal garden east of Eden, a park of trees.[60] The deity then puts the man into this garden to till and guard (2:8,15).[61] The garden represents the civilized order of the state, where fertility and prosperity can be found in abundance, as opposed to the chaos outside.[62] Moreover, as a place of unmediated access to the deity,[63] it also signifies a primordial time when there was no rift between the king and his people.

God prohibits the man from eating from the tree of the knowledge of good and evil in the center of the garden, under pain of death (Gen 2:17; 3:3). The precise meaning of this tree has generated much scholarly debate.[64] Arguments that favor the meaning of the "tree" as "offering the widest possible knowledge" are very strong. This divine knowledge would include becoming like the gods, moving toward civilization, and the knowledge of sexuality itself.[65] The divine command preventing the man from eating of the tree of knowledge reveals another symbolic differentiation between the divine and human realms, having its social correlate in the intellectual distance between the

king (and his royal court) and the people.[66] It is not mere coincidence
that Solomon, who strongly centralized the state and stratified his society, is considered to be the quintessential "wise" man. The ruling
elite hold the monopoly on wisdom, and according to their ideology,
the ignorance of the peasant is part and parcel of the created social
order. Should the peasant obtain a greater critical knowledge of the
real state of affairs governing his life, it would constitute a danger to
the elite's tight political control.[67] Genesis 6:1-4 and 11:1-9 are other
sections within the Yahwist narrative that manifest this same concern
over the separation between divine and human realms.

Adam and His Woman:
The Politics of the State

As I pointed out above in my extrinsic analysis, hierarchical relations
between the genders in a familial mode of production are magnified
in the transition to a tributary political economy. As the society itself
becomes more stratified in the division of the ruling elite and the
peasants, so relations between male and female become more hierarchically ranked. The increase in male status over the female in the
tributary mode of production becomes encoded in the literary production of Genesis 2.[68]

To overcome the man's loneliness, the deity creates from the
man's rib a "help corresponding to him" (Gen 2:18).[69] Within the ideology of the text, the "help" that the woman supplies is her sexual
ability to produce children.[70] Nevertheless, the priority of the male is
indicated by the fact that the primal woman is formed from *his* substance,[71] a reversal of the real state of affairs, in which women give
birth to men:

> This one shall be called Woman (*'iššâ*),
>   for out of Man (*'îš*) this one was taken. (2:23b)

Just as he names the animals, evincing his primacy over them, the
man names the woman *'iššâ*, expressing his authority over her.[72] As
the man is created by YHWH, a god, from the ground to serve and
tend the ground, the woman, built from the man, exists to serve and
tend the man.[73] The traditional interpretations of Genesis 2 that jus-

tify the subordination of women by appealing to this text are consistent with its thoroughgoing androcentrism.

The politics of state centralization can be seen in the man's poetic exclamation upon meeting the woman (2:23) and in its etiology regarding social relations (2:24). In acknowledging the woman as "bone of my bones and flesh of my flesh," the text describes the relations between the man and his woman according to the ideology of kinship.[74] Furthermore, the man abandons "his father and mother and clings to his wife and the two become one flesh." This verse has been taken to refer to: (1) the natural "love force" impelling the genders toward each other;[75] (2) the "human attitude" in which a son's emotional attachment to his parents is replaced by one to his wife;[76] (3) the "rich intimacy" of the couple's relationship—not just their physical union;[77] (4) a postexilic argument for monogamy;[78] (5) an echo of a former matriarchy;[79] and finally, (6) the man's abandonment of his parental clan to join with his wife's clan.[80] Justification for the first three meanings becomes quite clear if seen within the politics of state centralization.

Appropriating the familial idiom of kinship while simultaneously subverting it, the ideology of the text emphasizes the marital bond at the expense of the kinship bond. A man forsakes his patrilocal household and lineage, "his father and his mother," and becomes kin with his wife.[81] Instead of reflecting an earlier matriarchy or matrilocal residence, the ideological subversion of *patrilineal* kinship connections in favor of the state necessitates that the *man* leaves his parents to cling to his wife. The husband does not join his wife's clan. Rather, he and his wife, along with their subsequent children, bond together to form a nuclear family unit, thereby weakening lineage and extended family ties on both sides. The nuclear family owes its allegiance not to its kin-group connections but to the state. As a smaller, more independent social unit than the lineage, it poses no threat of rebellion against the state. It is significant that it is YHWH, a god, who brings the primal couple together (2:22). "If 'God' in this context is synonymous with, or the symbolic expression of, the state, the role of the state in subserving the solidarity of the husband-wife relationship at the expense of the lineage is unmistakable."[82] Rather than a hallmark of gender mutuality and equality, as some think,[83] Gen 2:23-24 can be seen as part of the state's sexual agenda in its ideological control over its populace.

The Fall: The Permanent Gulf
between God and Humanity/The King
and His People/The Man and His Woman

Structural analyses have detected binary oppositions in the male
mythology of Genesis 2–3: before versus after the fall, inside versus
outside the garden, immortality versus mortality, ignorance versus
knowledge, and so on. To resolve the contradiction between the oppositions and account for the transition from the former to the latter
in the "real" situation, some aspect of the latter (the "after," the "outside," mortality, knowledge) must have already existed in the former.
In the logic of myth, what facilitates the passage from former to latter is a "middle semantics" that mediates the fundamental oppositions.[84] This middle-ground category is abnormal, unnatural,
anomalous with respect to the other two,[85] and therefore ultimately
dangerous.

While both the man and the woman arrogate to themselves forbidden wisdom in the Genesis narrative, the woman represents this
mediating factor responsible for the move from before to after, from
inside to outside, from immortality to mortality, and from ignorance
to knowledge. Genesis 3 structures interactions among the trans-
gressing characters in chiastic fashion. The snake (A) tempts the
woman (B) who gives the fruit to the man (C; 3:1-7). In the politics
of blame, the man (C') accuses the woman (B'), who then turns
against the snake (A'; 3:8-12). God then curses the snake (A), punishes the woman (B) and then the man (C; 3:14-19). Note that the
woman consistently forms the middle ground between the snake and
the man (B/B'/B) and is ultimately responsible for the rupture in the
man's relationship with God.

In 3:1 the woman encounters the snake, described as being
craftier than all the other creatures that YHWH, a god, had made. The
wordplay between the snake's cunning (3:1, 'ārûm) and the couple's
unconscious nakedness (2:25, 'ārûmmîm) articulates the snake's role
in the ultimate recognition of their nakedness (3:7). In its ancient
Near Eastern context, the snake can symbolize evil and chaos,[86] as
well as healing, life, wisdom, and fertility.[87] As a "quintessentially
ambiguous" character,[88] the snake embodies perceived and actual
dangers to the state. The snake could represent the fertility cults observed in the Israelite population, offering "wisdom" that competed

with the royal ideology of the one God, יהוה.⁸⁰ As a veiled critique of Solomon's foreign policy, it could symbolize the external threats posed by Israel's political enemies.[90] On the other hand, it could also personify an internal threat, as James Kennedy argues, one in which dissatisfied elements of society pose a danger to the state by educating and encouraging peasants to independent action.[91]

Whatever dangers to the state the snake represents, it is through the woman that the snake accomplishes the rift between human beings and God and, by analogy, between the people and their king. The woman is the "mediating" factor that determines the man's passage from "inside" to "outside," from direct access to God to separation by a gulf. In a masterful move, the snake approaches her with a question: "Did God say, 'You shall not eat from any tree in the garden?'" (3:1). God had, in fact, prefaced his command to the man with the generous privilege of eating freely of every tree in the garden. Only the tree of the knowledge of good and evil was forbidden to him (2:16). By focusing on God's prohibition instead of God's generosity, the snake implies that God is an unreasonable and oppressive being.[92] The woman feels compelled to defend her God, but her response exhibits some reservations about what God had commanded:

> We may eat of the fruit of the trees in the garden; but God said, "You shall not eat of the fruit of the tree that is in the middle of the garden, nor shall you touch it, or you shall die." (3:2-3)

Picking up cues from the snake's innuendoes, the woman downplays the generosity and privilege of God's original command. The verb "we may eat" lacks the extravagance of God's permission, "you may freely eat." The woman makes no reference to "every" tree from which the couple may freely partake. Besides minimizing God's generosity, the woman adds to God's prohibition "nor touch it," thus augmenting the portrayal of the unreasonable God that the snake is trying to fabricate. Finally, the woman moderates the original death penalty. "For in the day that you eat of it you shall surely die" (2:17) becomes simply "or you shall die" (3:3).[93]

Read politically, the subtext of these verses is clear: "Forces antithetical to the state would have you (the peasant) believe that the king, our benefactor upon whom our very lives depend, who freely gives to us out of his bounty, is a capricious and restrictive leader. In fact, our king only withholds from us what belongs properly to him

(namely, the knowledge of good and evil) in order to rule us fairly."
Note that Solomon asked for wisdom from God to accomplish this
very aim: "Give your servant therefore an understanding mind to govern your people, able to discern *between good and evil*" (1 Kgs 3:9).
By having the woman, instead of the man, respond to the snake, the
subtext also implies that women are the ones most susceptible to
these forces threatening the state.

The snake counters God's threat of death with "You will not die"
(3:4). It then argues that the consequences of partaking of the fruit
will be very beneficial to the woman: "for God knows that when you
eat of it your eyes will be opened, and you will be like God, knowing
good from evil" (3:5). By introducing its remarks with "for God
knows," the snake insinuates dubious purposes behind God's prohibition. "The clear implication is that God acted out of fear and
envy."[94]

Desirous of the wisdom the tree would give, the woman takes and
eats of its fruit. She then gives some to the man, who evidently has
been with her during this dialogue with the snake (3:6). Immediately,
their eyes are opened and they realize their nakedness (3:7). Although
several scholars suggest a sexual awakening here,[95] the wisdom that
the couple unlawfully appropriates for themselves is one that is the
sole prerogative of the creator/sustainer God. In recognizing their
physical exposure, they also become cognizant of the gulf that sepa-
rates them from God. They perceive their humiliation and vulnerability before God because of their transgression.[96] In the ideology of
honor and shame, the couple, who felt no shame at their nakedness
before the fall (2:25), now feel shame before their absolute superior
by their crossing of boundaries.

God punishes the woman according to her "labor" in the social
order, in the area where she was created to be a "help" to the man: the
reproduction of offspring:

> I will greatly increase your pangs in childbearing;
>   in pain you shall bring forth children. (3:16a)[97]

Syntactically connected with these pains of childbearing[98] is God's
statement to the woman:

> Your desire shall be for your husband
>   and he shall rule over you. (3:16b)

The Hebrew noun *těšûqâ*, "desire," is found in only two other places in the Hebrew Bible. In Song 7:10, where the woman speaks of her lover's desire for her, "desire" has strong sexual connotations. In the very same terminology as that used in Gen 3:16b and 4:7 describes the desire of sin, lurking at the door, waiting to overcome Cain, a desire that Cain must "rule over." Based on the meaning of "desire" in 4:7, Susan Foh contends that the woman's desire in 3:16b refers to her desire to control or possess her husband, challenging his headship.[99]

Feminists and others have attempted to mitigate the androcentrism present in 3:16b.[100] However, just as the etiology in 2:23-24 should be read in the context of the political agenda to control sexuality in a nascent monarchy, so should the etiology of 3:16 be read in the broader context of social and familial structures redefined under a monarchy.[101] We have seen that 2:23-24 attempts to subvert patrilineages by emphasizing the nuclear family unit. Genesis 3:16 focuses on the nuclear family unit itself. Besides identifying the primary social role of the woman according to her childbearing functions, 3:16 enforces the woman's sexual fidelity to her husband. Consistent with the male ideology of honor and shame, a woman's sexual desire will be directed only toward her legitimate marriage partner, thus guaranteeing the paternity of his children. Moreover, as the king rules over the people, so will the husband rule over his wife under the increased stratification of the Israelite society.[102] Hierarchical relations between the genders, present during the premonarchic period, intensify during the new era of the state. If Foh is correct in arguing that "desire" refers to the woman's attempt to control her husband—which arises from her disobedience, a desire to subvert divinely ordained relationships—a symbolic parallel can also be drawn between the peasants' desire to rebel against the state and the state's justification in prevailing over them by whatever means.

As the woman is punished according to her "labor" in the social world, so too is the man. Utilizing the same word as that used to describe the woman's pain in childbearing,[103] the etiology in 3:17-19 justifies the continual suffering the male peasant will experience in tilling the ground. The relegation of the peasant to hard, menial work, in contrast to the relative leisure of the state, is now legitimized in the text's royal ideology. In contrast to his former easy life tending the garden, the peasant will now till the ground for his livelihood, a ground that becomes cursed because of his transgression.

Nevertheless, the cursing of the man's ground is prefaced by God's important qualifier:

> Because you have listened to the voice of your wife
>   and have eaten of the tree
> about which I commanded you
>   "You shall not eat of it . . ." (3:17)

The text does not narrate any conversation between the woman and the man when she gives him the fruit (3:6). However, the main point in the divine qualifier is that the man did not listen to *God's* voice, which commanded the man not to eat of the fruit (2:17). The notion of the woman as the temptress or seducer of the man away from God's commandments (and, by analogy, the laws of the state) is implied in God's statement, highlighting her mediation between the "before" and "after" of the man's existence. Because of the danger she represents (both to her man and to the state), the woman must be brought under the strict control of her husband (3:16).[104]

Just as the man's first naming of the woman, before the fall, should be contextualized in the politics of state centralization, so should the man's second naming of the woman, after the fall: "The man named his wife Eve, because she was the mother of all living" (3:20). The woman does not name herself. She is named by the man, who defines her identity. His exercise of power categorizes the woman strictly in her reproductive capacities within a larger system of hierarchical relations, of which he himself, as peasant, is very much a subordinate.

The subordinate status of the peasant vis-à-vis the king becomes particularly clear in the royal ideology expressed in 3:21-22. Verse 21 states that "YHWH, a god, made garments of skins for the man and for his wife, and he clothed them." Although God's covering the humans with clothes has been commonly interpreted as an expression of divine grace and compassion, Robert Oden convincingly shows that, in its ancient Near Eastern context, the act of dressing "is rather a significant symbolic act that firmly distinguishes humans from the divine."[105] Moreover, YHWH, a god, exclaims that "the man has become like one of us, knowing good and evil; and now, he might reach out his hand and take also from the tree of life, and eat, and live forever" (v 22). To prevent the man from seizing more divine prerogatives for himself, YHWH, a god, casts the man (and, presumably, his wife) out of the garden of Eden "to till the ground from which he was taken" (v 23) He places cherubim and a flaming sword to guard the way to the tree of life, making the chasm between himself and the man complete (v 24).

The ideological subtext of Genesis 2–3 accomplishes several things in service to the monarchy. First, it reveals that "once upon a time" the peasant enjoyed unmediated access to the king, as well as liberal privileges bestowed on him by his benefactor. He was forbidden only court wisdom, which the king required to rule effectively. Second, it affirms the nuclear family unit at the expense of the bonds of lineage. Within this unit, the male peasant retains his authority over his wife, whose "help" to him resides principally in her role in reproduction. Third, it explains and legitimizes the symbolic division between the king and the peasant during the Yahwist's time by attributing this great divide to the unlawful appropriation of the knowledge of good and evil by Adam, the primeval peasant. The violation of this prohibition is accomplished through his wife's mediation, thus subjecting her (and peasant women under the monarchy) to more pain in her childbearing and greater control by her husband.

Regarded as a rebellious threat to the royal court, the peasant needs to be controlled. In the symbolic act of investiture, the peasant's lower status is forever marked. He and his wife are banished from the king's presence, and state apparatuses—represented by the cherubim and sword—enforce the alienation. The man continues to till the ground, as he was created to do, but because of his transgression, he suffers in this menial labor "by the sweat of his brow" and through the royal extraction of his surpluses.

Summary

The analysis of gender relations and the symbolization of Eve as the vocal temptress in Genesis 2–3 reveals that one must take class relations into consideration in the literary production of the text. In the interests of the monarchy, the broader project of the Yahwist tries to resolve the inherent contradiction in Israel's regressing to a tributary mode of production, which it had rejected two hundred years previously when it became a tribal confederacy. It explains that the current relationship between the king and his people has its theological origin in the relationship between the divine and the human at the primordial beginning. YHWH, a god, creates the man for the express purpose of tilling the earth. He puts the man in his own garden, allowing him to eat freely of any of its trees—all except one: the tree of the knowledge of good and evil. At this point, the narrative describes the creation of a help for the man—a woman, who is intended to serve the man as the man serves the deity in tilling the garden. To legitimize royal interests, as well as to justify the current lower status of the peasant in the tributary economy, the Genesis story shifts the point of conflict from the public arena of class relations between men to the more private domain of household relations between men and women. While stressing the nuclear family and the marital bond in these domestic relations, the story simultaneously subverts lineages and other local power authorities that threaten the state.

Moreover, the introduction of the woman as the "middle semantics" that mediates the fundamental contradictions in the story emphasizes a gender conflict that displaces and obscures the very real class conflict. The gender confrontation functions like a symbolic alibi[106] for the class interests of the text, which become mystified and concealed through the theological cover of a story about origins and "the fall." The class struggle is shifted to the gender struggle, which is more predisposed to ideological manipulation during the monarchy, given the subordination of women to men even in a familial mode of production during the pre-state period. Through the process of ideological displacement, Genesis 2–3 shifts attention from its latent text, a class relationship that it signifies but cannot articulate, and focuses that attention on its manifest text, a gender relationship that it articulates but does not signify.[107] The woman becomes responsible for the man's violation of the single prohibition that the deity had imposed on him. In the politics of blame, the man, confronted by God with his transgression, diverts the crime to the woman: "The woman whom you gave to be with me, she gave me fruit from the tree, and I ate" (3:12). She becomes liable for the theological breach between the man and his God and the political breach between the peasant and his king. Because of her, the man is banished from God's presence. He is condemned to till the land in suffering, passing on this legacy to the present-day peasant, alienated from his king.

In the ideology of the text, the woman pays a big price. Renamed Hawwah/Eve by her husband, she becomes mother of all living. She can only become mother, however, through suffering. For her role in the man's transgression, God punishes her by increasing the pain of her childbearing. Her husband will rule over her, just as the king governs the peasant. Because her husband "listened to her voice," she becomes temptress, seducer, and the downfall of men. Moreover, as the history of interpretation of this text will reveal, women are condemned as the "poor banished children of Eve."[108]

5 Faithless Israel in Hosea: She Is Not My Wife and I Am Not Her Husband

The prophet Hosea is credited as the originator of the (in)famous depiction of God as faithful husband to Israel, his faithless wife. Succeeding prophets—for example, Jeremiah, Ezekiel,[1] and Malachi—adopt and enlarge upon this powerful and provocative but problematic metaphor. The marriage metaphor becomes an extraordinarily effective vehicle to communicate to and reinforce in the prophets' hearers the contours and demands of God's covenant with Israel: (1) that it is foremost an intimate, significant *relationship*; (2) that this relationship is between unequal parties, a dominant and a subordinate; (3) that it involves reciprocal commitments and responsibilities; and (4) that any violation by the subordinate of these commitments and responsibilities will result in punishment.[2]

That the marriage metaphor for God's covenant presents interpretive problems for modern readers is already well documented.[3] In the first place, the metaphor conflates the deity and the human husband: God becomes an all-forgiving male. Significantly for the present study, the sinful is thus embodied in the vivid image of a defiant, lubricious wife. Woman becomes the very epitome of evil as an adulteress in heat. Furthermore, by envisioning God humiliating and physically punishing his wife to make her repent, the metaphor comes dangerously close to sanctioning a husband's domestic violence against his wife.

This chapter investigates the material and sociohistorical conditions that give rise to such a metaphor, one capturing the imaginations of Hosea's male audience through a dramatic rhetoric of pain and pleasure. My *extrinsic analysis* highlights the native-tributary mode of production in eighth-century Israel and its effect on gender relations, the pluralistic cult, and emergent monolatry, with its marginalization of women's popular religion. The *intrinsic analysis* underscores the ideological dynamics of the marriage metaphor for God's covenant, the feminization of the ruling hierarchy, and the consequences of that feminization for the symbolization in Hosea of women as evil.

Before turning to the extrinsic analysis, I address first the difficult problems in dating the book of Hosea. Earlier biblical scholarship on Hosea tended to value what it saw as the *ipsissima verba,* or "authentic words," of the prophet.[4] Evidence of later editorial activity was regarded as secondary, not only chronologically but also in theological importance. More recent critical studies,[5] however, have recognized the significance of the work's later stages, those of the collectors and redactors. In their collection and arrangement of and commentary on the prophetic tradition they inherit, these later editors are responsible for the biblical work of Hosea as we have it today.

The authorship of the book of Hosea is a complex matter that is still disputed. Many scholars insist that most of the book originated with the prophet Hosea himself.[6] Others think that redactional activity occurred more extensively than previously thought.[7] Three major interpretive stages for Hosea's oracles can be detected in his book: an eighth-to-seventh-century collection of the prophet's oracles; a seventh-century Deuteronomistic redaction during the time of the Judean king Josiah; and a sixth-century Deuteronomistic redaction during the Babylonian exile (587–539 B.C.E.). Whether one thinks that Hosea's original oracles were particularly influential in these later interpretive periods or maintains that redactors expanded Hosea's original oracles during these later times with their own theologies, it is clear that these stages were critical in the book's formation. For the purposes of this chapter, I argue the first point: that the bulk of the oracles in the work is Hosean, having a particular theological thrust—a polemical monolatry, highlighting fidelity to YHWH among the gods—and that, building on this monolatry, later interpretive stages left their noticeable imprint on the oracles through their evolving monotheism.[8]

Extrinsic Analysis
of the Book of Hosea

The Sociopolitical Context
of Eighth-Century Israel

Very little is known about the northern prophet Hosea. The super-scription to his book (1:1), which was added later by a redactor,[9] identifies him as the son of Beeri, about whom nothing more can be said. The superscription situates Hosea between 750 and 724 B.C.E.—that is, between the last years of Jeroboam II (786–746) and the fall of Israel to the Assyrians in 721.

During this period, Israel operated under a native-tributary mode of production, into which a foreign-tributary mode of production intruded and made demands.[10] Because Israel was forced to pay tribute to foreign powers to secure its position in the wider political sphere, the native-tributary mode in the eighth-century northern kingdom had a much different configuration than the one under which the Yahwist who composed Genesis 2–3 in southern Judah operated (see chap. 4). Four major factors impinged on this mode of production in related, complex ways, directly affecting gender relations and Hosea's theological and social location in the YHWH-alone movement: agricultural intensification of royal cash crops; political instability within the Israelite royal court, coupled with the external threat of Assyrian invasion; conflicts within Israelite polytheism; and socioeconomic relations among the religious and political elite: the kings, priests, and prophets.

Royal Agricultural Intensification

Beginning with David's land grants of non-Israelite territories (for example, the fertile lowlands) to military supporters, two conflicting systems of land tenure with widely differing social values operated in ancient Israel.[11] Under the familial mode of production, highland farmers practiced a mixed, village-based agriculture that distributed risks of crop failure and optimized labor across a diverse spectrum of growing strategies.[12] Most importantly, villagers retained their surplus income and resources. Under the tributary mode of production, land grants in Israel's "breadbasket" regions became latifundia (large estates), passed on as patrimony in the hands of a few wealthy elites.[13] To gain access to the land, peasants paid enormous rent and/or taxes, turning their surpluses over to the landholders.

In order for the state to survive and compete with other ancient Near Eastern nations, agribusiness under the state's system of taxation focused on specific crops that were easily appropriated, storable, transportable, and liquid. These highly exportable and lucrative cash crops included oil, wine, and grain (cf. 1 Kgs 5:11; 2 Chr 2:10,15; Ezek 27:17).[14] Particularly during the eighth century, the monarchy imposed on highland villagers an increased demand for these crops.[15] In Hosea this desire for "grain, wine, and oil" becomes a signifier for the nation's promiscuity.[16]

Although this royal policy of crop intensification may have been more efficient in the short run, it had damaging effects on the highland mode of production in the long run. First, the tributary economy redistributed profits from grain, wine, and oil exportation among the ruling elite, leaving villages barely enough to carry on production.[17] Although the monarchy initially utilized this wealth for vital reasons, such as national security, the system eventually succumbed to corruption and extortion.[18] Second, the royal focus on specific crops conflicted with village strategies to spread risks—for example, crop rotation, staggered sowing, fallowing, and herd grazing.[19] Third, this policy impinged on village agriculture most directly by forcing its own agenda upon land use.[20] Formerly employed in multiple ways to spread risk, the highlands were gradually transformed through enormous peasant investment into terraces[21] of vineyards and olive trees to keep pace with the state's demand for wine and oil.[22] Because procedures to deal with crop failure were minimized, the highland villagers joined the lowland peasantry in being the hardest hit during lean years by economically ruinous cycles of tax and debt.[23]

Internal and External State Politics

Social, political, and economic developments in both Israel and Judah often resulted from external influences and pressures from the wider ancient Near Eastern context. A hiatus in Aramean hegemony and Assyrian westward expansion allowed Israel a time of relative peace and prosperity during the early to middle years of the eighth century under Jeroboam II. Nevertheless, wealth was primarily redistributed to the ruling classes. As the prophet Amos testifies, the ordinary citizen suffered under Jeroboam's vigorous reconstruction projects and policies (Amos 2:6-8; 3:9-10; 5:11).[24] Similar policies under the Omrides resulted in popular discontent, but with specific differences: the Omrides consolidated their power through intermarriage (1 Kgs 15:30-31) and profitable foreign trade agreements, while Jeroboam II seized the momentary lull in the broader ancient Near Eastern struggles for power to expand his holdings.[25]

If Hos 1:1 is correct, Hosea prophesied during a politically turbulent period after Jeroboam II's rule (cf. 2 Kgs 14:23—17:41).[26] The monarchy was plagued by a number of assassinations. Of the six kings to ascend the throne, all but one died violently (2 Kgs 15:8-31; 17:1-18). Continuing to benefit from the redistributive economy of Jeroboam II, the ruling elite exploited the system, causing rampant court corruption and partisan intrigue (Hos 6:8-10; 7:1-7). Furthermore, external pressures influenced Israelite domestic affairs. The northern kingdom not only contended with the western encroachment of Assyrian king Tiglath-pileser III but also clashed with its southern rival, Judah, during the Syro-Ephraimite war (735–733). Israel's foreign policy was often unpredictable. The nation curried favor with international powers, such as Egypt and Assyria, which competed with each other in the political arena (Hos 5:13; 7:8-15; 8:8-10; 10:6; 12:1). The tribute Israel paid to Assyria in the consecutive stages of their relations[27] exacted a considerable price from the elite (cf. 2 Kgs 15:20), who passed the burden on to an already hard-hit peasantry.[28] Thus the political struggles the Israelite elite faced in their own subordination to more powerful ancient Near Eastern countries affected the way they imposed an aggressive hegemony over their own countrymen and women.[29] Hosea labels Israel's contradictory and oppressive foreign and domestic policies with a sexual trope, "promiscuity."

The Cult in Eighth-Century Israel

Traditional reconstructions of ancient Israelite religion describe a monotheistic Yahwism, brought into Canaan by either conquering or immigrating nomads, that clashed with the indigenous fertility religions of the land.[30] In light of more recent analyses, this view must be revised. Scholars now regard the emergence of ancient Israel as a movement among the indigenous peoples within Canaan itself,[31] rather than as the result of an influx of an alien population into the land. These peoples were primarily agrarian,[32] steeped in religious beliefs and practices that focused on the fertility of the land, flock, and women.[33] The development of monotheism in ancient Israel comprises, therefore, a gradual internal process of both convergence with and differentiation from these diverse beliefs and practices of the Canaanite population.[34]

To understand Hosea, then, we must recognize that ancient Israelite religion had a strong heritage in the Canaanite religion itself. Early Israelite religion included the worship of several other deities in addition to YHWH. Veneration of the Canaanite deities El, Baal, and even the goddess Asherah was accepted or at least tolerated in the earlier stages of Israel's religious development.[35] What stands condemned as Baal worship in Hosea—for example, baal/s (2:8, 13, 17; 9:10; 13:1), cultic rites on the high places (4:13; 10:8), pillars (3:4; 10:1-2), divining rods (4:12), images (4:17; 8:4; 14:8), and calf figurines (8:5-6; 10:5; 13:2)—were, for centuries, accepted components of the worship of YHWH. In other words, Hosea condemns not Canaanite encroachment into Yahwism, but early Yahwism itself.[36] Although these practices had been taken over from foreign cults, their appropriation had occurred much earlier, and they were no longer regarded as syncretistic by the people.[37]

The theological position that Hosea advocates vis-à-vis the cult of his time can appropriately be called a *polemical* monolatry. In contrast to an *integrating* or *unpolemical monolatry*, which seemed to characterize the official and popular religion and cult of early Israel, a polemical monolatry venerated one deity without denying the existence or activity of other deities, but was intolerant or critical of them.[38] Hosea's theology would be decisive for the eventual later development of Israelite monotheism—the belief in the existence and veneration of a single solitary God[39]—during the exilic/postexilic periods.[40] His polemical monolatry is also a crucial factor in his gender-specific visualization of the deity and covenant community as a married couple.

Two particular religious practices that bear specifically on women's cultic participation and its relationship to the polemic behind Hosea's marriage metaphor need to be addressed: the worship of Asherah and the rituals of cultic prostitution. The former was most likely a feature of early Israelite cult; the latter was not, despite the traditional scholarly presumption that it was.

The Cult of Asherah

On the basis of archaeological and inscriptional evidence, it seems very probable that early Israel venerated the goddess Asherah, YHWH's consort, along with her cultic wooden symbol, the asherah.[41] Albertz speculates that "when Yahweh took over the place of El in the Israelite tribal alliance he also took his divine consort from him."[42] Although this is not a new speculation,[43] the discovery of *pithoi* inscriptions from the eighth-century site of Kuntillet 'Ajrud has sparked more recent interest in the goddess. These inscriptions recount a blessing on different individuals "by Yahweh of Samaria and by his/its asherah/Asherah." Moreover, from a pillar in a burial tomb near Khirbet el-Qôm comes the inscription: "May Uriyahu be blessed by Yahweh, my guardian [?], and his/its asherah/Asherah."[44] Along with other cultic artifacts not mentioned in the biblical texts,[45] the discovery of hundreds of terra-cotta female statuettes—"pillar figurines"—in the stratigraphy of domestic sites dated from the second half of the eighth to the seventh century reveals that a "nonconformist" cult existed alongside the official state cult.[46]

Several scholars argue that worship of the goddess was included in Hosea's polemic against the Israelite cult.[47] Some think that the goddess Asherah was the specific offending party behind Hosea's famous marriage metaphor.[48] However, Hosea does not explicitly refer to or condemn devotion to Asherah, her cult object, or the female figurines, even though the baals and bull calves face consistent censure (cf. Hos 2:8, 13, 17; 8:5-6; 9:10; 10:5; 13:1-2). The references to the goddess that scholars find in Hosea are quite oblique.[49] Thus the condemnation of the goddess should not be considered the determining factor in Hosea's symbolization of faithless Israel as female. However, it does form part of a more complex matrix that constituted Hosea's polemic (see below).

Theories of Cult Prostitution

"In manual after manual,"[50] scholars have persistently maintained belief in the alleged practice of cult prostitution in the Levant and Mesopotamia, involving a class of women who participated in *hieros gamos* (sacred marriage) ceremonies by representing the fertility goddess.[51] For example, one reads in John McKenzie's *Dictionary of the Bible*: "A peculiar feature of the Mesopotamian and Canaanite culture was ritual prostitution. To the temples of the goddess of fertility (Inanna, Ishtar, Astarte) were attached *bordellos* served by consecrated women who represented the goddess, the female principle of fertility. Intercourse with these women was communion with the divine as the principles of fertility."[52] In spite of admissions regarding "the meagerness of the data,"[53] the "fragmentary and somewhat contradictory" nature of the evidence,[54] and the lateness of the sources,[55] the notion of widespread sacred prostitution remains a standard presupposition in academic inquiries. Scholars contend that such sexual rites are at the very heart of prophetic use of the adulterous-wife symbol.[56]

After a critical examination of the available evidence, however, a number of scholars have questioned the existence and extensiveness of ancient Near Eastern cult prostitution. Ugaritic, Mesopotamian, and Egyptian texts offer no explicit information about sacred prostitution,[57] and testimonies used by some to support such an institution—for example, Herodotus and Strabo—are quite unreliable, because they were written at a far later date and are rather biased.[58] Though tongue-in-cheek, the remarks of Bernhard Lang highlight the colonialist bias of Western biblical scholars regarding the so-called Orient:

> Ancient authors such as Herodotus and modern novelists and orientalists even more so were obviously carried away by their erotic fantasies. Temple prostitution belonged to what came "easily to their daydreams packed inside Oriental clichés: harems, princesses, princes, slaves, veils, dancing girls and boys, sherbets, ointments, and so on." The modern as well as the ancient East was associated with licentious sex, untiring sensuality, unlimited desire, and deep generative energies; "the Orient was a place where one could look for sexual experience unobtainable in Europe."[59]

Scholarship and women have suffered immensely in the hands of academics who are unable to imagine any cultic role for women in antiquity that did not involve sexual intercourse.[60] Akkadian texts describe a number of cultic and other meanings for the *qadištu*—wet nurse, midwife, cult singer, archivist, and even sorceress—none of

which implies cultic prostitution. Yet the word *qadištu* has erro-
neously been translated as "female prostitute" on the basis of a mis-
reading of the Hebrew *qĕdēšâ*.[61] By a process of circular reasoning,
assumptions informed by exaggerations in later sources are read into
the biblical text. The biblical text is then used to explain terms found
in extrabiblical literature, which in turn are used to "validate" the
original interpretation of the biblical text.[62] Although, in the prophet's
mind, these rituals involved uncontrolled sexuality or prostitution, it
is difficult to accept this at face value.[63]

Robert Oden suggests that the phenomenon of cult prostitution
should be investigated as an accusation leveled by one society against
another as part of its process of self-definition. By this theory, the indictment that another society engages in cultic prostitution would reveal more about the society leveling the accusation than about the
other society.[64] Summarizing anthropologist Fredrik Barth, Oden
points out that ethnic groups categorize themselves directly in opposition to other groups. They may do so according to overt signals—
dress, language, eating habits, and so on—and they may do so
according to standards of morality and excellence that would distin-
guish them from other groups. Groups usually focus on certain areas
of conduct to demonstrate their difference from, and perhaps superiority to, other societies. It is significant for our discussion of cult
prostitution that one of these areas of conduct is sexual behavior: a
group can assert its distinctiveness by charging that other nations are
lax, excessive, or perverted in their sexual conduct.[65]

Expressed in Hosea, other prophets, and the Deuteronomist is a
politics of difference, defining Israel as being "distinct from," rather
than "in connection with," the other social groups. In Hosea's case
these groups include those involved in cults, the royal court, and foreign office. According to Hosea, Israelite self-definition lies in the exclusive worship of yhwh alone, to whom Israel is bound in covenant.
Operating under the distinction paradigm, Hosea may have exaggerated the worship practices in Israelite religious pluralism to include
cultic sexual service and all its depravities, in order to champion his
monolatrous position.

Relations among King, Cult, Priest, and Foreign Affairs

Neglected but certainly fruitful areas of study that contribute to our
understanding of Hosea's marriage metaphor include the complex

social, political, and economic relations among the king, cult, priest, and prophet, both at home and abroad in eighth-century Israel.[66] Scholars primarily interpret the adulterous-wife metaphor as Hosea's condemnation of Israel's "heterodox" cult.[67] However, Hosea also applies the metaphor to Israel's foreign allies and trading partners (8:8-10).[68] Cult and domestic and foreign affairs are not mutually exclusive, but converge in very real ways in the book of Hosea. Infractions in one sphere dramatically affect the others.

Particularly in Hosea 4–14, Hosea singles out the nation's leaders for rebuke and condemnation. These leaders include the king (5:1; 7:3, 5, 7; 8:4, 10; 10:7, 15; 13:10-11), priest (4:4-10; 5:1; 6:7-10; 7:1-7), prophet[69] (4:5; 6:5; cf. 9:7), and princes (7:3, 5, 16; 8:4, 10; 9:15). Their transgressions overlap in the areas of cult, state, and foreign affairs and are depicted metaphorically as *sexual* infractions. The prophet is condemned, along with the priest, for "stumbling," causing the people to be "destroyed for lack of knowledge" (4:5-6). Having devoted themselves to "fornication," priest and prophet permit a "spirit of promiscuity" to infect the people (4:10-12, 18-19).[70] Both priests and king fall under God's judgment (5:1), for Ephraim/Israel has "played the whore" (5:3). "A promiscuous spirit" defiles the nation, and it "does not know YHWH" (5:4). A murderous gang of priests (6:9) is responsible for the moral deterioration of the king and his royal court (7:3-7).[71] This decline in state affairs, instigated by priests described as "adulterers" (7:4),[72] directly affects external politics, where "Ephraim mixes himself with the peoples" (7:8). Ephraim becomes "a cake unturned," which foreigners devour (7:8-9). The relation between internal and external politics is achieved through the metaphors of the "oven," describing the internal intrigue (7:4-7), and that which is baked in the oven, "a half-baked cake" that foreigners consume (7:8-9). Ephraim's capricious foreign policy with Egypt and Assyria is likened to a silly, senseless dove (7:11-13). For grain and wine, the people gather themselves together and rebel against God (7:14).

Hosea 8:1-14 also underscores the cultic entanglements of kings and princes and their effects on foreign affairs.[73] The illegitimacy of royal leadership is closely linked with the royal forging of the idolatrous "calf of Samaria" from silver and gold (8:4-6). The description of the futility of this leadership[74] segues into the theme of unwise political alliances, described in sexual language as "hiring lovers" (8:9-

10). Ephraim is like a "wild ass," which, according to Jer 2:24, is characterized by unbridled sexuality: "In her heat sniffing the wind! Who can restrain her lust?" The tribute that Ephraim's king and princes offer the nations is like the fee a man negotiates with a prostitute (8:10). In 8:11-14 the theme of imprudent foreign treaties is juxtaposed with the condemnation of unlawful sacrifices. Ephraim's multiple altars to expiate sin have become the very sites at which sin is committed.

Hosea 10:1-15 contains similar interconnections among king (10:3-4, 7, 15), cult (10:1-2, 5-6, 8), and foreign politics (10:6, 10). God will break down Israel's altars and destroy its pillars because it does not acknowledge YHWH as king (10:1-4). The city inhabitants and the idolatrous priests will mourn and wail over the calf of Samaria (10:5). This "idolatrous" cult object will be carried off to Assyria as "tribute to the great king" (10:6). Then Samaria's illegitimate king shall perish (10:7, 15), just as the high places of Bethel are destroyed (10:8, 15). Foreign nations will be gathered against the people (10:10; cf. 10:14).

The interweaving of priestly, prophetic, and kingly crimes underscores the reality that Israelite religion, politics, and foreign affairs were inseparable.[75] Hosea symbolizes infractions in any of these domains through sexual imagery. Not only were royal bureaucracy and ideology legitimated by cult, but the cult itself functioned as an organ of the state.[76] Kings established sanctuaries not only as religious centers, but also as sites of administrative and economic activity.[77] Priests were state bureaucrats who had major fiscal responsibilities, especially during the harvest. According to Victor Matthews and Don Benjamin, priests adjudicated which state households were honored or shamed on the basis of their record of tax payments.[78] They assessed the productivity of a household's fields and herds by the amount of grain and animals it brought to the sanctuary. They collected tithes and taxes in the form of sacrifices and tributes. They offered or processed sacrifices for storage. They deposited sacrifices at the sanctuary treasury until the king redistributed them to workers and soldiers at home,[79] or in trade and tribute to foreign nations abroad.

Sacrifice was the central means of collecting revenue for the state (cf. 2 Chr 31:4-6; Neh 10:36-39).[80] In contrast to the standard depiction of the complete annihilation of offerings, only a token portion of grain and animals was usually consumed in the sacrificial fires. The remainder went to the priests and their households (cf. Lev 2:2-3; 6:14-17; 7:31-34). "In general, it would be better to understand sacrifice in Leviticus and Numbers as processing farm produce to be stored and redistributed rather than destroying it. At sanctuaries throughout Israel, priests slaughtered and butchered livestock, decanted wine and olive oil, and parched grain."[81]

Priests therefore had significant responsibilities in handling the monarchy's desired cash crops of grain, wine, and oil (cf. Deut 12:17; 14:23; 18:4; 2 Chr 31:5; Neh 10:39; 13:5, 12). According to Hos 4:8, the priests "feed on the sin of my people; they are greedy for their iniquity." Although this feeding could be figurative, it is quite plausible that Hosea meant it literally. The priests secured their economic livelihood from the practices of the cult.[82] Moreover, because of their role in sacrifices and food processing, priests were directly involved in the collection of tribute from the peasant classes to be delivered to the superpowers, Assyria and Egypt (5:13; 7:3-14; 8:9-10; 10:6; 12:1). The convergence of priestly and state interests in agricultural products, such as grain, wine, and oil, for both foreign and domestic purposes was branded by Hosea as "sexual promiscuity" (2:8-9; 4:11-17; 7:14; 9:1-2; 12:1).

The Social Location of the Prophet Hosea: The YHWH-Alone Movement

Hosea is singular in his attacks on the veneration of the baals and those cultic practices that had been regarded as compatible with the worship of YHWH, or at least tolerated. It is essential, however, to read these attacks within the broader context of domestic and foreign affairs and the complex interconnections among king, priest, and cult. Since he differentiated YHWH from the worship and cult of other deities, Hosea has been regarded as an important proponent of a so-called YHWH-alone movement, instrumental in the later development of Israelite monotheism.[83] This movement is thought to have originated in the ninth century B.C.E. with Elijah and Elisha and the ruthless coup d'état of Jehu. It continued in the eighth century, with Hosea as its "fanatical representative,"[84] and climaxed in Israelite monotheism during the exile.[85] Although the worship of YHWH alone eventually became the normative theological position, it was a conviction on the part of only a small minority group within the official polytheism of early Israelite religion and had different configurations over the course of the centuries. Nevertheless, the YHWH-alone movement was not simply a theological one; it was joined in complex ways to a wider sociopolitical environment through interconnections with monarchy, cult, and foreign policy.

Although the social, political, and economic climates in which they prophesied were different, Elijah and Hosea have some points of contact, which may help explain their differentiation of YHWH from other deities. For both, YHWH, not Baal, brings the thirst-quenching rains that are integral to an agrarian-based society (1 Kings 18; Hos 6:3; 10:12; 14:5). Although Ahab increased profitable foreign trade and political relations, his support of Jezebel's Phoenician cult of the Tyrian Baal in Israel, the building of a temple in Baal's honor (1 Kgs 16:31-32), the economic support of the god's 450 prophets at Jezebel's table (18:19), and the overall maintenance of the state system itself created an enormous burden on the populace, particularly during a time of famine (1 Kings 17–18).[86] Wealth from expanded foreign involvement was allocated primarily to the ruling elite. Elijah's stringent critique of the Naboth affair demonstrates the extent of the monarchy's exploitation of smallholders, instigated by the machinations of the foreign-born Jezebel (1 Kings 21).

For Elijah, YHWH moved from being a local god to one who had power and authority in the international arena.[87] YHWH worked beyond Israel's national borders—for example, in Zarephath for a Phoenician widow and her son (1 Kings 17) and on Mount Horeb (1 Kings 19). According to Mark Smith, this enlargement of YHWH's dominion promoted an early form of monolatrous faith, which would continue with Hosea, who proclaimed YHWH's power in both foreign and domestic affairs, and blossom fully as monotheism in the exilic period.[88]

Like Elijah, Hosea prophesied during a time when foreign affairs impinged on the administration of the Israelite state and dictated its domestic policy. The two prophets differ in that Elijah condemned a foreign baal, Baal Shamem,[89] while Hosea lambasted the worship of Israelite baals, which had long since converged with worship of YHWH.[90] These baals became subordinates in YHWH's host or assembly (cf. Hos 12:5), but Hosea maligns them as *foreign* deities. According to Baruch Halpern, the worship of the baals had political

ramifications for Hosea, resulting in Hosea's differentiation of YHWH
from other deities:

> The alternation in Hosea between foreign alliance and rural cult and
> "baal" suggests that the intellectual process involved is a denial both
> of subordinate gods and of foreign entanglements, or to put it differ-
> ently, of the equation of what is foreign (*and what is unjust*) with wor-
> ship of subordinate deities. In Hosea, the background for the
> intellectual developments of the late 8th and, later, 7th century is
> present. Indeed, the identification of the "baals" as gods of foreign na-
> tions, . . . as distinct from as gods subordinate to Yhwh, lies at the base
> of their rejection.[91]

For Hosea, the cult in eighth-century Israel embodied a mode of
production that was unjust and intolerable: an agricultural intensification, tied to a profitable foreign market and an aggressive foreign
hegemony that insistently imposed its will on Israelite internal affairs; and corrupt Israelite institutions of kingship, prophecy, and
priesthood that oversaw this agribusiness, funneling profits to their
own social sectors, and furthering the exploitation of the peasant
classes.[92] Hosea responded to the oppressive mode of production of
his time by proclaiming the exclusive worship of YHWH. His polemical
monolatry has its theological source in the exodus/wilderness period
of Israel's history:

> I have been the Lord your God
>   ever since the land of Egypt;
> you know no God but me,
>   and besides me there is no savior.
> It was I who fed you in the wilderness,
>   in the land of drought. (Hos 13:4-5)

Hosea's fondness for the exodus/wilderness period of Israelite history is well known. Through Moses, the prophet par excellence, God
brought Israel out of Egypt and guarded it (12:13). It was in the
wilderness that the wife/Israel first responded in covenantal fidelity to
the husband of her youth (2:14-15). When God chose Israel as partner in an exclusive relationship, it was like "finding grapes in the
wilderness" (9:10).[93] Through a metaphor of the caring parent of a

rebellious son, God called Israel from Egypt, adopted him in the wilderness, and performed a series of nurturing gestures on his behalf: teaching him to walk, carrying, healing, leading, lifting, and stooping down to feed the youngster (11:1-4).[94] After a revelation of the divine name, Ephraim is reminded that YHWH has been the nation's deity ("your God") ever since its enslavement in Egypt. Referring to shelters built during the Feast of Sukkoth, God will make the nation "live in tents again" (12:9). The threats Hosea makes against the present nation are framed in terms of "returning to Egypt" and the enslavement that this implies (8:13; 9:3, 6; 11:5; cf. 11:11).

The basic structures of Israelite religion tended toward exclusivity in the divine/human relations. This exclusivism had its source in the radical experience of being freed from Egyptian sociopolitical oppression to embark on a long sojourn in the wilderness, where Israel was covenanted with God. These dramatic events resulted in a close personal relationship between the exodus group and YHWH, its deliverer. In view of the many sociopolitical changes brought about by the Israelite transition from tribal alliance to the state, the extraordinary religious experience of being freed from state oppression to enter into an intense personal relationship with the saving deity *had to be rediscovered again*,[95] according to Hosea.

Elijah's sojourn to Mount Horeb (Sinai) after his slaughter of Jezebel's Baal prophets (1 Kgs 19:4-18) makes clear that he had strong affinities with this exodus/wilderness tradition in his own proclamation of YHWH alone.[96] For both Elijah and Hosea, the insistence on YHWH alone "was at the same time a fight against the social and political developments of the middle and late monarchy, against a disintegration of Israelite society into competing classes and its political alliances and the foreign infiltration into it. It was only in the course of this controversy that the prohibitions against alien gods were formulated."[97] Hosea reminds Israel that it arose out of a contest with a brutal regime. During his time, the Israelite kingship was using the cult supposedly dedicated to YHWH the liberator as a mechanism for state oppression. The cult supplied tribute and trade for a mercurial foreign policy, which imposed greater hardships on an already exploited underclass (see especially Hosea 8).[98] Such practices were totally opposed to the very theological principles on which the covenant with YHWH was founded—liberation from tyrannical foreign powers and the establishment of a just society under the one God, YHWH.[99]

The Marginalization
of Women's Popular Religion

In light of the convergence of cult, state politics, and foreign affairs, the effects of Hosea's polemical monolatry on the religious experiences of Israelite women can now be explored. Although lines between domestic and public spheres were blurred during the pre-state period, they became sharply demarcated with the rise of the monarchy.[100] Women were identified with the private matters of hearth and home, while men were associated with the official public arena. Women's participation in the official cult was restricted. Their own particular piety is difficult to determine from the biblical texts alone,[101] which focus much more on male cult matters. Attempting to reconstruct a "popular religion" based on the material culture recovered through archaeology, William Dever observes that women played a dominant role in this popular piety, which included: the making and use of (mostly female) images; the veneration of Asherah as the Mother Goddess and/or consort of Yahweh; rituals connected with conception, childbirth, lactation, and rites of passages; private prayer; and magic associated with maintenance of hearth and home and the security of the family patrimony.[102]

Hosea's polemical monolatry—his insistence on the worship of the one God YHWH—marginalized women's popular religion, particularly in its devotion to Asherah. Nevertheless, condemnation of women's popular religion was not the determinative factor in the formation of his adulterous-wife metaphor. The traditional dichotomy that sets the male god YHWH against the female fertility goddesses can no longer be maintained. At issue in Hosea is the plurality of the Israelite cult, *primarily where it intersects with the political and economic interests of the monarchy and foreign affairs.* Hosea was principally concerned with how the public male face of the cult, found in the sanctuary and priesthood, served the state. He condemned the way official cultic pluralism supported and legitimated the state's profitable but shortsighted agricultural agenda.

Veneration of the goddess Asherah was a major feature of Israelite religious pluralism, but Hosea did not mention or directly condemn it.[103] Perhaps one reason why Hosea passed over Asherah lies in the difference in kingship ideology between Judah and Israel. According to Susan Ackerman, since YHWH was regarded as the adopted father of the Judean king, it was possible that Asherah, as YHWH's consort, was looked upon as the king's adopted mother. If this was so, the queen mother (the king's human mother) could be seen as Asherah's earthly representative, which would explain the particular veneration of Asherah by the queen mothers of Judah. Given such divine sanction, the queen mother would become the second most powerful person in the royal assembly.[104] Since worship of Asherah did not intrude in royal matters of public politics in the northern kingdom, as it did in the south, Hosea did not castigate it.

Hosean monolatry marginalized women's popular religion only insofar as the religion overlapped with the pluralistic cult tied to state-run economic investments. Hosea censured neither Asherah nor her cult object, but rather the male "baals,"[105] primarily because their cult had taken on a more public role in the politics of the state. The bull-calf images found in Samaria (8:5-6) and Bethel (10:5), which had assimilated Baal worship,[106] stand condemned because of their connections with the king, his royal court (8:4; 10:3, 7), and foreign tribute (8:9-10; 10:6).[107] The material culture reveals that women evidently continued a fervent veneration of Asherah, along with other practices of female spirituality centered on the family household. However, even though Hosea did not single out worship of Asherah, it was ultimately suppressed, as Hosea's insistence on YHWH alone became the normative theological position. Along with the suppression of the goddess, other facets of women's piety were ignored, obscured, or skewed in the formation of the biblical text by male writers and redactors, who promulgated the official (male) position.

An extrinsic analysis reveals that, for the most part, the book of Hosea was produced during a time when Israel's native-tributary mode of production was adversely affected by political instability amid foreign encroachment, an agribusiness that exploited the peasantry and maximized ecological risks, and complex intersections among king, cult, priest, and foreign affairs. For Hosea the embodiment of this oppressive mode of production was the nation's veneration of the (male) baals, which had become identified with these domestic and foreign entanglements. To castigate this mode of production, Hosea proclaimed a religio-political ideology of YHWH alone, apparently initiated by Elijah during the previous century.

Intrinsic Analysis of Hosea 1–2

Hosea required a rhetorically effective metaphor to articulate his covenantal monolatry and critique of the religio-political dealings of the Israelite state. This metaphor had to embody the *exclusivity* of Israel's relationship with YHWH alone, as well as the *inequity* of that relationship. Israel had to relearn the covenantal truth that its existence depended only on YHWH. Ideologies of exclusivity and inequity were already embedded in the social and material practices of marriage in ancient Israel.[108] Hosea utilized the fullest rhetorical force of these ideologies as vehicles for his polemical monolatry. In the intrinsic analysis that follows I discuss the ideological dynamics of the marriage metaphor, how an emphasis on marital fidelity contributes to a monolatrous theology, and the consequences for the representation of women in Hosea.

The Feminization of the Israelite Ruling Hierarchy

In this analysis I focus primarily on Hosea 1–2, because scholars have traditionally identified these chapters with the marriage metaphor.[109] Even though other sections of Hosea extend the metaphor to a much broader and more complex sociopolitical arena, scholars typically associate the wife's/Israel's "lovers" in Hosea 1–2 with an idolatrous orgiastic fertility cult, seemingly isolated from the affairs of state.[110] One must now reread the sexual imagery embedded in Hosea 1–2 in light of Hosea's critique of Israel's oppressive and debilitating mode of production, which was intrinsic to the national cult.

Hosea aims his accusations primarily at a male audience: the king and his political and cultic elite. The marriage metaphor effectively *feminizes this male ruling hierarchy* by depicting its members collectively in the graphic image of a promiscuous wife. Hosea accomplishes several rhetorical goals through this feminization. First, the feminization epitomizes a radical loss of status for the elite. By reducing them not merely to the level of a male commoner but to that of a woman, Hosea strikes a heavy blow against their exalted male honor and prestige.[111] Since "masculinity" in Israelite society is typically defined against and regarded as superior to "femininity," Hosea symbolically "castrates" the elite by placing them in the "female" position with its lower status and power.[112] He sharpens the insult even further by portraying this "woman" as a sexually promiscuous wife, *the* most shameful individual of Israelite society, who brings the greatest dishonor to the world of men. To represent an elite group "penetrated" by foreigners, Hosea describes a libidinous wife who allows her body to be "penetrated" sexually by her lovers.

Second, Hosea is able to exploit the marriage metaphor theologically to proclaim his covenantal monolatry. In a culture where wives owe sexual fidelity to one husband, Hosea depicts the exclusivity of Israel's relationship with its "spouse," the one God YHWH. As wives are economically and socially dependent on their husbands, the marriage metaphor encodes similar relations of power. Hosea summons the ruling elite to trust in YHWH-alone, not in their agribusiness, foreign alliances, and military prowess. He thus utilizes the inequity and exclusivity of ancient Israelite marriage to make his monolatrous point.

Third, by underscoring this exclusivity and inequity, Hosea's metaphor invokes the personal experiences of the male elite as husbands—the superior partner in marital relations—to teach them the depths of YHWH's covenantal love. An adulterous wife and questionable paternity are exceedingly threatening to a society in which male notions of descent, inheritance, and honor are intimately entangled with fathering legitimate sons. Hosea rhetorically highlights the enormous effort an Israelite husband must make to forgive an unfaithful wife and accept her children as his own, especially if they were sired by another man. To stand by his wife and children, enduring the social stigma this entails, is one of the most difficult experiences for an Israelite male. Yet YHWH has precisely this kind of magnanimous love for Israel and its corrupt leadership.

Feminists have discussed the interpretive problems women have regarding this gender-specific metaphor for God's covenant, wherein God becomes the all-forgiving husband and Israel the sinful promiscuous wife.[113] Feminizing men in a marital relation with a male God reinscribes into the text the ideological and social links among women, subordination, shame, and sin. Howard Eilberg-Schwartz maintains that such masculine imagery for the deity is also problematic for men, because it destabilizes norms of "masculinity." In a society where heterosexuality is the rule and women are thus in theory more fitting partners for a male God, a homoerotic predicament arises when human males become the "Other" with respect to this God.

According to Eilberg-Schwartz, the biblical writers avoided this problem in two ways. First, they symbolically displaced male tensions and
contradictions onto women. The otherness of women is exaggerated
in order to minimize the ways men become the "Other" in a system
that validates male authority. Second, the biblical authors personified
Israelite males as female subjects.[114] Hosea combines these two ways
of dealing with divine/human homoeroticism. The elite are not simply
embodied in the person of an ordinary woman, but exaggerated into a
graphic depiction of an exceptionally promiscuous wife, one particularly frightening to men anxious about their paternity.

In order to humiliate and shame the elite, Hosea moves from the
public male arena of king and cult to the private domestic arena of
man and woman. By feminizing the ruling hierarchy as "Other," however, the marriage metaphor functions in Hosea 1–2 as a "symbolic
alibi"[115] that mystifies for and conceals from later interpreters the
conflicts between the prophet and the king and his elite, just as it simultaneously reinforces the subordination of Israelite women to
men. What one remembers from reading Hosea 1–2 is the conflict
between a faithful divine husband and his sinful wife/Israel, not the
clash between prophet and male aristocracy. In order to understand
Hosea's polemic correctly and rectify traditional (mis)readings of the
gendered metaphor, Hosea 1–2 must be reread as a conflict between
Hosea and the northern elite. The close reading of Hosea 1–2 that
follows presumes a polemic against the oppressive mode of production typified by eighth-century Israel, which Hosea characterizes as
sexually promiscuous.

Hosea 1: The Prophet's Dysfunctional Family

In Hos 1:2 YHWH commands Hosea to take a "promiscuous wife" and
bear "children of promiscuity." Hosea's true metaphor may be a familial rather than a marital one, using the centrality of the family unit
to criticize the deterioration of the larger social body as a result of the
self-serving policies of the ruling elite.[116] Following F. I. Andersen and
D. N. Freedman[117] and Phyllis Bird,[118] I translate 'ēšet zĕnûnîm as
"promiscuous woman." Previous translations of 'ēšet zĕnûnîm as "harlot" or "whore" have mistakenly identified Gomer as an ordinary prostitute, or as a cult prostitute involved in Canaanite fertility cults.[119]
Although marginalized in androcentric Israelite society, a prostitute is

still tolerated,[120] while an adulterous, promiscuous wife would never be. Because of the odiousness of her sin and her ultimate social disgrace, an adulteress provides a more effective metaphor to incarnate the elite's covenantal infidelity than does a prostitute.

Hosea is ordered to marry this promiscuous woman, because "the land fornicates away from YHWH" (1:2, translation mine). As a semantically loaded term, "land" could represent the nation of Israel, the physical territory, and all of its inhabitants—ruling elite, clergy, and populace. In light of our extrinsic analysis, however, "the land" acquires greater significance as the principal means of production in an oppressive mode thereof. It becomes the site of struggle, at which the religious and political elite who control the land[121] enforce a risky crop intensification of grain, wine, and oil, parlaying their exports among competitive foreign powers, making covenants with them, and growing rich at the expense of the peasantry who work the land.

Hosea describes royal (mis)use of the land through a sexual trope: it "fornicates away from YHWH" (1:2). By means of this trope, Hosea shrewdly exploits various interconnections among land, ownership, marriage, female sexuality, and procreation to articulate his critique of the ruling elite and promote his covenantal monolatry. Appropriating a convention identifying woman with the land,[122] Hosea correlates the feminized elite with the "land." As a wife belongs solely to her husband, so does the "land" belong not to the elite but to YHWH.

Themes of land, ownership, marriage, and procreation converge in the birth of Hosea and Gomer's first son, Jezreel, whose name means "God sows" (Hos 1:4). Jezreel (*yizrě'e'l*) is paronomastically similar to the nation's name, Israel (*yiśrā'ēl*). As the wife belongs to her husband and becomes the field that her husband alone "plows," so does Israel belong solely to YHWH and become the land that "God impregnates [or 'seeds']."[123] A faithful wife certifies the paternity of her husband's seed, providing legitimate sons who will eventually inherit the land.[124] The adulterous wife/Israel, however, sabotages the legitimacy of her divine husband's seed by allowing herself to be "plowed" and "seeded" by others (that is, the foreign nations). Jezreel's own legitimacy as Hosea's firstborn son becomes suspect because of Gomer's promiscuity.[125]

Besides highlighting themes of ownership, marriage, fertility, and legitimacy, Jezreel carries other associations that Hosea maximizes.[126] The Jezreel Valley was one of the most fertile agricultural regions of the state and probably an important source of the royal cash crops (cf. Hos 2:22). It was a significant region in Solomon's redivision of the kingdom into twelve districts, one that supplied enormous resources for the royal court (1 Kgs 4:12, 22ff.). It maintained an important trade route and strategic military highway, connecting Israel with its foreign-treaty partners. The area also had significant royal connections: David married Ahinoam of Jezreel (1 Sam 25:43), who may have been Saul's own wife.[127] The town of Jezreel included the royal palace of Ahab and Jezebel (1 Kgs 21:1) and of their son Joram (2 Kings 8–9). Jezreel thus played a critical economic, political, and military role in Israel's tributary mode of production.

Moreover, Jezreel embodied the treachery occurring in this mode of production. As the site of an infamous royal abuse of power, Jezreel was home to the landowner Naboth, whose vineyard Ahab coveted and seized through Jezebel's ruthless intervention (1 Kings 21). It was also the locale of Jehu's bloody massacre of Ahab's dynasty (2 Kings 8–10), as foretold by Hosea's predecessor, Elijah, who condemned Ahab's and Jezebel's victimization of Naboth (1 Kgs 21:17-19, 23). Hosea prophesies that God "will visit the bloodshed of Jezreel on the house of Jehu" (1:4). Ironically, just as Jehu exterminated the house of Omri through his violent coup at Jezreel, so would Jehu's own dynasty suffer extinction during Hosea's time, through the assassinations following the death of Jeroboam II (2 Kgs 15:8-31; 17:1-18; cf. Hos 7:4-7).[128] It is also ironic that the Jezreel Valley, which boasts a vital military route, would become the place where God would "break the bow of Israel" (1:5)—that is, destroy the elite's military power.[129]

In the extrinsic analysis above, I argued that Hosea's polemical monolatry had its theological roots in Israel's exodus/wilderness traditions. The monarchy and cult, which were meant to serve the interests of the liberating God, had become instruments of state oppression. Israel's ruling elite had to be reminded of the radical experience of being freed from Egyptian state tyranny to enter into an exclusive covenantal relationship in the wilderness with the saving God. The Hosean exodus/wilderness tradition first appears in the birth of Hosea and Gomer's third child, the son Lo-ammi: "Call his name Lo-ammi [not my people], for you are not my people and I am not I AM[130] to you" (Hos 1:9). The judgment Lo-ammi personifies is the negation of the covenant established between YHWH and Israel after their flight from Egypt (Lev 26:12-13; Jer 7:22-23; 11:4). The elite's inequitable domestic and foreign policies regarding the land were completely antithetical to the religious beliefs upon which this covenant was established—liberation from unjust foreign powers and the creation of a just society under the one God YHWH.

Hosea 2: God's Dysfunctional Family

Hosea 2 moves from the story of Hosea's dysfunctional family to God's story about dysfunctional Israel under the present rulership. Hosea's story resumes in chapter 3. Nevertheless, it is difficult to separate the stories of Hosea and Gomer and YHWH and Israel. Narratives of Hosea's family life in chapters 1 and 3 become stereoscoped with God's stormy relations with Israel in chapter 2, where Hosea presents YHWH as a husband who has been dishonored by his wife, whom he punishes for dalliances with her "lovers."

In the chapter's final redacted state, a prologue (1:11—2:1) and an epilogue (2:23) form an *inclusio* of hope and restoration around a story of violence and betrayal.[131] Both prologue and epilogue reverse the threats embodied in names of Hosea's children: Jezreel (the blood shed at Jezreel), "Unpitied" (Lo-ruhamah), and "Not My People" (Lo-ammi). The optimistic tone changes abruptly in 2:2, where these children are called to *rîb* with their mother. In an explicit parallel to 1:9, where the birth of Lo-ammi symbolizes the disintegration of the wilderness covenant, God proclaims: "She is not my wife, and I am not her husband" (2:2). Playing out the metaphor of marriage, 2:2 represents the broken covenant of 1:9 figuratively as a divorce because of the "wife's" infidelity.

The husband enjoins his children to plead with their mother that she "remove her promiscuity (*zĕnûnêhā*) from her face and her adultery (*wĕna'āpûpêhā*) from between her breasts" (2:2). The expressions "her promiscuity" and "her adultery" most likely refer to the cosmetics and jewelry used to make the wife attractive to her lovers (cf. 2:13; Isa 3:18-23; Jer 4:30; Ezek 23:40).[132] They may also be eroticized idioms for the luxury goods the elite derived from their agribusiness and foreign affairs (cf. Isa 1:21-23; 23:17-18). Describing punishment for aristocratic indifference to the wilderness covenant, Hosea draws on an apparent social practice. As an adulterous wife is publicly stripped and shamed,[133] so will the nobility be openly humiliated (2:3). A woman's slaughtered, naked body becomes a metaphor for God's punishment of the elite and their exploitative land-use projects. Ironically, the land they are identified with—the very land they abuse—will become a parched wilderness, because they have forgotten the intense wilderness experience during which their nation pledged itself to the one God.

Hosea teases out the interconnections among woman, land, and seed further in 2:4-5, where God has no pity on the woman's children because they are children of promiscuity. The wife is the land/field that only her husband plows with his "seed." The faithful wife guarantees the purity of her husband's "seed," producing legitimate sons who will inherit the patrimony. Because the wife/land/elite has been shameless in her promiscuity, the legitimacy of her children is suspect. They may not be of her husband's "seed." Hence he refuses to acknowledge paternity of her children. He will have no compassion upon them.

The wife articulates her own transgression in 2:5b: "I will go after my lovers." Scholars have traditionally interpreted "lovers" as the baals,[134] although this identification is not explicit.[135] Hosea's only clear identification of the lovers in Hosea appears in 8:9-10, where the lovers are "the nations" with whom Ephraim is foolishly allied. In 2:7 the wife will pursue (*rdp*) her lovers, but not overtake them. According to 12:1(2), Ephraim's treaties with Assyria and Egypt are as futile as pursuing (*rdp*) the wind. For J. A. Thompson, the references to "lovers" can have political nuances similar to those found in suzerainty treaty language for covenant partners.[136] In biblical texts Hiram of Tyre is considered a "lover" of David (2 Kgs 5:1). Ezekiel's allegories of the wife/Jerusalem in Ezekiel 16 and of the sister cities Samaria and Jerusalem in Ezekiel 23 both equate the women's lovers with the foreign nations (see also Jer 22:20, 22; 30:14).

Israel believes that the nations, not YHWH, supply its bread, water, wool, flax, oil, and drink (Hos 2:5b). These items may be commodities of trade (cf. 7:14; 12:1, 7-8). According to 2 Kgs 3:4, King Mesha of Moab used to deliver the wool of one hundred thousand rams to the king of Israel. Hans Walter Wolff thinks that the rare occurrences of "drink" (*šqwyym*) in the Hebrew Bible indicate a luxury "beyond the necessities of life."[137] Carl Friedrich Keil understands the pairing of "oil and drink" to refer to "everything that conduces to luxury and superfluity."[138] The list of gifts in 2:5 may thus include the expensive items the elite procure through their risky foreign trade agreements. I do not rule out the baals as the wife's lovers (see discussion of 2:13

below). They can be interpreted as such if one recognizes that they are the public cult symbols of the ruling class's foreign and domestic policies and not the objects of worship in some alleged orgiastic fertility cult.

Thus the elite did not depend on God but rather on their "lovers" —the nations—to supply the necessities and comforts of life. The Israelite rulers did not "know" (yd')[139] that it was YHWH who provided the cash crops ("grain, wine, and oil"), who secured their imported goods and "silver and gold which they made into Baal (*'āśû labbā'al*)" (2:8).[140] The reference to "silver and gold" also indicates Hosea's focus on the upper classes in his polemic, for only these classes traffic in "lavish" quantities of "silver and gold." In 8:4 Hosea attacks the "kings and princes" who "with their silver and gold made (*'āśû*) idols" (see also 13:1-2). The baals had become equated with profitable royal foreign entanglements and were thus rejected as idolatrous (cf. 10:5-6).[141]

The interconnected themes of the woman's nakedness and the land's destruction, which first appeared in 2:3, resurface in a series of threats in 2:9-13. The husband's duty to provide for the material welfare of his wife[142] simultaneously secured her dependence and her subordination. To punish his wife, then, the disgraced husband YHWH threatens to withdraw her food ("grain and wine") and clothing ("wool and flax, which were to cover her nakedness," 2:9). These threats are amplified in 2:12, where YHWH destroys her vines and fig trees, making them a forest devoured by wild beasts. As actions upon the land, these punishments imply a devastating famine, drying up the elite's sources of income (cf. 2:3; 4:3), or a military conquest destroying the nation (5:8-14; 10:7-8, 13-15; 13:15-16). However, Hosea describes these chastisements through a trope in which a husband physically punishes his wife.

After withdrawing the wife's food and clothing, God "will uncover her *nablût* in the sight of her lovers" (2:10). A polyvalent term, *nablût* can refer to the woman's genitalia,[143] the lewdness of her sexual behavior,[144] or the woman/land's deterioration.[145] Uncovering her genitals, YHWH reveals the literal site of the woman's pleasure, fertility, and transgression. The wife's exposed genitalia becomes a graphic image for the ruling class's breach of covenant and the land's decline. Unmasking their shared desires and sexual misconduct, the most vulnerable part of the wife's body will be displayed before her lovers, the nations.[146] Although the male gaze usually results in visual pleasure,[147] this is not the case here. The gaze of the nations/lovers reveals their own sexual and moral impotence in their inability to rescue Israel from its disgrace (2:10b; see also 5:12-14 and 7:11-12).[148]

God will put an end to "her festivals, her new moons, her sabbaths, and all her appointed festivals" (2:11). These cultic celebrations have usually been interpreted as the syncretistic services in which sexual acts allegedly occurred.[149] As we have discussed, however, the rampaging sexuality of these rites is probably fictional and therefore not Hosea's bone of contention. Rather, these sacred festivals served as major sources of income for the religious and political elite.[150] Pilgrimages brought the products of the land to various northern shrines (4:10, 15; 5:6-7; 8:11-13; 9:1-6; 10:1-2). By feminizing the elite as a wanton wife, Hosea labels their economic misuse of these festivals as *sexual* wrongdoing, describing the luxuries they acquire during these occasions as a hooker's fee (*'etnâ*), "which my lovers have given me" (2:12). Once God abolishes these festivals, however, their economic base dries up, threatening national security.

God will punish the elite for "the festival days of the baals" (2:13). Here Hosea makes explicit the identification of the woman's lovers as the baals. Nevertheless, the cultic veneration of the baals should not be isolated from the larger political sphere, in which festivals had become state occasions, particularly for the worship of the baals in their calf iconography (8:4-6; 10:3-6; 11:2; 13:1-3). References to the wife decking "herself with her ring and jewelry" and "going after her lovers" (2:13) indicate that these festivals were sumptuous public affairs through which the elite curried favor with the foreign nations (see especially 10:1-3). Once legitimate parts of YHWH's cult, the baals became equated with an unjust mode of production and are now condemned by Hosea.

YHWH levels at the wife the accusation that "she went after her lovers, *and forgot me*" (2:13b). What the elite forgot, Hosea insists, was the exclusive relationship Israel had with YHWH, a historical bond forged in the Sinai wilderness after YHWH had delivered them from their slavery in Egypt (9:10; 12:9; 13:4-5). Articulating his polemical monolatry, Hosea asserts that ever since Egypt, Israel "knew"[151] no other god or savior but YHWH (13:4; cf. 2:8, 20). It was YHWH alone who fed, taught, and healed Israel in the wilderness (11:1-4; 13:5). The elite had to relearn the lessons taught by these earlier experiences with the one God. National security depended on it.

The site of this reeducation is the wilderness itself, the place of the first intimate encounters between God and the people. For Hosea, then, the wilderness is both a threat and punishment for betrayal (2:3) and a place for hope and reconciliation. In the language of courtship, YHWH will seduce the nation into the wilderness and speak tenderly to her/it (2:14). The cash-crop vineyards that God destroyed (2:12) will be returned to the nation (2:15), reinforcing the notion that YHWH is the provider on whom Israel depends. Hosea envisions the renewal of the covenant when the nation responds to YHWH, "as in the days of her youth, as at the time when she came out of the land of Egypt" (2:15b).[152]

The source of Hosea's covenantal monolatry, the exodus/wilderness experience, becomes most explicit in 2:16: "On that day, says the Lord, you will call me, 'My Husband,' and no longer will you call me, 'My Baal.'" The motif of name-changing began in the prologue (1:11—2:1), continues here in 2:16, and will conclude in the epilogue of 2:23. For Halpern, the implied practice of referring to God as "baal" evidently inspired Hosea's marriage metaphor for the covenantal relationship, because "baal" not only indicates the deity Baal but can also mean "husband."[153] As a wife has only one husband, the elite have only one 'îš. Hosea completely rejects the veneration of a deity who had been a legitimate part of the state cult alongside YHWH. Baal had represented royal and elite interests so much that Hosea believed the cult of Baal had displaced the worship of the one God, YHWH. The cult had become an instrument of state oppression, totally opposed to the religious ideals upon which the wilderness covenant was based: freedom from foreign oppression and the creation of a just and equitable society. Some scholars interpret the title "My Husband" as suggesting that Israel has a more intimate partnership with God, rather than the ownership relation implied by the title "My Baal."[154] Such an interpretation dangerously imposes modern conceptions of marriage upon Hosea. Hosea utilizes the marriage metaphor to emphasize not only the exclusivity of Israel's relationship with YHWH alone, but also the inequity of that relationship. The very existence and continuance of the Israelite nation is dependent solely on YHWH, a reality forgotten by its aristocracy.

Hosea depicts covenantal renewal as the restitution of both cosmic world order and patriarchal authority in the family. The God-Israel covenant embraces the "wild animals, the birds of the air, and the creeping things of the ground" (2:18). Military strife will be ended.

God, the heavens, and the earth will reciprocate in answering one another in a cosmic chain reaction.[155] The earth's unique response to God is the production of "grain, wine, and oil" (2:21-22). Hosea thus reminds the elite that the land's freedom from armed conflict and its agricultural fertility and ability to yield crop revenue depend directly on their fidelity to YHWH alone. In the restoration of patriarchal authority, the husband becomes reconciled with his wife and takes her back (2:19-20). As husband and father, he is head of the family. His faithful wife (the elite) is his subordinate, protecting his seed and thereby legitimating his children. The notion of seed appears when the grain, wine, and oil answer Jezreel ("God sows," 2:22). In a play on words on "Jezreel" identifying the wife with the land, God sows "her" (the wife)[156] in the ground, impregnating her with his seed. No alien seed can sprout in the land in this new world order, because the wife will remain true to her spouse.

Finally, the children's paternity, which the husband questioned in 2:4-5, is resolved in 2:22-23. As part of this covenantal renewal, God acknowledges his wife's children as his own. God the husband becomes God the father. The children receive new names, symbolizing their change in status from suspected bastards to legitimate offspring. No longer embodying the murderous exploitation of the tributary mode (1:4-5), Jezreel becomes a place where God inseminates his wife after their reconciliation. God will have pity on his daughter Unpitied. He will say to his son Not My People, "You are my people," and his son will declare, "You are my God." In Hosea's depiction of covenantal renewal, then, the respective parties acknowledge and submissively accept their place within the cosmic and social order: the elite with their God, the woman with her husband, and the children with their father.

Summary

Hosea reacts against an oppressive mode of production, embodied in the cult of eighth-century Israel. This mode of production involved: (1) an intensive agribusiness producing grain, wine, and oil for export by the elite classes; (2) a volatile political situation coupled with a reckless foreign policy; (3) an intertwining of cult, kingship, and priesthood with foreign policy; and (4) an unpolemical monolatry whose male cultic veneration of Baal legitimated elite interests. Previous scholarship on Hosea 1–2 isolated Israelite cult from state interests and imagined licentious fertility cults of Baal that infected a pure Yahwism. In the rest of the book, however, Hosea's "lovers" are the foreign nations (as in Jeremiah and Ezekiel) with whom the elite are economically and politically entangled. Hosea thinks that the nation's aristocracy forgot that God freed Israel from oppression in Egypt to worship YHWH alone in a self-sustaining tribal fellowship. Instead, the elite administer an exploitative state that violates the very theological principles of their origins. Through unjust domestic and foreign policies, Israel seems to be "returning to Egypt" (8:13; 9:3).

How does Hosea pressure a powerful group of privileged men to recognize their oppression and return to the worship of YHWH alone? His first rhetorical strategy is feminizing them as a promiscuous wife, an action that symbolically castrates and shames them. He then exploits a full range of figurative identifications of the woman/wife with the land. The land can simultaneously represent the elite, the whole nation, the people, and the means of production for grain, wine, and oil. In addition, the woman becomes the fertile field or land that her husband plows and inseminates to produce legitimate sons. Famine, drought, and foreign invaders can destroy the woman/land. The woman/land thereby becomes a barren wilderness. The wilderness is also the site of God's seduction of the wife. As in the early days of the wilderness, Hosea predicts a return to YHWH alone. The wife will respond by proclaiming YHWH as "my husband" and by being faithful to him, allowing no foreign seed to contaminate her. God will respond in turn like a good husband, taking her back, providing for her material needs, and acknowledging paternity for her children.

A materialist reading thus grounds Hosea's polemical monolatry in specific material practices and social conditions. The worship of fertility goddesses and the perverse sexual practices of their cult do not inform Hosea's marriage metaphor and symbolization of woman as evil, as has been maintained in traditional scholarship. Rather, through a shaming, feminizing metaphor, Hosea directs a stringent critique against the nation's male leadership. However, this metaphorical feminization functions in Hosea 1–2 as a "symbolic alibi," which obscures for later interpreters Hosea's conflicts with this leadership while concurrently reinforcing the subordinate status of Israelite women to men. What one remembers from reading Hosea 1–2 is the conflict between a faithful divine husband and his sinful wife/Israel, not the clash between prophet and male aristocracy.

6 The Two Sisters in Ezekiel: They Played the Whore in Egypt

Ezekiel 16 and 23 have provoked a number of feminist readings because of their sexually violent pornographic content.[1] Nevertheless, because they focus primarily on gender and rhetoric, these studies have devoted little attention to situating the historical production of these extended metaphors[2] within the system of *colonial* relations that eventually led to the conquest and exile of the Judean elite.[3] By dehistoricizing the rhetoric of sexuality, these investigations overlook the "en-gendering" of these texts during brutal acts of empire. The pornography of these texts should be coded not simply as another form of patriarchal violence, but as colonial ethnic conflict framed as a sexualized encounter. The feminist critic must negotiate the "either/or" opposition between the colonized female body, symbolizing the nation, and the racialized male colonizer and conqueror constructed by the male prophet. In both texts the history of the nation is seen through the lens of a colonized male of the priestly elite during the final days of that nation and the exile of its upper-class sectors. The gender-specific metaphors of Ezekiel 16 and 23 are products of this personal and collective male experience of foreign colonization and conquest trauma.

In this chapter I focus on Ezekiel 23, because of its more detailed sexual descriptions of the foreign conquerors and its metaphor of promiscuous sisters for the nation, rather than that of the faithless wife.[4] In my examinations of sexualized tropes of nationhood, I am particularly indebted to the insights of feminist postcolonial theory and trauma studies in trying to grasp the experiences of prophet and

111

nation during periods of colonization, conquest, and exile. As in the case of most nationalisms, the gendered narrative of the nation's history in Ezekiel 23 originates from a masculine historical memory, an emasculinized humiliation, and remasculinized hope for a restored priestly hegemony.[5]

Extrinsic Analysis

The Empire Strikes Back:
The Fall and Exile of the Judean Elite

After Josiah's death in 609 B.C.E., Judah briefly came under the control of Egypt, marking its transition from a native-tributary to a foreign-tributary mode of production in Judah.[6] Agricultural surpluses were sent to a colonizing power via the Judean king, Jehoakim, who maintained his own royal lifestyle with this surplus. As an Egyptian vassal, Jehoiakim incurred a heavy tribute,[7] which he imposed on the "people of the land," the Judean landowners (2 Kgs 23:23-35). To keep pace with the tax, the landowners, in turn, extracted more from the peasants who worked their land. Jehoiakim's extravagant palace and use of corvée labor to build it depleted the land's economy even more.[8]

After defeating the Egyptians at the battle of Carchemish in 605 B.C.E., the Babylonian king Nebuchadnezzar gained control of Judah, and Jehoiakim became his vassal.[9] Jehoiakim (or more correctly, his already encumbered tax base) paid Judah's annual tribute to Babylonia for three years, but then rebelled in 601/600 (2 Kgs 24:1). Jehoiakim's withholding of tribute was most likely prompted by Nebuchadnezzar's military setback by the Egyptians under Neco during this time. It is also possible that Jehoiakim assumed Egyptian support against any Babylonian aggression, support that turned out to be a chimera (cf. 2 Kgs 24:7).[10]

Nebuchadnezzar's response to the rebellion was swift and lethal. According to 2 Kgs 24:2: "The Lord sent against [Jehoiakim] bands of the Chaldeans, bands of the Arameans, bands of the Moabites, and bands of the Ammonites; he sent them against Judah to destroy it, according to the word of the Lord that he spoke by his servants the prophets." The Babylonian Chronicle reports as follows on the occupation of Jerusalem after a brief siege during the seventh year of Nebuchadnezzar's rule (598/597): "In the month Kislev the king of Akkad mustered his army and marched to Hattu. He encamped against the city of Judah and on the second day of the month of Adar he captured the city (and) seized its king. A king of his own choice he appointed in the city (and) taking the vast tribute he brought it into Babylon" (TCS 5:102; also *ANET,* 564). The seized king was not Jehoiakim, but his teenage son Jehoiachin. Exactly how Jehoiakim died is disputed.[11] Along with his mother, other leading officials, and members of the artisan class, Jehoiachin surrendered to Nebuchadnezzar. According to 2 Kgs 23:14, ten thousand were exiled, leaving the "poorest people of the land." Ezekiel was most likely exiled during this first deportation in 597.[12] The reliability of this figure is difficult to assess.[13] Whatever the amount, those deported constituted only a small part of the total population.

After confiscating the royal treasury for the tribute denied him (2 Kgs 24:13), Nebuchadnezzar appointed Jehoiachin's twenty-one-year-old uncle Mattaniah to rule in Jerusalem and changed his name to Zedekiah (2 Kgs 24:17). Zedekiah faced difficulties in both domestic and foreign affairs. His native authority was undercut because the colonizer installed him while the legitimate king was in exile.[14] He was deprived of expert advisers because of the deportation, and left with shortsighted partisan chauvinists at court. Although exhorted by Jeremiah to submit to Babylon,[15] Zedekiah sided with the pro-Egyptian party and rebelled against Babylon (2 Kgs 24:30).[16]

In response to Zedekiah's insurrection, Nebuchadnezzar laid siege to Jerusalem in 589. Judah's hopes for Egyptian aid were apparently answered when Nebuchadnezzar withdrew from Jerusalem to confront Egyptian forces sent by Hophra (Jer 37:1-10; cf. Ezekiel 29). These hopes were short-lived, however, and the Babylonian siege of Jerusalem resumed. At the end of the two-year siege, Jerusalem ran out of food and the Babylonian forces breached its walls. Zedekiah was captured and his sons killed in his presence. He was blinded, chained, and shipped off to Babylon (2 Kgs 25:3-7). Nebuchadnezzar sacked the city, plundered and destroyed the temple, and exiled another portion of the population. Nebuchadnezzar's destruction of the temple was a significant part of his strategy to obtain economic and political authority over the conquered nation, as well as damaging national and religious morale.[17]

While estimates of deportees vary, what seems certain is that only a small minority of the population was exiled, restricted primarily to

the upper classes. Most of the population, especially the small
landowners and landless lower classes, remained in the land.[18] The
Babylonians evidently allowed the landless to take over the property
of the exiled landholders, in order to bring a semblance of order to a
war-torn country (cf. 2 Kgs 25:12; Jer 39:10; Ezek 11:15; 33:23-
29).[19] Although William F. Albright describes "a complete devastation
of Judah,"[20] and considered Judah to be "archaeological *tabula rasa*
for that period,"[21] this was probably not the case. Nebuchadnezzar
had *economic* reasons for leaving the Judean infrastructure intact:

> As [Nebuchadnezzar's] imperial system depended on the accumula-
> tion of wealth based on the production outside his own country, the
> total annihilation of a conquered territory would in fact be an act
> against his own interest. As his empire subsisted on already estab-
> lished forms of wealth production and accumulation, it would rather
> be in his interest to maintain, or even increase, the existing modes of
> production.[22]

Hans Barstad argues that the upper classes were not essential for
agricultural production in Judah. It was primarily the hill country
that underwent destruction and deportation by Nebuchadnezzar. The
rest of the population and farming areas were, for the most part, un-
changed.[23] Economic production in Judah probably went on as usual
not long after the catastrophic events of 587/586, supplying
Mesopotamia with exports of wine and olive oil.[24]

I turn now to the situation of the exiled elite in Mesopotamia in
order to contextualize Ezekiel's prophecies in their sociohistorical mi-
lieu. According to Bustenay Oded, the deported Judean elites were allowed personal freedom and autonomy, and property rights, while in
exile. They were able to assemble in communities and choose their
own leaders. In other words, they were able to preserve their Jewish
identity in a foreign land: "Therefore, the Jews in Babylonian Exile,
already before the Declaration of Cyrus (538 B.C.E.) were not dis-
persed marginal elements in the Mesopotamian society (or societies)
but constituted a stable and kinship based community with legal status, economic positions, hierarchical system of organization, unique
religious precepts and national consciousness."[25]

Although this complacent view of the exiles might characterize the
later period when the Jews were more settled in the Diaspora,[26] it is
very unlikely that it describes the conditions surrounding the first and

second deportations. Daniel Smith-Christopher disputes sanguine appraisals of Judah's exile, in light of comparative studies of the misfortunes of exiles throughout history and the evidence of trauma in the Hebrew Scriptures after the experience.[27] Along with the physical destruction wrought by the siege of Jerusalem, the deportees witnessed the horror of starvation and its attendant cannibalism (cf. Deut 28:52-57; 2 Kgs 6:28-30; 25:1-3; Jer 19:9; Lam 1:11; 2:20; 4:10). With no place to bury the dead, corpses rotted in the streets, eaten away by maggots and vermin (Jer 14:16; cf. Isa 5:25; 66:24). Because of lack of water for sanitation and adequate medical treatment for the wounded, plague festered in the city. When the walls were finally breached, the attackers violently plundered the city, mutilating and raping its women (cf. 2 Kgs 8:12; 15:16; Amos 1:13; Hos 13:15-16; Isa 13:16; Lam 5:11; Zech 14:2).[28] In recounting his defeat of a city, the Assyrian king Ashurnasirpal boasts that he cut off the arms and hands of captured troops, and their noses, ears, and limbs. He gouged out their eyes and made piles of their corpses and heads. Many heads he hung in trees around the city.[29] The horrible descriptions of mutilation and dismemberment are eerily similar to Ezekiel's prophecies against Oholibah/Jerusalem (Ezek 23:25-26; see below).

Besides the emotional and physical atrocities experienced in the defeat of the city, the deportees also had to contend with the trauma of exile. The harsh and oppressive strategy of exiling conquered peoples served economic and political purposes in consolidating the empire.[30] Traveling long distances, already difficult under normal conditions, was particularly agonizing for the captives. Many were undoubtedly malnourished after the long siege. If women had just been raped, their long, difficult journey was even more traumatic.[31] Assyrian reliefs depict the exiles being led away with hands, and sometimes feet, shackled with chains, leather straps, or ropes.[32] According to Oded, the Assyrians bound only those captives who were men of rank and status, like the king and the aristocracy, either to punish and humiliate them or to prevent their escape and organizing a rebellion.[33] There is no reason to suppose that the Neo-Babylonians differed in their treatment of upper-class prisoners of war.[34] Second Kings 25:7 describes Zedekiah as being blinded by the Babylonians and taken away in chains. Second Chronicles 36:6 notes that Jehoiachin was bound in fetters and taken to Babylon.

In assessing the condition of the deportees, one must reckon with the brutality of conquest and subsequent exile. Although the Judean elites were not slaves, as Africans were enslaved in the United States, they were most likely subject to corvée-labor practices for numerous building projects, which Oded himself acknowledges.[35] Some of the deported elites were assimilated into the Babylonian palace and cult bureaucracy. However, I am more concerned with those who were settled in rural sections of Mesopotamia, since Ezekiel was most likely one of them. Repopulating abandoned or desolate regions with deportees was a critical part of Assyrian policy to increase agricultural production and tax revenue.[36] It appears that Babylonia continued this practice. The rapid growth of the central floodplains of the Euphrates during the Neo-Babylonian period leads Robert Adams to conclude that "large masses of people were *involuntarily transferred* as part of intensive Neo-Babylonian efforts to rehabilitate the central region of a domain that previously had suffered severely."[37] The Judean elites were part of this transference. Although they were primarily urban professionals, many elites were put to intensive agricultural work and severely taxed, in order to increase the Babylonian treasury.[38] Moreover, they incurred the hostility of the local population in the areas where they were resettled.[39]

The Judean elites were not homogeneous in their socioeconomic and legal status while in exile: "There were masters and dependants, full freemen and chattel slaves, soldiers and civilians, labouring freemen and labouring dependant persons, townsmen and villagers, free peasants and dependant farmers, free landholders, tenants and *glebae adscripti.*"[40] Nevertheless, whatever socioeconomic level they managed to attain in exile, all deportees suffered a radical reduction of the elite status they possessed when they governed in Judah. Instead of living out their colonized status in their own native land, where they at least had some rank and privilege among their own countryfolk, they were transplanted forcibly to another part of the empire and made to submit to another drastic configuration of imperialist rule.

Ezekiel in His Colonial Context

Scholars commonly agree that the author of Ezekiel 23 was a priest, based on the superscription, Ezek 1:3.[41] In particular, he and the disciples who redacted and expanded his work were most likely members of the Zadokite priesthood,[42] which had dominated the Jerusalem

temple since the time of Solomon.[43] Given that he was stationed so-
ciologically among the upper tiers of Judean society, it is not surpris-
ing that he was exiled from Jerusalem during the first deportation of
the upper classes in 597.[44] He seemed to belong to that group of exiles who were forced to become farmers as a result of Babylonian intensification of agriculture in the central plains.[45] According to 1:3
and 3:15, he lived near an irrigation canal, Chebar, in the village of
Tel-abib. In contrast to those who were taken into the Babylonian
palace and temple bureaucracy, the elites who were forced into agricultural service suffered the greatest change in their lifestyles.

We can thus locate Ezekiel socially as a Zadokite priest of the now-
defunct Jerusalem temple. He was probably one of the first prophets
to have communicated his words through a written, rather than oral,
mode of production.[46] As such, his exilic message would have been
restricted to those who could read, namely, the upper classes. Moreover, he was a victim and survivor of state-sponsored terrorism.[47] We
may safely say that the wartime atrocities committed by the Assyrians
and Babylonians not only caused much physical pain, but were also
an effective form of psychological warfare against the victim.[48]
Ezekiel's theological (re)construction of Israelite history and his singularly pornographic descriptions of the nation as an adulterous and
defiled woman are framed by the trauma he experienced from the following acts of state-sponsored terrorism: (1) the barbaric conquest of
Jerusalem, (2) the destruction of the temple and his lifework, (3) his
exile to a foreign land, (4) his radical loss of status and prestige, and
(5) his forced labor in an unfamiliar occupation.

Intrinsic Analysis of Ezekiel 23

Ezekiel 23 relates the past history of Samaria and Jerusalem,
metonyms for the national states of Israel and Judah, through a narrative metaphor about two promiscuous sisters married to God. The
social sciences would describe their connubial relationship as an example of sororal polygyny, in which a man marries sisters, daughters
of the same mother (23:2) and therefore of equal status.[49] Several
questions tantalize and challenge us. Why does Ezekiel couch Israel's
and Judah's past in such a gender-specific narrative? Why is this
memory of the nation's history articulated in such sexually graphic
and violent imagery? In what specific ways is this imagery a symbolic

resolution of real social contradictions and conflicts facing a colonized and exiled male elite?[50]

In this intrinsic analysis, I explore Ezekiel's gendering of the rival
kingdoms as two promiscuous sisters by first examining "woman" as a
trope for nationhood in the male imagination. Second, I discuss how
this trope reflects and attempts to resolve contradictions in male
Judean/Babylonian colonial relations. I then examine how the
pornography of Ezekiel 23 arises from the author's attempt to work
through the personal and collective experience of conquest and exile
trauma. I argue that the gendered narrative of the nation's history is
produced by the collective male elite experience of humiliation and
emasculation by the victorious colonizer.

Woman as Trope of Nationhood

That "woman" has become a signifier for the land and the nation is
well known.[51] Feminist postcolonial studies, in particular, have
placed the trope of woman as land/nation under intensive critical
scrutiny.[52] The Hebrew Bible itself is no stranger to the metaphor of
woman as land/nation.[53] In the previous chapter, I demonstrated how
Hosea's/God's wife becomes identified with the land/nation itself.

Because women biologically reproduce members of ethnic entities, control of women and their sexuality is central to national and
ethnic polities.[54] In order to preserve ethnic and national boundaries,
male-generated laws and customs define with whom and under what
circumstances women can have sexual relations. Gender differences
between women and men also serve to define the *symbolic* limits of
national difference and power between men in male-constructed nationalisms.[55] As signifiers of ethnic/national differences, they become
a locus and sign in ideological discourses that construct, reproduce,
and transform ethnic/national categories.[56] Because they demarcate
national differences among nations, women literally and symbolically
designate the "porous frontiers" through which nation, ethnicity, and
culture can be penetrated.[57] One horrendous way in which women
literally mark the boundaries through which a nation can be penetrated is the systematic rape of enemy women by conquering armies.[58]

Women's elevated position in male idealizations and constructions
of nationhood does not, of course, translate into reality. While
women often figuratively represent the nation and embody its values

in the male imaginary, they are simultaneously prohibited by men from becoming public agents in determining its sociopolitical laws and governance: "Excluded from direct action as national citizens, women are subsumed symbolically into the national body politic as its boundary and metaphoric limit. . . . Women are typically constructed as the symbolic bearers of the nation, but are denied any direct relation to national agency."[59] Women become the literal and metaphorical sites where *male* controversies and struggles are played out, in which they have little voice or representation.

Colonial Subjects
and the Tangled Relations of Empire

Because women are so embedded in nationhood and national identity, sexual images often become tropes for colonial dominance—but not just because they graphically portray who is on the top and who is on the bottom. They are signifiers and markers for wider unequal distributions of power based on the class and race of the colonizers and colonized. The contradiction, whereby women and their bodies become national symbols of the elaborate power relations and colonial struggles among men, is fully evident in Ezekiel 23.

Ezekiel is a "subject" in two opposing senses. On the one hand, he is a *subject as a high-ranking agent* in his nation, a male elite priest. His sociopolitical subjectivity contrasts directly with that of women and lower-class men in his nation. On the other hand, he is a *subject as a subordinate vassal* under the power of Babylon. His male-constructed national history in Ezekiel 23, therefore, represents a tangled web of complicity and contradiction between the colonizer and the colonized. Both collude in sharing androcentric ideologies.[60] Further, within his own domain Ezekiel resides in the upper tiers of his society and shares the priestly ideology of his caste. Common ground therefore exists between Babylon and Ezekiel with respect to similar ideologies of gender and class superiority, although their power relationship is that of a Babylonian superior to his inferior. Within the intricate social complexes of gendered power, Ezekiel belongs to the superior sex and class in his native context. However, he also ranks as male subordinate to Babylonian male colonizers, to whom his class must pay tribute. This ethnic Other humiliates and eventually vanquishes him and his nation.

In chapter 23 Ezekiel attempts ideologically to resolve his contradictory double positioning as an elite male priest who is colonized,
conquered, and exiled from his national homeland by falling back on
androcentric ideologies of male superiority/female submission. What
results is an astonishingly pornographic projection of his historical
memory of trauma.

The Porno-Tropes of Trauma

Because Ezekiel 23 was written in response to a horrific event, studies on trauma literature can shed some light on Ezekiel 23 and its sexually graphic imagery.[61] Indeed, for Smith-Christopher, studies of
Ezekiel should be in dialogue with the literature on post-traumatic
stress disorder (PTSD), in order to obtain a more critical understanding of Ezekiel's so-called bizarre behavior and textual pronouncements.[62] Jay Geller also contends that trauma can be employed as a
notion internal to the production of biblical texts, in that their distinctive features may have been generated in the wake of some earlier
(un-worked-through) trauma.[63] "Trauma" refers not to the *injury* inflicted but to the *blow* that inflicted it, not to the *state of mind* that en-
sues but to the *event* that provoked it.[64] Memories of trauma exist as
"unassimilated scraps of overwhelming experiences, which need to be
integrated with existing mental schemes, and be transformed into
narrative language."[65] Bringing traumatic experiences to language is
essential in conceptually processing this integration. Narrativizing
trauma imposes some order upon the experience, making terrifying
memories of it more bearable.[66] Constructing a narrative from the
experiences of trauma enables the event to become "known."[67]
Telling the story of trauma is not merely a personally reconstitutive
act, but also an act of remaking one's political world.[68] As such, it is a
selective reinterpretation of the past that understands "historical
truth," not as exact replications of events, but as testimonies of one
who survives trauma and tries to cope with the past.[69]

Chapter 23 is Ezekiel's attempt to work through and integrate his
traumatic experience of colonization, conquest, and exile. Through it,
he addresses questions of meaning (Why did these events happen?)
and, in particular, theological understanding (Was our God powerless
to prevent these events?). It is one way in which Ezekiel coped with
and worked through the horrors of the conquest and exile, turning

frightening and uncontrollable events into a contained and predictable narrative.[70] I am concerned with how Ezekiel 23 may have resulted not from personal or individual trauma,[71] but rather from the collective trauma of a *specific group:* the male priestly caste of colonial Judah during exile.[72] We must continually keep in mind that in Ezekiel 23 the nation's history, presented in such a totalizing and sexually explicit fashion, reflects the interests of only a small, disgraced, and traumatized minority of Judean society in exile. The experiences of this small group become normative in the formation of the Hebrew canon.

Colluding with patriarchal ideologies that he shares with his colonizer, an upper-class Judahite priest stages his own horrendous experience of colonization, conquest, and exile as an extended metaphor about two rival promiscuous sisters. Ezekiel 23 reflects the collective trauma of Ezekiel's class and ethnic group as symbolic, if not physical, emasculation.[73] This male elite may have indeed witnessed the actual castration of their countrymen. Sennacherib claims that "With the bodies of their warriors I filled the plain, like grass. (Their) testicles I cut off, and tore out their privates like the seeds of cucumbers."[74] The threat of castration is certainly apparent in Isa 7:20, where the king of Assyria will act as God's razor to shave the head, beard, and "feet" or genitals of Judah. According to P. Kyle McCarter, the Ammonite shaving of the beards and exposing of the buttocks of David's servants suggests a symbolic castration in 2 Sam 10:4-5.[75]

Ezekiel 23 may be considered a testament to the nation's *emasculinity*, a nation stripped of its masculinity.[76] Its symbolic castration hallmarks the nation's *effemininity*. In Ezekiel's case, however, it is not the colonizer's discourse about its subjects, but a colonized individual's own discourse about his nation's upper classes and their fall from grace. Because of their humiliation and exile by foreigners, they are no longer men but women: effeminate, emasculine, castrated.

Moreover, it is not the effemininity that connotes the softness and languidity of women,[77] but a woman at her most nightmarish for an ancient Near Eastern society and priesthood: a wildly unfaithful, sexually amoral one. A story about nationhood, nationality, colonization, and conquest is retold through two significant ancient Near Eastern lenses: (1) the equation of male dishonor with female promiscuity, and (2) priestly notions of purity and defilement. In order to lambaste the nation's religio-political blunders, Ezekiel projects his own emasculating experience of being conquered and humbled by Babylonia in a (his)story about two promiscuous sisters. In this, Ezekiel differs from Hosea, with his trope of the faithless wife, used to feminize the Israelite elite in a rhetoric of prophetic critique.[78]

In dealing with extreme trauma, victims often use behavioral self-blame as a mechanism to reestablish a meaningful world.[79] By recognizing that one's own actions may have caused a traumatic event to occur, one can exert some control over a seemingly uncontrollable and intolerable situation. In chapter 23 Ezekiel blames the sins of the two nations for the events of conquest and exile. In order to resolve the contradiction of being a male elite under the thumb of a male colonizer, however, he resorts to androcentric ideologies to articulate this self-blame. To exercise control over his humiliating circumstances, he symbolizes the sociopolitical escapades of Israel's and Judah's male national leadership as lascivious women. In this act of transgendered self-blame, he thus reinscribes the male status quo and the entitlements of his assumptive elite world, in order to integrate his memories of trauma.[80] Avoiding blame by ducking behind a woman's body, Ezekiel thereby absolves simultaneously his own institutional complicity in sins of the nation and that of the male elite class to which he belongs. Blame falls metaphorically on the bodies of women, where male conflicts between victor and vanquished are played out.[81] In the national script, women symbolically become "the medium through which competing discourses represent their claims; a palimpsest written over with the text of other desires, other meanings."[82]

"A Pox on Both Your Houses": A Revisionist History of Israel and Judah

In wrestling with the problem of the marriage metaphor for the divine human relationship, I asked in a previous work, "To whose experience does the metaphor speak, and whose experience does the metaphor exclude?"[83] I now turn to an examination of the rhetoric of Ezek 23:1-35.[84]

At the beginning of his national history, Ezekiel emotionally titillates his audience with a glimpse of child porn:[85] as young girls, the two sisters Oholah and Oholibah play the whore (*znh*) in Egypt, and their young breasts are fondled and caressed by the Egyptians (23:3). The Egyptians are the first in a series of male racialized Others who play an erotic role in this national history. Ezekiel's descriptions of pedophilia are geared rhetorically to arouse his male elite audience sexually and to indict them at the same time.[86] If one follows the gist of the text carefully, the indictment is not about the Egyptians sexually molesting the sisters as children, which would have a historical referent in their economic exploitation of the Hebrews (Exod 1:1-14). Instead, the indictment is leveled at the two nations themselves, described later as enjoying this sexual abuse so much that they become exceedingly licentious in their adult life.[87]

Ezekiel makes no mention of Egyptian enslavement (or God's deliverance) in another revisionist history, Ezek 20:7-8. Here the people's relationship with God is characterized by rebellion and apostasy from their very beginnings in Egypt. In 20:7-8 Ezekiel is projecting back into the nation's prehistory Judah's political misalliances with Egypt under Jehoiakim and Zedekiah, labeling them as idolatry in Egypt.[88] By means of this negative twist on the exodus traditions, Ezekiel 23 excites and indicts its male audience by eroticizing and condemning simultaneously the nation's political favoritism of Egypt by tracing it back to its origins in Egypt. The people's time in Egypt becomes the source of national infidelity, symbolized by the sisters' juvenile promiscuity. The sisters were sexually licentious with foreign men even before marrying God and bearing his children (23:4).[89] Ezekiel reiterates these shameless origins in Egypt at important junctures of his revisionist history:

1. before Oholah is handed over to her lovers, the Assyrians (23:8);
2. when recounting Oholibah's flirtation with Egypt after her disgust with the Babylonians (23:19-20);
3. at the conclusion of Oholibah's shameless sexual history (23:21); and
4. concluding the husband's first denunciation of Oholibah (23:27)

The elder sister is called Oholah (lit. "her own tent"), a symbolic name for Samaria. The younger is named Oholibah (lit. "my tent in her"), representing Jerusalem (23:4). The cities are metonyms for the national states of Israel and Judah, respectively. The word "tent" in the names of both sisters has a polyvalent significance.[90] Theologically, the tent of meeting was the place where the presence of God dwelled during the people's wilderness sojourn. This presence is most clearly signified in Oholibah, where God's glory is thought to reside in the temple in Jerusalem ("my tent in her"). Economically, tents could refer to the various sanctuaries in the northern kingdom and the temple in Jerusalem as essential state mechanisms in the mode of production of both nations. As mentioned above, Nebuchadnezzar's destruction of the Jerusalem temple was a critical part of his strategy to gain economic and political control of Judah.

In addition, tents are typically female spaces of erotic expression or allusion. In the context of the sexual seduction of the Israelites by the women of Moab, Num 25:7-8 relates the priest Phinehas entering the women's quarters of a tent[91] and with a spear skewering the Israelite Zimri and the Midianite woman Cozbi, presumably in the act of sexual congress.[92] A number of scholars have already noted the sexuality surrounding Jael's invitation to Sisera to enter her tent (Judg 4:18-22).[93] A tent was pitched on the roof of David's palace, where Absalom had sexual relations with his father's concubines "in the sight of all Israel" (2 Sam 16:22).[94] Julie Galambush makes the sexuality implied by the tent reference in the sisters' names even more explicit by highlighting the metaphorical connection between tents/temples and female genitalia: "If the city is a woman, then the temple is her vagina, and the offense of Jerusalem's granting illicit 'access' to foreign men and competing gods becomes plain, both as a legal transgression and as a personal injury to the husband."[95]

Thus, in the national cartography of Ezekiel 23, the northern sanctuaries and the Jerusalem temple, symbolized by Oholah and Oholibah, are at once deposits of national treasure (economic production), sites of imperial contest (racial/ethnic difference and colonization), and spaces of female sexuality (gendered reproduction). This triangulation of class, race, and gender will govern the pornographic portrayal of Israel's and Judah's relations with their foreign Others.

As in most narratives of trauma, Ezekiel is quite selective in his rehearsal of the nation's history. He passes over the conquest and settlement in Canaan, and the periods of the judges, of the united monarchy, and of the Omrides during the divided monarchy. He dwells on a period during which another powerful racialized Other, Assyria, intruded in the affairs of the nation, beginning with Jehu's submission to Shalmaneser III (ca. 841 B.C.E.).[96]

The nation's history thus resumes with Oholah's adulterous escapades with Assyria. Her marital transgressions against God are highlighted by the detail that she "played the whore *while she was mine* [lit. 'under me']" (23:5). Hosea had already soundly condemned Israel's fickle foreign policies with Assyria.[97] In eroticizing these policies, Ezekiel focuses on Oholah's sexual lusting (*'gb*)[98] after a variety of elite Assyrian men: warriors, governors and commanders, and mounted horsemen (23:6).[99]

Visual tokens of masculine power, as well as the sexual desirability of these foreign elites, trigger Oholah's infatuation. The warriors are clothed in blue (*tĕkēlet*), one of the costliest dyes in the ancient world, the use of which was highly guarded.[100] Because of the expenses involved in the purchase and upkeep of horses, the cavalry formed an exclusive fighting unit.[101] That horses themselves are powerful symbols of sexuality heightens the masculine allure of these exotic equestrians.[102] To top things off, all of them are "handsome young men" (*bahûrê hemed kullām*) and the "choicest men of Assyria" (*mibhar bĕnê-'aššûr kullām*, 23:6-7).

Power is an aphrodisiac that irresistibly captivates Oholah. She dispenses sexual favors on these high-ranking foreign men and defiles herself (*nitmā'â*) with all their images (23:7).[103] The use of the verb *ṭāmē'*, "to become unclean," arises from Ezekiel's priestly notions of defilement. Purity and defilement are not restricted to cult, but extend to relations with the nations (*haggôyim*), who are the racial/ethnic Others of Israel. Condemning defilement among the nations, Lev 18:24-30 is significant for Ezekiel 23, coming as it does at the end of a series prohibiting certain types of sexual relations.[104] Personal relational defilement between the genders and communal political defilement among the nations become interchangeable. The theme of defilement with the nations will recur in Ezekiel's indictments of the sisters in 23:13, 17, and 30.

Ezekiel 23:8 is the first repetition of the nation's nymphomaniacal origins in Egypt, when young men slept with Oholah, squeezed her virgin nipples, and poured out their lust upon her. The reference to Egypt not only describes Oholah's immoral beginnings but may also refer to Israel's capricious foreign policy in Ezekiel's revisionist history. For Ezekiel, Samaria's vacillation between Egypt and Assyria toward the end of its rule under its last king, Hoshea,[105] simply perpetuates Israel's youthful depravity in Egypt.

Ezekiel eroticizes the violent end of the northern kingdom by describing the deity/husband delivering Oholah into "the hands of the Assyrians, for whom she lusted" (23:9). These former lovers rape

her,[106] exile her sons and her daughters, and kill her with the sword
(23:10). The sexual, military, and racial/ethnic violence that characterized the fall of Samaria converge in the image of the naked violated
body of Oholah. Nevertheless, by falling back on androcentric ideologies of male honor and female shame, Ezekiel foregrounds sexual
violence in this image. By becoming a byword among women, this
brutal picture of executed judgment stands as a cautionary tale for
ancient women who may be contemplating adulterous acts against
their husbands (cf. 16:41). This admonition becomes even more explicit later in 23:48: "all women may take warning and not commit
lewdness as you have done."[107]

Although both sisters follow similar paths of defilement (*derek
'eḥād*, 23:13), the primary target of Ezekiel's history is
Oholibah/Jerusalem.[108] Oholah's visual pleasure in the physical at-
tractiveness and military potency of the Assyrians will also infect her
younger sister, Oholibah. Taking the subject position of voyeur,[109]
Oholibah "saw" (*wattēre'*, 23:11), but what she saw is not simply the
lascivious spectacle of her older sister's (d)alliances with handsome
exotic males, but also God's horrendous judgment upon them. Rather
than take warning, however, as a respectable married woman would,
Oholibah becomes even more degenerate than her sister in her own
tireless nymphomania. Just like Oholah, Oholibah becomes sexually
obsessed with the physical trappings of power enjoyed by Assyrian
elite males (23:12). The historical referent here is most likely Ahaz's
alliance with Tiglath-pileser III during the Syro-Ephraimite war (2
Kgs 16:5-20; Isaiah 7–8).

Oholibah far exceeds her sister's carnality in her flirtations with
other elite foreigners besides the Assyrians. Like her sister's,
Oholibah's sexual obsession with the Babylonians begins with the act
of *seeing* (*wattēre'*, 23:14). Nevertheless, Oholibah is seduced not by
the Babylonian men themselves but by visual displays of Chaldean
potency.[110] She sees wall carvings of male figures, red images of
Chaldeans girded with belts around their loins, their heads covered
with turbans, all appearing to be a special royal class of warriors
(*šālišîm*).[111] All of these present "*a picture (dĕmût)* of Babylonians
whose native land was Chaldea" (23:15). This picture arouses her
lusts, and she sends out messengers to offer sexual invitations
(23:16). The Babylonians come to her love couch, where they mutually defile each other in their fornications (23:17).

The Babylonian wall carvings of males that Oholibah sees probably have historical referents.[112] However, Ezekiel's focus on the *visual* trappings of masculine power can also be illumined by trauma studies. In the structure of torture, the pain and suffering inflicted upon a person by a regime become objectified and translated into wholly convincing spectacles of power: "The physical pain is so incontestably real that it seems to confer its quality of 'incontestable reality' on that power that has brought it into being."[113] The victim who completely loses power internalizes what appears to be genuine power—namely, the power of the oppressor.[114]

To articulate his own suffering and that of his nation, Ezekiel objectifies and translates his own painful disempowerment into a vivid display of his conquerors' military and sexual strength. He (porno)graphically portrays these sisters as sexually cavorting with and being ravished by hypermasculine conquerors, who are ethnically Other. According to Sander Gilman, sexuality is the most conspicuous indicator of Otherness and is therefore symbolized in any racist or classist ideologies: "Fantasies of impotency are projected onto the Other as frigidity, fantasies of potency as hypersexuality."[115] This notion helps explain Ezekiel's fascination with the amazing military and sexual prowess of the conquerors. If Michelle Marcus is correct in arguing that Mesopotamian imperial imagery constitutes a strategy of "self-symbolization," representing oneself the way one would like to be seen,[116] then Ezekiel is internalizing and eroticizing the ideological self-image of his conquerors here. Perceptions of the "superior" empire and race are expressed in the language of exaggerated male sexuality, able to gratify a ravenous nymphomaniac.[117] The sexual virility of these conquerors is juxtaposed with the emasculinity of a small, humiliated, and traumatized group of exiled aristocrats.

As Oholibah turns away from her Babylonian lovers in disgust, God is alienated from her (23:18). Rejecting her Babylonian suitors and then rejected by her divine husband, Oholibah returns to her first paramours,[118] the Egyptians. This second reference to the shameless "days of her youth" in Egypt (23:19) most likely alludes not only to the oppressive Egyptian colonial relations during the time of Jehoiakim, but also to the seductive but unrealized hopes under Jehoiakim and Zedekiah in securing Egyptian help against the Babylonians. Although sexuality is implied in the Assyrians' and Babylonians' physical trappings of military and political power,[119] only the

Egyptians are described as having genital and ejaculatory largesse. Their "members (*bāśār*) were like those of donkeys" and their "emission (*zirmat*) was like that of stallions" (23:20; cf. 16:26 describing the Egyptians). A number of ancient texts credit members of the equine family with astonishing sexuality.[120]

There may be a cross-cultural explanation for limiting genital endowment to Egyptians. According to Gwendolyn Leick,[121] Enki is the only Mesopotamian deity with explicit phallic characteristics. Phallicism never flourished in Mesopotamian culture the way it did after the Aryan invasion of India, or even in pharaonic Egypt or classical antiquity. Archaeological remains of Mesopotamian phallic symbols are rare, although they are present in Egypt and its colonies. In this case the preoccupation with the size of Egyptian genitalia may allude to the ithyphallic Egyptian god Min-Amun, who is often portrayed with an erect penis.[122] Lawrence Stager discusses a number of Egyptian artifacts of Min found at Ashkelon, a Philistine stronghold destroyed by Nebuchadnezzar before his sack of Jerusalem. Among these artifacts are seven phallic-shaped *situlae* (bronze bottles), on which Min is the most prominent deity represented. On one of the *situlae,* Min is masturbating himself with his left hand while throwing his right hand up in a gesture of sexual pleasure. Stager thinks that these *situlae* may have contained semen or other liquids symbolizing generative power.[123] These artifacts corroborate the rhetorical connection Ezekiel draws between the Egyptians and large, ejaculatory penises.

Although the correlation between Min and Ezekiel's description of sexually well-endowed Egyptians is conjectural, Ezekiel clearly makes two points in his revisionist history regarding Oholibah's return to her Egyptians, with their tumescent phalli. First, these foreign men can only provide erotic attraction to Oholibah; they cannot compete with the military and political prowess of Mesopotamia.[124] Egyptian military assistance has been proven false historically at the times when Jerusalem needed it most, particularly before its destruction in 587 B.C.E.[125] Basically racialized stud-muffins for Oholibah, the Egyptians can make only love, not war.

Second, Ezekiel concludes the promiscuous history of Oholibah by returning to her origins in Egypt, following God's rejection of her. Oholibah reverts back to the time and place before her marriage to the deity. Ezekiel makes a wordplay on *zirmat* (ejaculations, 23:20) with Oholibah's longing for the *zimmat* (lewdness, 23.21) of her youth, when Egyptians fondled her breasts and squeezed her young nipples.[126] Ezekiel moves in binary categories from race/ethnicity to gender, and from gender to sex in wrapping up Oholibah's history: from Egyptian (foreign) to Judean (domestic), from male to female, from sources of male sexual pleasure (penises, *bāśār*; and ejaculations, *zirmat*) to those of the female (breasts, *šādayim*; and nipples, *daddîm*).[127] The repetition of "breasts" and "nipples" in 23:21 forms a distant chiasmus with "nipples" and "breasts" in 23:3, rhetorically marking off both Israel's and Judah's histories of moral and sexual deterioration. God's rejection of Oholibah and her return to her origins set up the next section, in which God pronounces judgment upon her (23:22-35).

Ezekiel formulates his judgment against Oholibah in two segments: 23:22-27, 28-35.[128] In the first part,[129] Ezekiel attempts to preserve the honor of the cuckolded deity by describing God as rousing up Oholibah's rejected lovers against her. The colonizers and conquerors of Jerusalem, the Babylonians, along with the Assyrians, become agents of marital payback in Ezekiel's revisionist history (23:22-23). The attractive foreign men are no longer clad in the finery that marks their elite status (23:6, 15). They are now decked out with the accoutrements of battle: shield, buckler, and helmet (23:24). Parade horses (23:5, 12) now become warhorses (23:23-24). God empowers these ethnic Others to judge their former lover according to their judgments (23:24). In their military atrocities, God the husband unleashes his own fury against his rebellious spouse (23:25).

While the marriage metaphor for the divine-human relationship takes its cues from the inequity and exclusivity of ancient Israelite marriage,[130] the punishment in 23:22-26 is probably not modeled on ancient Israelite penalties for adultery, as is usually presumed.[131] Descriptions of Oholibah's chastisement are more likely derived from the memories of trauma that Ezekiel experienced in the siege and conquest of Jerusalem. He assimilates these memories in this (his)story of the nation in order to process and cope with these painful events. To make this case, I use as a springboard Ashurnasirpal's gruesome exultation in his capture of a city:

In strife and conflict I besieged (and) conquered the city. I felled 3,000 of their fighting men with the sword. I carried off prisoners,

possessions, oxen (and) cattle from them. I burnt many captives from
them. I captured many troops alive: I cut off of some their arms (and)
hands; I cut off of others their noses, ears, (and) extremities. I gouged
out the eyes of many troops. I made one pile of the living (and) one of
heads. I hung their heads on trees around the city. I burnt their ado-
lescent boys (and) girls. I razed, destroyed, burnt, (and) consumed the
city.[132]

The parallels in table 2 make clear that memories of trauma, more
than the sentences for adultery, lie behind Ezekiel's depiction of
Oholibah's chastisement.

Ezekiel concludes the first section of Oholibah's punishment with
the final reference to her days of lewdness and whoring in the land of
Egypt (23:27). God will put an end to them definitively. Oholibah will
no longer lift her eyes for her days in Egypt or remember Egypt itself
anymore. Traditionally, Egypt connoted the place of God's liberation
of the people from slavery, the beginning of their election and God's
covenantal favor. Egypt was precisely the site where God's salvation
history was inaugurated and where the people were formed as a nation. In Ezekiel, however, Egypt occupies a much more sinister position at the beginning *and* at the end of the nation's history. Egypt
corrupted the nation's virtue from its infancy and continued to court
and seduce her shamelessly up to her violent termination.

We have seen that Oholah and Oholibah were enticed by the *visual* sight of their prospective partners throughout their shocking sexual histories. Just as Ashurnasipal "gouges out the eyes of many
troops," and Nebuchadnezzar puts out the eyes of Zedekiah (2 Kgs
25:7), God "blinds" Oholibah at the end of her history. She will no
longer "lift her eyes" to her lovers again, either with sexual desire or
to seek military aid (Ezek 23:27).[134]

Military, racial/ethnic, and sexual violence converge particularly in
the second section of Oholibah's sentencing (23:28-35).[135] God the
husband tells his licentious spouse that he will deliver her into the
hands of those she hated (*běyad 'ăšer śānē't*), into the hands of those
she turned from in disgust (23:28, *běyad 'ăšer noqʻâ napšēk mēhem*;
cf. 16:27, 37). According to 23:17, these are the Babylonians who
came to her bed of love and defiled her with their lust. After their sexual orgy, Oholibah turns from them in disgust (*wattēqaʻ napšâ
mēhem*), a metaphoric depiction of Judah's transfer of political allegiance from the Babylonia to Egypt. Her former lovers, the colonizers

Ashurnasirpal	Ezekiel 23
"I cut off of some their arms (and) hands; I *cut off* of others their *noses, ears*, (and) extremities."	23:25: "They shall *cut off* your *nose*[133] and your *ears*."
"I *felled* 3,000 of their fighting men with *the sword*."	23:25: "Your survivors shall *fall* by *the sword*."
"I *burnt* their *adolescent boys (and) girls*."	23:25: "They shall seize *your sons and your daughters*, and your survivors shall be *devoured by fire*."
"I *carried* off prisoners, *possessions, oxen (and) cattle* from them."	23:26: "They *shall also strip* you of *your clothes* and take away *your fine jewels*."
"I *gouged out* the *eyes* of many troops."	23:27: "She will *not lift up* her *eyes* to them."

Table 2: Parallels between Ashurnasirpal's military barbarities and those hurled against Oholibah.

she now hates, will turn that hatred back upon her in conquest and plunder (23:29, *wĕ'āśû 'ôtāk bĕśin'â*).

As she lived, so shall she die. Oholibah will be stripped naked and bare (*'êrōm wĕ'eryâ*).[136] Her whoring crotch (*'erwat zĕnûnayik*),[137] the site of her sexual pleasure, marital transgression, and economic livelihood, will be exposed (*wĕniglâ*). The expression used here, "to uncover nakedness/genitals," is a euphemism for copulation.[138] In the context of military invasion and pillaging, the expression "to uncover genitals" can refer only to sexual violence at its worst.[139] If Oholibah is Jerusalem and her vagina represents its temple,[140] the sack of the temple is sexualized as a brutal rape. Oholibah's foreign lovers become her gang rapists. This same image is found in Lam 1:10, another exilic text depicting the Babylonian assault upon the temple:

> Enemies have stretched out their hands (*yādô*)
>   over all her precious things;

> she has even seen the nations
>   invade (*yābō'û*) her sanctuary." (NRSV)

Scholars have noted the rape imagery in this verse, [141] interpreting "their hands" [142] as the invasive penis that pierces (*bw'*)[143] a rape victim. Given Ezekiel's own preoccupation with male sex organs (16:26; 23:20), his dual references in 23:28 to delivering Oholibah into the "hands" of her ex-lovers may also have sexual connotations of rape, as well as military overtones of conquest. The penis becomes a weapon of war.

In 23:30 Ezekiel blames Oholibah's sexually violent end on her sexually shameless life: "Your lewdness and your whorings have brought this upon you, because you played the whore with the nations (*gôyim*) and have polluted yourself with their images."[144] In order to process his own trauma from his nation's cruel destruction, Ezekiel scapegoats the political dealings of the Judean male elite with foreign nations onto the fractured, beaten, and sexually ravaged body of a woman. In an exercise of transgendered self-blame, he thus acquits himself of any institutional complicity in the actions of his male class.

Because Oholibah followed her corrupt sister's decadent lifestyle, God will give Oholah's cup into her hand (23:31). In many late pre-exilic and exilic texts, the "cup" refers to God's angry judgment in the form of military defeat and devastation inflicted upon Judah and the foreign nations.[145] Given Ezekiel's priestly background and the context of Oholibah's marital infidelities, the cup may also allude to the bitter waters given to a woman accused of adultery by her husband (Num 5:11-31).[146] In both texts the accused woman is married to a jealous husband.[147] In both texts the accused wife drinks from an earthenware vessel.[148] If found guilty, both women die a horrible death.[149] The cup of bitter waters Oholibah is forced to drink is "deep and wide" (Ezek 23:32), foreshadowing Jerusalem's extensive destruction by the invading armies. Like others who drink from God's cup of wrath, she will become an object of "scorn and derision" in her "drunkenness and grief" (23:32-33a).[150]

Ezekiel reiterates in 23:33b that the cup Oholibah drinks is the same as her sister Samaria. Oholibah frivolously dismissed her sister's horrible devastation and became even more licentious in her behavior toward the foreign nations. She must now suffer her sister's fate. The cup from which she must now drink is "a cup of horror and desolation" (*kôs šammâ ûšĕmāmâ*).[151] She must drink it to its dregs (23:34a; cf. Isa 51:17). According to Jer 25:16, those who imbibe in the cup "shall drink and stagger and go out of their minds[152] because of the sword that I am sending among them." Oholibah's crazed behavior is dreadfully manifested in oral and mammary self-mutilation: she will gnaw the cup's broken shards and use them to tear out her breasts (Ezek 23:34). The mouth that imbibes the cup is gashed; the breasts foreign men once enjoyed are lacerated.

The abhorrent images of Oholibah's bleeding mouth and gory breasts bring us full circle in the course of her promiscuous life. Her breasts provided salacious pleasure with the Egyptians from her beginnings (v 3) to her disastrous end (v 21). In vv 20-21 I noted Ezekiel's juxtaposition of male and female sources of sexual pleasure: penises and breasts. If one relates this juxtaposition to v 34, one may discern in Oholibah's tearing out of her breasts an implied castration, symbolic of the collective trauma experience by Ezekiel and his caste.[153] By depicting her injuries as self-inflicted, Ezekiel reinforces the blame he laid on her in v 30, and scapegoats the nation's sins upon her hacked-up body. She *herself* obliterates the bodily sites of her erotic pleasure and guilt. She *alone* is responsible for the tremendous agony she now endures. Oholibah's culpability is reinforced at the conclusion of this unit, where God the cuckold declares: "Therefore thus says the Lord God: Because you have forgotten me and cast me behind your back, therefore bear the consequences of your lewdness and whorings" (23:35). The consequences of her "lewdness and whorings" that she must bear are a destructive military siege and invasion by her foreign lovers, who leave a bloody carnage in their wake.

Summary

I have tried to situate the pornographic imagery of Ezek 23:1-35 historically in the collective trauma of disgraced priestly elite males, who suffered colonization, conquest, and exile during the first quarter of the sixth century B.C.E. This is not to condone or excuse the prophet's pornographic symbolization of the nation, but rather to contextualize it. Constructing a revisionist history of the nation in Ezekiel 23 was one way in which the prophet worked through his colonial and conquest trauma. Its symbolic and perhaps literal emasculation is inversely contrasted with an eroticized depiction of the ethnically different hypermasculine conquerors. To explain the humiliation of his class and process his trauma, Ezekiel projects the sins of the nations onto two sisters, promiscuous from their youth, who lust after these foreign lovers. The triangulation of gender, race/ethnicity, and class in the complex relations between colonizer and colonized, conqueror and conquered, must be reckoned with to understand and deal with Ezekiel's extremely offensive revisionist history. Like Genesis 2–3 and Hosea 1–2, Ezekiel 23 is another "symbolic alibi," in which Ezekiel and the elite class to which he belongs avoid blame for the nation's fall by concealing themselves behind the bodies of women.

7 The Other Woman in Proverbs: My Man's Not Home—He Took His Moneybag with Him

Proverbs 1–9 is the first in a series of postexilic theological reflections on God's own wisdom personified as a woman. In some of the rare instances in the Hebrew Bible in which an attribute of the deity is described as female,[1] Woman Wisdom is truly an awesome figure. She was present when God created the world and is the sanctioned mediator between the divine and human (Prov 3:19-20; 8:22-31).[2] By her, kings rule and sovereigns govern justly (8:15-16). Her counsel is better than silver or gold (3:14-16; 8:10). Fathers enjoin their young sons to pursue Wisdom as a lover pursues his beloved, and to cling to her once they have found her (4:5-9, 13; 7:4; cf. Wis 8:2; Sir 24:19-22). She becomes the tree of life for those who embrace her (Prov 3:18).

Woman Wisdom's powerful adversary in Proverbs 1–9 must necessarily be as mythically awesome. Like Wisdom, she is female, but those who embrace *her* charms are set on the pathways of death, never to return (Prov 2:18-19; 5:5-6; 7:27). Fathers caution their sons to avoid her at all costs, although her seductions are irresistible. She is the *'iššâ zārâ*, which I translate as the "Other Woman."[3] In Proverbs 1–9 she becomes the evil antithesis of Woman Wisdom personified.[4] Her Otherness is embodied in a number of ways that make her a most inappropriate marriage partner for a nice upper-class boy in the province of Yehud. She is the Other Woman in an illicit affair. She is Other because she is already married and therefore off-limits to any other male. She is Other because of her racial/ethnic foreignness. She is Other simply because "she is not our kind"—"our kind" defined, of course, by strictly constructed but often arbitrary and ever-shifting boundaries.

The extrinsic analysis of this chapter depends on the dating of Proverbs 1–9, which has been quite difficult to pin down. These chapters seem to have a timeless quality, and they lack references to historical events that would assist in dating. Nor does Proverbs 1–9 refer to theological themes of Israel's salvation history—such as God's promises to the ancestors of land, descendants and great name, the exodus and wilderness traditions, God's covenant with Israel, and so forth—that would help contextualize it. Traditionally, King Solomon (ca. 950 B.C.E.) is said to be the author of Proverbs (1:1; 10:1; 25:1), although Solomonic authorship is very unlikely.[5] Ben Sira, who often quotes, paraphrases, and explains the book of Proverbs, offers a *terminus ante quem* in the first quarter of the second century, circa 180 B.C.E.[6] The reference in Prov 25:1 to "the men of Hezekiah, king of Judah," who copied "other proverbs of Solomon" implies a *terminus a quo* in the late eighth to early seventh centuries for Proverbs 25–29, which was apparently added to the earlier Solomonic collection, Proverbs 10–22.[7] With respect to genre and language, however, Proverbs 1–9 and 31:10-31 differ considerably from these collections.[8]

Most scholars, however provisionally, date Proverbs 1–9 and 31:10-31 during the Persian period of the postexilic era, 538–333 B.C.E.[9] This dating has been strengthened recently in an illuminating study of the socioeconomic context of Woman Wisdom by Christine Yoder. Yoder argues convincingly for a reassessment of linguistic evidence to clarify the dating of Proverbs 1–9. Based on the presence of Late Biblical Hebrew, certain Aramaisms, the lack of Greek features that might suggest a Hellenistic date, and later MT orthography in Proverbs 1–9, she posits a dating somewhere between the early sixth century and the late third century B.C.E., most probably in the Persian period.[10]

An *extrinsic analysis* of Proverbs 1–9, then, would look to the Persian period for clues to the literary production of the Other Woman. As I argued in chapter 4 regarding Genesis 2–3, however, the precise historical dating of Proverbs 1–9 is not my critical focus. Instead, I concentrate on the particular mode of production at work during this period, with its various configurations, to construct these chapters. I discuss how imperial and economic policies during two centuries of Persian colonialism impinged upon the local conflicts and controversies among the populations and classes in the province of Yehud. My *intrinsic analysis* examines how Proverbs 1–9 attempts to resolve symbolically the socioeconomic conflicts and contradictions embedded in the dominant class during this period that help to produce the literary construction of the Other Woman. I investigate particularly Proverbs 7, in which the Other Woman verbalizes, herself, the dangers about which the sages warn young upper-class males.[11]

Extrinsic Analysis

Persian Imperial Politics

About fifty-eight years after the first deportation of exiles from Judah, the Persians under Cyrus emerged onto the ancient Near Eastern political scene to conquer the Babylonians and take over their vast empire (539–530 B.C.E.). Both the Jews who remained in Palestine and those deported to Babylonia fell under Persian sovereignty. Partly because of Second Isaiah's positive portrayals of Cyrus as God's messiah and his decision to allow the deported Jews to return to their homeland and rebuild the Jerusalem temple (Isa 45:1-3; cf. Ezra 1:1-4, 6:3-5; Isa 45:13), scholars have regarded Cyrus as rising above Neo-Assyrian and Neo-Babylonian despotism to be a tolerant, benign ruler.[12] This alleged Persian humanitarianism toward conquered peoples has been carried over into some Old Testament introductory textbooks.[13]

Unfortunately, these positive estimates skew the actual historical context of Achaemenid imperialism for those living in the various provinces of the empire. According to Amélie Kuhrt, the presumption that Persian imperialism was somehow more lenient than Assyrian tyranny is based on two factors: (1) the limited experience of one influential group in a very small community that managed to profit from Persian directives; and (2) royal propaganda successfully modeled on similar texts that earlier commended Ashurbanipal, a first-rate example of the much-condemned Assyrian imperialism.[14] Persian foreign policy was governed not so much by toleration and humanitarianism as by military strategy to strengthen and expand the imperial periphery, the economic taxation and exploitation of which primarily benefited the imperial center.[15] The main reason Cyrus allowed the deported Jews to return to Palestine was to ensure a sympathetic population along a strategic military supply route. These loyal residents acted as a buffer against the superpower at Persia's western front, Egypt (and later the Greeks).[16] They also provided for and housed Persia's armies when they entered the region. Cyrus returned the temple treasures taken by Nebuchadnezzar and supported the rebuilding of the Jerusalem temple primarily because such sanctuaries were economic centers for the accumulation and dissemination of taxes and tribute for the empire.[17] Temples also performed an ideological function in stabilizing a society when their cult personnel were loyal to the empire. Norman Gottwald states the matter of Achaemenid foreign affairs succinctly: "The survival and expansion of empires absolutely depended on their drawing from conquered regions surpluses that would at least offset the costs of their military and administrative investments and optimally would 'turn a profit.'"[18] If political support of the local elite did not achieve their military and economic goals, the Persians could be as ruthless and cruel to the colonies as the Assyrians and Babylonians had been.

Yehud under Persian Colonization

According to Charles Carter, the Persian province of Yehud was actually smaller and poorer than previous estimates had calculated. It was situated in the central hill country, "running along the Jerusalem corridor, from Bethel toward Hebron, and extending east to the Judean Desert."[19] The economy was essentially village-based agrarian, and Jerusalem was the provincial capital.[20] As in preexilic times, agricultural production focused primarily on the cultivation of three lucrative cash crops: grain, wine, and oil.[21]

During Babylonian colonization, Yehud experienced a change from a native-tributary mode of production[22] to a foreign-tributary mode of production, in which taxes and tribute were handed over to an outside power. However, its configuration during Achaemenid rule had elements of a native-tributary mode of production, in that taxes extracted from the peasants first passed through the hands of Persia's agents, the Jerusalem elite.[23] After taking their cut to support the local temple and an autonomous governmental bureaucracy, this elite then submitted their quotas to the Persian imperial treasury.[24] Although Carter is correct in saying that what changed in the transition from native- to foreign-tributary mode of production was the ultimate destination of the tribute,[25] the economic situation in Yehud had an added complexity. In the foreign tributary mode of production under the Persians, the two-tiered mode of extraction undoubtedly placed an additional burden on Yehud's already impoverished peasantry, in that it supported the lifestyles of two sets of elites—one foreign, the other domestic.

Changes in Persian imperial policy toward its colonies over the years directly affected this mode of production in postexilic Yehud.[26] The conservative maintenance of the empire by Cyrus's successor, Cambyses (530–522 B.C.E.), allowed Yehud to become a relatively autonomous and stable province, even though taxes were steep.[27] After assassinating Gaumata, who had usurped the throne after Cambyses died in 522, Darius (522–486) set about quelling a number of revolts that erupted in most of his territories and unifying the empire. He reorganized his kingdom into twenty satrapies, setting up local governing elites whose allegiance belonged to him. He adjusted the taxation of each satrapy to capitalize on what it could provide for the imperial center. One strategy for unification was the construction of temples throughout his kingdom, which increased employment and strengthened the collection of levies and tribute for imperial purposes. Support of these temples made Darius well liked and accepted among many in the colonies.[28] It was he who facilitated the construction of the Second Temple in Jerusalem through Zerubbabel, the governor that he appointed in Yehud (Ezra 3, 6). Under his administrative reorganization, imperial bureaucracy directly affected the autonomy Yehud had had under previous Persian rulers. Darius's administration demanded an increase in production and maximal taxation under the direction of loyal bureaucrats such as Zerubbabel. In addition, feeding Darius's expedition forces for his big military campaign against Egypt (519–517) contributed to a major depletion of Yehud's economic resources.

With the succession of Darius's son Xerxes to the throne (486–465), Persian priorities shifted negatively away from the colonies to the imperial center. Under Darius, local religions had enjoyed Persian support, especially in the construction and maintenance of temples throughout the empire, which enhanced local economies. Xerxes, however, not only eliminated these subsidies, but also actually destroyed sanctuaries in a shortsighted attempt to eliminate any religious nationalism that could foment rebellion in the colonies. Although the Jerusalem temple did not suffer such devastation, it is clear from the writings of the prophet Malachi that it experienced fiscal problems because of the decrease in Persian financial backing.[29] Xerxes diverted to the Persian imperial center the funds that would have gone to the local temples, while at the same time increasing the taxes of the colonies in the periphery. In contrast to his father, whose policies worked to intensify these outlying economies, Xerxes worked primarily to remove their surpluses.[30]

Artaxerxes I (465–423) carried on his father's program of not taxing the Persian center but increasing taxes in the Persian periphery. Nevertheless, Yehud temporarily benefited from Artaxerxes' rule, since Yehud was caught in the middle of conflicts between the Persian Empire and Egypt and Greece, which had formed an alliance on Persia's western front. In order to deal with the Egyptian and Greek threats, Artaxerxes fortified Persian outposts in Yehud, rebuilt the city walls of Jerusalem, dispatched competent and loyal governors to be in charge, and financed them with silver and gold. Ezra (ca. 458–446) and Nehemiah (ca. 445–432) were probably two of the functionaries whom Artaxerxes appointed.[31] Through them and through subsidies to the Jerusalem temple, Artaxerxes exploited the ideological potential of local religious leaders to influence and control the population. However, his attention to Yehud did not last during the second half of his rule: after defeating the Egypt/Greece coalition, he resumed his father's policies of colonial depletion.[32] Greece emerged as an economic factor in Yehud, as it engaged in trade for Yehud's cash crops. Unfortunately, Yehud's economy did not improve with this additional trading partner; indeed, it probably became weaker.[33] Yehud's fiscal decline was symptomatic of the increasing deterioration of the colonies throughout the Persian Empire.

Class and Conflict in Ancient Yehud

Social divisions in Yehud were directly affected by changes in imperial foreign policies. Jon Berquist distinguishes three interest groups of ethnic Jews, related in varying degrees of cooperation and conflict in Yehud during Achaemenid rule.[34] The first two consisted of immigrants from Babylon, who had probably served in the Babylonian cult or royal court and now enjoyed Persian support. Many had descended from the aristocrats, priests, upper-class landowners, and so on who had been deported to Babylonia years earlier.[35] The priestly immigrants had a vested interest in the rebuilding of the temple and oversight of the proper observance of holy days and ritual practice as they defined it. The political immigrants were more concerned about enhancing the economic productivity and prosperity of the region.

Supported by and in service to the Persian imperium, these two groups eventually formed an alliance as the *golah* community,[36] collaborating or clashing with the native population. Although numerically they were very much in the minority, they eventually became the wealthiest, dominant faction in Yehud, replicating the stratified, pyramidal social structure of preexilic times. Both groups shared an urban perspective, focusing on Jerusalem as the site of the new temple and political center. Both were allowed a certain religious and political autonomy to administer Yehud, as long they were loyal to the Persian government by collecting and rendering their quota of taxes and maintaining the socioeconomic stability in the area. They also worked to obtain special concessions from Persia for increased social, political, and religious autonomy and tax relief for the inhabitants of Yehud, although the political and economic interests of the imperium and those of Yehud were not easily harmonized in planning and carrying out their public policies.[37]

The third group was composed of those natives already living in the land when the exiles returned. As discussed in chapter 6,[38] when the minority elite was exiled, the bulk of Judah's population was left behind. Although the group probably included some smallholders, they were labeled the "poorest of the land" (2 Kgs 24:14; 25:12; Jer 39:10). However, their livelihood improved somewhat under Babylonian occupation. The Babylonians apparently allowed many of them to take possession of and work the lands of the deported landlords. While they did not achieve the high economic ranks of the exiled, some natives probably formed an "upper class" in Yehud that was accountable to the Babylonians.[39] For their appropriation of land, they were vilified by Ezekiel—and, undoubtedly, others—in exile (Ezek 11:15-21; 33:23-29; 36:1-7). This population would not have been thrilled about the return of the deportees, especially if it meant reverting back to their preexilic lower status.[40] They had been worshiping God their way for decades, and, unlike the returning priests, saw no need to rebuild the temple and subject themselves to priestly notions of proper ritual practice. They had been cultivating their land for years, and were suspicious of the political immigrants, whose material interests seemed to tilt toward the colonizer.[41] The two-tiered

extraction of surpluses in Yehud introduced by the returning deportees and the ever-increasing demand for more agricultural production
and imperial taxation played a major role in the exploitation and deterioration of the natives.

Inevitably, antagonisms developed between the local inhabitants
and the immigrants from Babylon who sought to reclaim their preexilic status and privileges in Yehud. Although clashes between the returning elite and the natives were often described in theological
terms (cf. Ezra 4:3; Neh 4:15; 6:12-14, 16), their conflicts were most
likely over socioeconomic issues. Imperial policies directly polarized
and exacerbated divisions in the social classes in Yehud. The peasantry shouldered most of the burden, as taxes and tribute became
more oppressive as the empire declined.[42] Darius's financial backing
of the temple created an upper class in Yehud composed of the
priestly and civic returnees, and his intensification policy also deep-
ened the economic rift in social classes. Although he provided partial
compensation for the cost of the food to feed and house his armies
as they passed through the area, this payment was not distributed to
those whose labors produced this food, but to the *golah* elite.[43] With
the cessation of temple support under Xerxes and with his policy of
colonial depletion, more surpluses were demanded of the lower
classes to finance temple operations, as were more imperial taxes.
This strategy preserved the income of the elites while diminishing
the assets of the rest of the population, thus widening the social
gap.[44]

If Nehemiah 5 is any indication,[45] economic abuses of the elite
against the natives came to a head during the latter part of the fifth
century under Artaxerxes I.[46] Nehemiah himself was aware that exploitation of the peasants by their leaders had been going on for some
time (Neh 5:15). Nehemiah 5:2-5 describes the drastic measures
farmers had to take to repay their debts to the *golah* landowners:
mortgaging their land if they owned any; taking out loans at high interest to pay imperial taxes; selling their sons and daughters into slavery[47] and risking the rape of their daughters by their creditors in
doing so.[48] Although Nehemiah's reforms seemed to bring temporary
relief to the peasantry, they did not change the systemic roots of the
exploitation: the elite monopoly of agricultural land, noncompensa-
tion for those who farmed it, stiff burdens on the peasantry to pay imperial taxes, costly tithes for the temple (10:32-39), and the priestly

elite's exemption from having to shoulder any portion of Persia's taxation (Ezra 7:24).[49] The great socioeconomic disparity in Yehud was symbolized in Nehemiah's rebuilding of the city walls of Jerusalem (Neh 2:11-20) and repopulating the city with leading families of the *golah* (7:5-73), creating an actual physical barrier between its upper and lower classes. "The rebuilt city exists for the urban elite and their cohorts from Persia; the outlying, unprotected countryside remains for the poorer inhabitants of the land."[50]

Economics, Endogamy, and Ideology: The Politics of the Other Woman

Proverbs 1–9, with its condemnation of the Other Woman, is often situated during the time of Ezra and Nehemiah and their interference in matters of intermarriage among the elite in Yehud. Accepting the Ezra-Nehemiah texts at face value, many think that ethnic and/or religious purity was the primary rationale for forbidding marriages to "foreign" women.[51] However, a growing number of scholars argue for underlying economic reasons for either marrying "foreign" women or prohibiting such marriages.[52] In this section, therefore, I investigate how economics and its abuses played a role in the problems surrounding intermarriage and how they interfaced with ideologies of ethnic and religious purity, in order to see how these may have influenced the literary construction of the Other Woman.

One of the earliest economic issues facing the immigrants was land tenure and gaining control of the principal means of production in Yehud from the natives.[53] After the Babylonian exile, the capital of Yehud was moved from Jerusalem to Mizpah, about twelve kilometers north of the latter (2 Kgs 25:23; Jeremiah 40–41). Through Persian financial backing, the capital returned to Jerusalem and regained its status as the urban home of the elite. Carter reassesses Kenneth Hoglund's earlier claim that settlement patterns during the Persian period do not support the presumption of a class struggle between the exiles and those who remained in the land.[54] Basing his findings on more recent data, Carter observes that new settlements around Jerusalem increased significantly during the Persian period, while those in other areas of Yehud did not. He concludes that the new data "call into question [Hoglund's] conclusion that the settlement patterns in and of themselves undermine the traditional view of intra-province struggles between returnees and those who had remained on the land."[55] The conflict would have occurred particularly over land held by the natives that surrounded the newly reestablished capital of Jerusalem.

The immigrants' hegemony over the Jerusalem temple enabled their efforts to take possession of the land and channel its surpluses.[56] Another means by which they regained land and other resources was through intermarriage.[57] According to Mary Douglas, "marriage was the obvious way for the new arrivals to insert themselves into the farming economy."[58] Initially, it was in the interests of the returning exiles to establish good relations with the natives of Yehud, even though, ideologically, the former understood themselves to be the superior. Many of the early returnees probably married into Yehud's landowning families.[59] Some of these families were ethnic Jews who formed the "upper class" among those who had remained in the land. Others were landowning non-Jews, foreigners in and surrounding the regions of Yehud. According to social-exchange theory, people review and weigh their relationships in terms of costs and rewards.[60] Forging alliances through intermarriage, the immigrant political and cultic elites exchanged or parlayed their high status as imperial agents in order to gain access to the land as a means of production through noncoercive means.[61] The natives exchanged their land to "marry up" into the ranks of the returning elite, their ethnic kinsfolk who had good connections with the Persian authorities.[62]

As we have seen, however, Persian support of the *golah* caused growing class divisions between the returnees and natives, which widened under the intensification and depletion policies of Darius and Xerxes. Certain ideologies buttressed these divisions, as well as the attempts on the part of the immigrants to take possession of the land. The first such ideology has come to be known as the "myth of the empty land": the land was essentially empty, because the "people of Israel" had been taken in captivity.[63] Neither Ezra nor Nehemiah gives any indication that the exiled elite constituted a small minority and that the major portion of the Jewish population remained in Judah.[64] Second—and intimately related to the "myth of the empty land"—was the ideological identification of those Jews who remained and their descendants as "people(s) of the land," whom the immigrants regarded as foreigners and adversaries (Ezra 4:1-4; 9:1, 11; 10:2, 11; Neh 9:24, 30; 10:28, 30-31).[65]

Third, lumping the natives in with their foreign neighbors (the Ammonites, Moabites, and Edomites) as the Other, the immigrants saw themselves as constituting the only "true Israel."[66] As the "children of the *golah*" (Ezra 4:1; 6:19-20; 8:35; 10:7, 16), they were the "holy seed" that would be sown in the new land to repopulate it (Ezra 9:2; Ezek 36:8-12). "Seed" also connotes the sperm necessary for the propagation of the male lineages of the elite returnees.[67] In the trope of "seed," sexual and agricultural reproduction converge with the intent of the returnees to take possession of the land. After all, the ancestors of those exiled had owned the land before their deportation, and therefore the immigrants now had a patrimonial right to it. They envisioned its repossession as a new exodus and conquest (Ezek 11:14-19; 33:23-27; 36:8-12; Jer 32:42-44; Ezra 9:10-11).[68]

The ideology of the returnees as the true Israel provided them with a sense of entitlement to the land—but they had to marry the natives in order to obtain it. This was a socioeconomic contradiction that needed to be resolved. By the time of Artaxerxes I generations later, when social chasms were exacerbated, previous marriages with the "peoples of the land" (both ethnic non-*golah* Jews and neighboring ethnic foreigners) stood condemned by Ezra.[69] Drawing an obvious parallel between the *golah* community and its Hebrew ancestors before the invasion of Canaan, Ezra proclaimed: "The land that you are entering to possess is a land unclean with the pollutions of the peoples of the lands, with their abominations" (Ezra 9:11). He enjoined the *golah* community to separate from the "peoples of the land . . . so that you may be strong and *eat the good of the land and leave it for an inheritance to your children forever*" (Ezra 9:12; cf. Ezek 36:12). Operating under a narrow ideological understanding of the true Israel, Ezra regarded marriages to non-*golah* Jewish women, like marriages to non-Jewish women, as "foreign."[70] Theological arguments masked the class issues involved in these marriages. The land had been consolidated into the hands of the returning elites through intermarriage; the concern now was to keep the land as an inheritance for the elites' own descendants and not to allow it to fall into the hands of those outside of the *golah* group.[71] In essence, *the elites practiced exogamy to obtain the land and endogamy to keep it.* They conveniently forgot that the land they now possessed for themselves and their children had been obtained generations before through intermarriage with these "peoples of the land." This socioeconomic contradiction was resolved through selective memory.

Tamara Eskenazi and Eleanore Judd cross-culturally illumine this shift in ethnic, religious, and class boundaries from acceptable wife to unacceptable wife by comparing the Ezra situation to the rise of the ultraorthodox Haredim ("tremblers"; cf. Ezra 10:3) in modern-day Israel. Like Yehud during Ezra's time, the modern land of Israel was ethnically, religiously, and politically diverse. Both were colonies under the superpowers of their respective times (Persia/Great Britain). Both occupied strategically important real estate that served the purposes of the empire. Both experienced tensions between the native population and the arriving immigrants. Both cases involved a shifting understanding of who is a Jew, moving from a broad definition to a narrow one. In both cases the religious self-understanding of one group of Jews categorized another group of Jews as Gentiles or foreigners, regarding a marriage with this other group as "mixed."[72]

Although Ezra 10 seems to present the *golah* community as acquiescing to Ezra's injunctions, it is quite probable that his anti-assimilationist policies were resisted by husbands who did not regard their marriages as "mixed."[73] Apart from the personal feelings the husbands had for their wives and children,[74] they were threatened with forfeiture of the very land for which they or their ancestors had married their wives if they did not assemble in Jerusalem and consent to divorce them (Ezra 10:7-8).[75] Furthermore, Ezra's policies undoubtedly offended the leading families of the women whose marriages were in jeopardy. Such social destabilization in Yehud during a politically vulnerable time would not have pleased Artaxerxes I and his associates. Ezra was most likely summoned abruptly back to Persia.[76]

If Neh 13:23-30 is any indication, the *golah* community continued to intermarry for socioeconomic reasons, particularly into ethnically foreign families. For Nehemiah, such intermarriages meant the threat of foreign influence on Yehud's internal affairs during a time of economic depletion by the Persian Empire. Land tenure was also an issue. If women could inherit during the postexilic period,[77] land could be transferred from the Jerusalem elite into ethnically foreign hands through marriages with foreign wives.[78] Furthermore, since the temple was crucial to the economic affairs of Yehud, intermarriage with foreign women among the priestly class, in particular (Neh 13:28-29), could permit unwelcome or detrimental influence on these affairs from the outside.[79]

Intrinsic Analysis

If women constitute the symbolic boundaries of a people's identity, as we saw in the last chapter,[80] they become here the vulnerable site at which the perceived "adversaries" of the *golah* could penetrate. What emerged in Yehud was an ideology of the "correct wife" needed to preserve the "holy seed" of the "true Israel" in the land of promise. Although the precise setting of Proverbs 1–9 and 31:10-31 (such as families of the landed nobility, court or temple schools, or the scribal class) is a matter of dispute, scholars usually locate these framing chapters (hereafter Proverbs 1–9)[81] within the male interests of the wealthy *golah* classes living in Jerusalem.[82] Preoccupations with securing the "correct wife" underlie the words of wisdom that the "father" imparts to his "son" in Proverbs 1–9. In the intrinsic analysis that follows, I deal first with the attribution of Solomonic authorship and its relationship to the ideological production of Proverbs 1–9. Second, I discuss the "myth of the classless society" as the ideological articulation of an ideal economics found in these chapters. Third, I show how ideologies of the "correct wife" and the Other Woman are located within the larger "myth of a classless society," with its ideal economics. Finally, I investigate how these ideologies of gender and economics are encoded in Proverbs 7.

"The Proverbs of Solomon, Son of David, King of Israel"

It is highly significant that the superscription of the book of Proverbs attributes authorship to King Solomon (1:1). In my discussion of Genesis 2–3, I noted that Solomon, who strongly centralized the state and stratified his society, was regarded as the quintessential "wise" man (1 Kgs 3:5-14; 4:29-34).[83] Parallels exist between the establishment of a native-tributary mode of production under Solomon and its reestablishment under a foreign-tributary mode of production during the Persian period. The returning elites wished to replicate, in the postexilic period, a social structure endemic to the preexilic era. During both periods, the centralization of power in Jerusalem, the (re)building of the temple, and the formation of a hierarchical society created circumstances of socioeconomic inequity in which the elite held the monopoly on wisdom along with material resources.[84] Attributing this wisdom book to a long-dead monarch has an ideological function: its elite male author appeals to this ancient king to validate his teachings and upper-class values and to legitimate his own social-class standing in Persian Yehud.[85]

Both a "real" and an "ideal" economics exist in Proverbs 1–9, but the ideal economics predominates, as it does in the Solomon narrative.[86] Although real economics works by exchange or trade, with any acquisition by one party diminishing another's store, ideal economics operates under the presumption of unlimited abundance: "Ideal economics entails a theory of 'surplus value,' according to which wealth can generate, of its own accord, a surplus over and above the value of anyone's labor. *Such a theory allows for one class to prosper without the necessity of interpreting their prosperity as being at anyone else's expense.*"[87]

I identify the ideal economics in Proverbs 1–9 as "the myth of the classless society," coinciding with the "myth of the empty land" in Ezra and Nehemiah, discussed above. Scholars have already remarked on the urban setting of Proverbs 1–9, its concerns about getting to the top, and the complete absence in it of the poor, poverty, or any hint of the ongoing socioeconomic crises described in Nehemiah 5.[88] In the words of R. N. Whybray, "Proverbs 1–9 thus represents the interests of the urban, wealthy, self-satisfied upper class to whom the plight of the urban poor in their midst as well as of the rural poor was of no interest whatever."[89] In Proverbs 1–9 elite class interests are masked under the idiom of family, in which a fictional "father" bestows words of wisdom upon a fictive "son." The paternal voice that speaks is not that of a rich landowner or a civic or cultic Persian functionary, but that of one's "father": "Families are not ideologically innocent places, but because everyone has one, they give the appearance of being so."[90] Although Walter Brueggemann describes the Solomonic period in the quotation below, his words are apropos for understanding the myth of a classless society in Proverbs 1–9 as a theodic settlement for its postexilic context:

> Behind every theodic crisis, there is a "theodic settlement"—a long-standing consensus about how life works, how society functions, how a system of benefits is allocated, what suffering must be tolerable and inescapably borne, and by whom it must be borne. The theodic settlement that decides who must "rightly" suffer is characteristically a

settlement authorized and imposed by those on the top of the heap, who benefit from the present social arrangement, so that the system can be legitimated as good, wise, and right. *For those who benefit, it is very difficult to notice that the theodic settlement may be for someone else a theodic crisis.*[91]

In Proverbs 1–9 the theodic crisis among those suffering under the native/foreign-tributary mode of production in postexilic Yehud is noticeably missing. The absence of economic class in Proverbs 1–9 symbolically resolves the ideological and material contradictions in Yehud society between rich and poor, between *golah* and non-*golah*.[92]

Claudia Camp draws intertextual connections between the book of Proverbs and the Solomon story in 1 Kings 1–11, whose final form she dates during the time of Ezra and Nehemiah.[93] Although the superscription introduces Proverbs as Solomon's wisdom words, he never appears in the book. For Camp, Solomon's disembodied voice finds corporeality in Woman Wisdom and the Other Woman. Both figurations reflect the ambiguous relationships *between* Solomon's own wisdom and "strangeness" during his rule and *with* women, wise and strange.[94]

The Other Woman in Proverbs 1–9

The *'iššâ zārâ* has been variously translated as "foreign woman," "strange woman," "loose woman," "outsider woman," and so forth. Instead of restricting the meaning of the word *zārâ* to the woman's ethnic, legal, religious, or social status, some more recent analyses have argued for a broader understanding of the *'iššâ zārâ*, one that encompasses a range of ethnic, social, religious, and economic Otherness.[95] Particularly in light of its postexilic context, the more inclusive definition of the Other Woman sees her not only as an ethnically foreign woman, devoted to foreign deities, but also, in an endogamous society, as any woman outside the family lineage. In addition, she can be a social outsider: the "other" woman in an adulterous affair, an adulteress herself, or a prostitute. She can simply be a woman considered "not our kind," although she may have once been "our kind" under a different set of rules. As a composite entity, then, the Other Woman is any woman who transgresses the values and socioeconomic prerogatives defined by the shifting standards of the *golah* community.[96]

Within the "classless" society of the *golah* exist ideologies of the "correct" wife and of marital endogamy to keep land and property, garnered earlier through intermarriage, in the family. In Proverbs the "correct" wife is embodied in the person of Woman Wisdom. The "incorrect" wife becomes incarnate in the Other Woman. Although seemingly opposites, Woman Wisdom and the Other Woman are actually two sides of the same coin:[97] male elite constructions of the "right" and "wrong" woman as potential mates. Class interests and divisions in Yehud's native/foreign-tributary mode of production are disguised by tropes of gender and sexuality in the ostensibly classless society envisioned in Proverbs 1–9. In postexilic Yehud the Other Woman represents a financially desirable but socially unacceptable potential wife for one of its upper-class sons. She is contrasted with the Woman of Substance, a *golah* woman of financial means whom young men are encouraged to pursue (see below).[98] Proverbs 1–9 pits an economically desirable *outsider* against an economically desirable *insider*.[99] Obviously, the demand for rich *golah* daughters will be greater than the supply. Therefore, the attractions of the Other Woman (rich, ethnically foreign women or wealthy, non-*golah* Jewish women) as marital partners become irresistible. The father's task in Proverbs 1–9 is to depict the Other Woman in the most dreadful fashion, so that his son does not succumb to her charms.

In a broader economic reading of Proverbs 1–9, adultery—the sexual transgression of the Other Woman in the book—functions on a figurative level as well as a literal one.[100] At the literal level, adultery is consensual sexual intercourse by a married woman with a man who is not her husband. The adulteress herself is a sexually transgressive woman who disrupts a patrilineal society and brings dishonor to her husband and family.[101] At the figurative level, adultery becomes a trope for marriage with the "wrong" woman. Because we are dealing with the problem of intermarriages during the postexilic period, Proverbs 1–9 utilizes adultery, rather than fornication or sex with prostitutes, as a trope to characterize such unacceptable marital alliances.[102] Adultery becomes multivalent, encompassing sexual intercourse with a married woman, sexual intercourse in marriage with an ethnically foreign woman, and sexual intercourse in marriage with a non-*golah* Jewish woman. The Other Woman inhabits these differing connotations of marital transgression, just as Woman Wisdom symbolizes marital fidelity to one's own wife and appropriate marriages within one's own kin group and economic class.

On both literal and figurative levels, adultery is projected to have dire economic consequences, which the father is quick to point out during each of his three warnings against the Other Woman.[103] Immediately after his first warning in 2:16-19, the father exhorts his son to keep to the paths of the righteous, "for the upright will inhabit the land, and men of integrity will remain in it; but the wicked will be cut off from the land, and the treacherous will be rooted out of it" (2:20-22). These verses encode issues that surrounded land tenure during the time of Ezra. In both cases, those who marry the "wrong" woman will be severed from the land as the means of production.[104] After his second warning against the seductive words of the Other Woman (5:3-8), the father relates that those foolish boys who listen to her risk losing their property to strangers and foreigners (zārîm and nokrî, 5:9-10) and utter ruin in the assembly (qāhāl) of the golah (5:14).[105] Behind this warning may be fears of the transferal of property into the hands of non-golah families (zārîm) or foreigners (nokrî) through the inheritance rights of their wives. The lesson: Exogamy will wreak financial ruin on the imprudent upper-class son. In his third warning, the father takes on adultery in its literal sense: he reminds his offspring that if an adulterer is caught with another man's wife (6:26-29), he must pay the cuckolded husband sevenfold, handing over all the wealth (hôn) of his house and suffering disgrace in the community (6:31-33). A number of scholars argue that the Other Woman is a function of the patriarchal need to control women's sexuality.[106] It seems more likely, however, that *male* sexuality is on the line here.[107] The father wishes to control the sexuality of his son in order to preserve his material assets and class status and that of his offspring. Within the boundaries of Persian-period economics, the son's sexuality finds legitimate expression with the "correct" wife, not the Other Woman.

The father depicts the pursuit of the "correct" wife in economic terms. She is lauded in the acrostic poem concluding the book of Proverbs (31:10-31). For Yoder, the 'ēšet-ḥayil (31:10a)—usually translated as "a good wife," "a capable wife," "a good housewife," and so on—should be rendered "a woman of substance," to foreground her socioeconomic strengths.[108] That there are not enough of these marriageable women to go around in the golah community is expressed by the qualifier "Who can find?" (31:10b). The "Woman of Substance" is a scarce commodity. However, although the initial investment for her is costly, since "her purchase price (mikrâ) is more than corals" (31:10b), she brings riches, property, and socioeconomic advantages to her spouse. He will have no lack of "booty" (*šālāl*, 31:11): "His 'plunder' from what she brings home makes him a wealthy man. As her husband, he is able to draw upon her dowry money and property for his own purposes and he profits from her additional earnings, inheritances, bequests, or supplemental dowry gifts. In short, he can live off of her."[109] If the son can harness his hormones and find such a woman, his status and prestige will be assured. He will be known at the city gates, sitting among the elders of the land (31:23).

Scholars have maintained that the "Woman of Substance" in 31:10-31 and Woman Wisdom in Proverbs 1–9 are actually one and the same: one literal, the other metaphorical.[110] As with the Woman of Substance, the search for Woman Wisdom is communicated in economic terms. In 23:23 the son is instructed: "Buy (*qěneh*) truth, and do not sell it; buy wisdom, instruction, and understanding." With the vocabulary of purchase, possession, and wealth, the father enjoins the son repeatedly to buy or acquire (*qnh*) Woman Wisdom, as one obtains a Woman of Substance:[111]

> Acquire (*qěneh*) Wisdom! Acquire (*qěneh*) Insight!
> > Do not forget or turn away from the words of my mouth.
> Do not forsake her, and she will keep you;
> > love her and she will guard you.
> The beginning of Wisdom is this: Acquire (*qěneh*) Wisdom.
> > With all your property (*běkol-qinyāněkā*), acquire (*qěneh*) Insight.
> Prize her highly, and she will exalt you.
> > She will honor you if you embrace her.
> She will place on your head a fair garland.
> > She will bestow on you a beautiful crown. (4:5-9)

Yoder crisply remarks: "[Woman Wisdom], *like the Woman of Substance, is regarded as both person and merchandise to be acquired.*"[112] Although, like the Woman of Substance, a man must give over all that he has (*běkol-qinyāněkā*) to "buy" Woman Wisdom, he will definitely be rewarded financially in the end. Wisdom imparts to the one who finds and acquires her a business profit (*saḥar*) better than earnings from silver,[113] and a revenue (*těbûʾâ*)[114] better than gold (3:13-14).

More precious than corals, she holds the key to long life in her right hand and to riches and honor in her left (3:15-16).

The fictional father constructs two ideologies of women who confront the average high-born male in Yehud and compete for his attention. Encoded in both are the social conflicts and contradictions of the economics of marriage in the *golah* community. An alliance with one or the other will dramatically affect a man's financial circumstances, either positively or negatively. Both women are portrayed in dangerously comparable ways; both make perilously similar pronouncements to attract the son to their respective domains.[115] Both attempt to seduce the son through their speeches. In a previous work,[116] I contended that the speeches of the various personages in Proverbs 1–9 are divided into two chiastically ordered groups. In the first, the structural chiasmus emphasizes the longer, weightier speeches of Woman Wisdom (B, 1:22-33) and her agent, the father's father (B', 5:1-11, 15-23), vis-à-vis the sinners (A, 1:11-14) and the unwise son (A', 5:12-14). Interlaced throughout this chiastic frame are the father's three warnings against the Other Woman. In the second group, the father contrasts the speeches of the Other Woman herself (A, 7:14-20; A', 9:16-17) with those of Woman Wisdom (B, 8:1-36; B', 9:5-6). Whereas, in the first group of speeches, the Other Woman is only a forbidding specter that the son must avoid, in this second group she actually appears and verbalizes the dangers she embodies for the son. Building on my earlier work, I now turn my attention to a materialist reading of Proverbs 7 and the seductive speech of the Other Woman.

His Absence Makes Her Heart Go Wander: The Other Woman in Proverbs 7

Feminist scholars have raised the possibility that the speaker of Proverbs 7 is female, perhaps a mother who addresses her son in 7:1.[117] Mothers did play an instructional role in the education of their sons (1:8; 6:20). In 31:1-9 Lemuel's mother exhorts her son to steer clear of bad women and strong wine, just as a mother would admonish her son to avoid the Other Woman, as in Proverbs 7. The image of a female looking out the window (7:6) has archaeological support in the Samaria ivories of a woman staring out a latticed window. It is possible that either a mother or a father sharing the same value system could be the son's lecturer in Proverbs 7.[118]

Nevertheless, I favor reading a father's voice in the didactic speeches of Proverbs 1–9. As I have mentioned, the superscription ascribes authorship of Proverbs 1–9 to the preexilic King Solomon, legitimating the male ideologies of a particular class in its conflicted postexilic context. The superscription literarily frames these chapters with a male voice. Furthermore, in 4:1-9 the speaker is clearly a son recalling his father's words. These verses claim that "wisdom" was handed down by the elite class from father to son, ostensibly since the time of Solomon the wise. Newsom summarizes the ideological maneuvers of this traditioning process: "All readers of this text, whatever their actual identities, are called upon to take up the subject position of son in relation to an authoritative father."[119] A female voice does complement the father's speeches—namely, that of Woman Wisdom. As the father's spokeswoman, she will have much to say to the son in Proverbs 8.

It is significant that the father introduces his son to the familial and erotic dimensions of Woman Wisdom only in 7:2-5. He urges the lad to call Wisdom "sister" (7:4). In Song 4:9, 10, 12; and 5:1, a lover addresses his beloved as "sister." In addition, the father tells his son to call Wisdom "kinswoman" (mōdāʻ).[120] The use of kinship language for Wisdom encodes an economics of marriage in which endogamy was encouraged for elite sons to preserve wealth. The father sets up Wisdom as the proper ideal bride, who will preserve the son "from the Other Woman, from the alien woman with her smooth words" (Prov 7:5).

The father sets the stage for the grand entry of the Other Woman and her seductive talk. In Prov 7:6-13 the urban elite setting of the father's narrative is readily apparent. The upper window from which the father looks out has a lattice, enabling him to observe the goings-on between the senseless boy[121] and the Other Woman without being seen.[122] The lad traverses streets (šûq, 7:8), roads (derek, 7:8), and corners (pinnâ, 7:8) that lie near the Other Woman's abode. The descriptors of nightfall heighten the eroticism of the proceedings (7:9). In Song 3:1 and 5:2, the lover also seeks the one she loves under the cloak of darkness.[123]

The woman comes out to meet the boy "dressed like a harlot" (Prov 7:10), a depiction that indicates not her profession but her shameless behavior. In her adultery she is like a common prostitute, only much worse. In 6:26 the father states that a man can hire a harlot "for peanuts,"[124] but an adulteress "stalks a man's very life." Since she is clothed as a harlot, the woman's real intent is hidden (*nĕṣurat lēb*, lit. "guarded of heart," 7:10).[125] We see in her deceptive speech (7:14-20) that she does not simply desire sex; she wishes the actual life of her victim. The description of her "feet" (*rgl*) as not staying at home (7:11) could refer to the fact that she refuses to be a proper wife, settled in her husband's house under his authority.[126] It could also be a carnal euphemism for being "on the prowl," seeking sexual quarry. In Ezek 16:25 the faithless wife/Jerusalem spreads her "feet" (legs or vagina, *rgl*) to anyone who passes.[127] Like the boy, the Other Woman is found in the city streets (*ḥûṣ*, Prov 7:12), in the squares (*rĕḥōbôt*, 7:12), and in corners (*pinnâ*, 7:12). These are precisely the places in which Woman Wisdom does her business (1:20-21; cf. 8:2-3), although in contrast to Wisdom, the Other Woman lies in wait for her prey (*te'ĕrōb*, 7:12). Using language evocative of rape,[128] the father describes the woman as *seizing* the young man (*heḥĕzîqâ bô*, 7:13), and brazenly kissing him.

She then opens her mouth, articulating in her own words the perils she represents to the father's son (7:14-20). Significantly, economic matters appear throughout her speech,[129] encoding issues surrounding money and marriage in postexilic Yehud (7:14, 20). Her first words in 7:14 are filled with ambiguity: "Well-being sacrifices I must make;[130] today I fulfill(ed) (*šillamtî*) my vows." The perfect tense of *šillamtî* can be rendered as a completed action: "I have fulfilled/paid my vows today."[131] Or *šillamtî* can have a modal sense:[132] "Today I am going to fulfill/pay my vows."[133] Both translations have their adherents, and I think that the speech intends both senses. The Other Woman's language is deliberately equivocal, disguising her true intention. The youth understands them in the first sense—that she has just paid her sacrificial vows. He hears them as an invitation to a feast, serving fresh meat from the sacrifice. Leviticus 7:15-17 specifies that sacrificial meat must be consumed on the day of the offering or on the next. The foolish lad might even assume that the invitation will be a prelude to sex.[134] However, what the woman really means is, "I am going to fulfill my vow." In other words, she has not yet slain her offering: her "offering" will be the boy himself.[135]

The ambiguity of her words is apparent as she addresses the youth as a true lover would speak to her beloved. Deceiving the boy into thinking she is inviting him to dinner, she proclaims: "Therefore, I have come out to meet you; to *seek* your face, and I have *found* you" (Prov 7:15). Throughout Proverbs 1–9, the father wishes the son to seek and find Woman Wisdom as a wife (2:4; 3:13; cf. 1:28; 8:17, 35). In Song 3:1-4 a lover seeks her beloved on their bed and continues her search until she finds him. When she does, she holds him and does not let him go until she brings him to the place where her own mother conceived her. The implication is that in her mother's bedroom, she and her man will join together in sexual union.

Proverbs 7:16-18 presents a caricature of this authentic love and sexual intimacy. Here economics, sexuality, and death intersect as the Other Woman hastens toward her seduction/destruction of the young man. The Other Woman possesses luxury items common only among the rich and prosperous. The fact that she can offer meat at her table bespeaks a wealthy household (cf. 23:20-21). She tells the boy that her love couch (*'ereś*)[136] is draped with expensive bedding,[137] colored linen imported from Egypt (7:16). She perfumes her bed (*miškāb*) with costly spices that come from afar—myrrh, aloes, and cinnamon (7:17).[138] Behind this depiction of the Other Woman's affluence lie the financially desirable but totally unacceptable women who daily confront young men of the *golah* community. The sexuality of the scene is underscored by the fact that the lavish goods are for her *bed*. For their own amatory intimacies, the two lovers in the Song of Songs avail themselves of all the erotic items in the Other Woman's arsenal. Their love couch is the grass beneath the trees.[139] The lover depicts her sweetheart as a bag of myrrh that lies between her breasts.[140] The man portrays the object of his affections as a garden filled with "henna with nard, nard and saffron, calamus and cinnamon, with all trees of frankincense, myrrh and aloes, with all chief spices."[141]

Although fancy spices and fine linens can be found in sexual encounters, they are also used in burial rituals.[142] Linen burial cloths wrapped Jesus' body and Lazarus's corpse.[143] John 19:39 records Nicodemus bringing a mixture of myrrh and aloes to be wrapped in Jesus' linen shroud.[144] Myrrh mixed with wine is offered to the dying Jesus as a painkiller (Mark 15:23). Mary of Bethany anoints Jesus' feet with an aromatic ointment of pure nard in preparation for his burial (John 12:3). Various spices are laid on King Asa's funeral bier, which goes up in smoke in his honor (2 Chr 16:14; cf. Jer 34:5). The Other Woman's seductive words thus become a murky brew of *oikonomia, eros,* and *thanatos* (economics, erotic love, and death), an aphrodisiac she serves up for the unsuspecting youth.

The Other Woman's sexual invitation becomes explicit in Prov 7:18, when she beckons the lad: "Come, let's drink our fill of love (*dōdîm*) till dawn; take our delight in making love (*'āhābîm*)." The word used in her invitation to "Come!" (*lĕkâ*) is the same used in 1:10-11 by the sinners to entice the son. *Dōdîm* and *'āhābîm* refer to the physical acts of sexual desire.[145] For the father, the proper contexts of these expressions of sexual arousal are with one's own spouse (5:15-23). But we discover in the climax of her speech that the Other Woman is already married! Her husband,[146] evidently a prosperous merchant, is away on a business trip. She reassures the youth that they will not get caught in flagrante delicto, because "hubby" will be gone until the moon is full (7:19-20).

Immediately following the words of the predator comes the fate of her prey. Proverbs 7:22-23 describes how the lad is misled by her "seductive speech and smooth talk." He follows her like an animal led to the slaughter, caught in traps and pierced by arrows. He does not realize (*lō' yāda'*) that *he* is the woman's sacrificial offering. He thinks he has been invited to dinner; he does not know he will *become* "dinner." Caught up in the Other Woman's equivocal words, he does not notice that she is preparing him for burial. His folly will cost him his very life, for her perfumed bed will become his coffin.[147]

Economics, sexuality, and death resurface in the father's final words to his sons (7:24-27).[148] His warning that they should avoid "her ways" (*dĕrākêhā*) and "her paths" (*bintîbôtêhā*) recalls the urban setting of his lecture (7:25; cf. 7:8, 12). Wisdom herself will stand along the "way" (*'ălê-dārek*) and on the "paths" (*nĕtîbôt*) by the gates and portals of the city for her own long speech that follows the Other Woman's (8:2-3). The urban context reminds us that the "myth of the classless society" presented in Proverbs is an illusion. The father informs the sons that the Other Woman has a history of bringing unsuspecting men to their demise: "All her slain are a mighty host" (7:26); "Her house is the way to Sheol,[149] going down to the chambers of death" (7:27). Here the father recalls his previous warnings against the Other Woman. In 2:18-19 the Other Woman's house "sinks down to death, and her paths to the shades. None who go to her (*bā'êhā*) come back, nor do they regain the paths of life." "To go to her" can be a euphemism for sexual intercourse,[150] but death is the end for the one who beds the Other Woman. In 5:3 the father depicts the lips of the Other Woman dripping honey with vivid sensuality: "Her mouth is slicker than olive oil."[151] But her "feet" (*raglêhā*) go down to death, and her steps follow the path to Sheol (5:5). We have seen that "feet" can be a sexual euphemism for legs or vagina. In the father's warning in 5:5, we again find the interface between Eros and Thanatos implicit in 7:24-27. Although what the Other Woman offers seems to be desirable, both financially and sexually, she can only lead to destruction. The safest course is to avoid her at all costs.

Summary

The analysis of the *'iššâ zārâ*, the Other Woman, should be placed within the wider sociopolitical context of Persian Yehud. During this time, Yehud operated under a foreign-tributary mode of production that had elements of a native-tributary mode of production. Persian imperial politics impinged upon Yehud to create a highly stratified society in which the small community of returning elites profited, even though they had to submit to foreign rule. What Persian support entailed, however, was exacerbated divisions between the returnees and the natives and increasing exploitation of the latter, especially during the later periods of Persia's depletion of the colonial periphery. The returnees married into the native population in order to secure agricultural land as a means of production. Generations later, the priestly and civic elite encouraged endogamy to keep land and property within the *golah* community. These socioeconomic concerns lay behind Ezra and Nehemiah's condemnation of intermarriage with Jewish women outside the *golah* group and with ethnically foreign women.

Proverbs 1–9 encodes these socioeconomic contradictions of Persian Yehud. One way in which Proverbs resolves them is through the "myth of the classless society" that permeates these chapters. Completely absent is any hint of the great economic disparities in the social order. A second way is the male construction of two symbolic women. One of these represents the "correct" or "acceptable" woman to marry—namely, a woman from a wealthy *golah* family. Such women are embodied in the personification of Woman Wisdom. This financially sought-after *insider* woman is juxtaposed with a financially attractive *outsider* woman, vividly brought to life in Proverbs in the figure of the Other Woman. In the father's instruction to his son, she is to be avoided at all costs. Sexually and financially desirable, she will nonetheless bring death to any man who falls under the spell of her words.

8 Conclusion

I write these remarks concurrently with an article I am doing on an Asian American reading of the woman warrior Yael in Judges 4–5. As I research a number of studies on the representations of Asian women in American orientalism[1]—such as the diabolically villainous Dragon Lady, the exotic hooker Suzy Wong, the seductive and coy geisha, the Mongol slave girl,[2] and so forth—I am struck by the cliché, "the more things change, the more they stay the same." These images were produced in Hollywood in various historical periods during the twentieth century, reflecting changes in U.S. foreign policy and social attitudes toward Asians. They were cultural representations that tried to resolve ideologically racist anxieties and fears in the United States in dealing with the influx of Asian immigrants during the late 1800s/early 1900s, the threats of Japanese imperialism before and during World War II, the takeover of China by the Communists, and Korean and Vietnam wars in the 1950s, 1960s, and 1970s. These were not depictions of "real" Asians or Asian Americans. In fact, the major roles on screen were performed by Caucasian actors in "yellowface."[3] Real Asians and Asian Americans who suffered various forms of political and cultural racism in the United States make up a double absence in these films, just as real women who endured and negotiated the androcentrism and ethnocentrism of ancient Israel remain a double absence in the Hebrew Bible. Instead of real Asian or Israelite women, we have ideological constructs that masked specific historical and socioeconomic subtexts. Hollywood films were following a long tradition, going as far back as ancient Israel, of using

women's bodies, especially foreign women's bodies, to inscribe the
contradictions and conflicts of their times.

Perhaps a subconscious reason why I focused particularly on economic issues as they are embedded in a gendered trope is that these
issues are an essential part of Asian American history. Ronald Takaki
lays out the problem of racism's collusion with economic exploitation
very well:

> "Color" in America operated within an economic context. Asian im-
> migrants came here to meet demands for labor—plantation workers,
> road crews, miners, factory operatives, cannery workers, and farm la-
> borers. Employers developed a dual-wage system to pay Asian laborers
> less than white workers and pitted the groups against each other in
> order to depress wages for both . . . [leading] white laborers to de-
> mand restriction of Asian workers already here in a segregated labor
> market of low-wage jobs and the exclusion of future Asian immi-
> grants. Thus the class interests of white capital as well as white labor
> needed Asians as "strangers."[4]

In this book I added gender and sexuality to the racial economics
of strangeness and Otherness by investigating the stereotypical constructions of woman as evil as they were manifested in four biblical
texts. I selected texts in which woman became a symbol or trope for a
sinful targeted group or nation. How woman embodied evil was qual-
itatively related to the sociohistorical period that produced the specific text. I consciously drew passages from four different periods of
ancient Israelite history, each operating under different modes of production, in order to see how each period reproduced the trope ideologically. The evilness embodied in the female form was constructed
out of the social, historical, and economic conflicts that needed ideological resolution through her symbolization. In all four cases this
symbolization originated from and was circulated among the literate
male elite classes. Also in each case, the focus on gender functioned
as a symbolic alibi for the class interests that gave rise to the text. The
voices of "real" women were absent and their experiences greatly
skewed. Brandishing weapons of the weak, women could indeed be
sexually manipulative, promiscuous, deceitful, recalcitrant, and so
forth, toward their men.[5] In analyzing the rhetorical encoding of
these weapons in the biblical text, however, one must recognize the
power imbalance in gender relations during each of these periods,

which compelled women to resort to such behavior to obtain their
ends.

*In what specific ways did woman become the incarnation of evil in
our texts?* In Genesis 2–3 she was the primordial Eve, by whose
agency man was expelled from paradise and became mortal. We discovered in chapter 4 that the depiction of Eve must be contextualized
in the politics of state centralization during the time of the Yahwist in
the tenth century. She represented the subordinate wife of the peasant, who "once upon a time" had familiar and easy access to the king
and tended his garden. Because he "listened to her voice" and par-
took of wisdom that belonged to the king alone, the peasant was cast
forth from the king's presence and relegated to the lower rungs of social hierarchy. Genesis 2–3 was produced from the conflicts that
arose when Israel moved from the familial mode of production of the
tribal period to the tributary mode of production of monarchic times.
It supplied the theological rationale for the social gulf between the
royal and peasant classes, and the economic exploitation of the latter
by the former. Class interests became obscured by the gender interests articulated in the text: "Your desire shall be for your husband,
and he shall rule over you" (3:16b). As the king ruled over the farmer,
so would a husband rule over his wife. This shift from class to gender,
from public arena to private, was related to the material and ideological attempt to weaken the bonds of kinship and lineage that threatened the state, and to bolster the marital bond and the nuclear family.
In the economic stratification of Israelite society during the monarchic period, women's status decreased and the wife became increasingly subject to her spouse, who himself became subordinate to a
higher elite. However, the focus on gender, and not class, is readily
apparent in the innumerable afterlives of the text, in which woman,
like Eve at the beginning, becomes responsible for bringing death
into the world and all our woe.

Chapter 5 investigated woman as the adulterous wife, the most
disruptive and threatening woman within a patrilineal social order. In
traditional readings of Hosea 1–2, the cheating wife represented the
northern kingdom of Israel, whose worship of the baals was symbolized in the wife's sexual infidelity to YHWH, her spouse, and the marital covenant between them. If examined in the eighth-century
context of the tributary mode of production that produced Hosea
1–2, however, this trope signified a very specific audience. During
this time, foreign nations compelled the northern elite to offer tribute

in exchange for nonaggression and political autonomy. This tribute was often in the form of portable cash crops of grain, wine, and oil, crops that this elite demanded from their peasantry to the detriment of highland cultivation. This peasant taxation was collected through the cult, the public state veneration of the baals, which for Hosea became identified with an unjust and insupportable mode of production. It involved a corrupt royal, priestly, and prophetic bureaucracy that oversaw an agribusiness, which exploited the farmer, whose surplus not only supported this elite, but also bore the brunt of the stiff tributes imposed by foreign powers. It was the male ruling elite whom Hosea feminized in the metaphor of the adulterous wife who runs after her lovers, the foreign nations. Hosea himself was most likely from the upper classes, a partisan of the YHWH-alone movement that would eventually become normative during the exile and beyond. To articulate the exclusivity and inequity of God's covenant with the nation, he adopted the trope of marriage to exploit ideologies of exclusivity and inequity, already entrenched in the social and material practices of Israelite marriage. Nevertheless, as in Genesis 2–3, the use of a gendered trope involving the domestic arena masked for later interpreters Hosea's conflicts with the male elite in the public domain. Foregrounded, instead, was the image of an adulterous wife and the faithful husband who must brutalize her in order to secure her repentance.

Ezekiel 23 appropriated the metaphor of the adulterous wife and doubled its rhetorical impact, by doubling not only the characters but also their prurient appetites. He depicted two sisters, wives of the deity, whose sexual insatiability he amplified pornographically. The sisters represented the two rival kingdoms, personified as Oholah (Samaria) and Oholibah (Jerusalem). Their lovers were the foreign nations, Egypt, Assyria, and Babylonia. I argued that Ezekiel 23 must be situated in the context of a foreign-tributary mode of production, in which *colonial* relations between Israel and Judah and these foreign powers eventually led to the conquest and exile of the Israelite and Judean elite. Ezekiel 23 furnished a way for the prophet to deal with the personal and collective trauma of the conquest and exile of the Judean royal and priestly aristocracy, of which he was a part. Nevertheless, because he shared androcentric ideologies of male domination/female submission with his colonizer, Ezekiel resorted to ideologies of gender to articulate the political history of Israel and Judah as colonial subjects. Along with his pornographic portrayal of the sisters' voracious lusts, what was also significant about this history was his racialization and sexualization of the sisters' foreign lovers. The hypermasculinity of these ethnic Others, with their impressive genitalia, contrasted inversely with the emasculated state of the male Judean leadership. These lovers became the agents of the divine husband's wrath in punishing his wayward spouses. Although admittedly anachronistic, the eroticized sadistic images of the (military) butchering of these sisters by these (foreign) paramours had the shock value of a snuff movie.

Social, racial/ethnic, and economic Otherness all intersected in the image of the *'iššâ zārâ*, the Other Woman, in the book of Proverbs. She is the personified antithesis of the "correct" wife/woman embodied in the figure of Woman Wisdom. The upper-class ideology of the Other Woman tried to resolve class contradictions and struggles in colonial Yehud during the Persian period. Operating under the "myth of the empty land," the early *golah* immigrants from Babylonia paradoxically had to intermarry with the natives of this allegedly "empty" land (ethnic Jews and ethnic foreigners) in order to secure that land as a means of production. During this time, Yehud labored under a mixed native- and foreign-tributary mode of production, in which the natives shouldered the burden of supporting both the lifestyle of the *golah* elite and the tribute to the Persian colonizer. Generations later, after the socioeconomic gulf between rich *golah* and the impoverished natives worsened, the *golah* wanted to preserve the land and inheritance within its own community by enforcing a prohibition of intermarriage with any non-*golah*. Not only racial/ethnic foreign women, but also non-*golah* Jewish women, were forbidden to *golah* sons. Because of a fluid, subjective definition of "foreignness," the civic and religious elite in Yehud collapsed non-*golah* Jewish women with ethnically foreign ones. In the book of Proverbs the Other Woman represented the economically desirable but socially "incorrect" non-*golah* women as potential mates for upper-class males in Yehud.

The symbolization of woman as evil was used in divergent ways both to uphold the elite status quo and to resist and censure it. Genesis 2–3, the story of the first couple, served the interests of the emerging monarchy by emphasizing the marriage bond over the kinship bond and the nuclear family over the extended family. It also legitimated the servitude of the peasant in the nascent tributary mode of production. In the "myth of the classless society" found in the book of Proverbs, elite class interests were concealed under the language of family, in which an imaginary father warns his son about the beguiling but perilous charms of the "wrong" woman. In Hosea 1–2, however, the prophet used the trope of the faithless wife to condemn the elite male leadership of Israel, who profited from an unjust mode of production that caused much suffering of the lower classes. In Ezekiel 23 the prophet blasted the mercurial and shortsighted foreign policies of both the northern and southern kingdoms that resulted in their downfall. Nevertheless, especially with respect to Hosea 1–2 and Ezekiel 23, the regrettable result of employing a gendered trope for a socioeconomic critique of the status quo was that issues of class and colonialism became obscured by gender for later interpreters. A condemnation of class exploitation, shortsighted foreign policies, and oppressive colonial relations was accomplished by perpetuating stereotypes of gender.

I suspect that the trope of gender provided an entrée for the biblical author to articulate issues of power and its asymmetry in class and colonial relations, because it replicated the material and ideological disparities found in male-female relations in ancient Israel. However, I definitely resist any privileging of gender as the fundamental category of analysis. As this study demonstrated, the focus on gender and the sexism embedded in the symbolizations of woman as evil masked sexism's complex interlinkages with classism, racism, colonialism, heterosexism, and so forth. Any further study of gender in the biblical text must encompass a broader systemic analysis, including class, race, and colonial relations.

I also write these concluding remarks at a time when the United States is on the verge of a seemingly pointless war with Iraq, and I am overwhelmed by the utter urgency for an ethics of reading the biblical text that confronts injustice and tyranny in its many obvious (and not-so-obvious) forms. As Danna Fewell and Gary Phillips remark,

> To a great degree, reading well is a matter of responding to and being responsible for the world the text imaginatively projects and the concrete world wherein reading, often done under duress, takes place. Our ability to maintain focus on both of these worlds, our concern to help others survive, and our skill and cleverness in discerning what is at stake enables us to read "behind the lines" in both a textual and military sense.[6]

Writing this book was not simply an intellectual, academic enter-prise for me. I found in the biblical text what I had already experi-enced in real life: that there are insidiously complex interconnections among religion—based on the biblical text—and the "-isms": sexism, racism, classism, colonialism, heterosexism, fundamentalism, and so forth. The Bible continues to be used to legitimate sinful realities. As biblical scholars, we are obligated ethically to challenge and confront social, economic, and religious systems that make it impossible for the majority of our families, congregations, and nations to experience the *shalom* that the Scriptures promise.

Notes

Chapter 1

1. *1 Enoch* 6–16; *Jub.* 4:21-23; 5:1-11; 7:21-25.

2. I put quotation marks around "foreign" here, because as we will see in chap. 7, the definition of "foreignness" in postexilic Yehud encompasses more than racial/ethnic foreignness.

3. Hesiod, *Works and Days* 59. For translation, see Joan O'Brien and Wilfred Major, eds., *In the Beginning: Creation Myths from Ancient Mesopotamia, Israel, and Greece*, AARASRS 11 (Chico, Calif.: Scholars Press, 1982), 114–21.

4. Hesiod, *Works and Days* 61–68.

5. Ibid., 83.

6. Ibid., 93–105. For further study of Pandora, see Dora Panofsky and Erwin Panofsky, *Pandora's Box: The Changing Aspects of a Mythical Symbol* (New York: Harper & Row, 1965).

7. Homer, *Odyssey* 12.39-54, 158-200.

8. *Vagina dentata*: the vagina with teeth. See Jill Raitt, "The *Vagina Dentata* and the *Immaculatus Uterus Divini Fontis*," *JAAR* 48 (1980) 415–31; Wolfgang Lederer, *The Fear of Women* (New York: Harcourt Brace Jovanovich, 1968), 44–52.

9. Anne Llewellyn Barstow, *Witchcraze: A New History of the European Witch Hunts* (San Francisco: Pandora, 1994); Joan Young Gregg, *Devils, Women, and Jews: Reflections of the Other in Medieval Sermon Stories* (Ithaca: State Univ. of New York Press, 1997); Christina Larner, *Witchcraft and Religion: The Politics of Popular Belief* (Oxford: Blackwell, 1984); Lederer, *Fear of Women*, 192–211; Kenneth P. Minkema, "Witchcraft and Gender Studies in the 1900s," *RSR* 26, no. 1 (2000) 13–19; George Mora,

"Reification of Evil: Witchcraft, Heresy, and the Scapegoat," in *Evil: Self and Culture,* ed. M. Nelson and M. Eigen (New York: Human Sciences Press, 1984), 36–60; Martha Reineke, "'The Devils Are Come Down upon Us': Myth, History, and the Witch as Scapegoat," in *The Pleasure of Her Text: Feminist Readings of Biblical and Historical Texts,* ed. Alice Bach (Philadelphia: Trinity Press International, 1990), 117–45; Walter Stephens, "Witches Who Steal Penises: Impotence and Illusion in *Malleus Maleficarum,*" *Journal of Medieval and Early Modern Studies* 28 (1998) 495–530.

10. María Herrera-Sobek, "The Treacherous Woman Archetype: A Structuring Agent in the Corrido," *Aztlán: International Journal of Chicano Studies* 13 (1982) 135–48; Manuel Peña, "Class, Gender, and Machismo: The 'Treacherous-Woman' Folklore of Mexican Male Workers," *Gender and Society* 5 (1991) 30–46.

11. Robert Briffault, *The Mothers,* 3 vols. (New York: Macmillan, 1927), 2:571, cited in Lederer, *Fear of Women,* 73–74, emphasis added.

12. See especially Lederer, *Fear of Women;* H. R. Hays, *The Dangerous Sex: The Myth of Feminine Evil* (New York: Pocket Books, 1972); John A. Phillips, *Eve: The History of an Idea* (San Francisco: Harper & Row, 1984).

Chapter 2

1. For briefer treatments of ideological criticism, see Gale A. Yee, "Ideological Criticism: Judges 17–21 and the Dismembered Body," in *Judges and Method: New Approaches in Biblical Studies,* ed. Gale A. Yee (Minneapolis: Fortress Press, 1995), 146–70; idem, "Ideological Criticism," in *Dictionary of Biblical Interpretation,* ed. John H. Hayes, 2 vols. (Nashville: Abingdon, 1999), 1:534–37.

2. See, for example, Norman K. Gottwald, *The Tribes of Yahweh* (Maryknoll, N.Y.: Orbis, 1979); idem, *The Hebrew Bible: A Socio-Literary Introduction* (Philadelphia: Fortress Press, 1985); Michel Clévenot, *Materialist Approaches to the Bible,* trans. William J. Nottingham (Maryknoll, N.Y.: Orbis, 1985); Fernando Belo, *A Materialist Reading of the Gospel of Mark,* trans. M. J. O'Connell (Maryknoll, N.Y.: Orbis, 1981); George V. Pixley, *On Exodus: A Liberation Perspective,* trans. Robert R. Barr (Maryknoll, N.Y.: Orbis, 1987); Kuno Füssel, "Materialist Readings of the Bible: Report on an Alternative Approach to Biblical Texts," in *God of the Lowly: Socio-Historical Interpretations of the Bible,* ed. Willy Schottroff and Wolfgang Stegemann, trans. Matthew J. O'Connell (Maryknoll, N.Y.: Orbis, 1984), 13–25; Ched Myers, *Binding the Strong Man: A Political Reading of Mark's Story of Jesus* (Maryknoll, N.Y.: Orbis, 1988); Itumeleng J. Mosala, *Biblical Hermeneutics and Black Theology in South Africa* (Grand Rapids: Eerdmans, 1989); G. H. Wittenberg, "The Ideological/Materialist Approach to the Old Testament," *OTE* 7 (1994) 167–72.

3. See David Jobling, "Feminism and 'Mode of Production' in Ancient Israel: Search for a Method," in *The Bible and the Politics of Exegesis: Essays in Honor of Norman K. Gottwald on His Sixty-Fifth Birthday,* ed. David Jobling, Peggy L. Day, and Gerald T. Sheppard (Cleveland: Pilgrim, 1991), 239–51; Tina Pippin, "Eros and the End: Reading for Gender in the Apocalypse of John," *Semeia* 59 (1992) 193–210.

4. Karl Marx and Frederick Engels, *The German Ideology. Part One, with Selections from Parts Two and Three,* ed. C. J. Arthur (repr. New York: International, 1985), 47.

5. Terry Eagleton, *Ideology: An Introduction* (New York: Verso, 1991), 28.

6. Ibid., 29.

7. Ibid.

8. Ibid., 29–30.

9. Ibid., 30.

10. Ibid.

11. Ibid., 102–3.

12. Ibid., 148–49.

13. Ibid., 194.

14. Ibid., 209. See also Michèle Barrett, "Ideology and the Cultural Production of Gender," in *Women's Oppression Today: The Marxist/Feminist Encounter,* rev. ed. (London: Verso, 1988), 97–98: "Ideology is a generic term for the processes by which meaning is produced, challenged, reproduced, transformed. Since meaning is negotiated primarily through means of communication and signification, it is possible to suggest that cultural production provides an important site for the construction of ideological processes. . . . Ideology is embedded historically in material practice but it does not follow *either* that ideology is theoretically indistinguishable from material practices *or* that it bears any direct relationship to them."

15. Eagleton, *Ideology,* 222–23.

16. Ibid., 223.

17. Ibid.

18. Barrett, "Ideology," 91–92.

19. Ibid., 92.

20. Eagleton, *Ideology,* 45.

21. Ibid., 45–46.

22. Ibid., 50.

23. Ibid., 52.

24. Ibid., 54.

25. Ibid., 55.

26. Ibid., 56.

27. Cf. Fredric Jameson, *The Political Unconscious: Narrative As a Socially Symbolic Act* (Ithaca: Cornell Univ. Press, 1981), 87.

28. Eagleton, *Ideology,* 58.

29. Barrett, "Ideology," 108.

30. For a theoretical study of stereotypes and their relationship to ideological production, see Teresa E. Perkins, "Rethinking Stereotypes," in *Ideology and Cultural Production,* ed. Michèle Barrett (New York: St. Martin's, 1979), 135–59.

31. Barrett, "Ideology," 109.

32. Cf. my own study, "'By the Hand of a Woman': The Biblical Metaphor of the Woman Warrior," *Semeia* 61 (1993) 99–132.

33. Barrett, "Ideology," 110–11.

34. Patrocinio Schweickart, "Reading Ourselves: Toward a Feminist Theory of Reading," in *Contemporary Literary Criticism: Literary and Cultural Studies,* ed. Robert Con Davis and Ronald Schleifer, 2nd ed. (New York: Longman, 1989), 127.

35. Barrett, "Ideology," 111.

36. Susan Faludi, *Backlash: The Undeclared War against American Women* (New York: Crown, 1991).

37. Cf. Jameson, *Political Unconscious,* 53–54, 77–79. Jameson refers here to the *text* as the imaginary resolution of a real contradiction. Within Eagleton's framework, however, ideology itself is an imaginary resolution of a real contradiction. Thus, when the text works on ideology in the production of itself as an ideological act, the text's resolution of the "real" becomes doubly complicated. This complication becomes apparent in Eagleton's categories for a materialist criticism that must analytically sort through these various productions, and has important implications for studying the symbolization of woman as evil. For an introductory discussion of Jameson's "strategies of containment," see William C. Dowling, *Jameson, Althusser, Marx: An Introduction to The Political Unconscious* (Ithaca: Cornell Univ. Press, 1984), 76–93.

38. Jameson, *Political Unconscious,* 20.

39. Terry Eagleton, *Criticism and Ideology: A Study in Marxist Literary Theory* (1976; repr. London: Verso, 1990), 64.

40. Ibid., 66.

41. Jameson, *Political Unconscious,* 76–79.

42. These very metaphors of the literary text are commonly used by biblical scholars. Cf. Stephen A. Geller, "Through Windows and Mirrors into the Bible: History, Literature, and Language in the Study of the Text," in *A Sense of Text: The Art of Language in the Study of Biblical Literature,* ed. Stephen A. Geller (Winona Lake, Ind.: Eisenbrauns, 1983), 3–40. For a critique of such metaphors of representation, see Myers, *Binding the Strong Man,* 22–26, a materialist investigation of the Gospel of Mark.

43. Eagleton, *Criticism and Ideology,* 68–69.

44. Ibid., 72.

45. Ibid., 44–45.

46. Norman K. Gottwald, "Sociology (Ancient Israel)," *ABD* 6:83.

47. Eagleton, *Criticism and Ideology*, 45.

48. Ibid., 50.

49. Compare Louis Althusser, "Ideology and Ideological State Apparatuses (Notes Towards an Investigation)," in *Lenin and Philosophy and Other Essays* (New York: Monthly Review Press, 1971), 142–48.

50. Eagleton, *Criticism and Ideology*, 54.

51. See above, p. 19.

52. Eagleton, *Criticism and Ideology*, 57.

53. Ibid., 59. Cf. Barrett, "Ideology," 106–7, regarding a critique of the unspoken assumption that literature is always a conscious rendering of authorial ideology.

54. Eagleton, *Criticism and Ideology*, 60.

55. Ibid., 63.

56. Ibid., 48.

57. Pierre Macherey, *A Theory of Literary Production*, trans. Geoffrey Wall (London: Routledge and Kegan Paul, 1978), 85.

58. Ibid., 155.

59. Cf. Jameson, *Political Unconscious*, 79–80.

60. Terry Eagleton, *Marxism and Literary Criticism* (Berkeley: Univ. of California Press, 1976), 35.

61. Eagleton, *Criticism and Ideology*, 88.

62. Fredric Jameson, "Metacommentary," in *Contemporary Literary Criticism: Modernism through Post-Structuralism*, ed. Robert Con Davis (New York: Longman, 1986), 121, emphasis added.

63. Cf. Myers, *Binding the Strong Man*, 31–38, who also utilizes an extrinsic and intrinsic criticism in his political reading of Mark's Gospel.

64. Jameson, *Political Unconscious*, 98–99.

65. For an extended discussion, see my study "The Author/Text/Reader and Power: Suggestions for a Critical Framework in Biblical Studies," in *Reading from This Place: Social Location and Biblical Interpretation*, vol. 1: *Social Location and Biblical Interpretation in the United States*, ed. Fernando F. Segovia and Mary Ann Tolbert (Minneapolis: Fortress Press, 1995), 109–18. See also Jane P. Tompkins, "The Reader in History: The Changing Shape of Literary Response," in *Reader-Response Criticism: From Formalism to Post-Structuralism*, ed. Jane P. Tompkins (Baltimore: Johns Hopkins Univ. Press, 1980), 201–32.

66. Eagleton, *Criticism and Ideology*, 89, discussing Macherey. Emphasis in original. See also Jameson, *Political Unconscious*, 60–61.

Chapter 3

1. Regarding the social-scientific study of the Bible, see Norman K. Gottwald, "Sociological Method in the Study of Ancient Israel," in *The Bible and Liberation: Political and Social Hermeneutics*, ed. Norman K. Gottwald

(Maryknoll, N.Y.: Orbis, 1983), 26–37; Ronald Clements, ed., *The World of Ancient Israel: Sociological, Anthropological and Political Perspectives* (Cambridge: Cambridge Univ. Press, 1989); David J. Chalcraft, ed., *Social Scientific Old Testament Criticism* (Sheffield: Sheffield Academic, 1997); Bruce J. Malina, *The New Testament World: Insights from Cultural Anthropology,* 3rd ed. (Louisville: Westminster John Knox, 2001); Carolyn Osiek, "The New Handmaid: The Bible and the Social Sciences," *TS* 50 (1989) 260–78; John W. Rogerson, *Anthropology and the Study of the Old Testament* (Sheffield: JSOT Press, 1984); Robert R. Wilson, *Sociological Approaches to the Old Testament,* GBS (Philadelphia: Fortress Press, 1984). For an annotated bibliography on the method, see Norman K. Gottwald, "Bibliography on the Social Scientific Study of the Old Testament," *American Baptist Quarterly* 2 (1983) 168–84; K. C. Hanson, "The Old Testament: Social Sciences and Social Description," www.kchanson.com/CLASSIFIEDBIB/otsocsci.html. For recent works using this method, see especially the essays in Ronald A. Simkins and Stephen L. Cook, eds., *The Social World of the Hebrew Bible: Twenty-Five Years of the Social Sciences in the Academy, Semeia* 87 (1999).

2. Phyllis Bird, "Women's Religion in Ancient Israel," in *Women's Earliest Records from Ancient Egypt and Western Asia,* ed. Barbara S. Lesko, BJS 166 (Atlanta: Scholars, 1989), 283–98; idem, "The Place of Women in the Israelite Culture," in *Ancient Israelite Religion: Essays in Honor of Frank Moore Cross,* ed. Patrick D. Miller Jr., Paul D. Hanson, and S. Dean McBride (Philadelphia: Fortress Press, 1987), 397–419; Carol Meyers, *Discovering Eve: Ancient Israelite Women in Context* (New York: Oxford Univ. Press, 1988), 11–23.

3. Bruce J. Malina, "The Social Sciences and Biblical Interpretation," in *Bible and Liberation,* ed. Gottwald, 12.

4. Distinguished from physical anthropology, which investigates the physiological connections between *Homo sapiens* and earlier hominids, cultural anthropology, as its name implies, focuses on all aspects of society and culture. See Wilson, *Sociological Approaches,* 17–22, for a brief discussion of the different subfields of cultural anthropology, which include ethnology, social anthropology, ethnography, archaeology, and structural anthropology.

I will discuss in detail the conclusions of feminist anthropologists that are specifically relevant to the symbolization of woman as evil. However, for a worthwhile general introduction to the issues examined in feminist cross-cultural research on gender, see Margo I. Duley and Mary I. Edwards, *The Cross-Cultural Study of Women: A Comprehensive Guide* (New York: Feminist Press, 1986); and Sandra Morgen, ed., *Gender and Anthropology: Critical Reviews for Research and Teaching* (Washington, D.C.: American Anthropological Association, 1989).

5. In the use here of the singular word "society," I do not presume a static, unchanging phenomenon. I use the word comprehensively to cover

the different forms and modes of production this society takes over the course of its history.

6. See Osiek, "New Handmaid," 275–77; Thomas Best, "The Sociological Study of the New Testament: Promise and Peril of a New Discipline," *SJT* 36 (1983) 181–94; Gary A. Herion, "The Impact of Modern and Social Science Assumptions on the Reconstruction of Israelite History," *JSOT* 34 (1986) 3–33; David Fiensy, "Using the Nuer Culture of Africa in Understanding the Old Testament," *JSOT* 44 (1989) 73–83.

7. Herion, "Impact," 24–25.

8. See the discussion of "double absence," above, p. 20.

9. See above, pp. 21–22.

10. The discussion of modes of production in ancient Israel is taken from Norman K. Gottwald, "Sociology (Ancient Israel)," *ABD* 6:79–89; idem, "Social Class As an Analytic and Hermeneutical Category in Biblical Studies," *JBL* 112 (1993) 3–22.

11. Marshall Sahlins, cited in David Jobling, "Feminism and 'Mode of Production' in Ancient Israel: Search for a Method," in *The Bible and the Politics of Exegesis: Essays in Honor of Norman K. Gottwald on His Sixty-Fifth Birthday,* ed. David Jobling, Peggy L. Day, and Gerald T. Sheppard (Cleveland: Pilgrim, 1991), 242.

12. The emergence of Israel in the pre-state period continues to be a topic of much debate. For helpful summaries of the state of the question, see Anthony J. Frendo, "Five Recent Books on the Emergence of Ancient Israel: Review Article," *PEQ* 124 (July–December 1992) 144–51; and James D. Martin, "Israel As a Tribal Society," in *World of Ancient Israel,* ed. Clements, 95–117. To get a taste of the argument, see Niels Peter Lemche, "Early Israel Revisited," *CRBS* 4 (1996) 9–34; William G. Dever, "Revisionist Israel Revisited: A Rejoinder to Niels Peter Lemche," *CRBS* 4 (1996) 35–50; and Norman K. Gottwald, "Triumphalist versus Anti-Triumphalist Versions of Early Israel: A Response to Articles by Lemche and Dever in Volume 4 (1996)," *CRBS* 5 (1997) 15–42.

13. Cf. Deut 7:13; Hos 2:8; and Joel 2:19.

14. Norman K. Gottwald, *The Tribes of Yahweh* (Maryknoll, N.Y.: Orbis, 1979), 462–63, 490–92, 608–49, 692–99. But see Niels Peter Lemche, *Early Israel: Anthropological and Historical Studies on the Israelite Society before the Monarchy,* VTSup 37 (Leiden: Brill, 1985), 202–44, for an incisive critique of Gottwald in this matter, particularly Gottwald's contention that premonarchic Israel was "egalitarian."

15. Gottwald, "Sociology (Ancient Israel)," 83.

16. Meyers, *Discovering Eve,* 122–88.

17. Gottwald, "Sociology (Ancient Israel)," 84.

18. See David Jobling, "Forced Labor: Solomon's Golden Age and the Question of Literary Representation," *Semeia* 54 (1991) 57–76.

19. For a more complete discussion of the Babylonian exile, see the extrinsic analysis in chap. 6 of this book, pp.112–16.

20. See chap. 7 of this book for a detailed discussion.

21. Gottwald, "Sociology (Ancient Israel)," 85.

22. Ibid., 86.

23. In my discussion of pre-state social structure, I rely primarily on the work of Lemche, *Early Israel*, 245–90. Lemche is quite critical of Gottwald's analysis of Israel's pre-state social structure in *Tribes of Yahweh*. Gottwald begins with the primary subdivision of the Israelite people—the šēbeṭ, or tribe (245ff.). He then moves to the smaller social units within the tribe: the mišpāḥâ (257ff.), which he defines as a "protective association of families," and the bêt 'āb (285ff.), which he describes as "the extended family." For Lemche the starting point of Israelite social structure is the bêt 'āb.

24. Lemche, *Early Israel*, 250–51.

25. Ibid., 269; Lawrence Stager, "The Archaeology of the Family in Ancient Israel," *BASOR* 260 (1985) 22.

26. Carol Meyers, "'To Her Mother's House': Considering a Counterpart to the Israelite Bêt 'āb," in *Bible and Politics of Exegesis*, ed. Jobling, Day, and Sheppard, 39–51, has suggested that a complement to the "father's house" existed in the "mother's house."

27. Lemche, *Early Israel*, 234, 264.

28. Ibid., 268–69. Gottwald, *Tribes of Yahweh*, 315, would concur in this respect.

29. Cf. 2 Sam 14:7.

30. John W. Rogerson, "Anthropology and the Old Testament," in *World of Ancient Israel*, ed. Clements, 30. Stager, "Archaeology of the Family," 24, thinks that biblical scholars should exercise greater caution in assigning tribal language and institutions to either the pre- or the postmonarchical periods.

31. Roger M. Keesing, *Kin Groups and Social Structure* (New York: Holt, Rinehart & Winston, 1975), 150.

32. See above, pp. 13–18, for a complete discussion of these strategies.

33. Salvatore Cucchiari, "The Gender Revolution and the Transition from Bisexual Horde to Patrilocal Bond: The Origins of Gender Hierarchy," in *Sexual Meanings: The Cultural Construction of Gender and Sexuality*, ed. Sherry B. Ortner and Harriet Whitehead (New York: Cambridge Univ. Press, 1981), 36. See also the essays in Jane Fishburne Collier and Sylvia Junko Yanagisako, eds., *Gender and Kinship: Essays toward a Unified Analysis* (Stanford: Stanford Univ. Press, 1987).

34. On the importance of male descent for Israelite priests, symbolized in the ritual of circumcision, see Howard Eilberg-Schwartz, "The Fruitful Cut: Circumcision and Israel's Symbolic of Fertility, Descent, and Gender," in *The Savage in Judaism: An Anthropology of Israelite Religion and Ancient Judaism* (Bloomington: Indiana Univ. Press, 1990), 141–76.

35. For a discussion of the group-bound individual as opposed to the self-

concerned individual, particularly in kinship practices, see Bruce J. Malina, "Dealing with Biblical (Mediterranean) Characters: A Guide for U.S. Consumers," *BTB* 19 (1989) 127–41.

36. Rainer Neu, "Patrilokalität und Patrilinearität in Israel: Zur ethnosoziologischen Kritik der These vom Matriarchat," *BZ* 34 (1990) 222–33; Stager, "Archaeology of the Family," 20; Meyers, *Discovering Eve*, 38; Naomi Steinberg, "Alliance or Descent? The Function of Marriage in Genesis," *JSOT* 51 (1991) 45–55; Tikva Frymer-Kensky, "Patriarchal Family Relationships and Near Eastern Law," *BA* 4 (1981) 209–14.

37. For discussions of endogamous marriages in ancient Israel, see Lemche, *Early Israel*, 224–29; Nathaniel Wander, "Structure, Contradiction, and 'Resolution' in Mythology: Father's Brother's Daughter Marriage and the Treatment of Women in Genesis 11–50," *JANESCU* 13 (1981) 75–99.

For anthropological studies on endogamy as practiced among Arab bedouin, see Robert F. Murphy and Leonard Kasdan, "The Structure of Parallel Cousin Marriage," *AmAnth* 61 (1959) 17–29. Raphael Patai, "The Structure of Endogamous Unilineal Descent Groups," *SWJA* 21 (1965) 325–50, presents a critique of Murphy and Kasdan. In turn, they refute Patai in Robert F. Murphy and Leonard Kasdan, "Agnation and Endogamy: Some Further Considerations," *SWJA* 23 (1967) 1–14. See also Joseph M. Whitmeyer, "Endogamy As a Basis for Ethnic Behavior," *Sociological Theory* 15, no. 2 (1997) 162–67.

38. The anthropological designation of the father's brother's daughter would be patrilateral parallel cousin.

39. Lila Abu-Lughod, *Veiled Sentiments: Honor and Poetry in a Bedouin Society* (Berkeley: Univ. of California Press, 1986), 78–81.

40. Cf. Patai, "Structure," 331–33.

41. Phyllis A. Bird, "Women (OT)," *ABD* 6:951–57; idem, "Images of Women in the Old Testament," in *Religion and Sexism: Images of Woman in the Jewish and Christian Traditions,* ed. Rosemary Radford Ruether (New York: Simon & Schuster, 1974), 41–88; Grace I. Emmerson, "Women in Ancient Israel," in *World of Ancient Israel,* ed. Clements, 371–94; Phyllis Trible, "Woman in the OT," *IDBSup,* 963–66; O. J. Baab, "Marriage," *IDB* 3:279–80.

42. A major part of this section is derived from my discussion in "Hosea," *WomBibCom,* 197–98.

43. Meyers, *Discovering Eve*, 183–88; Bird, "Women (OT)," 952.

44. Naomi Steinberg, "Gender Roles in the Rebekah Cycle," *USQR* 39 (1984) 185.

45. Cf. Judg 19:2-3.

46. See, for example, the stories about Jacob, Leah, and Rachel (Genesis 29–30). In this case, the two wives were not only of Jacob's patriline, but also sisters who competed for their husband's attention. Cf. J. Cheryl Exum, "The Mothers of Israel: The Patriarchal Narratives from a Feminist Perspective," *BRev* 2 (1986) 60–67.

47. Meyers, *Discovering Eve*, 166–67; Bird, "Images," 51.

48. Murphy and Kasdan, "Agnation and Endogamy," 13.

49. Wander, "Structure," 75–99; Steinberg, "Alliance or Descent?" 51–53.

50. Murphy and Kasdan, "Agnation and Endogamy," 10–12. See also Lemche, *Early Israel*, 228–31.

51. Murphy and Kasdan, "Agnation and Endogamy," 13.

52. Ibid., 12–13; Robert F. Murphy, "Social Distance and the Veil," *AmAnth* 66 (1964) 1257–74; Robert F. Murphy, "Tuareg Kinship," *AmAnth* 69 (1967) 163–70.

53. Wander, "Structure," 91–92.

54. Abu-Lughod, *Veiled Sentiments*, 81–82.

55. For an excellent presentation of the state of the question, see the essays in David D. Gilmore, ed., *Honor and Shame and the Unity of the Mediterranean* (Washington, D.C.: American Anthropological Association, 1987). Important for the role religion plays in honor/shame value systems is J. G. Peristiany and Julian Pitt-Rivers, eds., *Honor and Grace in Anthropology* (Cambridge: Cambridge Univ. Press, 1992). For two classic studies by these editors, see J. G. Peristiany, ed., *Honor and Shame: The Values of Mediterranean Society* (Chicago: Univ. of Chicago Press, 1966); and Julian Pitt-Rivers, ed., *The Fate of Shechem or the Politics of Sex: Essays in the Anthropology of the Mediterranean* (Cambridge: Cambridge Univ. Press, 1977). Connecting honor and shame with monotheism is Carol Delaney, "Seeds of Honor, Fields of Shame," in *Mediterranean,* ed. Gilmore, 35–48; and idem, *The Seed and the Soil: Gender and Cosmology in Turkish Village Society* (Berkeley: Univ. of California Press, 1991).

The most helpful analysis on honor and shame from a woman's perspective is Abu-Lughod, *Veiled Sentiments*, 78–166. Also worthwhile are idem, *Writing Women's Worlds: Bedouin Stories* (Berkeley: Univ. of California Press, 1993), 205–42; Gideon M. Kressel, "Shame and Gender," *AnthQ* 65 (1992) 34–46; Forouz Jowkar, "Honor and Shame: A Feminist View from Within," *Feminist Issues* 6, no. 1 (1986) 45–65; Nancy Lindisfarne, "Variant Masculinities, Variant Virginities: Rethinking 'Honour and Shame,'" in *Dislocating Masculinity: Comparative Ethnographies,* ed. Andrea Cornwall and Nancy Lindisfarne (New York: Routledge, 1994), 82–96; Sherry B. Ortner, "The Virgin and the State," *Feminist Studies* 4 (1978) 19–33; Carroll McC. Pastner, "Accommodations to Purdah: The Female Perspective," *Journal of Marriage and Family* 36 (1974) 408–14; idem, "A Social Structural and Historical Analysis of Honor, Shame and Purdah," *AnthQ* 45 (1972) 248–61; Jane Schneider, "Of Vigilance and Virgins: Honor, Shame and Access to Resources in Mediterranean Societies," *Ethnology* 9 (1971) 1–24; Unni Wikan, "Shame and Honor: A Contestable Pair," *Man* 19 (1984) 635–52; idem, "Honor and Self-Realization," in *Behind the Veil in Arabia: Women in Oman* (Chicago: Univ. of Chicago Press, 1984), 141–67.

56. For an early study of honor and shame in ancient Israel, see Johannes Pedersen, *Israel: Its Life and Culture*, vols. 1-2 (Copenhagen: Branner Og Korch, 1926), 213–44. For more recent investigations see the essays in Victor H. Matthews and Don C. Benjamin, eds., *Honor and Shame in the World of the Bible*, Semeia 68 (1994); Victor H. Matthews, "Hospitality and Hostility in Judges 4," *BTB* 21 (1991) 13–21; idem, "Hospitality and Hostility in Genesis 19 and Judges 19," *BTB* 22 (1992) 3–11; idem, "Honor and Shame in Gender-Related Legal Situations in the Hebrew Bible," in *Gender and Law in the Hebrew Bible and the Ancient Near East*, ed. Victor H. Matthews, Bernard M. Levinson, and Tikva Frymer-Kensky, JSOTSup 262 (Sheffield: Sheffield Academic, 1998), 97–112; P. J. Botha, "The Ideology of Shame in the Wisdom of Ben Sira: Ecclesiasticus 41:14—42:8," *OTE* 9 (1996) 353–71; Claudia V. Camp, "Understanding a Patriarchy: Women in Second-Century Jerusalem through the Eyes of Ben Sira," in *"Women Like This": New Perspectives on Jewish Women in the Greco-Roman World*, ed. Amy-Jill Levine, SBLEJL 1 (Atlanta: Scholars, 1991), 1–39; idem, "Honor, Shame, and the Hermeneutics of Ben Sira's Ms C," in *Wisdom, You Are My Sister: Studies in Honor of Roland E. Murphy, O.Carm., on the Occasion of His Eightieth Birthday*, ed. Michael L. Barré, S.S. (Washington, D.C.: Catholic Biblical Association of America, 1997), 157–71; David A. deSilva, "The Wisdom of Ben Sira: Honor, Shame, and the Maintenance of the Values of a Minority Culture," *CBQ* 58 (1996) 433–55; W. R. Domeris, "Shame and Honour in Proverbs: Wise Women and Foolish Men," *OTE* 8 (1995) 86–102; T. Raymond Hobbs, "Reflections on Honor, Shame, and Covenant Relations," *JBL* 116 (1997) 501–3; Lillian R. Klein, "Honor and Shame in Esther," in *A Feminist Companion to Esther, Judith and Susanna*, ed. Athalya Brenner, FCB 7 (Sheffield: Sheffield Academic, 1995), 149–75; Timothy S. Laniak, *Shame and Honor in the Book of Esther*, SBLDS 165 (Atlanta: Scholars, 1999); Margaret Odell, "The Inversion of Shame and Forgiveness in Ezekiel 16.59–63," *JSOT* 56 (1992) 101–12; idem, "An Exploratory Study of Shame and Dependence in the Bible and Selected Near Eastern Parallels," in *The Biblical Canon in Comparative Perspective*, ed. K. Lawson Younger Jr., William W. Hallo, and Bernard F. Batto (Lewiston, N.Y.: Mellen, 1991), 217–33; Saul M. Olyan, "Honor, Shame, and Covenant Relations in Ancient Israel and Its Environment," *JBL* 115 (1996) 201–18; Renata Rabichev, "The Mediterranean Concepts of Honour and Shame As Seen in the Depiction of the Biblical Women," *R&T* 3 (1996) 51–63; John J. Pilch, *Introducing the Cultural Context of the Old Testament* (Mahwah, N.J.: Paulist, 1991), 49–70; Johanna Stiebert, *The Construction of Shame in the Hebrew Bible: The Prophetic Contribution*, JSOTSup 346 (Sheffield: Sheffield Academic, 2002); Ken Stone, *Sex, Honor and Power in the Deuteronomistic History: A Narratological and Anthropological Analysis*, JSOTSup 234 (Sheffield: Sheffield Academic, 1997); idem, "Gender and Homosexuality in Judges 19: Subject-Honor, Object-Shame?" *JSOT* 67 (1995) 87–107.

For the NT period see Malina, "Honor and Shame: Pivotal Values of the First-Century Mediterranean World," in *New Testament World*, 27–57.

57. Julian Pitt-Rivers, "Honour and Social Status," in *Honour and Shame*, ed. Peristiany, 21.

58. Pierre Bourdieu, "The Sentiment of Honour in Kabyle Society," in *Honour and Shame*, ed. Peristiany, 191–241; Pitt-Rivers, "The Law of Hospitality," in *Fate of Shechem*, 94–112.

59. Robert Karen, "Shame," *Atlantic Monthly* (February 1992) 40–70; Gershen Kaufman, "The Meaning of Shame: Toward a Self-Affirming Identity," *Journal of Counseling Psychology* 21 (1974) 568–74.

60. Pitt-Rivers, "Honour and Social Status," 42.

61. Thus Peristiany, *Honor and Shame*, 9, in his introduction: "In this context it is the comparison of the male-female relationship and that of the roles of the sexes within these societies that points both to the significant analogies and to the equally significant differences." For the economics of sexuality, see in particular Schneider, "Of Vigilance and Virgins," 1–24; David D. Gilmore, "Introduction: The Shame of Dishonor," in *Mediterranean*, ed. Gilmore, 3–5; Abu-Lughod, *Veiled Sentiments*, 118–19; and Margaret M. Gilmore and David D. Gilmore, "'Machismo': A Psychodynamic Approach (Spain)," *Journal of Psychological Anthropology* 2 (1979) 281–300.

62. Pitt-Rivers, "Honour and Social Status," 44–46.

63. Ibid., 43.

64. Abou A. M. Zeid, "Honour and Shame among the Bedouins of Egypt," in *Honour and Shame*, ed. Peristiany, 243–59.

65. See Gilmore, "Introduction," 5–7.

66. Michael Herzfeld, "Honor and Shame: Problems in the Comparative Analysis of Moral Systems," *Man* 15 (1980) 339–51; idem, "The Horns of the Mediterraneanist Dilemma," *AmEth* 11 (1984) 439–54; idem, "'As in Your Own House': Hospitality, Ethnography, and the Stereotype of Mediterranean Society," in *Mediterranean*, ed. Gilmore, 75–89.

67. Wikan, "Shame and Honor," 635–37; idem, *Behind the Veil*, 141–67. See also Stanley Brandes, "Reflections on Honor and Shame in the Mediterranean," in *Mediterranean*, ed. Gilmore, 122.

The binary opposition of honor/shame = male/female has been appropriated by biblical scholars. Thus Malina, *New Testament World*, 49: "Actual conduct, daily concrete behavior, always depends upon one's sexual status. At this level of perception, when honor is viewed as an exclusive prerogative of one of the sexes, then honor is always male, and shame is always female." I argue, however, that this claim does not fit the OT evidence, where shame seems to connote the negative and is applicable to both genders. Moreover, I will show that two codes of honor are operative in the OT: one for the powerful and economically independent and one for the dependent.

68. Gilmore, "Introduction," 7.

69. *Kābēd:* Gen 13:2. Cf. Prov 13:18. *Kābôd:* Gen 31:1; Judg 9:9; 1 Kgs 3:13; Prov 8:18; 22:4; Eccl 6:2; 1 Chr 29:28; 2 Chr 1.11-12; 18:1; Esth 5:11; Hag 2:9; Dan 11:39. Cf. the *piel* of *kbd,* "to reward richly": Num 24:11. *Yĕqār:* Jer 20:5; Esth 1:4. *Tip'eret:* Esth 1:4.

70. *Tip'eret:* Prov 16:31; 20:29. *Hdr:* Lev 19:32; Lam 5:12. *Hôd:* Num 27:20. *Kābôd:* Prov 3:16; 1 Chr 29:28; 2 Chr 1:11.

71. *Kbd:* Exod 20:12; Deut 5:16; Mal 1:6.

72. *Yqr:* 1 Sam 18:30. *Tip'eret:* Prov 20:29.

73. *Kābôd:* Gen 45:13. Esth 5:11. *Yqr:* Esth 6:3-11. *Hdr:* Prov 25:6.

74. *Kbd:* 1 Sam 9:6.

75. *Kābôd:* Prov 3:35.

76. *Yqr:* Esth 1:20.

77. *Hādār:* Prov 31:25. *Kābôd:* Exod 20:12; Deut 5:16; Prov 11:16. Cf. Gen 30:20 and Prov 12:4.

78. *Herpâ:* 1 Sam 17:26. *Hrp:* 1 Sam 17:25; 2 Sam 21:21; 23:9. *Kĕlimmâ:* Ezek 32:24-25. *Qālôn* and *bôš:* Ps 83:16-17. See also the shame in stripping naked those who are defeated after a military conquest: Isa 20:4; Amos 2:16.

79. *Herpâ:* Isa 30:5; Jer 23:4, 9; 29:18; 42:18; 51:51. *Bôš:* 2 Sam 19:5; 2 Kgs 19:26 = Isa 37:27; Isa 30:5; Jer 48:39; Mic 7:16. *Hesed:* Prov 14:34.

80. *Herpâ:* Neh 1:3; 2:17.

81. *Herpâ:* Jer 15:15; Ps 22:6; 69:19; Job 16:10; 19:5. *Bôš:* Ps 22:6; 25:2; 69:7. *Kĕlimmâ* and *bōšet:* Ps 44:15; 69:19. *Kĕlimmâ:* Job 20:3. *Qālôn:* Job 10:15.

82. *Bôš:* Judg 3:25.

83. *Bôš:* Isa 42:17; 44:9; Jer 10:14; 51:17; Hos 10:6. *Bōšet:* Hos 9:10.

84. Prov 20:3; 26:1. *Qālôn:* Prov 3:35; 13:18. *Nĕbālâ:* Isa 9:17; 32:6; Job 42:8. Cf. 2 Sam 25:25. *Kĕlimmâ:* Prov 18:13.

85. *Qālôn:* Hab 2:16.

86. *Bôš:* Prov 19:26. Cf. Jer 31:19.

87. *Bôš:* Jer 2:26.

88. *Qālôn:* Prov 11:2. Cf. Prov 29:23.

89. *Herpâ:* Isa 4:1.

90. *Herpâ:* Gen 30:23. Cf. 2 Sam 6:20-23.

91. *Bôš:* Prov 12:4.

92. *Kābôd.*

93. Cf. Prov 14:31 and Isa 58:6-7.

94. See above (p. 40), n. 54.

95. Thus Pedersen, *Israel,* 1–2:222: "He [the man of honor] wants to be the one whose help is sought by others, to whom guests turn for shelter, and who distributes his gifts to all comers. Honour consists in independence. If one cannot give, then one can, at any rate, forbear receiving." The values of male independence and autonomy have also been a trademark of the Awlad 'Ali, according to Abu-Lughod, *Veiled Sentiments,* 78–117.

96. Zeid, "Honour and Shame," 252.

97. Gen 18:2; 19:1; 48:12; 1 Sam 24:8; 28:14; 2 Sam 9:6; 14:22; 15:5; 18:28; 24:20; 1 Kgs 1:53; 18:42; Esth 3:2 and passim.

98. Abu-Lughod, *Veiled Sentiments*, 276 n. 25: "I do not discuss the concept of shame that usually tags along with honor because, as I will argue, modesty is the more important concept to pair with honor, *being of the same order but applicable to women and the weak*" (emphasis added).

99. Note the descriptions of the "good" wife in Sir 26:13-18, 26; Prov 11:16; and 19:14. Cf. Prov 27:18 regarding servant-master relations. The servant will obtain honor in his care of the master.

100. Abu-Lughod, *Veiled Sentiments*, 104, emphasis added. Cf. Pedersen, *Israel*, 1–2:215.

101. Terry Eagleton, *Ideology: An Introduction* (London: Verso, 1991), 54.

102. See Gilmore, "Introduction," 4.

103. Meyers, *Discovering Eve*, 72–121.

104. Cf. Gen 15:3, where Abram's dishonor from Sarai's barrenness may result in forfeiting his material assets to his kin, Eliezer of Damascus.

105. Bird, "Images," 51–53.

106. Maureen J. Giovannini, "Female Chastity Codes in the Circum-Mediterranean: Comparative Perspectives," in *Mediterranean*, ed. Gilmore, 61–74; Schneider, "Of Vigilance and Virgins," 17–22; Zeid, "Honour and Shame," 256–57.

107. Particularly as this symbolism relates to endogamous marriages, see Delaney, "Seeds of Honor," 43–44.

108. Jon D. Levenson, "1 Samuel 25 As Literature and As History," *CBQ* 47 (1985) 27–28.

109. For studies of adultery in the ancient Near East, see Raymond Westbrook, "Adultery in Ancient Near Eastern Law," *RB* 97 (1990) 542–80; Elaine Adler Goodfriend, "Adultery," *ABD* 1:82–86. The latter also contains a good select bibliography.

110. Pitt-Rivers, *Fate of Shechem*, 78.

111. Meyers, *Discovering Eve*, 176.

112. Ibid., 41.

113. Ibid., 42.

114. Naomi Steinberg notes the distinction that anthropologists draw between conflict (a situation that arises from opposition) and conflict-indicating behavior (the means for communicating the presence of conflict) in "Conflict and Cooperation: Strategies of Domestic Power" (SBL Annual Meeting in New Orleans, 1990), 6–7. I thank Dr. Steinberg for a copy of her manuscript.

115. James Scott, *Weapons of the Weak: Everyday Forms of Peasant Resistance* (New Haven: Yale Univ. Press, 1985), xvi. See also Elizabeth Janeway, *Powers of the Weak* (New York: Knopf, 1980), 172, who reassesses the "shiftlessness" that Southern slaveholders attribute to their slaves as *purposive* "disguised disobedience."

116. Henrietta L. Moore, *Feminism and Anthropology* (Minneapolia: Univ. of Minnesota Press, 1989), 178–83,

117. Lila Abu-Lughod, "The Romance of Resistance: Tracing Transformations of Power through Bedouin Women," in *Beyond the Second Sex: New Directions in the Anthropology of Gender,* ed. Peggy Reeves Sanday and Ruth Gallagher Goodenough (Philadelphia: Univ. of Pennsylvania Press, 1990), 313–35.

118. Ibid., 316–17; idem, "A Community of Secrets: The Separate World of Bedouin Women," *Signs* 10 (1985) 644–65; Cynthia Nelson, "Public and Private Politics: Women in the Middle Eastern World," *AmEth* 1 (1974) 559.

119. Karen J. Brison, *Just Talk: Gossip, Meetings, and Power in a Papua New Guinea Village* (Berkeley: Univ. of California Press, 1992); Susan C. Rogers, "Female Forms of Power and the Myth of Male Dominance: A Model of Female/Male Interaction in Peasant Society," *AmEth* 2 (1975) 736; Louise Lamphere, "Strategies, Cooperation, and Conflict among Women in Domestic Groups," in *Women, Culture, and Society,* ed. Michelle Zimbalist Rosaldo and Louise Lamphere (Stanford: Stanford Univ. Press, 1974), 105–6; Susan Harding, "Women and Words in a Spanish Village," in *Toward an Anthropology of Women,* ed. Rayna R. Reiter (New York: Monthly Review, 1975), 297–305.

120. Harding, "Women and Words," 292–93.

121. Daisy Dwyer, "Ideologies of Sexual Inequality and Strategies for Change in Male-Female Relations," *AmEth* 5 (1978) 235.

122. Abu-Lughod, "Romance of Resistance," 317–20.

123. Ibid., 320–22.

124. Dwyer, "Ideologies of Sexual Inequality," 235; Evalyn Jacobson Michaelson and Walter Goldschmidt, "Females Roles and Male Dominance among Peasants," *SWJA* 27 (1971) 338–39; Lamphere, "Strategies," 105.

125. Dwyer, "Ideologies of Sexual Inequality," 235; Nelson, "Public and Privates Politics," 556–57, 559–60; Rogers, "Female Forms of Power," 737. See also Onunwa Udobata, "The Paradox of Power and 'Submission' of Women in African Traditional Religion and Society," *Journal of Dharma* 13 (1988) 31–38.

126. Margery Wolf, "Chinese Women: Old Skills in a New Context," in *Woman, Culture, and Society,* ed. Zimbalist Rosaldo and Lamphere, 159–61; Jane Fishburne Collier, "Women in Politics," in ibid., 89–96.

127. Moore, *Feminism and Anthropology,* 182; Michelle Zimbalist Rosaldo, "Women, Culture, and Society: A Theoretical Overview," in *Women, Culture, and Society,* 37.

128. Pitt-Rivers, *Fate of Shechem,* 80; Ernestine Friedl, "The Position of Women: Appearance and Reality," *AnthQ* 40 (1967) 108; Abu-Lughod, *Veiled Sentiments,* 147–48, 158; Michelle Zimbalist Rosaldo, "The Use and Abuse of Anthropology: Reflections on Feminism and Cross-Cultural Understanding," *Signs* 5 (1980) 413.

129. Rosaldo, "Women, Culture, and Society," 21.

130. Steinberg, "Conflict and Cooperation," 1–15.

131. Tikva Frymer-Kensky, *In the Wake of the Goddesses: Women, Culture, and the Biblical Transformation of Pagan Myth* (New York: Free Press, 1992), 128–40.

132. See especially the essays and responses in the *Semeia* 42 (1988) volume *Reasoning with the Foxes: Female Wit in a World of Male Power*. See also Esther Fuchs, "Who Is Hiding the Truth? Deceptive Women and Biblical Androcentrism," in *Feminist Perspectives on Biblical Scholars,* ed. Adela Yarbro Collins, SBLBSNA 10 (Chico, Calif.: Scholars, 1985), 137–44; Toni Craven, "Women Who Lied for the Faith," in *Justice and the Holy,* ed. Douglas A. Knight and Peter J. Paris, Homage Series (Atlanta: Scholars, 1989), 35–49; Ann W. Engar, "Old Testament Women As Tricksters," in *Mappings of the Biblical Terrain,* ed. Vincent L. Tollers and John Maier (Lewisburg, Pa.: Bucknell Univ. Press, 1990), 143–57; O. Horn Prouser, "The Truth about Women and Lying," *JSOT* 61 (1994) 15–28.

133. For analyses, see Amy-Jill Levine, "Sacrifice and Salvation: Otherness and Domestication in the Book of Judith," in *"No One Spoke Ill of Her"*: *Essays on Judith,* ed. James C. VanderKam, SBLEJL 2 (Atlanta: Scholars, 1992), 17–30; Pamela J. Milne, "What Shall We Do with Judith? A Feminist Reassessment of a Biblical 'Heroine,'" *Semeia* 62 (1993) 37–58; Mary Jacobus, "Judith, Holofernes, and the Phallic Woman," in *Reading Women: Essays in Feminist Criticism* (New York: Columbia Univ. Press, 1986), 110–36; Margarita Stocker, *Judith: Sexual Warrior Women and Power in Western Culture* (New Haven: Yale Univ. Press, 1998). For a study of irony in Judith's rhetorical strategies, see Carey A. Moore, *Judith,* AB 40B (Garden City, N.Y.: Doubleday, 1985), 78–85.

134. See in particular Sir 25:22; 26:3, 8, 24–26. For an extensive discussion of honor and shame in the book of Sirach, particularly as this value system relates to Sirach's notion of economics, see Camp, "Understanding a Patriarchy," 1–39.

135. For dating and authorship, see Howard Clark Kee, "Testaments of the Twelve Patriarchs (Second Century B.C.): A New Translation and Introduction," in *The Old Testament Pseudepigrapha,* ed. James H. Charlesworth, 2 vols. (Garden City, N.Y.: Doubleday, 1983–85), 1:777–78.

136. Collier, "Women in Politics," 96; Steinberg, "Conflict and Cooperation," 8.

137. Abu-Lughod, "Romance of Resistance," 324.

138. Rosaldo, "Women, Culture, and Society," 32.

139. Meyers, *Discovering Eve,* 142–64.

140. Cf. Harding, "Women and Words," 306–8, who lodges several general criticisms against those feminist anthropologists who think that male dominance is a myth that flatters and appeases men and obscures the fact women hold the real power in a society.

141. Cf. ibid., 293.

142. Meyers, *Discovering Eve*, 138–88.
143. Abu-Lughod, "Community of Secrets," 640.
144. Ibid., 640–41; Rogers, "Female Forms of Power," 741.
145. Nelson, "Public and Privates Politics," 559.
146. Abu-Lughod, "Community of Secrets," 644–45.
147. Dwyer, "Ideologies of Sexual Inequality," 235–36. Cf. Abu-Lughod, "Community of Secrets," 645.
148. Abu-Lughod, "Community of Secrets," 646.
149. Wikan, "Shame and Honor," 642–45.
150. Abu-Lughod, "Community of Secrets," 647.

Chapter 4

1. An abridged version of this chapter appeared as "Gender, Class, and the Social-Scientific Study of Genesis 2–3," *Semeia* 87 (1999) 177–92.

2. Jack Levison, "Is Eve to Blame? A Contextual Analysis of Sirach 25:24," *CBQ* 47 (1985) 617–23, challenges the interpretation that Sirach here refers to the person of Eve.

3. However, reflection on this enigmatic woman flowers during the so-called intertestamental period. See, for example, *Jubilees* 3–4; *Adam and Eve* (*Vita* and *Apocalypse*).

4. Against those who see in the Priestly version an egalitarian creation of male and female, Ilana Pardes, *Countertraditions in the Bible: A Feminist Approach* (Cambridge: Harvard Univ. Press, 1992), 22, 55–58, points out the invisibility of Eve and other mothers in the wider context of P's patrilineal genealogies in Genesis 5. See also Phyllis A. Bird, "'Male and Female He Created Them': Gen 1:27b in the Context of the Priestly Account of Creation," *HTR* 74 (1981) 129–59.

5. For the state of the question, see Albert de Pury, "Yahwist (J) Source," *ABD* 6:1012–20. For Gen 2:4b—3:24 in particular, see Claus Westermann, *Genesis 1–11: A Commentary*, trans. John J. Scullion, S.J., CC (Minneapolis: Augsburg, 1984), 186–90.

6. Carol Meyers, *Discovering Eve: Ancient Israelite Women in Context* (New York: Oxford Univ. Press, 1988), 120–21.

7. Jean Guichard, "Approche 'matérialiste' du récit de la chute: Genèse 3," *Lumière et Vie* 26 (1977) 57–90; Robert B. Coote and David Robert Ord, *The Bible's First History* (Philadelphia: Fortress Press, 1989), 28–30.

8. Walter Brueggemann, "David and His Theologian," *CBQ* 30 (1968) 156–81; Gerhard von Rad, *Genesis: A Commentary*, trans. John H. Marks, rev. ed., OTL (Philadelphia: Westminster, 1972), 98; Werner H. Schmidt, "A Theologian for the Solomonic Era? A Plea for the Yahwist," in *Studies in the Period of David and Solomon*, ed. Tomoo Ishida (Winona Lake, Ind.: Eisenbrauns, 1982), 55–73; Jacques Bernard, "Genèse 1 à 3: Lecture et Traditions de Lecture," *MScRel* 41 (1984) 109–28; Manfred Görg,

"Geschichte der Sünde—Sünde der Geschichte: Gen 3,1-7 im Licht Tendenzkritischen Beobachtungen," *MTZ* 41 (1990) 315–25; Knut Holter, "The Serpent in Eden As a Symbol of Israel's Political Enemies: A Yahwistic Criticism of the Solomonic Foreign Policy?" *SJOT* 1 (1990) 106–12; Howard N. Wallace, *The Eden Narrative*, HSM 32 (Atlanta: Scholars, 1985), 46–48.

9. George E. Mendenhall, "The Shady Side of Wisdom: The Date and Purpose of Genesis 3," in *A Light unto My Path: Old Testament Studies in Honor of Jacob M. Myers,* ed. Howard N. Bream, Ralph D. Heim, and Carey A. Moore (Philadelphia: Temple Univ. Press, 1974), 319–34; Nicholas Wyatt, "Interpreting the Creation and Fall Story in Genesis 2–3," *ZAW* 93 (1981) 10–21; John Van Seters, "The Creation of Man and the Creation of the King," *ZAW* 101 (1989) 333–42; Anne E. Gardner, "Genesis 2:4b—3: A Mythological Paradigm of Sexual Equality or of the Religious History of Pre-Exilic Israel?" *SJT* 43 (1990) 17.

10. Jacques Vermeylen, "Le Récit du Paradis et la Question des Origines du Pentateuque," *Bijdragen* 41 (1980) 230–50.

11. See Fredric Jameson, *The Political Unconscious: Narrative As a Socially Symbolic Act* (Ithaca: Cornell Univ. Press, 1981), 77–87; Keith W. Whitelam, "Between History and Literature: The Social Production of Israel's Traditions of Origin," *SJOT* 2 (1991) 66–69. Cf. Pamela J. Milne, "The Patriarchal Stamp of Scripture: The Implication of Structuralist Analyses for Feminist Hermeneutics," *JFSR* 5 (1989) 33.

12. See Richard H. Lowery, *The Reforming Kings: Cults and Society in First Temple Judah,* JSOTSup 120 (Sheffield: Sheffield Academic, 1991), 53–54, regarding competing modes of production in ancient Israel.

13. For other materialist studies of Genesis 2–3, see James M. Kennedy, "Peasants in Revolt: Political Allegory in Genesis 2–3," *JSOT* 47 (1990) 3–14. Cf. Guichard, "Approche 'matérialiste,'" 57–90.

14. See above, pp. 32–33.

15. Cf. Niels Peter Lemche, "Israel, History of (Premonarchic Period)," *ABD* 3:539; William G. Dever, "Israel, History of (Archaeology and the 'Conquest')," *ABD* 3:545–53; Robert B. Coote and Keith W. Whitelam, "The Emergence of Israel: Social Transformation and State Formation following the Decline in Late Bronze Age Trade," *Semeia* 37 (1986) 107–47; Norman K. Gottwald, *The Tribes of Yahweh* (Maryknoll, N.Y.: Orbis, 1979), 584–87.

16. Lemche, "Israel, History of," 536; Coote and Whitelam, "Emergence of Israel," 116–17.

17. Lemche, "Israel, History of," 537; Coote and Whitelam, "Emergence of Israel," 118–25. Both Mendenhall and Gottwald envision a "peasant revolt" against the urban elite. Although this theory is attractive, particularly in light of the present study, arguments against such a deliberate uprising are convincing. See Lemche, "Israel, History of," 540–41; and especially idem, *Early Israel: Anthropological and Historical Studies on the Israelite Society Before the Monarchy,* VTSup 37 (Leiden: Brill, 1985).

18. Lemche, "Israel, History of," 539.

19. Israel Finkelstein, "The Emergence of the Monarchy in Israel: The Environmental and Socio-Economic Aspects," *JSOT* 44 (1989) 61; Norman K. Gottwald, "The Participation of Free Agrarians in the Introduction of Monarchy to Ancient Israel: An Application of H. A. Landsberger's Framework for the Analysis of Peasants," *Semeia* 37 (1986) 87–88.

20. Coote and Whitelam, "Emergence of Israel," 135. Also Lemche, "Israel, History of," 542; Lawrence Stager, "The Archaeology of the Family in Ancient Israel," *BASOR* 260 (1985) 24–25.

21. David Hopkins, "Bare Bones: Putting Flesh on the Economics of Ancient Israel," in *The Origins of the Ancient Israelite States*, ed. Volkmar Fritz and Philip R. Davies, JSOTSup 228 (Sheffield: Sheffield Academic, 1996), 129–32; Paula M. McNutt, *Reconstructing the Society of Ancient Israel*, LAI (Louisville: Westminster John Knox, 1999), 164–71.

22. Coote and Whitelam, "Emergence of Israel," 135–38.

23. Lemche, "Israel, History of," 542.

24. Coote and Whitelam, "Emergence of Israel," 141. Also Gottwald, "Participation of Free Agrarians," 82–83; Marvin L. Chaney, "Systemic Study of the Israelite Monarchy," *Semeia* 37 (1986) 67–68.

25. Günther Wittenberg, "King Solomon and the Theologians," *Journal of Theology for Southern Africa* 63 (1988) 16–17.

26. John S. Holladay Jr., "The Kingdoms of Israel and Judah: Political and Economic Centralization in the Iron IIA-B (ca. 1000–750 B.C.E.)," in *The Archaeology of Society in the Holy Land*, ed. Thomas E. Levy (New York: Facts on File, 1995), 382.

27. Norman K. Gottwald, "Social Class As an Analytic and Hermeneutical Category in Biblical Studies," *JBL* 112 (1993) 6–9; idem, "Participation of Free Agrarians," 81–86; idem, "Sociology (Ancient Israel)," *ABD* 6:84; Chaney, "Systemic Study," 67–70.

28. Gottwald, "Sociology (Ancient Israel)," 82–83.

29. Cf. Guichard, "Approche 'matérialiste,'" 62–65.

30. Lemche, "Israel, History of," 539.

31. See especially Ps 2:7; 89:26-27; 2 Sam 7:14, where YHWH is described as "father" to the king, who becomes his "son" or "firstborn."

32. See Joseph Blenkinsopp, "The Family in First Temple Israel," in *Families in Ancient Israel*, ed. Leo G. Perdue et al. (Minneapolis: Fortress Press, 1997), 85–92, for a discussion of the effects of the state on the family household.

33. Cf. Henrietta L. Moore, "Women and the State," in *Feminism and Anthropology* (Minneapolis: Univ. of Minnesota Press, 1989), 128–85; Sherry B. Ortner, "The Virgin and the State," *Feminist Studies* 4 (1978) 19–33; Barbara S. Lesko, "Women of Egypt and the Ancient Near East," in *Becoming Visible: Women in European History*, ed. Renate Bridenthal, Claudia Koontz, and Susan Stuard, rev. ed. (Boston: Houghton Mifflin, 1987), 41–77; Ruby Rohrlich, "State Formation in Sumer and the Subjugation of

Women," *Feminist Studies* 6 (1980) 76–102; Ruby Rohrlich-Leavitt, "Women in Transition: Crete and Sumer," in *Becoming Visible*, 36–59.

34. Rohrlich, "State Formation," 76–102.

35. Lesko, "Women of Egypt," 62–63.

36. McNutt, *Reconstructing the Society of Ancient Israel*, 167; Meyers, *Discovering Eve*, 190.

37. Yehudi A. Cohen, "Ends and Means in Political Control: State Organization and the Punishment of Adultery, Incest, and the Violation of Celibacy," *AmAnth* 71 (1969) 661.

38. Ibid. In contrast to an inchoate incorporative state, a successful incorporative state has secured the transfer of loyalty and the exercise of authority from local nexuses to the state.

39. Ibid., 662.

40. Ibid., 665.

41. Naomi Steinberg, "The Deuteronomic Law Code and the Politics of State Centralization," in *Bible and the Politics of Exegesis: Essays in Honor of Norman K. Gottwald on His Sixty-Fifth Birthday*, ed. David Jobling, Peggy L. Day, and Gerald T. Sheppard (Cleveland: Pilgrim, 1991), 161–70; Louis Stulman, "Sex and Familial Crimes in the D Code: A Witness to Mores in Transition," *JSOT* 53 (1992) 47–64; idem, "Encroachment in Deuteronomy: Analysis of the Social World of the D Code," *JBL* 109 (1990) 613–32; Tikva Frymer-Kensky, "Deuteronomy," *WomBibCom*, 52–62. Cf. also Keith W. Whitelam, *The Just King: Monarchical Judicial Authority in Ancient Israel*, JSOTSup 12 (Sheffield: JSOT Press, 1979), 41–42.

42. Stulman, "Sex and Familial Crimes," 53.

43. Steinberg, "Deuteronomic Law Code," 166.

44. Ibid., 168; Stulman, "Sex and Familial Crimes," 62–63; Frymer-Kensky, "Deuteronomy," 61.

45. Frymer-Kensky, "Deuteronomy," 61.

46. This is not to say that the Yahwist does not mount a critique of the monarchy. It will be seen shortly that this critique is readily apparent within Genesis 2–3, as it tries to resolve the contradictions arising from a change in mode of production. Nevertheless, the Yahwist remains a particular voice within the dominant class, expressive of its values on the whole.

47. Earlier critiques of the sexism in Genesis 1–3 can be found in the writings of Shakespeare's contemporary Amelia Lanier (ca. 1570–1640), "Eve's Apology in Defense of Women," in *Salve Deus Rex Judaeorum*; and later in Elizabeth Cady Stanton's *The Woman's Bible* (1895).

48. See Phyllis Trible, "A Love Story Gone Awry," in *God and the Rhetoric of Sexuality*, OBT (Philadelphia: Fortress Press, 1978), 73–143. An earlier version can be found in idem, "Depatriarchalizing in Biblical Interpretation," *JAAR* 41 (1973) 30–48.

49. David J. A. Clines, "What Does Eve Do to Help? And Other Irredeemably Androcentric Orientations in Genesis 1–3," in *What Does Eve Do*

to Help? And Other Readerly Questions to the Old Testament, JSOTSup 94
(Sheffield: JSOT Press, 1990), 25–48; David Jobling, "Myth and Its Limits
in Genesis 2.4b—3.24," in *The Sense of Biblical Narrative: Structural Analyses in the Hebrew Bible,* ed. David Jobling, vol. 2, JSOTSup 39 (Sheffield:
JSOT Press, 1986), 17–43; Susan S. Lanser, "(Feminist) Criticism in the
Garden: Inferring Genesis 2–3," *Semeia* 41 (1988) 67–84; Milne, "Patriarchal Stamp of Scripture," 17–34; idem, "Feminist Interpretations of the
Bible: Then and Now," *BRev* 8, no. 5 (1992) 38–43, 52–55; idem, "Eve and
Adam: Is a Feminist Reading Possible?" *BRev* 4, no. 3 (1988) 12–21, 39;
Pardes, *Countertraditions in the Bible,* 13–38. See also the critique of Trible
in Gardner, "Genesis 2:4b—3," 3–15.

In her own reading of Genesis 2–3, Meyers, *Discovering Eve,* 72–121,
also attempts to recover a more positive interpretation for women by situating the text in its highland context. Nevertheless, both her contextualization
of the story during the premonarchic period and her neglect of the text as a
literary production within a particular socioeconomic mode of production
are problematic. See David Jobling, "Feminism and 'Mode of Production' in
Ancient Israel: Search for a Method," in *Bible and Politics of Exegesis,* ed.
Jobling, Day, and Sheppard, 246–47, and his critique of Meyers.

50. Terry Eagleton, *Criticism and Ideology: A Study in Marxist Literary
Theory* (1976; repr. London: Verso, 1990), 44–63.

51. Although conclusions regarding the dating of Genesis 2–3 and the interpretation of its royal elements vary, its Mesopotamian background and
royal symbolism have been consistently noted by biblical scholars. Cf. Manfred Hutter, "Adam als Gärtner und König (Gen 2:8-15)," *BZ* 30 (1986)
258–62; Walter Brueggemann, "From Dust to Kingship," *ZAW* 84 (1972)
1–18; Wallace, *Eden Narrative,* 65–99; Gardner, "Genesis 2:4b—3," 1–3;
Van Seters, "Creation of Man," 333–42; Wyatt, "Interpreting the Creation
and Fall," 14–15.

52. For a review of specific texts, see Westermann, *Genesis 1–11,* 221–22.

53. Wittenberg, "King Solomon," 25–28: "You will not die . . . you will be
like gods, knowing good from evil" (Gen 3:4).

54. For a fuller analysis see Guichard, "Approche 'matérialiste,'" 70–73.

55. *Yhwh ʾĕlōhîm:* 2:5, 7, et passim. For a literal translation as "YHWH, a
god," see Coote and Ord, *Bible's First History,* 51.

56. For the literary association of cultivated plants with man, see Terje
Stordalen, "Man, Soil, Garden: Basic Plot in Gen 2–3 Reconsidered," *JSOT*
53 (1992) 12–13.

57. Such as Meyers, *Discovering Eve,* 81–2; Mieke Bal, *Lethal Love: Feminist Literary Readings of Biblical Love Stories,* ISBL (Bloomington: Indiana
Univ. Press, 1987), 113–14.

58. Lanser, "(Feminist) Criticism," 72; Clines, "What Does Eve Do To
Help?" 40; Gardner, "Genesis 2:4b—3," 6–7; Jobling, "Myth and Its Limits,"
41; Beverly J. Stratton, *Out of Eden: Reading, Rhetoric, and Ideology in Gen-*

esis 2–3, JSOTSup 208 (Sheffield: Sheffield Academic, 1995), 105–8. Cf. Norman K. Gottwald, *The Hebrew Bible: A Socio-Literary Introduction* (Philadelphia: Fortress Press, 1985), 329.

59. Kennedy, "Peasants in Revolt," 5. Nicholas Wyatt, "When Adam Delved: The Meaning of Genesis iii 23," *VT* 38 (1988) 117–22; Van Seters, "Creation of Man," 333–42; and Brueggemann, "From Dust to Kingship," 1–18, argue that Adam is a royal figure. There are problems, however, with this interpretation, the foremost being that this royal figure is banished from the garden at the end of the story. According to Wallace, *Eden Narrative*, 162, "there is no convincing evidence that the man in Gen 2–3 is meant to be portrayed or understood in royal terms."

60. Cf. Ezek 31:8 and the vineyard King Ahab coveted for a vegetable garden in 1 Kgs 21:2. On the royal significance of the garden, see von Rad, *Genesis*, 77; Guichard, "Approche 'matérialiste,'" 71.

61. The structural analyses of Jobling, "Myth and Its Limits," 17–32; and Stordalen, "Man, Soil, Garden," 3–26, explore a narrative model, differing from the usual "creation and fall" model, that they argue would make more sense of the deep structures of the story. In this alternative model, the main plot is getting a man to till the earth. God becomes the "villain" who prevents the man from tilling the earth by taking the man to work in his garden.

62. Coote and Ord, *Bible's First History*, 54.

63. Wallace, *Eden Narrative*, 79.

64. Ibid., 115–32; Westermann, *Genesis 1–11*, 242–45. Cf. Guichard, "Approche 'matérialiste,'" 71, on the royal significance of the tree of the knowledge of good and evil.

65. Wallace, *Eden Narrative*, 129; J. A. Bailey, "Initiation and the Primal Woman in Gilgamesh and Genesis 2–3," *JBL* 89 (1970) 148; von Rad, *Genesis*, 81.

66. Kennedy, "Peasants in Revolt," 6–7; Coote and Ord, *Bible's First History*, 55; Wallace, *Eden Narrative*, 130–32.

67. Mendenhall, "Shady Side of Wisdom," 321–25; Kennedy, "Peasants in Revolt," 6–7.

68. Kennedy, "Peasants in Revolt," 8.

69. *ʿēzer kĕnegdô* does not imply equality between the genders (contra Trible), but rather a complementary entity of the same species. See Clines, "What Does Eve Do To Help?" 27–32; Gardner, "Genesis 2:4b—3," 5–7.

70. Clines, "What Does Eve Do To Help?" 34; Lisbeth Mikaelsson, "Sexual Polarity: An Aspect of the Ideological Structure in the Paradise Narrative, Gen 2,4—3,24," *Temenos* 16 (1980) 87. The focus on the biological role of woman in relation to man can be seen in 2:24, where the man becomes "one flesh" with his wife, which, on one level, signifies sexual intercourse. Moreover, in 3:20, the man names his woman Eve/Hawwah, which means "mother of all living," highlighting the biological result of this intercourse.

71. This is in keeping with the biological thinking of the time, in which the sperm was regarded as the person *in potentia*.

72. This is *contra* Trible, who argues that the phraseology of the naming (*qārā'* without the noun for "name," *šēm*) implies mutuality, not superiority. For a critique of this argument, see Lanser, "(Feminist) Criticism," 72–73; Gardner, "Genesis 2:4b—3," 8; Clines, "What Does Eve Do to Help?" 37–40; Mikaelsson, "Sexual Polarity," 87–88; Stratton, *Out of Eden*, 100–101.

73. Gardner, "Genesis 2:4b—3," 7, 9.

74. 2 Sam 5:1; 19:12-13; 1 Chr 11:1. Note the monarchical context.

75. Von Rad, *Genesis*, 85.

76. M. M. Bravmann, "The Original Meaning of '. . . A Man Leaves His Father and Mother . . . ,'" *Le Muséon* 88 (1975) 451.

77. Robert B. Lawton, "Genesis 2:24: Trite or Tragic," *JBL* 105 (1986) 98.

78. Angelo Tosato, "On Genesis 2:24," *CBQ* 52 (1990) 404–5.

79. See references in Westermann, *Genesis 1–11*, 233.

80. A. F. L. Beeston, "One Flesh," *VT* 36 (1986) 117.

81. Cohen, "Ends and Means," 667. Cf. Meyers, *Discovering Eve*, 86.

82. Cohen, "Ends and Means," 668.

83. Trible, *God and the Rhetoric of Sexuality*, 103–4.

84. Jobling, "Myth and Its Limits," 27–32.

85. Milne, "Patriarchal Stamp of Scripture," 24, following Leach.

86. K. R. Joines, "The Serpent in Genesis 3," *ZAW* 87 (1975) 1–11.

87. Wallace, *Eden Narrative*, 159–61.

88. William H. Propp, "Eden Sketches," in *The Hebrew Bible and Its Interpreters*, ed. William H. Propp, Baruch Halpern, and David Noel Freedman (Winona Lake, Ind.: Eisenbrauns, 1990), 197.

89. For the most extensive analysis, see Wallace, *Eden Narrative*, 161–72. See also pp. 155–59 on the identification of the serpent with the Asherah. On this relationship, see also Gardner, "Genesis 2:4b—3," 12–13; and Alberto J. Soggin, "The Fall of Man in the Third Chapter of Genesis," in *Old Testament and Oriental Studies*, BibOr 29 (Rome: Biblical Institute Press, 1975), 86–99.

90. Holter, "Serpent in Eden," 106–12.

91. Kennedy, "Peasants in Revolt," 8.

92. R. Walter Moberly, "Did the Serpent Get It Right?" *JTS* 39 (1988) 6.

93. Ibid., 6–7.

94. Ibid., 7.

95. See the review by Westermann, *Genesis 1–11*, 250–51. Also Coote and Ord, *Bible's First History*, 58–59; Robert Gordis, "The Significance of the Paradise Myth," *AJSL* 52 (1936) 86–94.

96. See 2 Sam 10:4; Isa 20:2-4; 47:2–3, where stripping enemies naked epitomizes their humiliation. As a symbol of vulnerability and powerlessness, see Isa 58:7; Ezek 16:4-5, 7; Job 1:21; 22:6; 24:7-10.

97. By stating that God "will greatly increase" the pains of childbearing, the text implies that this pain was always present. Along with many others, I read ʾiṣṣĕbônēk wĕhērōnēk as a hendiadys. For a reading of two separate words ("your toil and your pregnancies"), see Meyers, Discovering Eve, 95–105, who argues that they refer both to women's hard agrarian labor and to the demands of reproduction in the premonarchic settlement of the highlands.

98. The conjunction waw links 3:16a with 3:16b. Waw is most frequently rendered "and," but it can also mean "but," "yet," and "for," depending on context. In this context, I read waw as the conjunction "and," which further elaborates on the pains of childbearing that the woman will henceforth suffer. Irvin A. Busenitz, "A Woman's Desire for Man: Gen 3:16 Reconsidered," Grace Theological Journal 7 (1986) 203–12, does not think that the desire of the woman for the man and the fact that her husband will rule over her are part of God's punishment of the woman. Rather, they are the conditions under which the woman will suffer punishment.

99. Susan Foh, "What Is the Woman's Desire?" WTJ 37 (1975) 376–83.

100. Cf. Meyers, Discovering Eve, 109–17. John J. Schmitt, "Like Eve, Like Adam: mšl in Gen 3,16," Bib 72 (1991) 1–22, wants to read mšl as "to be like." The man is thus similar to the woman in his sexual desire for her. However, Schmitt does not deal satisfactorily with the preposition bĕ with mšl, which, in the majority of cases, means "to rule over." Schmitt also ignores the sociopolitical context of the text, which would affect his arguments.

101. Cf. Wallace, Eden Narrative, 143–44, 171.

102. Thus Guichard, "Approche 'matérialiste,'" 67. The construction mšl + bĕ describes the rule of kings or superiors over their subordinates: 1 Kgs 5:1; Josh 12:2; Neh 9:37; Isa 3:4; 19:4; Dan 11:3-5; Gen 37:8; Deut 15:6; Judg 8:22-23; 9:2; 14:4; 15:11. In arguing for a premonarchic provenance for the text, Meyers, Discovering Eve, 115, states: "It is intriguing to note that, except for the imperial dominion of David and Solomon or the eschatological hope for a similar extent of Judean control, the Israelite kings are never said to 'rule' over their people." However, I contend that the Davidic/Solomonic monarchy is the institution involved in the very production of this text and its ideology of social and gender relations.

103. 3:16, ʾiṣṣābônēk; 3:17, bĕʾiṣṣābôn.

104. See chap. 7, where the voice of woman will become an important trope in describing the verbal wiles and dangers represented in the book of Proverbs by the Other Woman, who seduces the foolish son away from God's laws.

105. Robert A. Oden Jr., "Grace or Status? Yahweh's Clothing of the First Humans," in The Bible without Theology: The Theological Tradition and Alternatives to It (San Francisco: Harper & Row, 1987), 104. Cf. also Gordon J. Wenham, Genesis 1–15, WBC 1 (Waco: Word, 1987), 84–85.

106. This is a description Manuel Peña uses of the "treacherous woman" theme found in Mexican folklore that "symbolically conflates class and gender by shifting the point of conflict from the public domain of the former to the domestic domain of the latter." Manuel Peña, "Class, Gender, and Machismo: The 'Treacherous-Woman' Folklore of Mexican Male Workers," *Gender and Society* 5 (1991) 30.

107. Ibid., 44.

108. This phrase is taken from a Roman Catholic Marian prayer, "Hail Holy Queen": "Hail Holy Queen, Mother of Mercy, our life our sweetness and Our hope. To thee do we cry, *poor banished children of Eve*; to thee do we send up our sighs, mourning and weeping in this valley of tears. Turn then, most gracious advocate, thine eyes of mercy toward us and after this our exile show unto us the blessed fruit of thy womb, Jesus. O clement, O loving, O sweet Virgin Mary! Pray for us, O Holy Mother of God, that we may be made worthy of the promises of God."

Chapter 5

1. See chap. 6 of this volume for an extended study of this metaphor in Ezekiel.

2. From Renita J. Weems, *Battered Love: Marriage, Sex, and Violence in the Hebrew Prophets* (Minneapolis: Fortress Press, 1995), 17–18.

3. Athalya Brenner, "Pornoprophetics Revisited: Some Additional Reflections," *JSOT* 70 (1996) 63–86; J. Cheryl Exum, "The Ethics of Biblical Violence against Women," in *The Bible in Ethics: The Second Sheffield Colloquium*, ed. John W. Rogerson et al., JSOTSup 207 (Sheffield: Sheffield Academic, 1995), 248–71; Harold Fisch, "Hosea: A Poetics of Violence," in *Poetry with a Purpose: Biblical Poetics and Interpretation*, ed. Harold Fisch, ISBL (Bloomington: Indiana Univ. Press, 1988), 136–57, 192–93; John Goldingay, "Hosea 1–3, Genesis 1–4, and a Masculist Interpretation," *HBT* 17 (1995) 37–44; Naomi Graetz, "God Is to Israel As Husband Is to Wife: The Metaphoric Battering of Hosea's Wife," in *A Feminist Companion to the Latter Prophets*, ed. Athalya Brenner, FCB 8 (Sheffield: Sheffield Academic, 1995), 126–45; F. Rachel Magdalene, "Ancient Near Eastern Treaty-Curses and the Ultimate Texts of Terror: A Study of the Language of Divine Sexual Abuse in the Prophetic Corpus," in *Feminist Companion to Latter Prophets*, 326–52; T. Drorah Setel, "Prophets and Pornography: Female Sexual Imagery," in *Feminist Interpretation of the Bible*, ed. Letty M. Russell (Philadelphia: Westminster, 1985), 86–95; Renita J. Weems, "Gomer: Victim of Violence or Victim of Metaphor?" *Semeia* 47 (1989) 87–104; Weems, *Battered Love*; Gale A. Yee, "Hosea," *WomBibCom*, 195–202; idem, "The Book of Hosea: Introduction, Commentary, and Reflections," *NIB* 7:195–297. Nelly Stienstra, *YHWH Is the Husband of His People: An Analysis of a Biblical*

Metaphor with a Special Reference to Translation (Kampen: Kok Pharos, 1993), simply glosses over these interpretive problems.

4. The classic example is that of T. H. Robinson, *Prophecy and the Prophets in Ancient Israel* (London: Duckworth, 1923), 52–58. On Hosea in particular see idem, *Die zwölf kleinen Propheten,* HAT 14 (Tübingen: Mohr/Siebeck, 1938), 1–2. For a review of the literature, see Graham I. Davies, *Hosea,* OTG (Sheffield: JSOT Press, 1993), 94–96.

5. Grace I. Emmerson, *Hosea: An Israelite Prophet in Judean Perspective,* JSOTSup 28 (Sheffield: JSOT Press, 1984); Martti Nissinen, *Prophetie, Redaktion und Fortschreibung im Hoseabuch: Studien zum Werdegang eines Prophetenbuches im Lichte von Hos 4 und 11,* AOAT 231 (Neukirchen-Vluyn: Neukirchener Verlag, 1991); Thomas Naumann, *Hoseas Erben: Strukturen der Nachinterpretation im Buch Hosea,* BWANT 131 (Stuttgart: Kohlhammer, 1991); Brian Peckham, "The Composition of Hosea," *HAR* 11 (1987) 331–53; idem, *History and Prophecy: The Development of Late Judean Literary Tradition,* ABRL (New York: Doubleday, 1993); and finally, my own work, *Composition and Tradition in the Book of Hosea: A Redaction Critical Investigation,* SBLDS 102 (Atlanta: Scholars, 1987).

6. For example, Francis I. Andersen and David Noel Freedman, *Hosea,* AB 24 (Garden City, N.Y.: Doubleday, 1980), 59; Douglas Stuart, *Hosea–Jonah,* WBC 31 (Waco: Word, 1987), 8; Thomas Edward McComiskey, *The Minor Prophets: An Exegetical and Expository Commentary,* vol. 1: *Hosea, Joel, and Amos* (Grand Rapids: Baker, 1992).

7. See Yee, *Composition,* 1–25, for a review of the literature.

8. This stands in contrast to my prior work on Hosea (*Composition*), where I argue that an exilic redactor was responsible for much of the work.

9. Yee, *Composition,* 55–57.

10. Norman K. Gottwald, "From Tribal Existence to Empire: The Socio-Historical Context for the Rise of the Hebrew Prophets," in *God and Capitalism: A Prophetic Critique of Market Society,* ed. J. Mark Thomas and Vernon Visick (Madison: AR Editions, 1991), 17; idem, "Sociology (Ancient Israel)," *ABD* 6:84–85. For an overview of the economy of the monarchy, see Richard H. Lowery, *The Reforming Kings: Cults and Society in First Temple Judah,* JSOTSup 120 (Sheffield: JSOT Press, 1991), 393–461.

11. Marvin L. Chaney, "Systemic Study of the Israelite Monarchy," *Semeia* 37 (1986) 67–68; Rainer Albertz, *A History of Israelite Religion in the Old Testament Period,* vol. 1: *From the Beginnings to the End of the Monarchy,* trans. John Bowden, OTL (Louisville: Westminster John Knox, 1994), 159–60; Judith A. Todd, "The Pre-Deuteronomistic Elijah Cycle," in *Elijah and Elisha in Socioliterary Perspective,* ed. Robert B. Coote, SemeiaSt (Atlanta: Scholars, 1992), 5–8; Joseph Blenkinsopp, *Sage, Priest, Prophet: Religious and Intellectual Leadership in Ancient Israel,* LAI (Louisville: Westminster John Knox, 1995), 149–54.

12. David C. Hopkins, "The Dynamics of Agriculture in Monarchical Israel," *SBLSP 1983*, 187–93; idem, "Bare Bones: Putting Flesh on the Economics of Ancient Israel," in *The Origins of the Ancient Israelite States*, ed. Volkmar Fritz and Philip R. Davies, JSOTSup 228 (Sheffield: Sheffield Academic, 1996), 133.

13. D. N. Premnath, "Latifundialization and Isaiah 5.8-10," *JSOT* 40 (1988) 49–54; Keith W. Whitelam, "King and Kingship," *ABD* 4:40.

14. Hopkins, "Dynamics of Agriculture," 196; Marvin L. Chaney, "Bitter Bounty: The Dynamics of Political Economy Critiqued by the Eighth-Century Prophets," in *Reformed Faith and Economics*, ed. Robert L. Stivers (Lanham, Md.: Univ. Press of America, 1989), 22–27; Alice A. Keefe, "The Female Body, the Body Politic and the Land: A Sociopolitical Reading of Hosea 1–2," in *Feminist Companion to Latter Prophets*, ed. Brenner, 94.

15. Hopkins, "Dynamics of Agriculture," 199–202; Chaney, "Bitter Bounty," 22–23; Gottwald, "From Tribal Existence to Empire," 17.

16. Hos 2:8-9; 7:14; 12:1; cf. 2:5, 22; 8:7; 9:2. Keefe, "Female Body," 70–100, correlates Hosea's sexually charged critique with this form of agribusiness.

17. John Andrew Dearman, *Property Rights in the Eighth-Century Prophets: The Conflict and Its Background*, SBLDS 106 (Atlanta: Scholars, 1988), 132–33, notes that instead of the "anonymous rich and powerful of popular reconstruction," those profiteering from surplus income were mostly state officials and functionaries. See also Blenkinsopp, *Sage, Priest, Prophet*, 153–54; Bernhard Lang, *Monotheism and the Prophetic Minority: An Essay in Biblical History and Sociology*, SWBA 1 (Sheffield: Almond, 1983), 114–27.

18. See Dearman, *Property Rights*, 132–35, on a redistributing economy. See also Albertz, *History of Israelite Religion*, 1:161–62.

19. Hopkins, "Dynamics of Agriculture," 187–93. For a more extended discussion, see idem, *The Highlands of Canaan*, SWBA 3 (Sheffield: Almond, 1985), 213–61.

20. Hopkins, "Dynamics of Agriculture," 200.

21. See ibid., 181–83, for the labor, social cooperation, and support needed for terrace construction.

22. Chaney, "Bitter Bounty," 24.

23. Gottwald, "Sociology (Ancient Israel)," 84; Chaney, "Bitter Bounty," 25–26; Albertz, *History of Israelite Religion*, 1:160–61; Lang, *Monotheism*, 114–27. See Norman K. Gottwald, "A Hypothesis about Social Class in Monarchic Israel in the Light of Contemporary Studies of Social Class and Social Stratification," in *The Hebrew Bible in Its Social World and in Ours*, SemeiaSt (Atlanta: Scholars, 1993), 139–64, for an extended analysis of ruling-class extraction of surplus during the Israelite monarchy.

24. Dearman, *Property Rights*, 132–33, 140; Albertz, *History of Israelite Religion*, 1:165–67; Lowery, *Reforming Kings*, 11.

25. Tamis Hoover Rentería, "The Elijah/Elisha Stories: A Socio-Cultural Analysis of Prophets and People in Ninth-Century B.C.E. Israel," in *Elijah and Elisha in Socioliterary Perspective,* ed. Robert B. Coote, SemeiaSt (Atlanta: Scholars, 1992), 89–95; Dearman, *Property Rights,* 136–37.

26. See J. Maxwell Miller and John H. Hayes, *A History of Ancient Israel and Judah* (Philadelphia: Westminster, 1986), 326–37; John H. Hayes and Jeffrey K. Kuan, "The Final Years of Samaria (730–720)," *Bib* 72 (1991) 153–81.

27. See Miller and Hayes, *History of Ancient Israel and Judah,* 320–22; Hayes and Kuan, "Final Years," 153–81. Cf. 2 Kgs 15:19-20; 17:3-4; Hos 5:13; 7:8-12; 8:10; 10:6; 12:1. For an analysis of the economic complexities of the Assyrian Empire, see J. N. Postgate, "The Economic Structure of the Assyrian Empire," in *Power and Propaganda: A Symposium on Ancient Empires,* ed. Mogens Trolle Larsen (Copenhagen: Akademisk Forlag, 1979), 193–221.

28. Wesley I. Toews, *Monarchy and Religious Institution in Israel under Jeroboam I,* SBLMS 47 (Atlanta: Scholars, 1993), 166.

29. Albertz, *History of Israelite Religion,* 1:162–63. See also the analysis of Mario Liverani, "The Ideology of the Assyrian Empire," in *Power and Propaganda,* ed. Larsen, 297–317, on the hierarchical structure and dynamics of colonization, which can be applied to the Israelite scene.

30. For example, Helmer Ringgren, *Israelite Religion,* trans. David Green (Philadelphia: Fortress Press, 1966), 41–54. For a critique of these positions, see Delbert R. Hillers, "Analyzing the Abominable: Our Understanding of Canaanite Religion," *JQR* 75 (1985) 253–69; Albertz, *History of Israelite Religion,* 1:172–75.

31. Major scholars proposing this model include George E. Mendenhall, "The Hebrew Conquest of Palestine," *BA* 25 (1962) 66–87; and Norman K. Gottwald, *The Tribes of Yahweh: A Sociology of the Religion of Liberated Israel, 1250–1050 B.C.* (Maryknoll, N.Y.: Orbis, 1979). See also the critique and modification of Gottwald by Niels Peter Lemche, *Early Israel: Anthropological and Historical Studies on the Israelite Society before the Monarchy,* VTSup 37 (Leiden: Brill, 1985). For a review of the literature, see J. D. Martin, "Israel As a Tribal Society," in *The World of Ancient Israel: Sociological, Anthropological and Political Perspectives,* ed. R. E. Clements (Cambridge: Cambridge Univ. Press, 1989), 95–118.

32. William G. Dever, "Unresolved Issues in the Early History of Israel: Toward a Synthesis of Archaeological and Textual Reconstructions," in *The Bible and the Politics of Exegesis: Essays in Honor of Norman K. Gottwald on His Sixty-Fifth Birthday,* ed. David Jobling, Peggy L. Day, and Gerald T. Sheppard (Cleveland: Pilgrim, 1991), 195–208.

33. Regarding YHWH as a God directly involved with fertility from the beginning of Israelite worship, see Albertz, *History of Israelite Religion,* 1:89–90.

34. Mark S. Smith, *The Early History of God: Yahweh and the Other Deities in Ancient Israel*, 2nd ed. (Grand Rapids: Eerdmans, 2002), 6–14.

35. Ibid., 160–99; and the essays by Coogan, McCarter, Dever, and Holladay in Patrick D. Miller Jr., Paul D. Hanson, and S. Dean McBride, eds., *Ancient Israelite Religion: Essays in Honor of Frank Moore Cross* (Philadelphia: Fortress Press, 1987). Also, consult the review article by William G. Dever, "'Will the Real Israel Please Stand Up?' Part II: Archaeology and the Religions of Ancient Israel," *BASOR* 298 (1995) 37–58.

36. Robert Karl Gnuse, *No Other Gods: Emergent Monotheism in Israel*, JSOTSup 241 (Sheffield: Sheffield Academic, 1997), 73.

37. Albertz, *History of Israelite Religion*, 1:172–75.

38. For this distinction see J. Andrew Dearman, *Religion and Culture in Ancient Israel* (Peabody, Mass.: Hendrickson, 1992), 36. Regarding Hosea, see Smith, *Early History of God*, 190; Lang, *Monotheism*, 30–36; Morton Smith, *Palestinian Parties and Politics That Shaped the Old Testament* (New York: Columbia Univ. Press, 1971), 42–45.

39. David L. Petersen, "Israel and Monotheism: The Unfinished Agenda," in *Canon, Theology, and Old Testament Interpretation: Essays in Honor of Brevard S. Childs*, ed. Gene M. Tucker, David L. Petersen, and Robert R. Wilson (Philadelphia: Fortress Press, 1988), 97; Smith, *Early History of God*, 1–3.

40. Smith, *Early History of God*, 11, 191–99; Lang, *Monotheism*, 13–56; and several essays in W. Dietrich and M. A. Klopfenstein, eds., *Ein Gott allein? JHWH-Verehrung und biblischer Monotheismus im Kontext der israelitischen und altorientalischen Religionsgeschichte* (Freiburg: Universitätsverlag Freiburg, 1994). Baruch Halpern, "'Brisker Pipes Than Poetry': The Development of Israelite Monotheism," in *Judaic Perspectives on Ancient Israel*, ed. Jacob Neusner, Baruch A. Levine, and Ernest S. Frerichs (Philadelphia: Fortress Press, 1987), 77–115, distinguishes an unself-conscious monotheism in early Israel that was monolatrous and henotheistic from a later, radically self-conscious monotheism. Mark S. Smith, "Yahweh and Other Deities in Ancient Israel: Observations on Old Problems and Recent Trends," in *Ein Gott allein?* 225–26, argues against this lack of terminological precision.

41. For the secondary literature see J. A. Emerton, "'Yahweh and His Asherah': The Goddess or Her Symbol?" *VT* 49 (1999) 315–37; Albertz, *History of Israelite Religion*, 1:85–87; Georg Braulik, O.S.B., "The Rejection of the Goddess Asherah in Israel: Was the Rejection as Late as Deuteronomistic and Did It Further the Oppression of Women in Israel?" in *The Theology of Deuteronomy*, trans. Ulrika Lindblad (N. Richland Hills, Tex.: BIBAL, 1994), 167–71; John Day, "Asherah," *ABD* 1:483–87; idem, "Asherah in the Hebrew Bible and Northwest Semitic Literature," *JBL* 105 (1986) 385–408; William G. Dever, "Asherah, Consort of Yahweh? New Evidence from Kuntillet 'Ajrûd," *BASOR* 255 (1984) 21–37; David Noel Freedman, "Yahweh of

Samaria and His Asherah," *BA* 50 (1987) 241–49; Judith M. Hadley, "Yahweh and 'His Asherah': Archaeological and Textual Evidence for the Cult of the Goddess," in *Ein Gott allein?* ed. Dietrich and Klopfenstein, 235–68; Judith M. Hadley, "From Goddess to Literary Construct: The Transformation of Asherah into Ḥokmah," in *A Feminist Companion to Reading the Bible: Approaches, Methods and Strategies,* ed. Athalya Brenner and Carole Fontaine, FCB 11 (Sheffield: Sheffield Academic, 1997), 360–99; Patrick D. Miller Jr., "The Absence of the Goddess in Israelite Religion," *HAR* 10 (1986) 239–48; Saul M. Olyan, *Asherah and the Cult of Yahweh in Israel,* SBLMS 34 (Atlanta: Scholars, 1988); Smith, *Early History of God,* xxx–xxxv, 108–47; idem, "God Male and Female in the Old Testament: Yahweh and His 'Asherah,'" *TS* 48 (1987) 333–40. Ze'ev Meshel, "Did Yahweh Have a Consort?" *BAR* 5 (1979) 31, is open to the possibility of a consort for Yahweh, finding it "a thoroughly blasphemous notion, but one that seems consistent with the diverse religious influences at Kuntillet 'Ajrud." For iconography of the goddess, see the massive study of Urs Winter, *Frau und Göttin: Exegetische und ikonographische Studien zum weiblichen Gottesbild im Alten Israel und in dessen Umwelt,* OBO 53 (Göttingen: Vandenhoeck & Ruprecht, 1983).

42. Albertz, *History of Israelite Religion,* 1:85.

43. Cf. Raphael Patai, *The Hebrew Goddess* (Philadelphia: Ktav, 1967).

44. Ziony Zevit, "The Khirbet el-Qôm Inscription Mentioning a Goddess," *BASOR* 255 (1984) 39–47.

45. William G. Dever, "Ancient Israelite Religion: How to Reconcile the Differing Textual and Artifactual Portraits?" in *Ein Gott allein?* ed. Dietrich and Klopfenstein, 111.

46. John S. Holladay Jr., "Religion in Israel and Judah under the Monarchy: An Explicitly Archaeological Approach," in *Ancient Israelite Religion,* ed. Miller et al., 275–82; Braulik, "Rejection," 171.

47. See G. I. Emmerson, "A Fertility Goddess in Hosea IV 17-19?" *VT* 24 (1974) 492–97; Helgard Balz-Cochois, "Gomer oder die Macht der Astarte. Versuch einer feministischen Interpretation von Hos 1–4," *Evangelische Theologie* 42 (1982) 37–65; J. Day, "Asherah," 486; Braulik, "Rejection," 165–82; F. Gangloff and J.-C. Haelewyck, "Osée 4,17-19: Un Marzeah en l'honneur de la déesse 'Anat?" ETL 71 (1995) 370–82; Marie-Theres Wacker, "Traces of the Goddess in the Book of Hosea," in *Feminist Companion to Latter Prophets,* ed. Brenner, 219–41.

48. Judith McInlay, "Bringing the Unspeakable to Speech in Hosea," *Pacifica* 9 (1996) 121–33; William D. Whitt, "The Divorce of Yahweh and Asherah in Hos 2.4—7.12ff," *SJOT* 6 (1992) 31–67. See the critique of Whitt by John J. Schmitt, "Yahweh's Divorce in Hosea 2—Who Is That Woman?" *SJOT* 9 (1995) 119–32. Whitt (57) claims: "In Hosea's metaphoric speech, Yahweh is 'divorcing' the mother goddess Asherah because the Israelites act out fertility rites in which she and Baal have sexual intercourse to give the land fertility. As Yahweh's wife, Asherah is committing

'adultery.' Hosea is angry because the Israelites believe that even though she is properly Yahweh's wife, it is she and Baal who are responsible for the fertility of the land."

According to Olyan, *Asherah*, 38–61, however, Asherah was never the consort of Baal in the piety of ancient Israel. She became associated with Baal only in the Deuteronomistic polemic that condemned both deities.

49. Emmerson, "Fertility Goddess," 492–97; Balz-Cochois, "Gomer," 37–65; J. Day, "Asherah," 385–408; Braulik, "Rejection," 165–82; Gangloff and Haelewyck, "Osée 4,17-19," 370–82; and Wacker, "Traces of the Goddess," 219–41, single out Hos 4:12, 17-19; 9:13; and 14:8 (MT 9), where ambiguous feminine references and wordplay, they argue, indicate the presence of the goddess.

50. This is the critique of M. Arnaud, "La Prostitution sacrée en Mésopotamie, un mythe historiographique?" *RHR* 183 (1973), 111, on the academic study of "sacred prostitution." He argues that the supposed ancient practice was "a historiographic myth."

51. Cf. Michael C. Astour, "Tamar the Hierodule: An Essay in the Method of Vestigial Motifs," *JBL* 85 (1966) 185–96; O. J. Baab, "Prostitution," *IDB* 3:932–34; Beatrice S. Brooks, "Fertility Cult Functionaries in the OT," *JBL* 60 (1941) 227–53; Louis M. Epstein, "Sacred Prostitution," in *Sex Laws and Customs in Judaism* (New York: Bloch, 1948), 152–57; Edwin O. James, *The Cult of the Mother-Goddess: An Archaeological and Documentary Study* (New York: Praeger, 1959), 81–84; Lang, *Monotheism*, 24; Bonnie MacLachlan, "Sacred Prostitution and Aphrodite," *Studies in Religion* 21 (1991) 145–62; Edwin M. Yamauchi, "Cultic Prostitution: A Case Study in Cultural Diffusion," in *Orient and Occident: Essays Presented to Cyrus H. Gordon,* ed. Harry A. Hoffner, AOAT 22 (Neukirchen-Vluyn: Neukirchener Verlag, 1973), 213–22.

52. John L. McKenzie, *Dictionary of the Bible* (New York: Macmillan, 1965), 700, emphasis added.

53. Baab, "Prostitution," 933.

54. Yamauchi, "Cultic Prostitution," 222.

55. Epstein, "Sacred Prostitution," 154.

56. Cf. Stienstra, YHWH *Is the Husband*, 98–100, 139–41; Irene Kerasote Rallis, "Nuptial Imagery in the Book of Hosea: Israel As the Bride of Yahweh," *St. Vladimir's Theological Quarterly* 34 (1990) 197–219; F. C. Fensham, "The Marriage Metaphor in Hosea for the Covenant Relationship between the Lord and His People," *JNSL* 12 (1984) 71–87; Hans Walter Wolff, *Hosea,* trans. Gary Stansell, Hermeneia (Philadelphia: Fortress Press, 1974), 14–15; James Luther Mays, *Hosea,* OTL (Philadelphia: Westminster, 1969), 25–26; Balz-Cochois, "Gomer," 37–65; P. A. Kruger, "Israel, the Harlot (Hos. 2:4-9)," *JNSL* 11 (1983), 107–16; Gerrie Snyman, "Social Reality and Religious Language in the Marriage Metaphor in Hosea 1–3," *OTE* 6 (1993) 90–112; and others.

57. Albertz, *History of Israelite Religion,* 1:172–73.

58. For a review and critique of the unfounded claims of thinkers past and present regarding sacred prostitution, see Arnaud, "La Prostitution sacrée," 111–15; E. J. Fisher, "Cultic Prostitution in the Ancient Near East? A Reappraisal," *BTB* 6 (1976) 225–36; Winter, *Frau und Göttin,* 334–42; Robert A. Oden Jr., "Religious Identity and the Sacred Prostitution Accusation," in *The Bible without Theology: The Theological Tradition and Alternatives to It* (San Francisco: Harper & Row, 1987), 135–53; Hillers, "Analyzing the Abominable," 253–69; Mayer I. Gruber, "Hebrew *Qedeshah* and Her Canaanite and Akkadian Cognates," *UF* 18 (1986) 133–48; Jo Ann Hackett, "Can a Sexist Model Liberate Us? Ancient Near Eastern 'Fertility' Goddesses," *JFSR* 5 (1989) 65–76; Tikva Frymer-Kensky, *In the Wake of the Goddesses: Women, Culture, and the Biblical Transformation of Pagan Myth* (New York: Free Press, 1992), 199–202; Joan Goodnick Westenholz, "Tamar, *Qĕdēšâ, Qadištu,* and Sacred Prostitution in Mesopotamia," *HTR* 82 (1989) 245–65; Richard A. Henshaw, *Female and Male: The Cultic Personnel: The Bible and the Rest of the Ancient Near East,* Princeton Theological Monograph Series 31 (Allison Park, Pa.: Pickwick, 1994), 218–56.

59. Bernhard Lang, *Wisdom and the Book of Proverbs: A Hebrew Goddess Redefined* (New York: Pilgrim, 1986), 98. The quotations Lang cites are by cultural critic Edward W. Said, *Orientalism* (New York: Vintage, 1979), 190.

60. Gruber, "Hebrew *Qedeshah,*" 138.

61. Ibid., 138–48; and Fisher, "Cultic Prostitution," 227–28. *Qĕdēšâ* in Hos 4:14b is customarily translated "cult prostitute," although the word means literally "holy one." *Qĕdēšâ* does have particular associations with the cult, but the word does not inherently have sexual connotations.

62. Fisher, "Cultic Prostitution," 228.

63. This is not to say that female sexuality was never part of the fertility cults. Phyllis Bird, "The Place of Women in the Israelite Cultus," in *Ancient Israelite Religion,* ed. Miller et al., 406; idem, "'To Play the Harlot': An Inquiry into an Old Testament Metaphor," in *Gender and Difference in Ancient Israel,* ed. Peggy L. Day (Minneapolis: Fortress Press, 1989), 87–88; and Renate Jost, "Von 'Huren und Heiligen': Ein sozialgeschichtlicher Beitrag," in *Feministische Hermeneutik und Erstes Testament: Analysen und Interpretationen,* ed. Hedwig Jahnow (Stuttgart: Kohlhammer, 1994), 135, allow for the possibility that rituals of the *qĕdēšôt* (hierodules) may have included sexuality, but may not have been regarded as "prostitution" by the performers.

64. Oden, "Religious Identity," 132–33.

65. Ibid., 133–35.

66. Although scholars have noted the connections between cult and king (see, e.g., Robert Gnuse, "Calf, Cult, and King: The Unity of Hosea 8:1-13," *BZ* 26 [1982] 83–92), they have not made correlations of cult and king with the husband/wife metaphor.

67. Thus Kruger, "Israel, the Harlot," 109 n. 8, who argues that *znh* "is not once applied to [Israel's] external politics," He glosses over 8:9-10 by commenting that Hosea only "hints at the idea of harlotry in a political sphere." He also overlooks the fact that the image of the "wild ass" in Hos 8:9 has deeply sexual connotations (Jer 2:24). Moreover, one should not restrict the use of *znh* in Hos 9:1 to the cult. The reference to the threshing floor and wine vat could refer to the state's agricultural intensification of grain, wine, and oil, as I argue below.

68. In Yee, *Composition*, 289, 305–6, I correlated the *earliest* tradition of the "harlot" metaphor in the book of Hosea with Israel's foreign policy. Later redactors interpreted this metaphor as the "polluted" cult.

69. See Margaret S. Odell, "Who Were the Prophets in Hosea?" *HBT* 18 (1996) 78–95, regarding the institutional prophets condemned by Hosea.

70. See also Jer 2:8, in which priest, prophet, *and* leaders are grouped together in a divine accusation.

71. The perpetrator of political intrigue in 7:1-7 seems to be the "gang of priests" described in 6:9. See Yee, "Hosea," *NIB* 7:255–57.

72. The use of "adulterers" (*mĕnāʾăpîm*) to describe the priests, rather than "promiscuity" (*zny*), which is usually employed, is due to the wordplay on "baker" (*ʾōpeh*) in 7:4, a figure associated with the oven metaphor that appears throughout 7:4-7.

73. On the unity of the chapter, see Gnuse, "Calf, Cult, and King," 83–92.

74. This futility is dramatized in 8:7 through a literary device known as "pseudo-sorites." See M. O'Connor, "The Pseudo-Sorites in Hebrew Verse," in *Perspectives on Language and Text: Essays and Poems in Honor of F. I. Andersen's Sixtieth Birthday*, ed. E. W. Conrad and E. W. Newing (Winona Lake, Ind.: Eisenbrauns, 1987), 239–53.

75. Lowery, *Reforming Kings*, 119–120; Karel van der Toorn, "Theology, Priests, and Worship in Canaan and Ancient Israel," *CANE* 3:2440–41.

76. Cf. Gösta W. Ahlström, *Royal Administration and National Religion in Ancient Palestine*, SHANE 1 (Leiden: Brill, 1982), 8: "From what has been said above, it should be evident that religion was an arm of the royal administration. By sending out and placing military personnel and civil servants, including priests, in district capitals, at strategic points, in store cities, and in the national sanctuaries, the central government saw to it that both civil and cultic laws were upheld and that taxes were paid." For a study of the cultic legitimation of kingship in Hosea, see Helmut Utzschneider, *Hosea, Prophet vor dem Ende*, OBO 31 (Göttingen: Vandenhoeck & Ruprecht, 1980). Regarding the relationship between religion and the northern kingdom of Israel, see Toews, *Monarchy*.

77. Holladay, "Religion in Israel and Judah," 249–99; Lowery, *Reforming Kings*, 112–16. Regarding Bethel and Samaria, see Ahlström, *Royal Administration*, 58–62.

78. For what follows see Victor H. Matthews and Don C. Benjamin, *Social World of Ancient Israel: 1250–587* B.C.E. (Peabody, Mass.: Hendrickson, 1993), 187–95.

79. Cf. Deut 14:28-29 and 26:12, which speak of a "poor tithe" that is not deposited in the central sanctuary during the third year of a growing cycle, but is distributed to the needy in one's area.

80. Matthews and Benjamin, *Social World*, 188; Lowery, *Reforming Kings*, 80; and Blenkinsopp, *Sage, Priest, Prophet*, 152.

81. Matthews and Benjamin, *Social World*, 192.

82. Cf. Yee, "Hosea," *NIB* 7:239; Davies, *Hosea*, 24–25.

83. Smith, *Palestinian Parties*, 34–37, 43–48; Lang, *Monotheism*, 13–56; Smith, *Early History of God*, 195–96; Joseph Blenkinsopp, *A History of Prophecy in Israel: From the Settlement in the Land to the Hellenistic Period* (Philadelphia: Westminster, 1983), 104–5; Albertz, *History of Israelite Religion*, 1:61–62; Petersen, "Israel and Monotheism," 94–95; W. S. Boshoff, "Yahweh As God of Nature: Elements of the Concept of God in the Book of Hosea," *JNSL* 18 (1992) 33; Else Kragelund Holt, *Prophesying the Past: The Use of Israel's History in the Book of Hosea*, JSOTSup 194 (Sheffield: Sheffield Academic, 1995), 107–14; Gunther H. Wittenberg, "Amos and Hosea: A Contribution to the Problem of the 'Prophetenschweigen' in the Deuteronomistic History (Dtr)," *OTE* 6 (1993) 302–9.

84. Smith, *Palestinian Parties*, 35–36.

85. Smith, *Early History of God*, 187; Lang, *Monotheism*, 30–49.

86. See Lang, *Monotheism*, 27–28, for a consideration of the financial impact of Jezebel's cult in Israel. For an analysis of Israel's socioeconomic and political situation during the time of Elijah and Elisha, see Rentería, "Elijah/Elisha Stories," 83–95.

87. Smith, *Early History of God*, 187. It may be fair to say that a correlation exists between Omride promotion and strengthening of international ties and Elijah's proclamation of a more universal YHWH.

88. Smith, *Early History of God*, 187.

89. See ibid., 65–71.

90. Albertz, *History of Israelite Religion*, 1:172–73.

91. Baruch Halpern, "The Baal (and the Asherah) in Seventh-Century Judah: Yhwh's Retainers Retired," in *Konsequente Traditionsgeschichte: Festschrift für Klaus Baltzer zum 65. Geburtstag*, ed. Rüdiger Bartelmus, Thomas Krüger, and Helmut Utzschneider, OBO 126 (Göttingen: Vandenhoeck & Ruprecht, 1993), 148–49, emphasis added. Also idem, "Development of Israelite Monotheism," 93–94; Toews, *Monarchy*, 153–54.

92. Toews, *Monarchy*, 166; Keefe, "Female Body," 91–93. Blenkinsopp, *Sage, Priest, Prophet*, 150, summarizes the political and religious circumstances of Hosea's time succinctly: "By the eighth century B.C.E., [Israel and Judah] were moving inexorably toward a situation in which the coercive

power of the state, supported by a class of nouveaux riches parasitical on the monarchy and court, legitimated by state cults exercising their own forms of hierocratic coercion, and resting on a broad basis of peasant serfdom and slavery, was reaching out into every sphere of social life. That this process did not work its way to its anticipated term was due in the first place to Assyrian intervention, which terminated the existence of one kingdom and reduced the other to vassalage. But it was also the result of sustained protest coming not from the peasant class, which lacked the resources and leadership to generate it, but from the educated and literate stratum, in some instances within the 'system' itself." According to Blenkinsopp, Hosea (along with Amos, Isaiah, and Micah) belonged to this group of upper-class intellectual dissidents, who considered themselves heirs to the prophets of old but demurred at describing themselves as prophets because of the monarchy's institutionalization of prophecy to legitimate its own ends (pp. 142–43).

93. Hos 9:10-17 was most likely proclaimed during the Feast of Sukkoth. See Yee, "Hosea," *NIB* 7:265–70. The God who remembers focuses on two themes that Sukkoth commemorates: the wilderness period and fertility.

94. Cf. Deut 32:10-14; Ezek 16:6-14.

95. Albertz, *History of Israelite Religion,* 1:62–64.

96. See Marsha C. White, *The Elijah Legends and Jehu's Coup,* BJS 311 (Atlanta: Scholars, 1997), 3–11, for a discussion of the similarities between Moses and Elijah.

97. Albertz, *History of Israelite Religion,* 1:64.

98. Ibid., 1:122; Norman K. Gottwald, *The Hebrew Bible: A Socio-Literary Introduction* (Philadelphia: Fortress Press, 1985), 361.

99. Toews, *Monarchy,* 166; Albertz, *History of Israelite Religion,* 1:174–77; Gottwald, "From Tribal Existence to Empire," 18–20.

100. Carol Meyers, *Discovering Eve: Ancient Israelite Women in Context* (New York: Oxford Univ. Press, 1988), 189–96.

101. Phyllis Bird, "Women's Religion in Ancient Israel," in *Women's Earliest Records from Ancient Egypt and Western Asia,* ed. B. S. Lesko, BJS 166 (Atlanta: Scholars, 1989), 285–88. Bird offers an excellent attempt at reconstructing the religious experiences of Israelite women in "Place of Women," 397–419.

102. Dever, "Will the Real Israel," 45–48, 53. See also Bird, "Place of Women," 397–419; idem, "Women's Religion in Ancient Israel," 283–98; idem, "Israelite Religion and the Faith of Israel's Daughters: Reflections on Gender and Religious Definition," in *Bible and Politics of Exegesis,* ed. Jobling, Day, and Sheppard, 97–108. Holladay, "Religion in Israel and Judah," 269, remarks that the social function of "nonconformist" religion is an attempt by certain individuals or groups to rectify perceived weaknesses in the established religion—for example, the exclusion of women or the "unclean" from important aspects of cult. For the worship of Asherah in royal

circles, especially among the queen mothers in Judah, see Olyan, *Asherah*, 6–8; and Susan Ackerman, "The Queen Mother and the Cult in Ancient Israel," *JBL* 112 (1993) 385–401.

103. Olyan, *Asherah*, 22.

104. Ackerman, "Queen Mother," 400–401.

105. Hos 2:8, 13, 17; 11:2; 13:1. I am assuming with Halpern, "Baal (and the Asherah)," 130, that the expression "the baal" (2:8) should be understood as a collective plural.

106. Albertz, *History of Israelite Religion*, 1:144–45.

107. Toews, *Monarchy*, 166–68.

108. Ideology is understood here not simply as a set of ideas, but as material practices embodied within patterns of social behavior and social institutions.

109. I did not include Hosea 3 in this analysis, primarily because its dating is so disputable, and because my argument regarding the interrelations between cult, monarchy, and marital ideology can already be made by focusing on Hosea 1–2.

110. See, e.g., those cited in n. 56.

111. Consult chap. 3 of this book for a detailed discussion of how ideologies of honor and shame bolstered male social structures of patrilineality, patrilocality, and patrimony.

112. See especially Ken Stone, *Sex, Honor and Power in the Deuteronomistic History: A Narratological and Anthropological Analysis*, JSOTSup 234 (Sheffield: Sheffield Academic, 1997), 74–84; Athalya Brenner, *The Intercourse of Knowledge: On Gendered Sex and Desire in the Hebrew Bible*, BibIntSer 26 (Leiden: Brill, 1997), 138–43, on the dynamics of male rape for male-male power relations. The raped man is violently cast into the passive position of the female.

113. See authors cited in n. 3.

114. Howard Eilberg-Schwartz, *God's Phallus and Other Problems for Men and Monotheism* (Boston: Beacon, 1994), 20, 97–102.

115. Such was the case for Genesis 2–3, which also functions as a "symbolic alibi," concealing the conflicts between the ruling elite and the peasant under the cover of a clash between man and woman. See chap. 4. Francis Landy, *Hosea*, RNBC (Sheffield: Sheffield Academic, 1995), 37, describes this shift in gender as "mystification," "displacement," and misogyny in drag.

116. So argues Keefe, "Female Body," 76, 97.

117. Andersen and Freedman, *Hosea*, 157–62.

118. Bird, "To Play the Harlot," 80–89.

119. See H. H. Rowley, "The Marriage of Hosea," in *Men of God* (London: Nelson, 1963), 66–97; and Davies, *Hosea*, 79–92, for fuller discussions.

120. Phyllis A. Bird, "The Harlot As Heroine: Narrative Art and Social Presupposition in Three Old Testament Texts," *Semeia* 46 (1989) 121.

121. Whitelam, "King and Kingship," 40.

122. Marvin H. Pope, *Song of Songs*, AB 7C (Garden City, N.Y.: Double-day, 1977), 323–36, cites a number of ancient Near Eastern references in which women become the land or held, plowed by the male. See also Carol Delaney, "Seeds of Honor, Fields of Shame," in *Honor and Shame and the Unity of the Mediterranean,* ed. David D. Gilmore (Washington, D.C.: American Anthropological Association, 1987), 38–43, for cross-cultural examples.

123. Besides the references cited by Pope, *Song of Songs*, regarding the woman as the field plowed by the male, see also Sir 26:19-21 and the eroticization of Wisdom in Sir 6:19. For other ancient Near Eastern material see, Tikva Frymer-Kensky, "The Planting of Man: A Study in Biblical Imagery," in *Love and Death in the Ancient Near East: Essays in Honor of Marvin H. Pope,* ed. John H. Marks and Robert M. Good (Guilford, Conn.: Four Quarters, 1987), 129–36.

124. See especially Delaney, "Seeds of Honor," 39, who argues that a woman's fertility (her ability to produce children) is not the issue in the Turkish society that she investigates. If it were, less weight would be put on female virginity and sexual purity. Rather, the issue is "a woman's ability to guarantee the seed of a particular man: it is because of this that she *becomes* valuable." See also Joan Frigolé Reixach, "Procreation and Its Implications for Gender, Marriage, and Family in European Rural Ethnography," *AnthQ* 71 (1998) 38.

125. William Rainey Harper, *A Critical and Exegetical Commentary on Amos and Hosea,* ICC (Edinburgh: T. & T. Clark, 1905), 211, for example, argues that Jezreel is not Hosea's legitimate son.

126. H. G. M. Williamson, "Jezreel in the Biblical Texts," *Tel Aviv* 18 (1991) 72–92.

127. Jon D. Levenson and Baruch Halpern, "The Political Import of David's Marriages," *JBL* 99 (1980) 507–18.

128. A number of scholars interpret Hos 1:4 as a prediction of God's punishment on Jehu's dynasty for his killing spree at Jezreel. See a review of recent interpretations in Stuart A. Irvine, "The Threat of Jezreel (Hosea 1:4-5)," *CBQ* 57 (1995) 494–503. However, Thomas Edward McComiskey, "Prophetic Irony in Hosea 1.4: A Study of the Collocation *Pqd ʾl* and Its Implications for the Fall of Jehu's Dynasty," *JSOT* 58 (1993) 93–101, argues persuasively that Hos 1:4 is an instance of prophetic irony.

129. N. M. Waldman, "The Breaking of the Bow," *JQR* 79 (1978) 82–86.

130. The background for this translation comes in Exod 3:14-15, where the liberating God reveals the divine name YHWH to Moses through a word-play on *hāyâ*, "to be, become": "I AM WHO I AM.... Say this to the people of Israel, 'I AM (*'ehyeh*) has sent me to you.'" For a further discussion of the Hosean wordplays on *'ehyeh*, see Yee, *Composition*, 69–71.

131. For a detailed discussion of this prologue and epilogue, see Yee, *Composition*, 71–76.

132. The NRSV translation, "put away her whoring from her face," is misleading. It suggests that the wife is either an actual prostitute, ostensibly

wearing some sort of signs on her face to broadcast her profession, or a cultic prostitute, adorned with ritual insignia. We have very little evidence about what prostitutes actually wore. In order to convey the full force of the disintegration of the wilderness covenant, the metaphor necessitates an adulterous wife, not a prostitute.

133. The usual punishment for adultery was death by stoning (Lev 20:10; Deut 22:22; cf. John 7:53—8:11). However, Hos 2:3, along with Jer 13:26 and Ezek 16:37-39, apparently offers another method of marital chastisement.

134. See, e.g., Andersen and Freedman, *Hosea*, 230; Harper, *Amos and Hosea*, 229; Kruger, "Israel, the Harlot," 113; Mays, *Hosea*, 39; Stuart, *Hosea*, 48; Wolff, *Hosea*, 35.

135. The "lovers" appear in Hos 2:5, 10, 12, 13; 8:9. The "lovers" can refer to the baals in 2:13, although they may also be interpreted as the "nations."

136. J. A. Thompson, "Israel's 'Lovers'," *VT* 27 (1977) 475–81.

137. Wolff, *Hosea*, 35.

138. Carl Friedrich Keil, *The Twelve Minor Prophets*, vol. 1, trans. James Martin (Edinburgh: T. & T. Clark, 1900), 54.

139. Or better, "forgot"; see 2:13. As Andersen and Freedman, *Hosea*, 242, point out, the lack of "knowledge" is not simply ignorance, but the result of "rejecting" knowledge, just as "forgetting" is a sin, not just a mental lapse.

140. According to Harper, *Amos and Hosea*, 229–30, the silver and gold came from the sale of the grain, wine, and oil.

141. Halpern, "Baal (and the Asherah)," 148–49.

142. Exod 21:10-11.

143. See those cited in Saul M. Olyan, "'In the Sight of Her Lovers': On the Interpretation of *Nablut* in Hos 2,12," *BZ* 36 (1992) 255–56 n. 1.

144. Andersen and Freedman, *Hosea*, 248–49.

145. Thus argues Olyan, "In the Sight of Her Lovers," 260–61, exploring the sense of *nbl* as "to languish, wither, fade."

146. See also Ezek 16:37, where the nations are the paramours who gaze on the wife/Jerusalem's nakedness.

147. Laura Mulvey, "Visual Pleasure and Narrative Cinema," in *Feminisms: An Anthology of Literary Theory and Criticism*, ed. Robyn R. Warhol and Diane Price Herndl (New Brunswick: Rutgers Univ. Press, 1991), 432–42.

148. Andersen and Freedman, *Hosea*, 249, correlate 2:10b with the larger political arena expressed in 5:12-14, where the king of Assyria will be unable to protect Ephraim and Judah. Nevertheless, they "hesitate to give the word 'lovers' too many meanings," preferring to limit the word to the alleged sexual activity of the Canaanite cult.

149. Harper, *Amos and Hosea*, 233; Mays, *Hosea*, 42–43; Stuart, *Hosea*, 51; Wolff, *Hosea*, 38, Rallis, "Nuptial Imagery," 108–9, 207.

150. Besides the extrinsic analysis (above), see also Shigeyuki Nakanose, *Josiah's Passover: Sociology and the Liberating Bible* (Maryknoll, N.Y.: Orbis, 1993), 93–112.

151. Regarding the covenantal character of the "knowledge" of God, see R. Crotty, "Hosea and the Knowledge of God," *Australian Biblical Review* 19 (1971) 1–16; Herbert B. Huffmon, "The Treaty Background of Hebrew *YADA*," *BASOR* 181 (1966) 131–77; Hans Walter Wolff, "'Wissen um Gott' bei Hosea als Urform von Theologie," in *Gesammelte Studien zum Alten Testament*, ThBü 22 (Munich: Kaiser, 1964), 182–205.

152. The verb '*nh* (to answer, respond) refers to the nation's covenant response at Sinai, described in Exod 19:5-6, 8: "If you keep my covenant, you shall be my treasured possession among all the peoples. . . . All the people responded ('*nh*) as one: 'Everything that the Lord has spoken, we will do.'"

153. Halpern, "Baal (and the Asherah)," 122, 148.

154. Stuart, *Hosea*, 57; Wolff, *Hosea*, 49, Mays, *Hosea*, 48. According to the NJB, "The transition from 'my master' to 'my husband' hints that the emphasis will henceforth be on marital intimacy rather than on the subordination of wife to husband" (1499 n. r).

155. According to Smith, *Early History of God*, 74–75, Hosea's words in 2:21-23 recall the Canaanite literary tradition of Baal's blessings on the cosmos.

156. Some scholars have emended the MT to have "him" (Jezreel) sown in the land. Cf. NRSV. However, the MT is perfectly clear if one understands the sexual connotation of "sowing."

Chapter 6

1. Gerlinde Baumann, "Connected by Marriage, Adultery and Violence: The Prophetic Marriage Metaphor in the Book of the Twelve and in the Major Prophets," *SBLSP 1999*, 552–69; Athalya Brenner, "Pornoprophetics Revisited: Some Additional Reflections," *JSOT* 70 (1996) 63–86; Katheryn Pfisterer Darr, "Ezekiel's Justifications of God: Teaching Troubling Texts," *JSOT* 55 (1992) 97–117; idem, "Ezekiel," *WomBibCom*, 183–90; Linda M. Day, "Rhetoric and Domestic Violence in Ezekiel 16," *BibInt* 8 (2000) 205–30; Peggy L. Day, "The Bitch Had It Coming to Her: Rhetoric and Interpretation in Ezekiel 16," *BibInt* 8 (2000) 231–54; idem, "Adulterous Jerusalem's Imagined Demise: Death of a Metaphor in Ezekiel XVI," *VT* 50 (2000) 285–309; Carol J. Dempsey, "The 'Whore' of Ezekiel 16: The Impact and Ramifications of Gender-Specific Metaphors in Light of Biblical Law," in *Gender and Law in the Hebrew Bible and the Ancient Near East*, ed. Victor H. Matthews, Bernard M. Levinson, and Tikva Frymer-Kensky, JSOTSup 262 (Sheffield: Sheffield Academic, 1998), 57–78; J. Cheryl Exum, "The Ethics of Biblical Violence against Women," in *The Bible in Ethics: The Second Sheffield Colloquium*, ed. John W. Rogerson et al., JSOTSup 207

(Sheffield: Sheffield Academic, 1995), 248–71; idem, "Prophetic Pornography," in *Plotted, Shot, and Painted: Cultural Representations of Biblical Women*, JSOTSup 215 (Sheffield: Sheffield Academic, 1996), 101–28; Julie Galambush, *Jerusalem in the Book of Ezekiel: The City As Yahweh's Wife*, SBLDS 130 (Atlanta: Scholars, 1992); Christl Maier, "Jerusalem als Ehebrecherin in Ezechiel 16: Zur Verwendung und Funktion einer biblischen Metapher," in *Feministische Hermeneutik und Erstes Testament: Analysen und Interpretationen* (Stuttgart: Kohlhammer, 1994), 85–105; Mary E. Shields, "Multiple Exposures: Body Rhetoric and Gender Characterization in Ezekiel 16," *JFSR* 14 (1998) 5–18; idem, "An Abusive God? Identity and Power/Gender and Violence in Ezekiel 23," in *Postmodern Interpretations of the Bible: A Reader*, ed. A. K. M. Adam (St. Louis: Chalice, 2001), 129–51; Gail Corrington Streete, *The Strange Woman: Power and Sex in the Bible* (Louisville: Westminster John Knox, 1997), 85–98; Jan William Tarlin, "Utopia and Pornography in Ezekiel: Violence, Hope, and the Shattered Male Subject," in *Reading Bibles, Writing Bodies: Identity and the Book*, ed. Timothy K. Beal and David M. Gunn (New York: Routledge, 1997), 175–83; Fokkelien van Dijk-Hemmes, "The Metaphorization of Woman in Prophetic Speech: An Analysis of Ezekiel 23," in *On Gendering Texts: Female and Male Voices in the Hebrew Bible*, ed. Athalya Brenner and Fokkelien van Dijk-Hemmes (Leiden: Brill, 1993), 167–76; Renita J. Weems, *Battered Love: Marriage, Sex, and Violence in the Hebrew Prophets* (Minneapolis: Fortress Press, 1995), 58–64.

2. I initially understood both these texts as allegories, but have been persuaded by Galambush that both chapters should be analyzed as metaphors; see Galambush, *Jerusalem*, 10–11. Linda Day, "Rhetoric and Domestic Violence," 205 n. 1; Peggy Day, "Adulterous Jerusalem's Imagined Demise," 232 n. 5; and van Dijk-Hemmes, "Metaphorization of Woman," 167–76, are of the same opinion.

3. One study that does attend to the historical circumstances that produced the text is Corrine Patton, "'Should Our Sister Be Treated like a Whore?' A Response to Feminist Critiques of Ezekiel 23," in *The Book of Ezekiel: Theological and Anthropological Perspectives*, ed. Margaret S. Odell and John T. Strong, SBLSymSer 9 (Atlanta: SBL, 2000), 221–38.

4. The metaphor of the faithless wife was examined in chap. 5 above on Hosea 1–2. Scholars typically view Ezekiel 23 as being more focused on the political, while Ezekiel 16 accused the nation's religious or cultic infractions. See Daniel I. Block, *The Book of Ezekiel: Chapters 1–24*, NICOT (Grand Rapids: Eerdmans, 1997), 729; Walther Eichrodt, *Ezekiel: A Commentary*, trans. Cosslett Quin, OTL (Philadelphia: Westminster, 1970), 324, 329; Galambush, *Jerusalem*, 80 n. 12, 110; Moshe Greenberg, *Ezekiel 21–37: A New Translation with Introduction and Commentary*, AB 22A (New York: Doubleday, 1997), 491; Walther Zimmerli, *Ezekiel 1*, trans. Ronald E.

Clements, Hermeneia (Philadelphia: Fortress Press, 1979), 482. Nevertheless, in light of the complex interconnections between cult and politics that we saw in Hosea, a case can be made that Ezekiel 16's emphasis on cult does not at all preclude politics.

Although similarities exist between Ezekiel 16 and 23, there are also a number of key differences. Ezekiel 16 is apparently focused on cultic infractions, chap. 23 on political misalliances. Ezekiel 16 attributes Jerusalem's promiscuity to her foreign parentage, chap. 23 to her sexual precocity in Egypt. While Samaria is only referred to sketchily with respect to the main character Jerusalem in chap. 16, Samaria is a main character alongside her sister Jerusalem in chap. 23. In chap. 16 Jerusalem is the object of the male gaze; in chap. 23 Jerusalem is the subject of the gaze, eying her male lovers. Ezekiel 16 concludes on a relatively positive note with the restoration of the covenant, while this does not happen in chap. 23.

5. See Anne McClintock, *Imperial Leather: Race, Gender, and Sexuality in the Colonial Contest* (New York: Routledge, 1995), 352–53. Although I concentrate primarily on the colonial situation that produced the text, orientalist readings of Ezekiel 16 and 23 in the texts' "afterlives" are not uncommon. For example, Marten Woudstra quips that the "obscenities" in 16:1-43 were due to the fact that "the oriental mind was probably more accustomed to a frank discussion of the sexual life than we are" ("The Everlasting Covenant in Ezekiel 16:59–63," *Calvin Theological Journal* 6 [1971] 23). For a critique of orientalist depictions of the alleged sexual decadence of the East, see Edward W. Said, *Orientalism* (New York: Vintage, 1979), 180–90.

6. Regarding a foreign-tributary mode of production, see Norman K. Gottwald, "Sociology (Ancient Israel)," *ABD* 6:85–86.

7. One hundred talents of silver and a talent of gold.

8. Jeremiah soundly condemned this excess (22:13-19). See John Bright, *A History of Israel*, 3rd ed. (Philadelphia: Westminster, 1981), 325–26.

9. Regarding the royal ideology behind Nebuchadnezzer's empire, see David Stephen Vanderhooft, *The Neo-Babylonian Empire and Babylon in the Latter Prophets*, HSM 59 (Atlanta: Scholars, 1999), 33–51.

10. D. J. Wiseman, "Babylonia 605–539 B.C.," in *Cambridge Ancient History*, vol. 3, ed. John Boardman, 2nd ed. (Cambridge: Cambridge Univ. Press, 1991), 232.

11. J. Maxwell Miller and John H. Hayes, *A History of Ancient Israel and Judah* (Philadelphia: Westminster, 1986), 408.

12. Cf. Ezek 1:1; 33:21; 40:1.

13. Peter R. Ackroyd, *Exile and Restoration: A Study of Hebrew Thought of the Sixth Century B.C.*, OTL (Philadelphia: Westminster, 1968), 22–23 n. 24; Hans M. Barstad, *The Myth of the Empty Land: A Study in the History and Archaeology of Judah During the 'Exilic' Period*, SO 28 (Oslo: Scandinavian Univ. Press, 1996), 33–34.

14. According to Bustenay Oded, "Observations on the Israelite/Judean Exiles in Mesopotamia during the Eighth-Sixth Centuries B.C.E.," in *Immigration and Emigration within the Ancient Near East: Festschrift E. Lipiński*, ed. K. van Lerberghe and Antoon Schoors, Orientalia Lovaniensia Analecta 65 (Leuven: Peeters, 1995), 210, Nebuchadnezzar used Jehoiachin to exert pressure on Zedekiah to keep him loyal to Babylon.

15. Jer 27:12-15; 37:1-10, 16-21; 38:14-28.

16. See Miller and Hayes, *History of Ancient Israel and Judah*, 411–13, for a discussion the achievements of Psammetichus II that swayed many in Judah to ally with Egypt.

17. Barstad, *Myth of the Empty Land*, 69–70.

18. Rainer Albertz, *A History of Israelite Religion in the Old Testament Period*, vol. 2: *From the Exile to the Maccabees*, trans. John Bowden, OTL (Louisville: Westminster John Knox, 1994), 371; Barstad, *Myth of the Empty Land*, 42–43; Bustenay Oded, "Judah and the Exile," in *Israelite and Judaean History*, ed. John H. Hayes and J. Maxwell Miller, OTL (Philadelphia: Westminster, 1977), 479. Cf. Daniel L. Smith, *The Religion of the Landless: The Social Context of the Babylonian Exile* (Bloomington, Ind.: Meyer-Stone, 1989), 31–32.

19. Albertz, *History of Israelite Religion*, 2:371; William H. Brownlee, "The Aftermath of the Fall of Judah according to Ezekiel," *JBL* 89 (1970) 395; Morton Smith, *Palestinian Parties and Politics That Shaped the Old Testament* (New York: Columbia Univ. Press, 1971), 100–101; Smith, *Religion of the Landless*, 188–97. It is also very possible, following Enno Janssen, *Juda in der Exilszeit: Ein Beitrag zur Frage der Entstehung des Judentums*, FRLANT 69 (Göttingen: Vandenhoeck & Ruprecht, 1956), 54, that those who were left in the land and prospered came into conflict with the returning exiles and were regarded as "foreigners" by Third Isaiah. See also Meindert Dijkstra, "The Valley of Dry Bones: Coping with the Reality of the Exile in the Book of Ezekiel," in *The Crisis of Israelite Religion: Transformation of Religious Tradition in Exilic and Post-Exilic Times*, ed. Bob Becking and Marjo C. A. Korpel, OtSt 42 (Leiden: Brill, 1999), 120–25, on the antagonism between those in Israel and the exiles.

20. William F. Albright, "The Seal of Eliakim and the Latest Preëxilic History of Judah," *JBL* 51 (1932) 104.

21. William F. Albright, *From the Stone Age to Christianity: Monotheism and the Historical Process*, 2nd ed. (Garden City, N.Y.: Doubleday, 1957), 322.

22. Barstad, *Myth of the Empty Land*, 67–68.

23. Thus Israel Finkelstein and Neil Asher Silberman, *The Bible Unearthed: Archaeology's New Vision of Ancient Israel and the Origin of Its Sacred Texts* (New York: Free Press, 2001), 306–7.

24. Barstad, *Myth of the Empty Land*, 42–71, 234–35. For a different opinion, see Vanderhooft, *Neo-Babylonian Empire*, 81–114, who argues that

the economic viability of the region was secondary to Nebuchadnezzar's desire to eliminate Egyptian hegemony in the region. Nevertheless, Vanderhooft maintains that for the Judean prophets, speaking for a subjugated minority, it was the "propagandistic interpretation of economic arrangements in the empire" that was significant (114).

25. Oded, "Observations," 212.

26. However, see J. M. Wilkie, "Nabonidus and the Later Jewish Exiles," *JTS* 2 (1951) 36–44, who argues that the later Jewish exiles received harsh treatment under the last Babylonian king, Nabonidus.

27. Daniel Smith-Christopher, "Reassessing the Historical and Sociological Impact of the Babylonian Exile (597/587–539 B.C.E.)," in *Exile: Old Testament, Jewish, and Christian Perspectives*, ed. James M. Scott, JSJSup 56 (Leiden: Brill, 1997), 23–31.

28. See T. R. Hobbs, "Aspects of Warfare in the First Testament World," *BTB* 25 (1995) 83–85; idem, *A Time for War: A Study of Warfare in the Old Testament* (Wilmington, Del.: Glazier, 1989), 177–81; Paul Bentley Kern, *Ancient Siege Warfare* (Bloomington: Indiana Univ. Press, 1999), 62–85; and Mordechai Cogan, "'Ripping Open Pregnant Women' in Light of an Assyrian Analogue," *JAOS* 103 (1983) 755–57, on the terrible effects of war and the siege, in particular, on soldiers and civilians alike. For analyses of rape in war, in particular, see F. W. Dobbs-Allsopp and Tod Linafelt, "The Rape of Zion in Thr 1, 10," *ZAW* 113 (2001) 77–81; Pamela Gordon and Harold C. Washington, "Rape As a Military Metaphor in the Hebrew Bible," in *A Feminist Companion to the Latter Prophets*, ed. Athalya Brenner, FCB 8 (Sheffield: Sheffield Academic, 1995), 308–25; Alice Keefe, "Rapes of Women/Wars of Men," *Semeia* 61 (1993) 79–97; F. Rachel Magdalene, "Ancient Near Eastern Treaty-Curses and the Ultimate Texts of Terror: A Study of the Language of Divine Sexual Abuse in the Prophetic Corpus," in *Feminist Companion to Latter Prophets*, 326–52; Susan Thistlethwaite, "'You May Enjoy the Spoil of Your Enemies': Rape As a Biblical Metaphor for War," *Semeia* 61 (1993) 59–75.

29. Cited in A. Kirk Grayson, "Assyrian Rule of Conquered Territory in Ancient Western Asian," *CANE* 2:961. For further discussion of Assyrian cruelty, see Erika Bleibtreu, "Grisly Assyrian Record of Torture and Death," *BAR* 17, no. 1 (1991) 52–61, 75; Kern, *Ancient Siege Warfare*, 68–76. See I. J. Gelb, "Prisoners of War in Early Mesopotamia," *JNES* 32 (1972) 70–98, on the abusive and exploitative treatment of foreign captives in early Mesopotamia (second half of third millennium).

30. See Bustenay Oded, *Mass Deportations and Deportees in the Neo-Assyrian Empire* (Wiesbaden: Reichert, 1979), 41–74, on the aims and objectives of mass deportation.

31. On effects of war on women and children in particular, see Kern, *Ancient Siege Warfare*, 80–85.

32. Yigael Yadin, *The Art of Warfare in Biblical Lands,* trans. M. Pearlman, 2 vols. (New York: McGraw-Hill, 1963), 2:462–63; Bleibtreu, "Grisly Assyrian Record," 61.

33. Oded, *Mass Deportations,* 34–36.

34. Ibid., 41–45. We have less information on the Babylonian system of deportation, although its sociopolitical objectives were not that different from those of Assyrian deportation. According to Oded, "Judah and the Exile," 475, there were two main differences between Babylonian and Assyrian deportation practices. The Babylonians did not settle new populations in the areas depleted by exile, and they preferred to appoint a local governor rather than a Babylonian to govern the population remaining on the land. However, see Oded, *Mass Deportations,* 45, where he acknowledges that the Babylonians continued the Assyrian policy of replacing exiled officials with their own people.

35. Oded, "Observations," 208; idem, *Mass Deportations,* 54–59, 90–91.

36. Oded, *Mass Deportations,* 67–74.

37. Robert McCormick Adams, *Heartland of Cities: Surveys of Ancient Settlement and Land Use on the Central Floodplain of the Euphrates* (Chicago: Univ. of Chicago Press, 1981), 177, italics added. See also I. Eph'al, "The Western Minorities in Babylonia in the 6th–5th Centuries B.C.: Maintenance and Cohesion," *Orientalia* 47 (1978) 81–82.

38. Jon L. Berquist, *Judaism in Persia's Shadow: A Social and Historical Approach* (Minneapolis: Fortress Press, 1995), 15–17; Oded, "Observations," 205; Smith-Christopher, "Reassessing," 23–25; idem, "Ezekiel on Fanon's Couch: A Postcolonialist Dialogue with David Halperin's *Seeking Ezekiel,*" in *Peace and Justice Shall Embrace: Power and Theopolitics in the Bible: Essays in Honor of Millard Lind,* ed. Ted Grimsrud and Loren L. Johns (Telford, Pa.: Pandora, 1999), 120–26; James D. Purvis and Eric M. Meyers, "Exile and Return: From the Babylonian Destruction to the Reconstruction of the Jewish State," in *Ancient Israel: From Abraham to the Roman Destruction of the Temple,* ed. Hershel Shanks, rev. ed. (Washington, D.C.: Biblical Archaeology Society, 1999), 205–6.

39. Oded, *Mass Deportations,* 46.

40. Ibid., 115.

41. I am assuming Ezekiel 23 is exilic, written by one of the deportees in Babylonia, whom I will call "Ezekiel" for the sake of convenience. For a concise survey of the historical context of Ezekiel and his book, see Thomas Renz, *The Rhetorical Function of the Book of Ezekiel,* VTSup 76 (Leiden: Brill, 1999), 27–55. On Ezekiel as a literary construct, see Corrine Patton, "Priest, Prophet and Exile: Ezekiel As a Literary Construct," *SBLSP 2000,* 700–727.

42. Regarding the school of Ezekiel, see Zimmerli, *Ezekiel 1,* 68–74.

43. Stephen L. Cook, *Prophecy and Apocalypticism: The Postexilic Social Setting* (Minneapolis: Fortress Press, 1995), 97; Marvin L. Sweeney,

"Ezekiel: Zadokite Priest and Visionary Prophet of the Exile," *SBLSP 2000*, 728–51.

44. Although the book does not explicitly mention that Ezekiel was part of the first deportation, scholars assume that he was. Cf. Block, *Ezekiel*, 9; Moshe Greenberg, *Ezekiel, 1–20*, AB 22 (Garden City, N.Y.: Doubleday, 1983), 1, 40; Henry McKeating, *Ezekiel*, OTG (Sheffield: Sheffield Academic, 1995), 23; Zimmerli, *Ezekiel 1*, 16; Albertz, *History of Israelite Religion*, 2:428; Cook, *Prophecy and Apocalypticism*, 97–98.

45. Berquist, *Judaism in Persia's Shadow*, 15–16.

46. Ellen F. Davis, *Swallowing the Scroll: Textuality and the Dynamics of Discourse in Ezekiel's Prophecy*, JSOTSup 78 (Sheffield: Almond, 1989). See also Terry Eagleton, *Criticism and Ideology: A Study in Marxist Literary Theory* (1976; repr. London: Verso, 1990), regarding a literary mode of production.

47. According to Gorst-Unsworth, state-sponsored terrorism can be defined as "the act of a state against an individual or group, with the aim of achieving specific psychological changes (directly) in their victims and often (indirectly) in their communities. . . . The survivor of torture has not merely been the accidental victim of physical injury or threat of death such as might occur, for example, in a natural disaster or accident. . . . He or she has received the focused attention of an adversary determined to cause the maximal psychological change." Cited in Smith-Christopher, "Ezekiel on Fanon's Couch," 124–25.

48. Thus Grayson, "Assyrian Rule," 961. Cf. Cogan, "Ripping Open Pregnant Women," 756. From a psychiatric perspective, see Judith Lewis Herman, "Complex PTSD: A Syndrome in Survivors of Prolonged and Repeated Trauma," *Journal of Traumatic Stress* 5 (1992) 383–85.

49. As in the case of Jacob, Leah, and Rachel. See Naomi Steinberg, *Kinship and Marriage in Genesis: A Household Economics Perspective* (Minneapolis: Fortress Press, 1993), 115–34.

50. Gale A. Yee, "Ideological Criticism: Judges 17–21 and the Dismembered Body," in *Judges and Method: New Approaches in Biblical Studies*, ed. Gale A. Yee (Minneapolis: Fortress Press, 1995), 151.

51. Bronwyn Davies, *(In)Scribing Body/Landscape Relations* (Walnut Creek, Calif.: AltaMira, 2000); Darby Lewes, *Nudes from Nowhere: Utopian Sexual Landscapes* (Lanham, Md.: Rowman & Littlefield, 2000); Susan Stanford Friedman, *Mappings: Feminism and the Cultural Geographics of Encounter* (Princeton: Princeton Univ. Press, 1998); Stacy Alaimo, *Undomesticated Ground: Recasting Nature As Feminist Space* (Ithaca: Cornell Univ. Press, 2000).

52. See McClintock, "Introduction: Postcolonialism and the Angel of Progress," and "The Lay of the Land: Genealogies of Imperialism," in *Imperial Leather*, 1–51; Laura Chrisman, "The Imperial Unconscious?: Representations of Imperial Discourse," in *Colonial Discourse and Post-Colonial*

Theory: A Reader, ed. Patrick Williams and Laura Chrisman (New York: Columbia Univ. Press, 1994), 498–516; Jean Franco, "Beyond Ethnocentrism: Gender, Power and the Third-World Intelligentsia," in *Colonial Discourse,* 359–69; Deniz Kandiyoti, "Identity and Its Discontents: Women and the Nation," in *Colonial Discourse,* 376–91; Kadiatu Kanneh, "Feminism and the Colonial Body," in *The Post-Colonial Studies Reader,* ed. Bill Ashcroft, Gareth Griffiths, and Helen Tiffin (New York: Routledge, 1995), 346–48; Ania Loomba, *Colonialism/Post-Colonialism* (New York: Routledge, 1998), 72–81, 151–72; Anne McClintock, Aamir Mufti, and Ella Shohat, eds., *Dangerous Liaisons: Gender, Nation, and Postcolonial Perspectives* (Minneapolis: Univ. of Minnesota Press, 1997); Revathi Krishnaswamy, *Effeminism: The Economy of Colonial Desire* (Ann Arbor: Univ. of Michigan Press, 1998), 1–13; José Rabasa, "Allegories of *Atlas,*" in *Post-Colonial Studies Reader,* 358–64; Jenny Sharpe, "The Unspeakable Limits of Rape: Colonial Violence and Counter-Insurgency," in *Colonial Discourse,* 221–43; Ann Laura Stoler, "Carnal Knowledge and Imperial Power: Gender, Race, and Morality in Colonial Asia," in *Gender at the Crossroads of Knowledge: Feminist Anthropology in the Postmodern Era,* ed. Micaela di Leonardo (Berkeley: Univ. of California Press, 1991), 51–101.

53. For example, according to Susan Niditch, "The 'Sodomite' Theme in Judges 19–20: Family, Community, and Social Disintegration," *CBQ* 44 (1982) 371–73; and Keefe, "Rapes of Women," 85–86, the concubine's raped and mutilated body in Judges 19 becomes an ideological symbol of tribal disintegration.

54. Yehudi A. Cohen, "Ends and Means in Political Control: State Organization and the Punishment of Adultery, Incest, and the Violation of Celibacy," *AmAnth* 71 (1969) 658–87; Nira Yuval-Davis and Floya Anthias, eds., *Woman—Nation—State* (New York: St. Martin's, 1989), 7, 8–9.

55. McClintock, *Imperial Leather,* 354.

56. Yuval-Davis and Anthias, *Woman—Nation—State,* 7, 9–10.

57. Loomba, *Colonialism/Post-Colonialism,* 159.

58. Cf. Claudia Card, "Rape As a Weapon of War," *Hypatia* 11, no. 4 (1996) 5–18, and the references cited in n. 28 above.

59. McClintock, *Imperial Leather,* 354.

60. Leela Gandhi, *Postcolonial Theory: A Critical Introduction* (New York: Columbia Univ. Press, 1998), 164: "Colonising as well as anti-colonial men, while being otherwise opposed, have often shared certain attitudes to women."

61. I especially thank Won-Jae Hur, who graciously shared his work on trauma with me and helped me immensely with the bibliography on this important area of studies: Won-Jae Hur, "Voicing the Wound: Trauma, Language, and the Theology of *Han*" (M.Div. thesis, Episcopal Divinity School, 2000). See Paul Antze and Michael Lambek, eds., *Tense Past: Cultural Essays in Trauma and Memory* (London: Routledge, 1996); Dan Bar-On, *The Inde-*

scribable and the Undiscussable: Reconstructing Human Discourse after Trauma (Budapest: Central European Univ. Press, 1999), Bessel A. van der Kolk, Alexander C. McFarlane, and Lars Weisaet, eds., *Traumatic Stress: The Effects of Overwhelming Experience on Mind, Body, and Society* (New York: Guilford, 1996); Cathy Caruth, *Unclaimed Experience: Trauma, Narrative, and History* (Baltimore: Johns Hopkins Univ. Press, 1996); Judith Lewis Herman, *Trauma and Recovery: The Aftermath of Violence—from Domestic Abuse to Political Terror,* with a new afterword by the author (New York: Basic, 1997); idem, "Complex PTSD," 377–91; Ronnie Janoff-Bulman, *Shattered Assumptions: Towards a New Psychology of Trauma* (New York: Free Press, 1992); Laurence J. Kirmayer, "Landscapes of Memory: Trauma, Narrative, and Dissociation," in *Tense Past,* ed. Antze and Lambek, 173–98; Martha Minow, *Between Vengeance and Forgiveness: Facing History after Genocide and Mass Violence* (Boston: Beacon, 1998); Elaine Scarry, *The Body in Pain: The Making and Unmaking of the World* (New York: Oxford Univ. Press, 1985); Kalí Tal, *Worlds of Hurt: Reading the Literatures of Trauma* (New York: Cambridge Univ. Press, 1996); Ernst van Alphen, "Symptoms of Discursivity: Experience, Memory, and Trauma," in *Acts of Memory: Cultural Recall in the Present,* ed. Mieke Bal, Jonathan Crewe, and Leo Spitzer (Hanover, N.H.: Univ. Press of New England, 1999), 24–38.

62. Smith-Christopher, "Ezekiel on Fanon's Couch," 135–44; idem, "Reassessing," 23–33.

63. Jay Geller, "Trauma," in *Handbook of Postmodern Biblical Interpretation,* ed. A. K. M. Adam (St. Louis: Chalice, 2000), 264. Cf. Caruth, *Unclaimed Experience,* 10–11.

64. Kai Erikson, "Notes on Trauma and Community," in *Trauma: Explorations in Memory,* ed. Cathy Caruth (Baltimore: Johns Hopkins Univ. Press, 1995), 184.

65. Bessel A. van der Kolk and Onno van der Hart, "The Intrusive Past: The Flexibility of Memory and the Engraving of Trauma," in *Trauma,* ed. Caruth, 176. Also Caruth, *Unclaimed Experience,* 5.

66. Janoff-Bulman, *Shattered Assumptions,* 108–9.

67. Dori Laub, "Bearing Witness or the Vicissitudes of Listening," in *Testimony: Crises of Witnessing in Literature, Psychoanalysis, and History,* ed. Shoshana Felman and Dori Laub (New York: Routledge, 1992), 57; van Alphen, "Symptoms of Discursivity," 25.

68. Tal, *Worlds of Hurt,* 121; Janoff-Bulman, *Shattered Assumptions,* 105–6. See also the essays in Antze and Lambek, eds., *Tense Past,* which maintain that memory of trauma is a social product of wider discourses. They interrogate the different ways in which this memory operates in society and how it is used in collective and individual practice.

69. See Laub, "Bearing Witness," 59–63. In the face of the historical fact that only one chimney was blown up at Auschwitz by the Canada commando, Laub defended a woman's testimony that she saw four destroyed.

"She was testifying not simply to empirical historical facts, but to the very secret of survival and of resistance to extermination" (62).

70. Tal labels the taming of the traumatic event through successive retelling as "mythologization," one of the three strategies of cultural coping with trauma. The other two are medicalization (positing that trauma victims suffer from an "illness" and can be "cured" medically) and disappearance (a denial of the existence of a particular trauma). See Tal, *Worlds of Hurt*, 6.

71. In this I depart from David J. Halperin's oedipal reading of the sexual pathology in Ezekiel 23 (and 16) as arising from Ezekiel's frustrated childhood love for his mother and sexual abuse as a child. See Halperin, *Seeking Ezekiel: Text and Psychology* (University Park: Univ. of Pennsylvania Press, 1993), 141–83.

72. For studies in collective trauma and its aftermath, see Eduardo Duran and Bonnie Duran, *Native American Postcolonial Psychology* (Albany: State Univ. of New York Press, 1995); Erikson, "Notes on Trauma and Community," 183–99; and Ellen S. Zinner and Mary Beth Williams, eds., *When a Community Weeps: Case Studies in Group Survivorship* (Philadelphia: Brunner/Mazel, 1999).

73. Patton, "Should Our Sister?" 233–38. Also S. Tamar Kamionkowski, "Gender Ambiguity and Subversive Metaphor in Ezekiel 16" (Ph.D. dissertation, Brandeis University, 2000), 73–96, regarding Ezekiel 16. For an analysis of the cultural significance of castration throughout history, see Gary Taylor, *Castration: An Abbreviated History of Western Manhood* (New York: Routledge, 2000).

74. Cited in Bleibtreu, "Grisly Assyrian Record," 60.

75. P. Kyle McCarter Jr., *II Samuel,* AB 9 (Garden City, N.Y.: Doubleday, 1984), 270 n. 4. See also Taylor, *Castration,* 150–51, on beardlessness and effeminacy.

76. See Gandhi, *Postcolonial Theory*, 98, regarding the colonial encounter as a struggle between competing masculinities, where colonial and colonized women become the symbolic mediators of this male contest. In the case of Ezekiel, Judah becomes emasculated by the conquest of Babylonia.

77. As the British colonials described the men of India; see Krishnaswamy, *Effeminism*, 15–52.

78. See above, pp. 98–99.

79. In contrast to characterological self-blame (which is focused on one's individual character or qualities), behavioral self-blame is control-related. Blame is focused on one's own behavior, the acts or omissions a person believes caused or contributed to the trauma. See Janoff-Bulman, *Shattered Assumptions*, 125–26.

80. See ibid., 115–41, regarding the different strategies trauma victims use to integrate old realities with the new.

81. Deryn Guest, "Hiding Behind the Naked Women in Lamentations: A Recriminative Response," *BibInt* 7 (1999) 413–48, demonstrates how the shifting of blame to women's bodies is found in the book of Lamentations.

82. Gandhi, *Postcolonial Theory*, 90.

83. Gale A. Yee, "Hosea," *WomBibCom*, 200.

84. I limit my analysis to Ezek 23:1-35 for reasons of manageability. Scholars usually regard 23:1-35 as the original oracle, with 23:36-49 as a secondary addition. See Aelred Cody, O.S.B., *Ezekiel, with an Excursus on Old Testament Priesthood*, OTM (Wilmington, Del.: Glazier, 1984), 114; George Albert Cooke, *A Critical and Exegetical Commentary on the Book of Ezekiel*, ICC (Edinburgh: T. & T. Clark, 1936), 256; Eichrodt, *Ezekiel*, 332; Ronald M. Hals, *Ezekiel*, FOTL 19 (Grand Rapids: Eerdmans, 1989), 166; D. M. G. Stalker, *Ezekiel*, Torch Bible Commentaries (London: SCM, 1968), 194; John W. Wevers, *Ezekiel*, NCBC (repr. Grand Rapids: Eerdmans, 1982), 133; Zimmerli, *Ezekiel 1*, 480.

85. See Robert Carroll, "Desire under the Terebinths: On Pornographic Representation in the Prophets—a Response," in *Feminist Companion to Latter Prophets*, ed. Brenner, 275–307, who criticizes the designation of "pornographic" for Ezekiel 16 and 23. Responding to Carroll, see Athalya Brenner, "On 'Jeremiah' and the Poetics of (Prophetic?) Pornography," in *On Gendering Texts*, ed. Brenner and van Dijk-Hemmes, 177–93; idem, "Pornoprophetics Revisited," 63–86; idem, "On Prophetic Propaganda and the Politics of 'Love,'" in *Reflections on Theology and Gender*, ed. Fokkelien van Dijk-Hemmes and Athalya Brenner (Kampen: Kok Pharos, 1994), 87–107; idem, *The Intercourse of Knowledge: On Gendered Sex and Desire in the Hebrew Bible*, BibIntSer 26 (Leiden: Brill, 1997), 153–74. In a later work, Carroll seems to acknowledge that the discourses in Ezekiel 16 and 23 are pornographic: Robert Carroll, "Whorusalamin: A Tale of Three Cities As Three Sisters," in *On Reading Prophetic Texts: Gender-Specific and Related Studies in Memory of Fokklien Van Dijk-Hemmes*, ed. Bob Becking and Meindert Dijkstra, BibIntSer 18 (Leiden: Brill, 1996), 62–82. For other discussions of prophetic pornography, see T. Drorah Setel, "Prophets and Pornography: Female Sexual Imagery," in *Feminist Interpretation of the Bible*, ed. Letty M. Russell (Philadelphia: Westminster, 1985), 86–95; Exum, "Prophetic Pornography," 101–28; Gordon and Washington, "Rape As a Military Metaphor," 310–13; Tarlin, "Utopia and Pornography in Ezekiel," 175–83.

86. Contra Block, *Ezekiel*, 734, who attempts to erase the child abuse and blame the victim by asserting that the sisters actively "offered their breasts and nipples to the men of Egypt."

87. A point made by van Dijk-Hemmes, "Metaphorization of Woman," 171–73. Unfortunately, one of the most dreadful consequences of child abuse is, in fact, adult promiscuity. See Robert J. Timms and Patrick Connors, "Adult Promiscuity Following Childhood Sexual Abuse: An Introduction," *Psychotherapy Patient* 8, nos. 1–2 (1992) 19–27; Cathy Spatz Widom and Joseph B. Kuhns, "Childhood Victimization and Subsequent Risk for Promiscuity, Prostitution, and Teenage Pregnancy: A Prospective Study," *American Journal of Public Health* 86, no. 11 (1996) 1607–12; Elizabeth

Oddone Paolucci, Mark L. Genuis, and Claudio Violato, "A Meta-Analysis of the Published Research on the Effects of Child Sexual Abuse," *Journal of Psychology* 135, no. 1 (2001) 17–36. This fact, however, is not the intent of Ezekiel's critique.

88. Corrine Patton, "'I Myself Gave Them Laws That Were Not Good': Ezekiel 20 and the Exodus Traditions," *JSOT* 69 (1996) 76–77; idem, "A Dragon in the Seas: Egypt in the Book of Ezekiel" (paper read at the Catholic Biblical Association annual meeting, Scranton, Pa., 1998), 2–4. I thank Dr. Patton for a copy of this paper.

89. Although the two sisters are not designated as brides, this seems to be implied in "they became mine."

90. See the discussions by Block, *Ezekiel*, 735–36; Eichrodt, *Ezekiel*, 321–22.

91. The rare word *qubbâ* is used here, not *'ōhel*. According to William L. Holladay, *A Concise Hebrew and Aramaic Lexicon of the Old Testament* (Grand Rapids: Eerdmans, 1971), 311, *qubbâ* refers to the "women's quarters" in a tent.

92. Helena Z. Sivan, "The Rape of Cozbi (Numbers XXV)," *VT* 51 (2001) 69–80.

93. Mieke Bal, *Murder and Difference: Gender, Genre, and Scholarship on Sisera's Death* (Bloomington and Indianapolis: Indiana Univ. Press, 1988), 122–23; Susan Niditch, "Eroticism and Death in the Tale of Jael," in *Gender and Difference in Ancient Israel*, ed. Peggy L. Day (Minneapolis: Fortress Press, 1989), 43–57; Gale A. Yee, "'By the Hand of a Woman': The Biblical Metaphor of the Woman Warrior," *Semeia* 61 (1993) 116.

94. Ken Stone, *Sex, Honor and Power in the Deuteronomistic History: A Narratological and Anthropological Analysis*, JSOTSup 234 (Sheffield: Sheffield Academic, 1997), 119–27.

95. Galambush, *Jerusalem*, 87 and 111 n. 58. See Alan Mintz, "The Rhetoric of Lamentations and the Representation of Catastrophe," *Prooftexts* 2 (1982) 4; and Dobbs-Allsopp and Linafelt, "Rape of Zion," 78–80, on the collocation of temple and vagina in Lamentations. See also discussion below on Ezek 23:28–29.

96. For a thorough study of Israel's Assyrian period, see Jeffrey Kah-jin Kuan, *Neo-Assyrian Historical Inscriptions and Syria-Palestine*, Jian Dao Dissertation Series 1 (Hong Kong: Alliance Bible Seminary, 1995). Also Miller and Hayes, *History of Ancient Israel and Judah*, 289–376; Morton Cogan, *Imperialism and Religion: Assyria, Judah, and Israel in the Eighth and Seventh Centuries B.C.E.*, SBLMS 19 (Missoula, Mont.: Scholars, 1974).

97. Hos 5:13; 7:11; 8:9; 9:3; 10:6; 12:1.

98. Along with *znh*, Ezekiel utilizes *'gb* in his repertoire of the sisters' sexual wrongdoings in 23:7, 9, 11, 12, 16, 20.

99. It is unclear whether *pārāšîm rōkĕbê sûsîm* refers to charioteers or cavalry, but the point that we are dealing with elite military units remains the same.

100. Carol Bier, "Textile Arts in Ancient Western Asia," *CANE* 3:1575.

101. 1 Kgs 10:28–29; 2 Chr 1:16-17. See Yadin, *Art of Warfare,* 2:382–85.

102. Cf. Jer 3:8. See also the discussion of Ezek 23:20 below.

103. *Gillûlîm* often refers to "idols" in Ezekiel, but according to Block, *Ezekiel,* 740, the term is not confined to images of deity, but can represent images of men (cf. 23:13-14, which refers to "images of Chaldeans," *ṣalmê kāśdîm*). This connotation coheres with Oholah's *visual* attraction to the Assyrians in the previous verses.

104. See also Lev 20:22-26, which follows similar sexual injunctions.

105. Hos 7:11; 8:9; 12:1; 2 Kgs 17:3-4. See Greenberg, *Ezekiel 21–37,* 476.

106. That rape is described here in v 10 with the expression *glh 'erwâ,* "uncover nakedness," see discussion above on 23:29.

107. Commenting on this passage, Carroll, "Whorusalamin," 76, remarks: "Throughout the two discourses there is an interweaving of fantasy and socially realistic images which makes it very difficult for modern readers to determine where fantasy ends and realism begins."

108. This fact is supported rhetorically by the greater number of verses devoted to Oholibah's transgressions (23:11-21) and to her punishment (23:22-35), and the three references to Oholibah's licentious origins in Egypt (23:19-20, 21, 27), as opposed to Oholah's single one (23:8).

109. Laura Mulvey, "Visual Pleasure and Narrative Cinema," in *Feminisms: An Anthology of Literary Theory and Criticism,* ed. Robyn R. Warhol and Diane Price Herndl (New Brunswick, N.J.: Rutgers Univ. Press, 1991), 432–42. For a discussion of the "gaze" of Oholibah, see Galambush, *Jerusalem,* 115–16.

110. See Michelle I. Marcus, "Art and Ideology in Ancient Western Asia," *CANE* 4:2487–98, on the relationship of Mesopotamian art and relief carvings with imperial ideology.

111. Donald G. Schley, "The *Shalishim:* Officers or Special Three-Man Squads?" *VT* 40 (1990) 326.

112. See Greenberg, *Ezekiel 21–37,* 478–79, for possibilities.

113. Scarry, *Body in Pain,* 27, 51–59.

114. Duran and Duran, *Native American Postcolonial Psychology,* 29. See also Hussein Abdilahi Bulhan, *Frantz Fanon and the Psychology of Oppression* (New York: Plenum, 1985), 123–24, regarding internalized oppression.

115. Sander Gilman, *Differences and Pathology: Stereotypes of Sexuality, Race, and Madness* (Ithaca: Cornell Univ. Press, 1985), 25–26. See also Lynne Segal, "Competing Masculinities (III): Black Masculinity and the White Man's Black Man," in *Slow Motion: Changing Masculinities, Changing Men* (New Brunswick, N.J.: Rutgers Univ. Press, 1990), 168–204. On the biblical text see Randall C. Bailey, "They're Nothing but Incestuous Bastards: The Polemical Use of Sex and Sexuality in Hebrew Canon Narratives," in *Reading from This Place,* vol. 1: *Social Location and Biblical Interpretation*

in the United States, ed. Fernando F. Segovia and Mary Ann Tolbert (Minneapolis: Fortress Press, 1995), 121–38.

116. Marcus, "Art and Ideology," 2492.

117. Omitted in Ezekiel 23 are references to the insatiability of Jerusalem with her foreign lovers, found in 16:28-29.

118. Lit. "concubines" (*pilagšîm*, 23:20), usually found in feminine form in the Hebrew Bible.

119. Perhaps a modern-day analogue is the popular notion that young women are sexually attracted to men in uniform.

120. Jer 2:24; 5:8; Hos 8:9; *1 En.* 86:4; 88:3; 90:21; cf. Jer 13:27 and 50:11.

121. Gwendolyn Leick, *Sex and Eroticism in Mesopotamian Literature* (London: Routledge, 1994), 21.

122. Patton, "Dragon in the Seas," 25.

123. Lawrence E. Stager, "The Fury of Babylon: Ashkelon and the Archaeology of Destruction," *BAR* 22, no. 1 (1996) 61. Leick also remarks that the emphasis on the phallus and ejaculations of Enki and Enlil underscores the reproductive potency of these gods (Leick, *Sex and Eroticism*, 49). In Ezekiel 23, however, the sisters' endless copulations do not result in pregnancy or motherhood.

124. Greenberg, *Ezekiel 21–37*, 492; Eichrodt, *Ezekiel*, 329–30.

125. Zedekiah's switch of allegiance from Babylonia to Egypt was the catalyst for the destruction of Jerusalem and the second deportation of Judah in 587 B.C.E.; see 2 Kgs 24:20—25:1.

126. For *daddîm* as "nipples," see Block, *Ezekiel*, 733 n. 14; Greenberg, *Ezekiel 21–37*, 474.

127. I also note the movement from general to specific in localizing the sources of sexual pleasure: penises > ejaculations, breasts > nipples.

128. Greenberg, *Ezekiel 21–37*, 489; Block, *Ezekiel*, 747.

129. Beginning with an introductory *lākēn* (therefore).

130. Gale A. Yee, "'She Is Not My Wife, and I Am Not Her Husband': A Materialist Analysis of Hosea 1–2," *BibInt* 9 (2001) 369–71.

131. This point is forcibly argued by Peggy Day, "Adulterous Jerusalem's Imagined Demise," 308–9; idem, "Bitch," 231–54, for Ezekiel 16.

132. Cited in Grayson, "Assyrian Rule," 961.

133. According to Shalom M. Paul, "Biblical Analogues to Middle Assyrian Law," in *Religion and Law: Biblical-Judaic and Islamic Perspectives*, ed. Edwin B. Firmage, Bernard G. Weiss, and John W. Welch (Winona Lake, Ind.: Eisenbrauns, 1990), 344–46, Middle Assyrian Law (MAL) A:15 states that if a man catches his wife in adultery and both partners are convicted before the king or judges, he may kill both, let his wife and thus her partner go free, or cut off his wife's nose and make her partner a eunuch. For Paul, Oholibah is thus punished according to the ordinances of her conquerors (Ezek 23:24). However, there is no mention in the law about the cutting off

of "ears," nor does Ezekiel refer to the legally sanctioned castration of Oholibah's lovers in crime. We are on safer ground, therefore, in contextualizing the cutting off of the nose in atrocities of war rather than in the punishments for adultery.

134. Greenberg, *Ezekiel 21–37*, 482, notes that *tiśʾî ʿênayik ʾĕlêhem* can have both connotations of "looking amorously at" and "look for help to."

135. Beginning with the introductory formula *kî kōh ʾāmar ʾădōnāy yhwh*, "for thus says the Lord yhwh." Most scholars regard this section as a secondary expansion: Eichrodt, *Ezekiel*, 330; Wevers, *Ezekiel*, 137; Walther Zimmerli, *Ezekiel 2*, trans. James D. Martin, Hermeneia (Philadelphia: Fortress Press, 1983), 490.

136. Cf. Ezek 16:7, 22, 39, where the expression *ʿērōm wĕʿeryâ* is a literary tripling device characteristic of Ezekiel 4–7. See Lawrence Boadt, "Rhetorical Strategies in Ezekiel's Oracles of Judgment," in *Ezekiel and His Book: Textual and Literary Criticism and Their Interrelation*, ed. Johan Lust, BETL 74 (Leuven: Leuven Univ. Press, 1986), 188, on Ezekiel's tripling. In Ezekiel 23 this rhetorical strategy is found in the three occurrences of *ʿerwâ* (nakedness, genitals) in vv 10, 18, and 29, the verse under discussion.

137. According to Jacob Milgrom, *Leviticus 17–22*, AB 3A (New York: Doubleday, 2000), 1534, *ʿerwâ* (usually translated as "nakedness") is a euphemism for genitals. However, when it is coupled with *zĕnûnayik* in Ezek 23:29, one can reasonably assume a franker designation.

138. Leviticus 18 and 20. See Milgrom, *Leviticus 17–22*, 1534, on *lĕgallôt ʿerwâ*.

139. See also Isa 47:3; Lam 1:8; Nah 3:5; and Ezek 16:36-37, where the expression is used to describe other female embodiments of a nation whose trauma in war is sexualized.

140. See Ezek 23:37-38, 44, where the identification of vagina and sanctuary is even clearer.

141. Mintz, "Rhetoric of Lamentations," 4; Dobbs-Allsopp and Linafelt, "Rape of Zion," 77–81; Guest, "Hiding," 418; Kathleen M. O'Connor, *Lamentations and the Tears of the World* (Maryknoll, N.Y.: Orbis, 2002), 23.

142. The Hebrew *yād* (hand) is a euphemism for "penis": Isa 58:8–10; Song 5:4. For discussion of *yād*, see Marvin H. Pope, *Song of Songs*, AB 7C (Garden City, N.Y.: Doubleday, 1977), 517–19.

143. *Bwʾ* (to enter) is an often-used graphic allusion to sexual intercourse: Ezek 23:44; Gen 6:4; 16:2; 19:31.

144. For the translation of *gillûlîm* as "images," see n. 103 above.

145. Jer 25:15-29; 49:12; 51:7; Hab 2:16; Lam 4:21; Isa 51:17, 21-22. For a discussion see G. Mayer, "*Kôs*," *TDOT* 7:101–4.

146. Noted by Michael Fishbane, "Accusations of Adultery: A Study of Law and Scribal Practice in Numbers 5:11–31," in *Women in the Hebrew Bible: A Reader*, ed. Alice Bach (New York: Routledge, 1999), 497.

147. *Qinʾâ*, Num 5:14; Ezek 23:25; cf.16:42.

148. *Ḥ ereš*, Num 5:17; Ezek 23:34.

149. According to Martin Noth, *Numbers*, trans. James D. Martin, OTL (Philadelphia: Westminster, 1968), 52, the woman dies according to the capital punishment for adulteresses: by public stoning. Perhaps the potion itself results in death for the suspected woman. Alice Bach, "Good to the Last Drop: Viewing the Sotah (Numbers 5.11-31) as the Glass Half Empty and Wondering How to View It Half Full," in *Women in the Hebrew Bible: A Reader*, ed. Alice Bach (New York: Routledge, 1999), 512–17, notes that many rabbis assumed that a woman who drank the bitter waters died. She demonstrates how modern interpreters minimize the lethal consequences for the suspected wife who drinks.

150. Cf. Jer 25:18, 27; 49:13.

151. *Šammâ* is also used to describe the cup given to Judah and Jerusalem in Jer 25:17.

152. The *hithpoel* of *hll* is found in 1 Sam 21:14, "to pretend to be insane." Here in Jer 25:16 it means "to behave as if insane or crazed. See Holladay, *Concise Lexicon*, 81.

153. I thank Dr. Benny Liew for pointing this sexual insight out to me at the 2002 spring meeting of the Ethnic Chinese Biblical Colloquium at Princeton Theological Seminary.

Chapter 7

1. Some scholars trace her origins to the ancient goddesses, perhaps an ancient Hebrew goddess. See Bernhard Lang, *Wisdom and the Book of Proverbs: A Hebrew Goddess Redefined* (New York: Pilgrim, 1986); Judith M. Hadley, "Wisdom and the Goddess," in *Wisdom in Ancient Israel: Essays in Honour of J. A. Emerton*, ed. John Day et al. (Cambridge: Cambridge Univ. Press, 1995), 234–43; Michael D. Coogan, "The Goddess Wisdom—'Where Can She Be Found?' Literary Reflexes of Popular Religion," in *Ki Baruch Hu: Ancient Near Eastern, Biblical, and Judaic Studies in Honor of Baruch A. Levine*, ed. Robert Chazan et al. (Winona Lake, Ind.: Eisenbrauns, 1999), 203–9. We will see, however, that both Woman Wisdom and the Other Woman are probably elite male literary constructions of their composite perceptions of real women.

2. For an analysis, see Gale A. Yee, "An Analysis of Prov 8:22-31 According to Style and Structure," *ZAW* 94 (1982) 58–66.

3. Writings focusing on the "Otherness" of the *'iššâ zārâ* can be found in Athalya Brenner, "Proverbs 1–9: An F Voice?" in *On Gendering Texts: Female and Male Voices in the Hebrew Bible*, ed. Athalya Brenner and Fokkelien van Dijk-Hemmes, BibIntSer 1 (Leiden: Brill, 1993), 121–26; Christl Maier, "Conflicting Attractions: Parental Wisdom and the 'Strange Woman' in Proverbs 1–9," in *Wisdom and Psalms*, ed. Athalya Brenner and Carole R. Fontaine, FCB 2/2 (Sheffield: Sheffield Academic, 1998), 95–105; Carol A.

Newsom, "Women and the Discourse of Patriarchal Wisdom: A Study of Proverbs 1–9," in *Gender and Difference in Ancient Israel*, ed. Peggy L. Day (Minneapolis: Fortress Press, 1989), 14–49; L. A. Snijders, "The Meaning of *Zar* in the Old Testament," *OtSt* 10 (1954) 99, 104; Harold C. Washington, "The Strange Woman (*'shh zrh/nkryh*) of Proverbs 1–9 and Post-Exilic Judaean Society," in *Second Temple Studies*, vol. 2: *Temple and Community in the Persian Period*, ed. Tamara C. Eskenazi and Kent H. Richards, JSOTSup 175 (Sheffield: Sheffield Academic, 1994), 229–30; Jane S. Webster, "Sophia: Engendering Wisdom in Proverbs, Ben Sira and the Wisdom of Solomon," *JSOT* 78 (1998) 67.

4. In this I disagree with Michael V. Fox, *Proverbs 1–9*, AB 18A (New York: Doubleday, 2000), 262, who thinks that the Strange Woman is the antithesis of one's own wife. He believes that personified folly is personified wisdom's counterpart.

5. R. N. Whybray, *The Book of Proverbs: A Survey of Modern Study*, History of Biblical Interpretation 1 (Leiden: Brill, 1995), 1. The attribution of the work to Solomon is significant, however, because it signals the ideological bias of the chapter's author. See above, 147–49.

6. Patrick W. Skehan and Alexander A. Di Lella, O.F.M., *The Wisdom of Ben Sira*, AB 39 (New York: Doubleday, 1987), 10, 43–45.

7. Richard J. Clifford, *Proverbs: A Commentary*, OTL (Louisville: Westminster John Knox, 1999), 3–4, 219.

8. Proverbs 10–29 is composed for the most part in poetic sentences formulated in antithetic structure. Proverbs 1–9 is composed of didactic speeches of a father to his son and the speeches of Woman Wisdom.

9. Clifford, *Proverbs*, 6; Robert Gordis, "The Social Background of Wisdom," in *Poets, Prophets, and Sages: Essays in Biblical Interpretation* (Bloomington: Indiana Univ. Press, 1971), 162; Roland E. Murphy, *The Tree of Life: An Exploration of Biblical Wisdom*, ABRL (New York: Doubleday, 1990), 19; Leo G. Perdue, *Proverbs*, IBC (Louisville: Westminster John Knox, 2000), 56; Leo G. Perdue, "Wisdom Theology and Social History in Proverbs 1–9," in *Wisdom, You Are My Sister: Studies in Honor of Roland E. Murphy, O.Carm., on the Occasion of His Eightieth Birthday*, ed. Michael L. Barré, S.S., CBQMS 29 (Washington, D.C.: Catholic Biblical Association of America, 1997), 80; Raymond C. Van Leeuwen, "The Book of Proverbs: Introduction, Commentary, and Reflections," *NIB* 5:20–21; Harold C. Washington, *Wealth and Poverty in the Instruction of Amenemope and the Hebrew Proverbs*, SBLDS 142 (Atlanta: Scholars, 1994), 133. But see Claudia V. Camp, *Wise, Strange, and Holy: The Strange Woman and the Making of the Bible*, JSOTSup 320 (Sheffield: Sheffield Academic, 2000), 59–71; and R. B. Y. Scott, *Proverbs. Ecclesiastes: Introduction, Translation, and Notes*, AB 18 (Garden City, N.Y.: Doubleday, 1965), xxxvii–xxxviii, who argue for a later date at the end of the Persian period, closer to the Hellenistic period.

10. Christine Roy Yoder, *Wisdom As a Woman of Substance: A Socioeconomic Reading of Proverbs 1–9 and 31:10-31*, BZAW 304 (Berlin: de Gruyter, 2001), 15–38.

11. This chapter builds on my earlier work on Proverbs 1–9, "'I Have Perfumed My Bed with Myrrh': The Foreign Woman in Proverbs 1–9," *JSOT* 43 (1989) 53–68. In a response to a reprinting of this article, I outlined the parameters of what will be developed in this chapter in "A Socio-Literary Production of the Foreign Woman in Proverbs," in *A Feminist Companion to Wisdom Literature*, ed. Athalya Brenner, FCB 9 (Sheffield: Sheffield Academic, 1995), 127–30.

12. Amélie Kuhrt, "The Cyrus Cylinder and Achaemenid Imperial Policy," *JSOT* 25 (1983) 83–84, points out that Cyrus was also regarded favorably by both Herodotus and Xenophon, and even by historical personages in the more recent past, such as Arnold Toynbee, David Ben-Gurion, and the Shah of Iran.

13. J. Kenneth Kuntz, *The People of Ancient Israel: An Introduction to Old Testament Literature, History, and Thought* (New York: Harper & Row, 1974), 397; Lawrence Boadt, *Reading the Old Testament: An Introduction* (New York: Paulist, 1984), 435–36; Peter C. Craigie, *The Old Testament: Its Background, Growth, and Content* (Nashville: Abingdon, 1986), 287. See also T. Cuyler Young Jr., "Cyrus," *ABD* 1:1232.

14. Kuhrt, "Cyrus Cylinder," 94–95.

15. Lester L. Grabbe, *Judaism from Cyrus to Hadrian*, vol. 1: *The Persian and Greek Periods* (Minneapolis: Fortress Press, 1992), 23, 115; Jon L. Berquist, *Judaism in Persia's Shadow: A Social and Historical Approach* (Minneapolis: Fortress Press, 1995), 26; Charles E. Carter, *The Emergence of Yehud in the Persian Period: A Social and Demographic Study*, JSOTSup 294 (Sheffield: Sheffield Academic, 1999), 293–94; Washington, *Wealth and Poverty*, 162.

16. Joseph Blenkinsopp, "Temple and Society in Achaemenid Judah," in *Second Temple Studies*, vol. 1: *Persian Period*, ed. Philip R. Davies, JSOTSup 117 (Sheffield: Sheffield Academic, 1991), 50–51.

17. Ibid., 22–40; James M. Trotter, "Was the Second Jerusalem Temple a Primarily Persian Project?" *SJOT* 15 (2001) 276–94; Carter, *Emergence of Yehud*, 304–5; Perdue, *Proverbs*, 57.

18. Norman K. Gottwald, *The Politics of Ancient Israel*, LAI (Louisville: Westminster John Knox, 2000), 224.

19. Carter, *Emergence of Yehud*, 76, 246–47.

20. Ibid., 216–17, 249; Grabbe, *Judaism*, 1:23, 118.

21. Carter, *Emergence of Yehud*, 255–56.

22. During the time of the divided monarchy, foreign nations impinged upon this native mode of production by demanding tribute. However, most of the surplus remained with the native elite. See the extrinsic analysis of the book of Hosea above, pp. 83–85.

23. Norman K. Gottwald, "Sociology (Ancient Israel)," *ABD* 6:85.

24. Carter, *Emergence of Yehud*, 281, 309–10; Grabbe, *Judaism*, 1:115,
25. Carter, *Emergence of Yehud*, 281.
26. For a more detailed discussion of the various foreign policies of specific emperors, see Berquist, *Judaism in Persia's Shadow*, 23–127, from which this section of the chapter primarily draws.
27. Ibid., 49–50.
28. Indeed, subsidizing the rebuilding of the Sais temple under Udjahorresnet in Egypt (ca. 520 B.C.E.) allowed him to take possession of that country without military conquest.
29. Berquist, *Judaism in Persia's Shadow*, 89, 92–102; Grabbe, *Judaism*, 1:129.
30. Berquist, *Judaism in Persia's Shadow*, 93.
31. Kenneth Hoglund, "The Achaemenid Context," in *Second Temple Studies*, ed. Davies, 1:54, 64; Berquist, *Judaism in Persia's Shadow*, 110–11; D. Bodi, "La clémence des Perses envers Néhémie et ses compatriotes: faveur ou opportunisme politique?" *Transeu* 21 (2001) 69–86.
32. Berquist, *Judaism in Persia's Shadow*, 105–9.
33. Ibid., 109.
34. Ibid., 65–79.
35. Blenkinsopp, "Temple and Society," 50–51; Richard A. Horsley, "The Slave Systems of Classical Antiquity and Their Reluctant Recognition by Modern Scholars," *Semeia* 83/84 (1998) 170. However, Philip R. Davies, *In Search of 'Ancient Israel,'* JSOTSup 148 (Sheffield: Sheffield Academic, 1992), 81–82, raises the issue that the "returnees" may not necessarily have been Judean exiles returning home.
36. *Golah:* those deported into exile, the exiles. The *golah* community refers to those ethnically Jewish families who returned to Yehud from the Babylonian exile. See Ezra 1:11; 2:1; 4:1; 6:19-20; 10:6-8, and passim. See Berquist, *Judaism in Persia's Shadow*, 79; Washington, *Wealth and Poverty*, 164–65; Joseph Blenkinsopp, "The Social Context of the 'Outsider Woman' in Proverbs 1–9," *Bib* 72 (1991) 472.
37. Gottwald, *Politics of Ancient Israel*, 238–39; Perdue, *Proverbs*, 56–57.
38. See above, pp. 113–14.
39. Daniel L. Smith, "The Politics of Ezra: Sociological Indicators of Postexilic Judaean Society," in *Second Temple Studies*, ed. Davies, 1:95–96.
40. Grabbe, *Judaism*, 1:117, 121.
41. Berquist, *Judaism in Persia's Shadow*, 78.
42. Rainer Albertz, *A History of Israelite Religion in the Old Testament Period*, vol. 2: *From the Exile to the Maccabees*, trans. John Bowden, OTL (Louisville: Westminster John Knox, 1994), 448.
43. Berquist, *Judaism in Persia's Shadow*, 62.
44. Ibid., 113.
45. This assumes, with a number of scholars, the beginning of Nehemiah's governorship in Yehud in 445 B.C.E. during the rule of Artaxerxes I. For a summary of the debate, see H. G. M. Williamson, "The Chronological

Order of Ezra and Nehemiah," in *Ezra and Nehemiah,* OTG (Sheffield: Sheffield Academic, 1987), 55–69.

46. For an excellent class analysis of Nehemiah 5, see Norman K. Gottwald, "The Expropriated and the Expropriators in Nehemiah 5," in *Concepts of Class in Ancient Israel,* ed. Mark R. Sneed, SFSHJ 204 (Atlanta: Scholars, 1999), 1–19.

47. In the wider imperial context, Berquist, *Judaism in Persia's Shadow,* 115, points out that if Yehud's inhabitants sold their children to the Greeks to pay off debts, Persia's depletion policy diminished Yehud's labor force while simultaneously strengthening that of its enemy.

48. According to H. G. M. Williamson, *Ezra, Nehemiah,* WBC 16 (Waco: Word, 1985), 238, the detail of the daughters' molestation suggests that they may have been sexually abused as payment for delaying foreclosure on loans.

49. Gottwald, "Expropriated," 9, 12; Albertz, *History of Israelite Religion,* 2:496–97.

50. Berquist, *Judaism in Persia's Shadow,* 114.

51. David Bossman, O.F.M., "Ezra's Marriage Reform: Israel Redefined," *BTB* 9 (1979) 36–38; F. Charles Fensham, *The Books of Ezra and Nehemiah,* NICOT (Grand Rapids: Eerdmans, 1982), 124; Christine Hayes, "Intermarriage and Impurity in Ancient Jewish Sources," *HTR* 92 (1999) 3–36; Hyam Maccoby, "Holiness and Purity: The Holy People in Leviticus and Ezra-Nehemiah," in *Reading Leviticus: A Conversation with Mary Douglas,* ed. John F. A. Sawyer, JSOTSup 227 (Sheffield: Sheffield Academic, 1996), 153–70; Mark A. Throntveit, *Ezra–Nehemiah,* IBC (Louisville: Westminster John Knox, 1992), 57; and those discussed in Daniel Smith, "Politics of Ezra," 90–93.

52. Blenkinsopp, "Social Context," 457–73; Willa Mathis Johnson, "Ethnicity in Persian Yehud: Between Anthropological Analysis and Ideological Criticism," *SBLSP 1995,* 177–86; Washington, "Strange Woman," 217–42; Berquist, *Judaism in Persia's Shadow,* 118–19; Maier, "Conflicting Attractions," 100–102; Hoglund, "Achaemenid Context," 67; Yoder, *Wisdom,* 105.

53. Washington, "Strange Woman," 232; Mary Douglas, "Responding to Ezra: The Priests and the Foreign Wives," *BibInt* 10 (2002) 11; Yoder, *Wisdom,* 104–6.

54. Hoglund, "Achaemenid Context," 59.

55. Carter, *Emergence of Yehud,* 248.

56. Ezra 4:1-3; 6:6-12. Cf. 10:8. See Joseph Blenkinsopp, "Did the Second Jerusalemite Temple Possess Land?" *Transeu* 21 (2001) 61–68; Washington, *Wealth and Poverty,* 160; Carter, *Emergence of Yehud,* 292; Washington, "Strange Woman," 233.

57. Edmund Leach, *Genesis As Myth and Other Essays* (London: Jonathan Cape, 1969), 57; Daniel Smith, "Politics of Ezra," 96; Tamara C. Eskenazi,

"Out from the Shadows: Biblical Women in the Postexilic Era," *JSOT* 54 (1992) 35; Blenkinsopp, "Social Context," 472.

58. Douglas, "Responding to Ezra," 11. See also Daniel Smith, "Politics of Ezra," 96; Daniel L. Smith-Christopher, "The Mixed Marriage Crisis in Ezra 9–10 and Nehemiah 13: A Study of the Sociology of the Post-Exilic Judean Community," in *Second Temple Studies*, ed. Eskenazi and Richards, 2:245.

59. Douglas, "Responding to Ezra," 11; Tamara C. Eskenazi and Eleanore P. Judd, "Marriage to a Stranger in Ezra 9–10," in *Second Temple Studies*, ed. Eskenazi and Richards, 2:285. Blenkinsopp comments on Mal 2:10-16: "The most plausible fifth-century setting for this indictment would be the situation of those Babylonian *olim* who, on their return to the homeland, abandoned the wives they brought with them for native women, and one important motive for doing so may well have been the acquisition or reacquisition of property deeded to these women" (Blenkinsopp, "Social Context," 471).

60. Smith-Christopher, "Mixed Marriage Crisis," 248–49.

61. Ibid., 260–61. I disagree with his notion that the returnees exchanged their low status as "exiles" for participation in the aristocratic society of Yehud. I would argue, instead, that the returnees exchanged or exploited their high status under Persian sponsorship in order to gain access to the natives' land.

62. Douglas, "Responding to Ezra," 12.

63. Hans M. Barstad, *The Myth of the Empty Land: A Study in the History and Archaeology of Judah During the 'Exilic' Period*, SO 28 (Oslo: Scandinavian Univ. Press, 1996); Robert P. Carroll, "The Myth of the Empty Land," *Semeia* 59 (1992) 79–93.

64. Barstad, *Myth of the Empty Land*, 39, 44; Lester L. Grabbe, *Ezra and Nehemiah* (London: Routledge, 1998), 136–38; idem, "Triumph of the Pious or Failure of the Xenophobes: The Ezra-Nehemiah Reforms and Their *Nachgeschichte*," in *Jewish Local Patriotism and Self-Identification in the Graeco-Roman Period*, ed. Siân Jones and Sarah Pearce, JSPSup 31 (Sheffield: Sheffield Academic, 1998), 56–57.

65. Blenkinsopp, "Social Context," 460; H. G. M. Williamson, "The Concept of Israel in Transition," in *The World of Ancient Israel: Sociological, Anthropological and Political Perspectives*, ed. R. E. Clements (Cambridge: Cambridge Univ. Press, 1989), 155; Grabbe, "Triumph of the Pious," 57.

66. Washington, "Strange Woman," 232; Blenkinsopp, "Social Context," 460; Grabbe, *Ezra and Nehemiah*, 138; Daniel L. Smith-Christopher, "Between Ezra and Isaiah: Exclusion, Transformation, and Inclusion of the 'Foreigner' in Post-Exilic Biblical Theology," in *Ethnicity and the Bible*, ed. Mark G. Brett, BibIntSer 19 (Leiden: Brill, 1996), 126.

67. H. D. Preuss, "*Zāra'; Zera'*," *TDOT* 4:143–62.

68. Washington, "Strange Woman," 232; Carter, *Emergence of Yehud*, 311.

69. I focus primarily on Ezra here, because in Nehemiah's case the women were ethnically foreign, while Ezra operated under different criteria for "foreignness."

70. Washington, "Strange Woman," 230–32; Smith-Christopher, "Mixed Marriage Crisis," 247; idem, "Between Ezra and Isaiah," 126; Eskenazi and Judd, "Marriage to a Stranger," 285.

71. Johnson, "Ethnicity in Persian Yehud," 182–83; Joseph Blenkinsopp, *Ezra-Nehemiah: A Commentary*, OTL (Philadelphia: Westminster, 1988), 176–77; Berquist, *Judaism in Persia's Shadow*, 118; Perdue, *Proverbs*, 57–58.

72. Eskenazi and Judd, "Marriage to a Stranger," 266–85.

73. Carter, *Emergence of Yehud*, 311; Smith-Christopher, "Mixed Marriage Crisis," 247; Grabbe, "Triumph of the Pious," 57; Douglas, "Responding to Ezra," 5.

74. See Smith-Christopher, "Mixed Marriage Crisis," 253–55, on the factor of romance in "mixed" marriages.

75. Blenkinsopp, "Did the Second Jerusalemite Temple Possess Land?" 63–68; idem, "Social Context," 468–69.

76. Blenkinsopp, *Ezra-Nehemia*, 179; Eskenazi and Judd, "Marriage to a Stranger," 271.

77. Eskenazi, "Out from the Shadows," 35; Yoder, *Wisdom*, 49–58; Washington, "Strange Woman," 235–36. Cf. Num 27:1-11; 36:1-9.

78. Berquist, *Judaism in Persia's Shadow*, 117–18.

79. Blenkinsopp, *Ezra-Nehemia*, 176–77.

80. See above, pp. 118–19.

81. Although I refer in the following to Proverbs 1–9, I also include Prov 31:10-31 and its encomium of praise for the idealized wife. Scholars have noted that these chapters comprise a later redactional frame around the sentence collections.

82. Perdue, *Proverbs*, 15–27; idem, "Liminality As a Social Setting for Wisdom Instructions," *ZAW* 93 (1981) 114–15; Gordis, "Social Background of Wisdom," 162–63; Mark Sneed, "The Class Culture of Proverbs: Eliminating Stereotypes," *SJOT* 10 (1996) 296–308; Perdue, *Proverbs*, 17–22; Washington, *Wealth and Poverty*, 166; Albertz, *History of Israelite Religion*, 2:511; Fox, *Proverbs 1–9*, 11; R. N. Whybray, *Wealth and Poverty in the Book of Proverbs*, JSOTSup 99 (Sheffield: Sheffield Academic, 1990), 99–106; James L. Crenshaw, "Poverty and Punishment in the Book of Proverbs," in *Urgent Advice and Probing Questions: Collected Writings on Old Testament Wisdom* (Macon, Ga.: Mercer Univ. Press, 1995), 398–99; Maier, "Conflicting Attractions," 103–4; G. H. Wittenberg, "The Situational Context of Statements concerning Poverty and Wealth in the Book of Proverbs," *Scriptura* 21 (1987) 1–23; Yoder, *Wisdom*, 103–4; J. David Pleins, "Poverty in the Social World of the Wise," *JSOT* 37 (1987) 61–78; R. N. Whybray, "City Life

in Proverbs 1–9," in *"Jedes Ding hat seine Zeit . . ."*: *Studien zur israelitischen und altorientalischen Weisheit, Diethelm Michel zum 65. Gehurtrtag,* ed. Anja A. Diesel et al., BZAW 241 (Berlin. de Gruyter, 1996), 243–50.

Carter, *Emergence of Yehud,* 285–90, raises the question of the literary mode of production in Yehud: How could the social and religious elite of a small, impoverished province carry on the literary production ascribed to the Persian period? Based on historical and sociological parallels, he concludes that "the level of literary creativity traditionally attributed to the Persian period need not be questioned on the grounds either of a small province or a small Jerusalem."

83. See above, pp. 69–70.

84. See Walter A. Brueggemann, "The Social Significance of Solomon As a Patron of Wisdom," in *The Sage in Israel and the Ancient Near East,* ed. John G. Gammie and Leo G. Perdue (Winona Lake, Ind.: Eisenbrauns, 1990), 123–29, on the operations of this mode of production that tradents remembered of Solomon's rule.

85. Perdue, *Proverbs,* 18–19, 64–65; idem, "Wisdom Theology and Social History," 92–93. Cf. Brueggemann, "Social Significance of Solomon," 129.

86. For an analysis of these economics at work in 1 Kings 1–11, see David Jobling, "Forced Labor: Solomon's Golden Age and the Question of Literary Representation," *Semeia* 54 (1991) 57–76, reprinted with some modification in idem, "The Value of Solomon's Age for the Biblical Reader," in *The Age of Solomon: Scholarship at the Turn of the Millennium,* ed. Lowell K. Handy, SHCANE 11 (Leiden: Brill, 1997), 470–92.

87. Jobling, "Forced Labor," 62, emphasis added.

88. See those cited in n. 82.

89. Whybray, "City Life in Proverbs 1–9," 249. See also idem, *Wealth and Poverty,* 99–106.

90. Newsom, "Women," 144.

91. Brueggemann, "Social Significance of Solomon," 130, emphasis added.

92. See above, p. 24, on the notion of "absence" in the text that must marginalize other voices in order to give itself voice. This textual voice symbolically resolves the real social contradictions that produce the text itself.

93. Camp, *Wise, Strange, and Holy,* 154–55, 180–86. See also Jobling, "Value of Solomon's Age," 470, 487.

94. Camp, *Wise, Strange, and Holy,* 155–81. These wise and strange women in 1 Kings 1–11 include Abishag and Bathsheba, the two prostitute mothers, Pharaoh's daughter, the Queen of Sheba, and Solomon's innumerable foreign wives.

95. Newsom, "Women," 148; Brenner, "Proverbs 1–9," 121–23; Washington, "Strange Woman," 229–30; Maier, "Conflicting Attractions," 93–94; Camp, *Wise, Strange, and Holy,* 40–43; Blenkinsopp, "Social Context," 473; Perdue, *Proverbs,* 87; Webster, "Sophia," 55–56. Nevertheless, interpreting

the *'iššâ zārâ* as representing ethnically foreign cult or wisdom still has its adherents. See John Barclay Burns, "Proverbs 7,6-27: Vignettes from the Cycle of Astarte and Adonis," *SJOT* 9 (1995) 20–36; and Johann Cook, "'*iššâ Zārâ* (Proverbs 1–9 Septuagint): A Metaphor for Foreign Wisdom?" *ZAW* 106 (1994) 458–76. Fox, *Proverbs 1–9*, 134–41, identifies her only as another man's wife.

96. Camp, *Wise, Strange, and Holy*, 32, thinks that the Strange Woman is too multidimensional to be linked with one historical moment. In a sense I agree, but for different reasons. I prefer to connect the literary construction of the Other Woman with a particular mode of production found that had particular historical configurations in postexilic Yehud, rather than with a particular historical moment.

97. Claudia V. Camp, "Wise and Strange: An Interpretation of the Female Imagery in Proverbs in Light of Trickster Mythology," *Semeia* 42 (1988) 28–29.

98. Blenkinsopp, "Social Context," 467, maintains that the personification of wisdom is "a secondary elaboration, a counter to the Outsider Woman, in the context of the exogamy-endogamy issue in the early Second Temple period."

99. Yoder, *Wisdom*, 105–6. I therefore disagree with Maier, "Conflicting Attractions," 104, that "the male 'outsider' transgresses conventional behaviour in economic matters" and "the female 'outsider' transgresses the sexual mores." Issues surrounding the Other Woman are also economic, and are cloaked in tropes of sexuality.

100. Cf. Perdue, *Proverbs*, 92–93.

101. See Elaine Adler Goodfriend, "Adultery," *ABD* 1:82–86; Raymond Westbrook, "Adultery in Ancient Near Eastern Law," *RB* 97 (1990) 542–80; Robert Gordis, "On Adultery in Biblical and Babylonian Law," *Judaism* 33 (1984) 210–11; Henry McKeating, "Sanctions against Adultery in Ancient Israelite Society, with Some Reflections on Methodology in the Study of Old Testament Ethics," *JSOT* 11 (1979) 52–72; Anthony Phillips, "Another Look at Adultery," *JSOT* 20 (1981) 3–25. See also above, pp.47–48, in which I discuss adultery at some length.

102. See chaps. 5 and 6 above, in which I discuss the use of adultery as a trope to describe idolatry, an oppressive mode of production, and alliances with foreign nations in both Hosea and Ezekiel, all in the context of the deity's covenant with the nation in its depiction as a marriage.

103. See Yee, "I Have Perfumed My Bed," 55, to see how these three warnings are interspersed in the chiastic structure of the speeches in Proverbs 1–6.

104. Ezra 10:8a. See Blenkinsopp, "Social Context," 468; Perdue, *Proverbs*, 94–95. The class bias in Proverbs regarding possessing and being

cut off from the land resembles that in the wisdom psalm, Psalm 37. See Walter Brueggemann, "Theodicy in a Social Dimension," *JSOT* 33 (1985) 24 n. 39.

105. Cf. Ezra 10:8b.

106. Claudia V. Camp, "What's So Strange about the Strange Woman?" in *The Bible and the Politics of Exegesis: Essays in Honor of Norman K. Gottwald on His Sixty-Fifth Birthday,* ed. David Jobling, Peggy L. Day, and Gerald T. Sheppard (Cleveland: Pilgrim, 1991), 27; idem, "The Strange Woman of Proverbs: A Study in the Feminization and Divinization of Evil in Biblical Thought," in *Women and Goddess Traditions in Antiquity and Today,* ed. Karen L. King (Minneapolis: Fortress Press, 1997), 321; Washington, "Strange Woman," 218; Brenner, "Proverbs 1–9," 125–26.

107. See Alice Ogden Bellis, "The Gender and Motives of the Wisdom Teacher in Proverbs 7," in *Wisdom and Psalms,* ed. Brenner and Fontaine, 82–83; Maier, "Conflicting Attractions," 102; Fox, *Proverbs 1–9,* 260.

108. For a detailed socioeconomic analysis of Prov 31:10-31, see Yoder, *Wisdom,* 75–91.

109. Ibid., 78.

110. Thomas P. McCreesh, O.P., "Wisdom As Wife: Proverbs 31:10-31," *RB* 92 (1985) 25–46; Claudia V. Camp, *Wisdom and the Feminine in the Book of Proverbs,* BibLitSer 11 (Decatur, Ga.: Almond, 1985), 90–93, 186–91; Murphy, *Tree of Life,* 27; Whybray, *Book of Proverbs,* 102–3, 105–8; Clifford, *Proverbs,* 274; Yoder, *Wisdom,* 91–101.

111. Cf. Ruth 4:10: "Also Ruth the Moabitess, the widow of Mahlon, I have bought (*qānîtî*) to be my wife, to perpetuate the name of the dead in his inheritance" (rsv).

112. Yoder, *Wisdom,* 96.

113. Cf. Prov 31:18, where the Woman of Substance "perceives that her business profit is good" (*kî-ṭôb saḥrāh*).

114. Proverbs 3:9-10 reveals the importance of the land and its income-generating commodities (*tĕbû'â*) in the economy of Yehud for the elite: "Honor the Lord with your wealth (*mēhônekā*) and with the first fruits of your land's revenue/yield (*tĕbû'ātekā*); then your barns will be filled with plenty, and your vats will be bursting with wine."

115. On the similarities of the two women, see J. N. Aletti, "Séduction et parole en Proverbes I–IX," *VT* 27 (1977) 129–44; Yee, "I Have Perfumed My Bed," 53–68.

116. Yee, "I Have Perfumed My Bed," 53–68.

117. Fokkelien van Dijk-Hemmes, "Traces of Women's Texts in the Hebrew Bible," in *On Gendering Texts,* ed. Brenner and van Dijk-Hemmes, 57–62; Brenner, "Proverbs 1–9," 120; Mieke Heijerman, "Who Would Blame Her? The 'Strange' Woman of Proverbs 7," in *Reflections on Theology*

and Gender, ed. Fokkelien van Dijk-Hemmes and Athalya Brenner (Kampen: Kok Pharos, 1994), 21; Bellis, "Gender and Motives," 79–91. In the Septuagint a woman does peer out the window, but it is the seductive woman, not the mother. See Michael V. Fox, "The Strange Woman in Septuagint Proverbs," *JNSL* 22 (1996) 36–37.

118. Both Maier, "Conflicting Attractions," 104–5; and Gerlinde Baumann, "A Figure with Many Facets: The Literary and Theological Functions of Personified Wisdom in Proverbs 1–9," in *Wisdom and Psalms,* ed. Brenner and Fontaine, 51, are open to this possibility.

119. Newsom, "Women," 143–44.

120. Crawford H. Toy, *A Critical and Exegetical Commentary on the Book of Proverbs,* ICC (New York: Scribner's, 1908), 145; W. O. E. Oesterley, *The Book of Proverbs,* Westminster Commentaries 17 (London: Methuen, 1929), 50. *Mōdā'* occurs otherwise only in Ruth 2:1 and 3:2, where Boaz is described as a kinsman of Naomi. Naomi exploits this relationship in order to maneuver Boaz into marrying Ruth.

121. The descriptor, "a young man without sense (*ḥāsar lēb*)," is the same as the one the father uses to portray the adulterer in 6:32.

122. Toy, *Proverbs,* 146; William McKane, *Proverbs: A New Approach,* OTL (Philadelphia: Westminster, 1970), 335; Fox, *Proverbs 1–9,* 242.

123. For parallels between the Song of Songs and Proverbs 7, see Daniel Grossberg, "Two Kinds of Sexual Relationships in the Hebrew Bible," *Hebrew Studies* 35 (1994) 7–25.

124. Lit. "loaf of bread," or subsistence rations. Oesterley, *Proverbs,* 47; McKane, *Proverbs,* 329.

125. Fox, *Proverbs 1–9,* 244.

126. Oesterley, *Proverbs,* 149; Fox, *Proverbs 1–9,* 244.

127. Commenting on Song 5:3, "I had bathed my feet, how could I soil them?" Carey Ellen Walsh, *Exquisite Desire: Religion, the Erotic, and the Song of Songs* (Minneapolis: Fortress Press, 2000), 110–11, argues that "feet" can be a double entendre, referring to the vaginal lips surrounding the opening into which her lover's "hand" will thrust (Song 5:4).

128. Cf. Deut 22:25; Judg 19:25; 2 Sam 13:11, 14.

129. See Karel van der Toorn, "Female Prostitution in Payment of Vows in Ancient Israel," *JBL* 108 (1989) 193–205; Heijerman, "Who Would Blame Her?" 24, 27–28; and van Dijk-Hemmes, "Traces of Women's Texts," 60–61, who argue that the woman is in need of money to pay for her vows and resorts to prostitution to obtain it.

130. Lit. "are upon me" (*'ālāy*).

131. Thus RSV; NRSV; Toy, *Proverbs,* 150–51; Oesterley, *Proverbs,* 52; Jacques Berlinerblau, *The Vow and the 'Popular Religious Groups' of Ancient Israel: A Philological and Sociological Inquiry,* JSOTSup 210 (Sheffield: Sheffield Academic, 1996), 127 n. 5; Fox, *Proverbs 1–9,* 245–46.

132. That is, it can be an action that belongs to the near future but that is represented as being performed at the time of utterance.

133. Thus Gustav Boström, *Proverbiastudien: Die Weisheit und das fremde Weib in Spr. 1–9*, Lunds universitets årsskrift 30 (Lund: Gleerup, 1935), 105–7; McKane, *Proverbs*, 337; van der Toorn, "Female Prostitution," 197–98; Clifford, *Proverbs*, 88–89.

134. It is not unthinkable that the invitation to a meal could have been the female equivalent of "Come up and see my etchings"—a perversion of "The way to a man's heart is through his stomach."

135. Clifford, *Proverbs*, 88–89, discusses the ambiguity of meaning from the two senses of *šillamtî*.

136. See Amos 6:4 regarding the opulent couches (*'erēś*) of the elite, upon which they idle away their days.

137. Cf. the royal purple coverings (*marbad*) that the Woman of Substance makes for herself in Prov 31:22.

138. For a discussion of these high-priced items, see Victor H. Matthews, "Perfumes and Spices," *ABD* 5:226–28; Robert H. O'Connell, "Proverbs VII 6-17: A Case of Fatal Deception in a 'Woman and the Window' Type-Scene," *VT* 41 (1991) 237–38; Fox, *Proverbs 1–9*, 247–48. Cf. the great quantity of spices that the Queen of Sheba and other monarchs bring to Solomon's court in 1 Kgs 10:2, 10, 25.

139. *'erēś* in Song 1:16.

140. Song 1:13. See also 3:6; 4:6; 5:1, 5, 13.

141. Song 4:13-14.

142. As noted by O'Connell, "Proverbs VII 6–17," 238; and Clifford, *Proverbs*, 89.

143. Matt 27:59; Mark 15:46; Luke 23:53; John 11:44; 19:40; 20:6-7.

144. Mark 16:1 and Luke 24:1 note unspecified "spices." Luke 23:56 has "spices and perfumes."

145. *Dōdîm*: Ezek 16:8; 23:17; Song 1:2, 4; 4:10, and passim; *'ăhābîm*: Prov 5:19. Cf. Hos 8:9.

146. The MT refers only to *hā'îš*, "the man" not in his house. For another reading that allows for the possibility that "the man" is not the Other Woman's husband, see Brenner, "Proverbs 1–9," 124, who suggests that "the man" could be a male relative and custodian, as well as a husband.

147. Cf. 2 Chr 16:14, where Asa's funeral bier is a bed (*miškāb*) "which had been filled with various kinds of spices prepared by the perfumer's art."

148. For the variation between singular and plural for "son," see Fox, *Proverbs 1–9*, 250.

149. Sheol is the Hebrew abode of the dead.

150. See 6:29 and Judg 15:1. Clifford, *Proverbs*, 48; and Fox, *Proverbs 1–9*, 122, see a sexual connotation in *bā'ēhā*.

151. See Van Leeuwen, "Book of Proverbs," 66, for this rendering.

Chapter 8

1. On the phenomenon of American orientalism, see Sheng-Mei Ma, *The Deathly Embrace: Orientalism and Asian American Identity* (Minneapolis: Univ. of Minnesota Press, 2000); Henry Yu, *Thinking Orientals: Migration, Contact, and Exoticism in Modern America* (Oxford: Oxford Univ. Press, 2001); Robert G. Lee, *Orientals: Asian Americans in Popular Culture* (Philadelphia: Temple Univ. Press, 1999); and Helen Zia, "Gangsters, Gooks, Geishas, and Geeks," in *Asian American Dreams: The Emergence of an American People* (New York: Farrar, Straus & Giroux, 2000), 109–35.

2. For an analysis and critique of the American exoticization of Asian women, see Aki Uchida, "The Orientalization of Asian Women in America," *Women's Studies International Forum* 21 (1998) 161–74. The Asian Woman fetish of white men has been explored in the novel by Mako Yoshikawa, *One Hundred and One Ways* (New York: Bantam, 1999). "One hundred and one ways" refers to the number of ways a geisha was supposedly able to "unlock [men's] bodies with a groan" (9).

3. See Yen Le Espiritu, "Ideological Racism and Cultural Resistance," in *Asian American Woman and Men* (Thousand Oaks, Calif.: Sage, 1997), 86–107; Gina Marchetti, *Romance and the "Yellow Peril": Race, Sex, and Discursive Strategies in Hollywood* (Berkeley: Univ. of California Press, 1993); Peter X. Feng, ed., *Screening Asian Americans* (New Brunswick, N.J.: Rutgers Univ. Press, 2002); Chüng Hsing, *Asian America through the Lens: History, Representations, and Identity* (Walnut Creek, Calif.: Alta Mira, 1998); Darrell Y. Hamamoto, *Monitored Peril: Asian Americans and the Politics of TV Representation* (Minneapolis: Univ. of Minnesota Press, 1994). For a helpful one-hour video, containing clips of Hollywood depictions of Asians, see Deborah Gee, producer and director, *Slaying the Dragon* (San Francisco: NAATA Distribution, 1995).

4. Ronald Takaki, *Strangers from a Different Shore: A History of Asian Americans* (New York: Penguin, 1989), 13.

5. It goes without saying that men, too, can adopt similar behavior, when in a hierarchically subordinate position.

6. Danna Nolan Fewell and Gary A. Phillips, "Ethics, Bible, Reading As If," *Semeia* 77 (1997) 2. This essay introduces the volume, which is devoted to the theme "Bible and the Ethics of Reading."

Bibliography

Abu-Lughod, Lila. "A Community of Secrets: The Separate World of Bedouin Women." *Signs* 10 (1985) 637–57.

———. "The Romance of Resistance: Tracing Transformations of Power through Bedouin Women." In *Beyond the Second Sex: New Directions in the Anthropology of Gender.* Edited by Peggy Reeves Sanday and Ruth Gallagher Goodenough, 313–37. Philadelphia: Univ. of Pennsylvania Press, 1990.

———. *Veiled Sentiments: Honor and Poetry in a Bedouin Society.* Berkeley: Univ. of California Press, 1986.

———. *Writing Women's Worlds: Bedouin Stories.* Berkeley: Univ. of California Press, 1993.

Ackerman, Susan. "The Queen Mother and the Cult in Ancient Israel." *JBL* 112 (1993) 385–401.

Ackroyd, Peter R. *Exile and Restoration: A Study of Hebrew Thought of the Sixth Century B.C.* OTL. Philadelphia: Westminster, 1968.

Adams, Robert McCormick. *Heartland of Cities: Surveys of Ancient Settlement and Land Use on the Central Floodplain of the Euphrates.* Chicago: Univ. of Chicago Press, 1981.

Ahlström, G. W. *Royal Administration and National Religion in Ancient Palestine.* SHANE 1. Leiden: Brill, 1982.

Alaimo, Stacy. *Undomesticated Ground: Recasting Nature As Feminist Space.* Ithaca: Cornell Univ. Press, 2000.

Albertz, Rainer. *A History of Israelite Religion in the Old Testament Period.* 2 vols. Translated by John Bowden. OTL. Louisville: Westminster John Knox, 1994.

Albright, William F. *From the Stone Age to Christianity: Monotheism and the Historical Process.* 2nd ed. Garden City, N.Y.: Doubleday, 1957.

————. "The Seal of Eliakim and the Latest Preëxilic History of Judah." *JBL* 51 (1932) 77–106.

Aletti, J. N. "Séduction et parole en Proverbes I–IX." *VT* 27 (1977) 129–44.

Althusser, Louis. "Ideology and Ideological State Apparatuses (Notes Towards an Investigation)." In *Lenin and Philosophy and Other Essays*, 127–86. New York: Monthly Review, 1971.

Andersen, Francis I., and David Noel Freedman. *Hosea*. AB 24. Garden City, N.Y.: Doubleday, 1980.

Antze, Paul, and Michael Lambek, eds. *Tense Past: Cultural Essays in Trauma and Memory*. London: Routledge, 1996.

Arnaud, M. "La Prostitution sacrée en Mésopotamie, un mythe historiographique?" *RHR* 183 (1973) 111–15.

Astour, Michael C. "Tamar the Hierodule: An Essay in the Method of Vestigial Motifs." *JBL* 85 (1966) 185–96.

Baab, O. J. "Marriage." In *IDB* 3:279–80.

————. "Prostitution." In *IDB* 3:932–34.

Bach, Alice. "Good to the Last Drop: Viewing the Sotah (Numbers 5.11-31) as the Glass Half Empty and Wondering How to View It Half Full." In *Women in the Hebrew Bible: A Reader*. Edited by Alice Bach, 503–22. New York: Routledge, 1999.

Bailey, J. A. "Initiation and the Primal Woman in Gilgamesh and Genesis 2–3." *JBL* 89 (1970) 137–50.

Bailey, Randall C. "They're Nothing but Incestuous Bastards: The Polemical Use of Sex and Sexuality in Hebrew Canon Narratives." In *Reading from This Place*. Vol. 1: *Social Location and Biblical Interpretation in the United States*. Edited by Fernando F. Segovia and Mary Ann Tolbert, 121–38. Minneapolis: Fortress Press, 1995.

Bal, Mieke. *Lethal Love: Feminist Literary Readings of Biblical Love Stories*. ISBL. Bloomington: Indiana Univ. Press, 1987.

————. *Murder and Difference: Gender, Genre, and Scholarship on Sisera's Death*. ISBL. Bloomington: Indiana Univ. Press, 1988.

Balz-Cochois, Helgard. "Gomer oder die Macht der Astarte. Versuch einer feministischen Interpretation von Hos 1–4." *Evangelische Theologie* 42 (1982) 37–65.

Bar-On, Dan. *The Indescribable and the Undiscussable: Reconstructing Human Discourse after Trauma*. Budapest: Central European Univ. Press, 1999.

Barrett, Michèle. "Ideology and the Cultural Production of Gender." In *Women's Oppression Today: The Marxist/Feminist Encounter*, 84–113. Rev. ed. London: Verso, 1988.

Barstad, Hans M. *The Myth of the Empty Land: A Study in the History and Archaeology of Judah during the 'Exilic' Period*. SO 28. Oslo: Scandinavian Univ. Press, 1996.

Barstow, Anne Llewellyn. *Witchcraze: A New History of the European Witch Hunts*. San Francisco: Pandora, 1994.

Baumann, Gerlinde. "Connected by Marriage, Adultery and Violence: The Prophetic Marriage Metaphor in the Book of the Twelve and in the Major Prophets." In *SBLSP* 38 (1999) 552–69.

———. "A Figure with Many Facets: The Literary and Theological Functions of Personified Wisdom in Proverbs 1–9." In *Wisdom and Psalms*. Edited by Athalya Brenner and Carole R. Fontaine, 44–78. FCB 2/2. Sheffield: Sheffield Academic, 1998.

Beeston, A. F. L. "One Flesh." *VT* 36 (1986) 115–17.

Bellis, Alice Ogden. "The Gender and Motives of the Wisdom Teacher in Proverbs 7." In *Wisdom and Psalms*. Edited by Athalya Brenner and Carole R. Fontaine, 79–91. FCB 2/2. Sheffield: Sheffield Academic, 1998.

Belo, Fernando. *A Materialist Reading of the Gospel of Mark*. Translated by M. J. O'Connell. Maryknoll, N.Y.: Orbis, 1981.

Berlinerblau, Jacques. *The Vow and the 'Popular Religious Groups' of Ancient Israel: A Philological and Sociological Inquiry*. JSOTSup 210. Sheffield: Sheffield Academic, 1996.

Bernard, Jacques. "Genèse 1 à 3: Lecture et Traditions de Lecture." *MScRel* 41 (1984) 109–28.

Berquist, Jon L. *Judaism in Persia's Shadow: A Social and Historical Approach*. Minneapolis: Fortress Press, 1995.

Best, Thomas. "The Sociological Study of the New Testament: Promise and Peril of a New Discipline." *SJT* 36 (1983) 181–94.

Bier, Carol. "Textile Arts in Ancient Western Asia." In *Civilizations of the Ancient Near East*. Edited by Jack M. Sasson, 3:1567–88. New York: Scribner's, 1995.

Bird, Phyllis A. "The Harlot As Heroine: Narrative Art and Social Presupposition in Three Old Testament Texts." *Semeia* 46 (1989) 119–39.

———. "Images of Women in the Old Testament." In *Religion and Sexism: Images of Woman in the Jewish and Christian Traditions*. Edited by Rosemary Radford Ruether, 41–88. New York: Simon & Schuster, 1974.

———. "Israelite Religion and the Faith of Israel's Daughters: Reflections on Gender and Religious Definition." In *The Bible and the Politics of Exegesis: Essays in Honor of Norman K. Gottwald on His Sixty-Fifth Birthday*. Edited by David Jobling, Peggy L. Day, and Gerald T. Sheppard, 97–108. Cleveland: Pilgrim, 1991.

———. "'Male and Female He Created Them': Gen 1:27b in the Context of the Priestly Account of Creation." *HTR* 74 (1981) 129–59.

———. "The Place of Women in the Israelite Cultus." In *Ancient Israelite Religion: Essays in Honor of Frank More Cross*. Edited by Patrick D. Miller Jr., Paul D. Hanson, and S. Dean McBride, 397–419. Philadelphia: Fortress Press, 1987.

————. "'To Play the Harlot': An Inquiry into an Old Testament Metaphor." In *Gender and Difference in Ancient Israel*. Edited by Peggy L. Day, 75–94. Minneapolis: Fortress Press, 1989.

————. "Women (OT)." In *ABD* 6:951–57.

————. "Women's Religion in Ancient Israel." In *Women's Earliest Records from Ancient Egypt and Western Asia*. Edited by Barbara S. Lesko, 283–98. BJS 166. Atlanta: Scholars, 1989.

Bleibtreu, Erika. "Grisly Assyrian Record of Torture and Death." *BAR* 17, no. 1 (1991) 52–61, 75.

Blenkinsopp, Joseph. "Did the Second Jerusalemite Temple Possess Land?" *Transeu* 21 (2001) 61–68.

————. *Ezra-Nehemiah: A Commentary*. OTL. Philadelphia: Westminster, 1988.

————. "The Family in First Temple Israel." In *Families in Ancient Israel*. Edited by Leo G. Perdue et al., 48–103. Families, Religion, and Culture. Louisville: Westminster John Knox, 1997.

————. *A History of Prophecy in Israel: From the Settlement in the Land to the Hellenistic Period*. Philadelphia: Westminster, 1983.

————. *Sage, Priest, Prophet: Religious and Intellectual Leadership in Ancient Israel*. LAI. Louisville: Westminster John Knox, 1995.

————. "The Social Context of the 'Outsider Woman' in Proverbs 1–9." *Bib* 72 (1991) 457–73.

————. "Temple and Society in Achaemenid Judah." In *Second Temple Studies*. Vol. 1: *Persian Period*. Edited by Philip R. Davies, 22–53. JSOTSup 117. Sheffield: Sheffield Academic, 1991.

Block, Daniel I. *The Book of Ezekiel: Chapters 1–24*. NICOT. Grand Rapids: Eerdmans, 1997.

Boadt, Lawrence. *Reading the Old Testament: An Introduction*. New York: Paulist, 1984.

————. "Rhetorical Strategies in Ezekiel's Oracles of Judgment." In *Ezekiel and His Book: Textual and Literary Criticism and Their Interrelation*. Edited by Johan Lust, 182–200. BETL 74. Leuven: Leuven Univ. Press, 1986.

Bodi, D. "La clémence des Perses envers Néhémie et ses compatriotes: faveur ou opportunisme politique?" *Transeu* 21 (2001) 69–86.

Boshoff, W. S. "Yahweh As God of Nature: Elements of the Concept of God in the Book of Hosea." *JNSL* 18 (1992) 13–24.

Bossman, David, O.F.M. "Ezra's Marriage Reform: Israel Redefined." *BTB* 9 (1979) 32–38.

Boström, Gustav. *Proverbiastudien: Die Weisheit und das fremde Weib in Spr. 1–9*. Lunds universitets årsskrift 30. Lund: Gleerup, 1935.

Botha, P. J. "The Ideology of Shame in the Wisdom of Ben Sira: Ecclesiasticus 41:14—42:8." *OTE* 9 (1996) 353–71.

Bourdieu, Pierre. "The Sentiment of Honour in Kabyle Society." In *Honour and Shame: The Values of Mediterranean Society.* Edited by J. G. Peristiany, 191–241. Chicago: Univ. of Chicago Press, 1966.

Brandes, Stanley. "Reflections on Honor and Shame in the Mediterranean." In *Honor and Shame and the Unity of the Mediterranean.* Edited by David D. Gilmore, 121–34. Washington, D.C.: American Anthropological Association, 1987.

Braulik, Georg, O.S.B. "The Rejection of the Goddess Asherah in Israel: Was the Rejection as Late as Deuteronomistic and Did It Further the Oppression of Women in Israel?" In *The Theology of Deuteronomy,* 165–82. Translated by Ulrika Lindblad. N. Richland Hills, Tex.: BIBAL, 1994.

Bravmann, M. M. "The Original Meaning of '. . . A Man Leaves His Father and Mother . . .'." *Le Muséon* 88 (1975) 449–53.

Brenner, Athalya. *The Intercourse of Knowledge: On Gendered Sex and Desire in the Hebrew Bible.* BibIntSer 26. Leiden: Brill, 1997.

———. "On 'Jeremiah' and the Poetics of (Prophetic?) Pornography." In *On Gendering Texts: Female and Male Voices in the Hebrew Bible.* Edited by Athalya Brenner and Fokkelien van Dijk-Hemmes, 177–93. BibIntSer 1. Leiden: Brill, 1993.

———. "On Prophetic Propaganda and the Politics of 'Love.'" In *Reflections on Theology and Gender.* Edited by Fokkelien van Dijk-Hemmes and Athalya Brenner, 87–107. Kampen: Kok Pharos, 1994.

———. "Pornoprophetics Revisited: Some Additional Reflections." *JSOT* 70 (1996) 63–86.

———. "Proverbs 1–9: An F Voice?" In *On Gendering Texts: Female and Male Voices in the Hebrew Bible.* Edited by Athalya Brenner and Fokkelien van Dijk-Hemmes, 113–30. BibIntSer 1. Leiden: Brill, 1993.

Briffault, Robert. *The Mothers.* 3 vols. New York: Macmillan, 1927.

Bright, John. *A History of Israel.* 3rd ed. Philadelphia: Westminster, 1981.

Brison, Karen J. *Just Talk: Gossip, Meetings, and Power in a Papua New Guinea Village.* Studies in Melanesian Anthropology 11. Berkeley: Univ. of California Press, 1992.

Brooks, Beatrice S. "Fertility Cult Functionaries in the OT." *JBL* 60 (1941) 227–53.

Brownlee, William H. "The Aftermath of the Fall of Judah according to Ezekiel." *JBL* 89 (1970) 393–404.

Brueggemann, Walter. "David and His Theologian." *CBQ* 30 (1968) 156–81.

———. "From Dust to Kingship." *ZAW* 84 (1972) 1–18.

———. "The Social Significance of Solomon As a Patron of Wisdom." In *The Sage in Israel and the Ancient Near East.* Edited by John G. Gammie and Leo G. Perdue, 117–32. Winona Lake, Ind.: Eisenbrauns, 1990.

———. "Theodicy in a Social Dimension." *JSOT* 33 (1985) 3–25.

Bulhan, Hussein Abdilahi. *Frantz Fanon and the Psychology of Oppression.* New York: Plenum, 1985.

Burns, John Barclay. "Proverbs 7,6-27: Vignettes from the Cycle of Astarte and Adonis." *SJOT* 9 (1995) 20–36.

Busenitz, Irvin A. "A Woman's Desire for Man: Gen 3:16 Reconsidered." *Grace Theological Journal* 7 (1986) 203–12.

Camp, Claudia V. "Honor, Shame, and the Hermeneutics of Ben Sira's Ms C." In *Wisdom, You Are My Sister: Studies in Honor of Roland E. Murphy, O.Carm., on the Occasion of His Eightieth Birthday.* Edited by Michael L. Barré, S.S., 157–71. CBQMS 29. Washington D.C.: Catholic Biblical Association of America, 1997.

———. "The Strange Woman of Proverbs: A Study in the Feminization and Divinization of Evil in Biblical Thought." In *Women and Goddess Traditions in Antiquity and Today.* Edited by Karen L. King, 310–29. Studies in Antiquity and Christianity. Minneapolis: Fortress Press, 1997.

———. "Understanding a Patriarchy: Women in Second-Century Jerusalem through the Eyes of Ben Sira." In *"Women Like This": New Perspectives on Jewish Women in the Greco-Roman World.* Edited by Amy-Jill Levine, 1–39. SBLEJL 1. Atlanta: Scholars, 1991.

———. "What's So Strange about the Strange Woman?" In *The Bible and the Politics of Exegesis: Essays in Honor of Norman K. Gottwald on His Sixty-Fifth Birthday.* Edited by David Jobling, Peggy L. Day, and Gerald T. Sheppard, 17–31. Cleveland: Pilgrim, 1991.

———. *Wisdom and the Feminine in the Book of Proverbs.* BibLitSer 11. Decatur, Ga.: Almond, 1985.

———. "Wise and Strange: An Interpretation of the Female Imagery in Proverbs in Light of Trickster Mythology." *Semeia* 42 (1988) 14–36.

———. *Wise, Strange, and Holy: The Strange Woman and the Making of the Bible.* JSOTSup 320. Sheffield: Sheffield Academic, 2000.

Card, Claudia. "Rape As a Weapon of War." *Hypatia* 11, no. 4 (1996) 5–18.

Carroll, Robert P. "Desire under the Terebinths: On Pornographic Representation in the Prophets—a Response." In *A Feminist Companion to the Latter Prophets.* Edited by Athalya Brenner, 275–307. FCB 8. Sheffield: Sheffield Academic, 1995.

———. "The Myth of the Empty Land." *Semeia* 59 (1992) 79–93.

———. "Whorusalamin: A Tale of Three Cities As Three Sisters." In *On Reading Prophetic Texts: Gender-Specific and Related Studies in Memory of Fokklien Van Dijk-Hemmes.* Edited by Bob Becking and Meindert Dijkstra, 67–82. BibIntSer 18. Leiden: Brill, 1996.

Carter, Charles E. *The Emergence of Yehud in the Persian Period: A Social and Demographic Study.* JSOTSup 294. Sheffield: Sheffield Academic, 1999.

Caruth, Cathy. *Unclaimed Experience: Trauma, Narrative, and History.* Baltimore: Johns Hopkins Univ. Press, 1996.

Chalcraft, David J., ed. *Social Scientific Old Testament Criticism.* BibSem 47. Sheffield: Sheffield Academic, 1997.

Chaney, Marvin L. "Bitter Bounty: The Dynamics of Political Economy Critiqued by the Eighth-Century Prophets." In *Reformed Faith and Economics*. Edited by Robert L. Stivers, 15–30. Lanham, Md.: Univ. Press of America, 1989.

———. "Systemic Study of the Israelite Monarchy." *Semeia* 37 (1986) 53–76.

Chrisman, Laura. "The Imperial Unconscious? Representations of Imperial Discourse." In *Colonial Discourse and Post-Colonial Theory: A Reader*. Edited by Patrick Williams and Laura Chrisman, 498–516. New York: Columbia Univ. Press, 1994.

Clements, R. E., ed. *The World of Ancient Israel: Sociological, Anthropological and Political Perspectives*. Cambridge: Cambridge Univ. Press, 1989.

Clévenot, Michel. *Materialist Approaches to the Bible*. Translated by William J. Nottingham. Maryknoll, N.Y.: Orbis, 1985.

Clifford, Richard J. *Proverbs: A Commentary*. OTL. Louisville: Westminster John Knox, 1999.

Clines, David J. A. "What Does Eve Do to Help? And Other Irredeemably Androcentric Orientations in Genesis 1–3." In *What Does Eve Do to Help? And Other Readerly Questions to the Old Testament*, 25–48. JSOTSup 94. Sheffield: JSOT Press, 1990.

Cody, Aelred, O.S.B. *Ezekiel, with an Excursus on Old Testament Priesthood*. OTM 11. Wilmington, Del.: Glazier, 1984.

Cogan, Mordechai. "'Ripping Open Pregnant Women' in Light of an Assyrian Analogue." *JAOS* 103 (1983) 755–57.

Cogan, Morton. *Imperialism and Religion: Assyria, Judah, and Israel in the Eighth and Seventh Centuries* B.C.E. SBLMS 19. Missoula, Mont.: Scholars, 1974.

Cohen, Yehudi A. "Ends and Means in Political Control: State Organization and the Punishment of Adultery, Incest, and the Violation of Celibacy." *AmAnth* 71 (1969) 658–87.

Collier, Jane Fishburne. "Women in Politics." In *Women, Culture, and Society*. Edited by Michelle Zimbalist Rosaldo and Louise Lamphere, 89–96. Stanford: Stanford Univ. Press, 1974.

Collier, Jane Fishburne, and Sylvia Junko Yanagisako, eds. *Gender and Kinship: Essays Toward a Unified Analysis*. Stanford: Stanford Univ. Press, 1987.

Coogan, Michael D. "The Goddess Wisdom—'Where Can She Be Found?' Literary Reflexes of Popular Religion." In *Ki Baruch Hu: Ancient Near Eastern, Biblical, and Judaic Studies in Honor of Baruch A. Levine*. Edited by Robert Chazan, William W. Hallo, and Lawrence H. Schiffman, 203–9. Winona Lake, Ind.: Eisenbrauns, 1999.

Cook, Johann. "'Iššâ Zārâ (Proverbs 1–9 Septuagint): A Metaphor for Foreign Wisdom?" *ZAW* 106 (1994) 458–76.

Cook, Stephen L. *Prophecy and Apocalypticism: The Postexilic Social Setting*. Minneapolis: Fortress Press, 1995.

Cooke, George Albert. *A Critical and Exegetical Commentary on the Book of Ezekiel*. ICC. Edinburgh: T. & T. Clark, 1936.

Coote, Robert B., and David Robert Ord. *The Bible's First History*. Philadelphia: Fortress Press, 1989.

Coote, Robert B., and Keith W. Whitelam. "The Emergence of Israel: Social Transformation and State Formation following the Decline in Late Bronze Age Trade." *Semeia* 37 (1986) 107–47.

Craigie, Peter C. *The Old Testament: Its Background, Growth, and Content*. Nashville: Abingdon, 1986.

Craven, Toni. "Women Who Lied for the Faith." In *Justice and the Holy: Essays in Honor of Walter Harrelson*. Edited by Douglas A. Knight and Peter J. Paris, 35–49. Homage Series. Atlanta: Scholars, 1989.

Crenshaw, James L. "Poverty and Punishment in the Book of Proverbs." In *Urgent Advice and Probing Questions: Collected Writings on Old Testament Wisdom*, 396–405. Macon, Ga.: Mercer Univ. Press, 1995.

Crotty, R. "Hosea and the Knowledge of God." *Australian Biblical Review* 19 (1971) 1–16.

Cucchiari, Salvatore. "The Gender Revolution and the Transition from Bisexual Horde to Patrilocal Bond: The Origins of Gender Hierarchy." In *Sexual Meanings: The Cultural Construction of Gender and Sexuality*. Edited by Sherry B. Ortner and Harriet Whitehead, 31–70. New York: Cambridge Univ. Press, 1981.

Darr, Katheryn Pfisterer. "Ezekiel." In *The Women's Bible Commentary*. Edited by Carol A. Newsom and Sharon H. Ringe, 192–200. Rev. ed. Louisville: Westminster John Knox, 1998.

———. "Ezekiel's Justifications of God: Teaching Troubling Texts." *JSOT* 55 (1992) 97–117.

Davies, Bronwyn. *(In)Scribing Body/Landscape Relations*. Walnut Creek, Calif.: AltaMira, 2000.

Davies, Graham I. *Hosea*. OTG. Sheffield: JSOT Press, 1993.

Davies, Philip R. *In Search of 'Ancient Israel.'* JSOTSup 148. Sheffield: Sheffield Academic, 1992.

Davis, Ellen F. *Swallowing the Scroll: Textuality and the Dynamics of Discourse in Ezekiel's Prophecy*. JSOTSup 78. Sheffield: Almond, 1989.

Day, John. "Asherah." In *ABD* 1:483–87.

———. "Asherah in the Hebrew Bible and Northwest Semitic Literature." *JBL* 105 (1986) 385–408.

Day, Linda M. "Rhetoric and Domestic Violence in Ezekiel 16." *BibInt* 8 (2000) 205–30.

Day, Peggy L. "Adulterous Jerusalem's Imagined Demise: Death of a Metaphor in Ezekiel XVI." *VT* 50 (2000) 285–309.

———. "The Bitch Had It Coming to Her: Rhetoric and Interpretation in Ezekiel 16." *BibInt* 8 (2000) 231–54.

———, ed. *Gender and Difference in Ancient Israel*. Minneapolis: Fortress Press, 1989.

Dearman, John Andrew. *Property Rights in the Eighth-Century Prophets.* SBLDS 106. Atlanta: Scholars, 1988.

———. *Religion and Culture in Ancient Israel.* Peabody, Mass.: Hendrickson, 1992.

Delaney, Carol. *The Seed and the Soil: Gender and Cosmology in Turkish Village Society.* Comparative Studies on Muslim Societies 11. Berkeley: Univ. of California Press, 1991.

———. "Seeds of Honor, Fields of Shame." In *Honor and Shame and the Unity of the Mediterranean.* Edited by David D. Gilmore, 35–48. Washington, D.C.: American Anthropological Association, 1987.

Dempsey, Carol J. "The 'Whore' of Ezekiel 16: The Impact and Ramifications of Gender-Specific Metaphors in Light of Biblical Law." In *Gender and Law in the Hebrew Bible and the Ancient Near East.* Edited by Victor H. Matthews, Bernard M. Levinson, and Tikva Frymer-Kensky, 57–78. JSOTSup 262. Sheffield: Sheffield Academic, 1998.

deSilva, David A. "The Wisdom of Ben Sira: Honor, Shame, and the Maintenance of the Values of a Minority Culture." *CBQ* 58 (1996) 433–55.

Dever, William G. "Ancient Israelite Religion: How to Reconcile the Differing Textual and Artifactual Portraits?" In *Ein Gott allein? JHWH-Verehrung und biblischer Monotheismus im Kontext der israelitischen und altorientalischen Religionsgeschichte.* Edited by Walter Dietrich and Martin A. Klopfenstein, 235–68. OBO 139. Göttingen: Vandenhoeck & Ruprecht, 1994.

———. "Asherah, Consort of Yahweh? New Evidence from Kuntillet 'Ajrûd." *BASOR* 255 (1984) 21–37.

———. "Israel, History of (Archaeology and the 'Conquest')." In *ABD* 3:545–53.

———. "Revisionist Israel Revisited: A Rejoinder to Niels Peter Lemche." *CRBS* 4 (1996) 35–50.

———. "Unresolved Issues in the Early History of Israel: Toward a Synthesis of Archaeological and Textual Reconstructions." In *The Bible and the Politics of Exegesis: Essays in Honor of Norman K. Gottwald on His Sixty-Fifth Birthday.* Edited by David Jobling, Peggy L. Day, and Gerald T. Sheppard, 195–207. Cleveland: Pilgrim, 1991.

———. "'Will the Real Israel Please Stand Up?' Part II: Archaeology and the Religions of Ancient Israel." *BASOR* 298 (1995) 37–58.

Dietrich, Walter, and Martin A. Klopfenstein, eds. *Ein Gott allein? JHWH-Verehrung und biblischer Monotheismus im Kontext der israelitischen und altorientalischen Religionsgeschichte.* OBO 139. Göttingen: Vandenhoeck & Ruprecht, 1994.

Dijkstra, Meindert. "The Valley of Dry Bones: Coping with the Reality of the Exile in the Book of Ezekiel." In *The Crisis of Israelite Religion: Transformation of Religious Tradition in Exilic and Post-Exilic Times.* Edited by Bob Becking and Marjo C. A. Korpel, 114–33. OtSt 42. Leiden: Brill, 1999.

Dobbs-Allsopp, F. W., and Tod Linafelt. "The Rape of Zion in Thr 1, 10." *ZAW* 113 (2001) 77–81.

Domeris, W. R. "Shame and Honour in Proverbs: Wise Women and Foolish Men." *OTE* 8 (1995) 86–102.

Douglas, Mary. "Responding to Ezra: The Priests and the Foreign Wives." *BibInt* 10 (2002) 1–23.

Dowling, William C. *Jameson, Althusser, Marx: An Introduction to The Political Unconscious*. Ithaca: Cornell Univ. Press, 1984.

Duley, Margo I., and Mary I. Edwards. *The Cross-Cultural Study of Women: A Comprehensive Guide*. New York: Feminist, 1986.

Duran, Eduardo, and Bonnie Duran. *Native American Postcolonial Psychology*. SUNY Series in Transpersonal and Humanistic Psychology. Albany: State Univ. of New York Press, 1995.

Dwyer, Daisy. "Ideologies of Sexual Inequality and Strategies for Change in Male-Female Relations." *AmEth* 5 (1978) 227–40.

Eagleton, Terry. *Criticism and Ideology: A Study in Marxist Literary Theory*. 1976. Reprinted London: Verso, 1990.

———. *Ideology: An Introduction*. London: Verso, 1991.

———. *Marxism and Literary Criticism*. Berkeley: Univ. of California Press, 1976. Reprinted with a new introduction, London: Routledge, 2002.

Eichrodt, Walther. *Ezekiel: A Commentary*. Translated by Cosslett Quin. OTL. Philadelphia: Westminster, 1970.

Eilberg-Schwartz, Howard. *God's Phallus and Other Problems for Men and Monotheism*. Boston: Beacon, 1994.

———. *The Savage in Judaism: An Anthropology of Israelite Religion and Ancient Judaism*. Bloomington: Indiana Univ. Press, 1990.

Emerton, J. A. "'Yahweh and His Asherah': The Goddess or Her Symbol?" *VT* 49 (1999) 315–37.

Emmerson, Grace I. "A Fertility Goddess in Hosea IV 17-19?" *VT* 4 (1974) 492–97.

———. *Hosea: An Israelite Prophet in Judean Perspective*. JSOTSup 28. Sheffield: JSOT Press, 1984.

———. "Women in Ancient Israel." In *The World of Ancient Israel: Sociological, Anthropological and Political Perspectives*. Edited by R. E. Clements, 371–94. Cambridge: Cambridge Univ. Press, 1989.

Engar, Ann W. "Old Testament Women As Tricksters." In *Mappings of the Biblical Terrain*. Edited by Vincent L. Tollers and John Maier, 143–57. Lewisburg, Pa.: Bucknell Univ. Press, 1990.

Eph'al, I. "The Western Minorities in Babylonia in the 6th–5th Centuries B.C.: Maintenance and Cohesion." *Orientalia* 47 (1978) 74–90.

Epstein, Louis M. "Sacred Prostitution." In *Sex Laws and Customs in Judaism*, 152–57. New York: Bloch, 1948. Reprinted New York: Ktav, 1967.

Erikson, Kai. "Notes on Trauma and Community." In *Trauma: Explorations in Memory*. Edited by Cathy Caruth, 183–99. Baltimore: Johns Hopkins Univ. Press, 1995.

Eskenazi, Tamara C. "Out from the Shadows: Biblical Women in the Postexilic Era." *JSOT* 54 (1992) 25–43.

Eskenazi, Tamara C., and Eleanore P. Judd. "Marriage to a Stranger in Ezra 9–10. In *Second Temple Studies*. Vol. 2: *Temple and Community in the Persian Period*. Edited by Tamara C. Eskenazi and Kent H. Richards, 266–85. JSOTSup 175. Sheffield: Sheffield Academic, 1994.

Exum, J. Cheryl. "The Ethics of Biblical Violence against Women." In *The Bible in Ethics: The Second Sheffield Colloquium*. Edited by John W. Rogerson et al., 248–71. JSOTSup 207. Sheffield: Sheffield Academic, 1995.

———. "The Mothers of Israel: The Patriarchal Narratives from a Feminist Perspective." *BRev* 2, no. 1 (1986) 60–67.

———. "Prophetic Pornography." In *Plotted, Shot, and Painted: Cultural Representations of Biblical Women*, 101–28. JSOTSup 215. Sheffield: Sheffield Academic, 1996.

Faludi, Susan. *Backlash: The Undeclared War against American Women*. New York: Crown, 1991.

Fensham, F. C. *The Books of Ezra and Nehemiah*. NICOT. Grand Rapids: Eerdmans, 1982.

———. "The Marriage Metaphor in Hosea for the Covenant Relationship between the Lord and His People." *JNSL* 12 (1984) 71–87.

Fewell, Danna Nolan, and Gary A. Phillips. "Ethics, Bible, Reading As If." *Semeia* 77 (1997): 1–21.

Fiensy, David. "Using the Nuer Culture of Africa in Understanding the Old Testament." *JSOT* 44 (1989) 73–83.

Finkelstein, Israel. "The Emergence of the Monarchy in Israel: The Environmental and Socio-Economic Aspects." *JSOT* 44 (1989) 43–74.

Finkelstein, Israel, and Neil Asher Silberman. *The Bible Unearthed: Archaeology's New Vision of Ancient Israel and the Origin of Its Sacred Texts*. New York: Free Press, 2001.

Fisch, Harold. "Hosea: A Poetics of Violence." In *Poetry with a Purpose: Biblical Poetics and Interpretation*. Edited by Harold Fisch, 136–57, 192–93. ISBL. Bloomington: Indiana Univ. Press, 1988.

Fishbane, Michael. "Accusations of Adultery: A Study of Law and Scribal Practice in Numbers 5:11-31." In *Women in the Hebrew Bible: A Reader*. Edited by Alice Bach, 487–502. New York: Routledge, 1999.

Fisher, E. J. "Cultic Prostitution in the Ancient Near East? A Reappraisal." *BTB* 6 (1976) 225–36.

Foh, Susan. "What Is the Woman's Desire?" *WTJ* 37 (1975) 376–83.

Fontaine, Carole R. "A Heifer from Thy Stable: On Goddesses and the Status of Women in the Ancient Near East." In *The Pleasure of Her Text: Feminist Readings of Biblical and Historical Texts*. Edited by Alice Bach, 69–95. Philadelphia: Trinity Press International, 1990.

Fox, Michael V. *Proverbs 1–9*. AB 18A. New York: Doubleday, 2000.

———. "The Strange Woman in Septuagint Proverbs." *JNSL* 22 (1996) 31–44.

Franco, Jean. "Beyond Ethnocentrism: Gender, Power and the Third-World Intelligentsia." In *Colonial Discourse and Post-Colonial Theory: A Reader*. Edited by Patrick Williams and Laura Chrisman, 359–69. New York: Columbia Univ. Press, 1994.

Freedman, David Noel. "Yahweh of Samaria and His Asherah." *BA* 50 (1987) 241–49.

Frendo, Anthony J. "Five Recent Books on the Emergence of Ancient Israel: Review Article." *PEQ* 124 (1992) 144–51.

Friedl, Ernestine. "The Position of Women: Appearance and Reality." *AnthQ* 40 (1967) 97–108.

Friedman, Susan Stanford. *Mappings: Feminism and the Cultural Geographics of Encounter*. Princeton: Princeton Univ. Press, 1998.

Frymer-Kensky, Tikva. "Deuteronomy." In *The Women's Bible Commentary*. Edited by Carol A. Newsom and Sharon H. Ringe, 57–68. Rev. ed. Louisville: Westminster John Knox, 1998.

———. *In the Wake of the Goddesses: Women, Culture, and the Biblical Transformation of Pagan Myth*. New York: Free Press, 1992.

———. "Patriarchal Family Relationships and Near Eastern Law." *BA* 4 (1981) 209–14.

———. "The Planting of Man: A Study in Biblical Imagery." In *Love and Death in the Ancient Near East: Essays in Honor of Marvin H. Pope*. Edited by John H. Marks and Robert M. Good, 129–36. Guilford, Conn.: Four Quarters, 1987.

Fuchs, Esther. "Who Is Hiding the Truth? Deceptive Women and Biblical Androcentrism." In *Feminist Perspectives on Biblical Scholars*. Edited by Adela Yarbro Collins, 137–44. SBLBSNA 10. Chico, Calif.: Scholars, 1985.

Füssel, Kuno. "Materialist Readings of the Bible: Report on an Alternative Approach to Biblical Texts." In *God of the Lowly: Socio-Historical Interpretations of the Bible*. Edited by Willy Schottroff and Wolfgang Stegemann, 13–25. Maryknoll, N.Y.: Orbis, 1984.

Galambush, Julie. *Jerusalem in the Book of Ezekiel: The City As Yahweh's Wife*. SBLDS 130. Atlanta: Scholars, 1992.

Gandhi, Leela. *Postcolonial Theory: A Critical Introduction*. New York: Columbia Univ. Press, 1998.

Gangloff, F., and J.-C. Haelewyck. "Osée 4,17-19: Un Marzeah en l'honneur de la déesse 'Anat?" *ETL* 71 (1995) 370–82.

Gardner, Anne E. "Genesis 2:4b-3: A Mythological Paradigm of Sexual Equality or of the Religious History of Pre-Exilic Israel?" *SJT* 43 (1990) 1–18.

Gelb, I. J. "Prisoners of War in Early Mesopotamia." *JNES* 32 (1972) 70–98.

Geller, Jay. "Trauma." In *Handbook of Postmodern Biblical Interpretation.* Edited by A. K. M. Adam, 261–67. St. Louis: Chalice, 2000.

Geller, Stephen A. "Through Windows and Mirrors into the Bible: History, Literature, and Language in the Study of the Text." In *A Sense of Text: The Art of Language in the Study of Biblical Literature.* Edited by Stephen A. Geller, 3–40. JQRSup. Winona Lake, Ind.: Eisenbrauns, 1983.

Gilman, Sander. *Differences and Pathology: Stereotypes of Sexuality, Race, and Madness.* Ithaca: Cornell Univ. Press, 1985.

Gilmore, David D. "Introduction: The Shame of Dishonor." In *Honor and Shame and the Unity of the Mediterranean.* Edited by David D. Gilmore, 2–21. Washington, D.C.: American Anthropological Association, 1987.

———, ed. *Honor and Shame and the Unity of the Mediterranean.* Washington, D.C.: American Anthropological Association, 1987.

Gilmore, Margaret M., and David D. Gilmore. "'Machismo': A Psychodynamic Approach (Spain)." *Journal of Psychological Anthropology* 2 (1979) 281–300.

Giovannini, Maureen J. "Female Chastity Codes in the Circum-Mediterranean: Comparative Perspectives." In *Honor and Shame and the Unity of the Mediterranean.* Edited by David D. Gilmore, 61–74. Washington, D.C.: American Anthropological Association, 1987.

Gnuse, Robert. "Calf, Cult, and King: The Unity of Hosea 8:1-13." *BZ* 26 (1982) 83–92.

———. *No Other Gods: Emergent Monotheism in Israel.* JSOTSup 241. Sheffield: Sheffield Academic, 1997.

Goldingay, John. "Hosea 1–3, Genesis 1–4, and a Masculist Interpretation." *HBT* 17 (1995) 37–44.

Goodfriend, Elaine Adler. "Adultery." In *ABD* 1:82–86.

Gordis, Robert. "On Adultery in Biblical and Babylonian Law." *Judaism* 33 (1984) 210–11.

———. "The Significance of the Paradise Myth." *AJSL* 52 (1936) 86–94.

———. "The Social Background of Wisdom." In *Poets, Prophets, and Sages: Essays in Biblical Interpretation,* 160–97. Bloomington: Indiana Univ. Press, 1971.

Gordon, Pamela, and Harold C. Washington. "Rape As a Military Metaphor in the Hebrew Bible." In *A Feminist Companion to the Latter Prophets.* Edited by Athalya Brenner, 308–25. FCB 8. Sheffield: Sheffield Academic, 1995.

Görg, Manfred. "Geschichte der Sünde—Sünde der Geschichte: Gen 3, 1-7 im Licht Tendenzkritischen Beobachtungen." *MTZ* 41 (1990) 315–25.

Gottwald, Norman K. "Bibliography on the Social Scientific Study of the Old Testament." *American Baptist Quarterly* 2 (1983) 168–84.

―――. "The Expropriated and the Expropriators in Nehemiah 5." In *Concepts of Class in Ancient Israel*. Edited by Mark R. Sneed, 1–19. SFSHJ 201. Atlanta: Scholars, 1999.

―――. *The Hebrew Bible: A Socio-Literary Introduction*. Philadelphia: Fortress Press, 1985. Edition with CD-ROM, 2003.

―――. "A Hypothesis about Social Class in Monarchic Israel in the Light of Contemporary Studies of Social Class and Social Stratification." In *The Hebrew Bible in Its Social World and in Ours*, 139–64. SemeiaSt. Atlanta: Scholars, 1993.

―――. "The Participation of Free Agrarians in the Introduction of Monarchy to Ancient Israel: An Application of H. A. Landsberger's Framework for the Analysis of Peasants." *Semeia* 37 (1986) 77–106.

―――. *The Politics of Ancient Israel*. LAI. Louisville: Westminster John Knox, 2000.

―――. "Social Class As an Analytic and Hermeneutical Category in Biblical Studies." *JBL* 112 (1993) 3–22.

―――. "Sociological Method in the Study of Ancient Israel." In *The Bible and Liberation: Political and Social Hermeneutics*. Edited by Norman K. Gottwald, 26–37. Maryknoll, N.Y.: Orbis, 1983.

―――. "Sociology (Ancient Israel)." In *ABD* 6:79–89.

―――. *The Tribes of Yahweh: A Sociology of the Religion of Liberated Israel, 1250–1050* B.C.E. Maryknoll, N.Y.: Orbis, 1979.

―――. "Triumphalist versus Anti-Triumphalist Versions of Early Israel: A Response to Articles by Lemche and Dever in Volume 4 (1996)." *CRBS* 5 (1997) 15–42.

Grabbe, Lester L. *Ezra and Nehemiah*. OTR. London: Routledge, 1998.

―――. *Judaism from Cyrus to Hadrian*. Vol. 1: *The Persian and Greek Periods*. Minneapolis: Fortress Press, 1992.

―――. "Triumph of the Pious or Failure of the Xenophobes: The Ezra-Nehemiah Reforms and Their *Nachgeschichte*." In *Jewish Local Patriotism and Self-Identification in the Graeco-Roman Period*. Edited by Siân Jones and Sarah Pearce, 50–65. JSPSup 31. Sheffield: Sheffield Academic, 1998.

Graetz, Naomi. "God Is to Israel As Husband Is to Wife: The Metaphoric Battering of Hosea's Wife." In *A Feminist Companion to the Latter Prophets*. Edited by Athalya Brenner, 126–45. FCB 8. Sheffield: Sheffield Academic, 1995.

Grayson, A. Kirk. "Assyrian Rule of Conquered Territory in Ancient Western Asia." In *Civilizations of the Ancient Near East*. Edited by Jack M. Sasson, 2:959–68. New York: Scribner's, 1995.

Greenberg, Moshe. *Ezekiel 1–20*. AB 22. Garden City, N.Y.: Doubleday, 1983.

―――. *Ezekiel 21–37*. AB 22A. New York: Doubleday, 1997.

Gregg, Joan Young. *Devils, Women, and Jews: Reflections of the Other in Medieval Sermon Stories*. Ithaca: State Univ. of New York Press, 1997.

Grossberg, Daniel. "Two Kinds of Sexual Relationships in the Hebrew Bible." *Hebrew Studies* 35 (1994) 7–25.

Gruber, Mayer I. "Hebrew *Qedeshah* and Her Canaanite and Akkadian Cognates." *UF* 18 (1986) 133–48.

Guest, Deryn. "Hiding Behind the Naked Women in Lamentations: A Recriminative Response." *BibInt* 7 (1999) 413–48.

Guichard, Jean. "Approche 'matérialiste' du récit de la chute: Genèse 3." *Lumière et Vie* 26 (1977) 57–90.

Hackett, Jo Ann. "Can a Sexist Model Liberate Us? Ancient Near Eastern 'Fertility' Goddesses." *JFSR* 5 (1989) 65–76.

Hadley, Judith M. "From Goddess to Literary Construct: The Transformation of Asherah into Ḥokmah." In *A Feminist Companion to Reading the Bible: Approaches, Methods and Strategies.* Edited by Athalya Brenner and Carole Fontaine, 360–99. FCB 11. Sheffield: Sheffield Academic, 1997.

———. "Wisdom and the Goddess." In *Wisdom in Ancient Israel: Essays in Honour of J. A. Emerton.* Edited by John Day et al., 234–43. Cambridge: Cambridge Univ. Press, 1995.

———. "Yahweh and 'His Asherah': Archaeological and Textual Evidence for the Cult of the Goddess." In *Ein Gott allein? JHWH-Verehrung und biblischer Monotheismus im Kontext der israelitischen und altorientalischen Religionsgeschichte.* Edited by Walter Dietrich and Martin A. Klopfenstein, 235–68. OBO 139. Göttingen: Vandenhoeck & Ruprecht, 1994.

Halperin, David J. *Seeking Ezekiel: Text and Psychology.* University Park: Univ. of Pennsylvania Press, 1993.

Halpern, Baruch. "The Baal (and the Asherah) in Seventh-Century Judah: Yhwh's Retainers Retired." In *Konsequente Traditionsgeschichte: Festschrift für Klaus Baltzer zum 65. Geburtstag.* Edited by Rüdiger Bartelmus, Thomas Krüger, and Helmut Utzschneider, 115–54. OBO 126. Göttingen: Vandenhoeck & Ruprecht, 1993.

———. "'Brisker Pipes Than Poetry': The Development of Israelite Monotheism." In *Judaic Perspectives on Ancient Israel.* Edited by Jacob Neusner, Baruch A. Levine, and Ernest S. Frerichs, 77–115. Philadelphia: Fortress Press, 1987.

Hals, Ronald M. *Ezekiel.* FOTL 19. Grand Rapids: Eerdmans, 1989.

Hanson, K. C. "BTB Readers Guide: Kinship." *BTB* 24 (1994) 183–94.

———. "The Herodians and Mediterranean Kinship. Part 1: Genealogy and Descent." *BTB* 19 (1989) 75–84.

———. "The Herodians and Mediterranean Kinship. Part 2: Marriage and Divorce." *BTB* 19 (1989) 142–51.

———. "The Herodians and Mediterranean Kinship. Part 3: Economics." *BTB* 20 (1990) 10–21.

———. "The Old Testament: Social Sciences and Social Description." 'http://www.kchanson.com/CLASSIFIEDBIB/otsocsci.html'

Harding, Susan. "Women and Words in a Spanish Village." In *Toward an Anthropology of Women*. Edited by Rayna R. Reiter, 283–308. New York: Monthly Review, 1975.

Harper, William Rainey. *A Critical and Exegetical Commentary on Amos and Hosea*. ICC. Edinburgh: T. & T. Clark, 1905.

Hayes, Christine. "Intermarriage and Impurity in Ancient Jewish Sources." *HTR* 92 (1999) 3–36.

Hayes, John H., and Jeffrey K. Kuan. "The Final Years of Samaria (730–720)." *Bib* 72 (1991) 153–81.

Heijerman, Mieke. "Who Would Blame Her? The 'Strange' Woman of Proverbs 7." In *Reflections on Theology and Gender*. Edited by Fokkelien van Dijk-Hemmes and Athalya Brenner, 21–31. Kampen: Kok Pharos, 1994.

Henshaw, Richard A. *Female and Male: The Cultic Personnel: The Bible and the Rest of the Ancient Near East*. Princeton Theological Monograph Series 31. Allison Park, Pa.: Pickwick, 1994.

Herion, Gary A. "The Impact of Modern and Social Science Assumptions on the Reconstruction of Israelite History." *JSOT* 34 (1986) 3–33.

Herman, Judith Lewis. "Complex PTSD: A Syndrome in Survivors of Prolonged and Repeated Trauma." *Journal of Traumatic Stress* 5 (1992) 377–91.

———. *Trauma and Recovery: The Aftermath of Violence: From Domestic Abuse to Political Terror,* with a new afterword by the author. New York: Basic, 1997.

Herrera-Sobek, María. "The Treacherous Woman Archetype: A Structuring Agent in the Corrido." *Aztlán: International Journal of Chicano Studies* 13 (1982) 135–48.

Herzfeld, Michael. "'As in Your Own House': Hospitality, Ethnography, and the Stereotype of Mediterranean Society." In *Honor and Shame and the Unity of the Mediterranean*. Edited by David D. Gilmore, 75–89. Washington, D.C.: American Anthropological Association, 1987.

———. "Honor and Shame: Problems in the Comparative Analysis of Moral Systems." *Man* 15 (1980) 339–51.

———. "The Horns of the Mediterraneanist Dilemma." *AmEth* 11 (1984) 439–54.

Hillers, Delbert R. "Analyzing the Abominable: Our Understanding of Canaanite Religion." *JQR* 75 (1985) 253–69.

Hobbs, T. Raymond. "Aspects of Warfare in the First Testament World." *BTB* 25 (1995) 79–90.

———. *A Time for War: A Study of Warfare in the Old Testament*. Old Testament Studies 3. Wilmington, Del.: Glazier, 1989.

———. "Reflections on Honor, Shame, and Covenant Relations." *JBL* 116 (1997) 501–3.

Hoglund, Kenneth. "The Achaemenid Context." In *Second Temple Studies*. Vol. 1: *Persian Period*. Edited by Philip R. Davies, 54–72. JSOTSup 117. Sheffield: Sheffield Academic, 1991.

Holladay, John S., Jr. "The Kingdoms of Israel and Judah: Political and Economic Centralization in the Iron IIA-B (ca. 1000–750 B.C.E.)." In *The Archaeology of Society in the Holy Land*. Edited by Thomas E. Levy, 368–98. New York: Facts on File, 1995.

———. "Religion in Israel and Judah under the Monarchy: An Explicitly Archaeological Approach." In *Ancient Israelite Religion: Essays in Honor of Frank Moore Cross*. Edited by Patrick D. Miller Jr., Paul D. Hanson, and S. Dean McBride, 249–99. Philadelphia: Fortress Press, 1987.

Holladay, William L. *A Concise Hebrew and Aramaic Lexicon of the Old Testament*. Grand Rapids: Eerdmans, 1971.

Holt, Else Kragelund. *Prophesying the Past: The Use of Israel's History in the Book of Hosea*. JSOTSup 194. Sheffield: Sheffield Academic, 1995.

Holter, Knut. "The Serpent in Eden As a Symbol of Israel's Political Enemies: A Yahwistic Criticism of the Solomonic Foreign Policy?" *SJOT* 1 (1990) 106–12.

Hopkins, David C. "Bare Bones: Putting Flesh on the Economics of Ancient Israel." In *The Origins of the Ancient Israelite States*. Edited by Volkmar Fritz and Philip R. Davies, 121–39. JSOTSup 228. Sheffield: Sheffield Academic, 1996.

———. "The Dynamics of Agriculture in Monarchical Israel." *SBLSP* 22 (1983) 177–202.

———. *The Highlands of Canaan: Agricultural Life in the Iron Age*. SWBA 3. Sheffield: Almond, 1985.

Horsley, Richard A. "Empire, Temple and Community But No Bourgeoisie! A Response to Blenkinsopp and Petersen." In *Second Temple Studies*. Vol. 1: *Persian Period*. Edited by Philip R. Davies, 163–74. JSOTSup 117. Sheffield: Sheffield Academic, 1991.

Huffmon, H. "The Treaty Background of Hebrew YADA'." *BASOR* 181 (1966) 131–77.

Hur, Won-Jae. "Voicing the Wound: Trauma, Language, and the Theology of Han." M.Div. thesis, Episcopal Divinity School, 2000.

Hutter, Manfred. "Adam als Gärtner und König (Gen 2:8-15)." *BZ* 30 (1986) 258–62.

Irvine, Stuart A. "The Threat of Jezreel (Hosea 1:4-5)." *CBQ* 57 (1995) 494–503.

Jacobus, Mary. "Judith, Holofernes, and the Phallic Woman." In *Reading Women: Essays in Feminist Criticism*, 110–36. New York: Columbia Univ. Press, 1986.

James, Edwin O. *The Cult of the Mother-Goddess: An Archaeological and Documentary Study*. New York: Praeger, 1959.

Jameson, Fredric. "Metacommentary." In *Contemporary Literary Criticism: Modernism through Post-Structuralism*. Edited by Robert Con Davis, 111–23. New York: Longman, 1986.

———. *The Political Unconscious: Narrative As a Socially Symbolic Act.* Ithaca: Cornell Univ. Press, 1981.

Janeway, Elizabeth. *Powers of the Weak*. New York: Knopf, 1980.

Janoff-Bulman, Ronnie. *Shattered Assumptions: Towards a New Psychology of Trauma*. New York: Free Press, 1992.

Janssen, Enno. *Juda in der Exilszeit: Ein Beitrag zur Frage der Entstehung des Judentums*. FRLANT 51. Göttingen: Vandenhoeck & Ruprecht, 1956.

Jobling, David. "Feminism and 'Mode of Production' in Ancient Israel: Search for a Method." In *The Bible and the Politics of Exegesis: Essays in Honor of Norman K. Gottwald on His Sixty-Fifth Birthday*. Edited by David Jobling, Peggy L. Day, and Gerald T. Sheppard, 239–51. Cleveland: Pilgrim, 1991.

———. "Forced Labor: Solomon's Golden Age and the Question of Literary Representation." *Semeia* 54 (1991) 57–76.

———. "Myth and Its Limits in Genesis 2.4b—3.24." In *The Sense of Biblical Narrative: Structural Analyses in the Hebrew Bible*, vol. 2. Edited by David Jobling, 17–43. Sheffield: JSOT Press, 1986.

———. "The Value of Solomon's Age for the Biblical Reader." In *The Age of Solomon: Scholarship at the Turn of the Millennium*. Edited by Lowell K. Handy, 470–92. Leiden: Brill, 1997.

Jobling, David, Peggy L. Day, and Gerald T. Sheppard, eds. *The Bible and the Politics of Exegesis: Essays in Honor of Norman K. Gottwald on His Sixty-Fifth Birthday*. Cleveland: Pilgrim, 1991.

Johnson, Willa Mathis. "Ethnicity in Persian Yehud: Between Anthropological Analysis and Ideological Criticism." *SBLSP* 34 (1995) 177–86.

Joines, K. R. "The Serpent in Genesis 3." *ZAW* 87 (1975) 1–11.

Jost, Renate. "Von 'Huren und Heiligen': Ein sozialgeschichtlicher Beitrag." In *Feministische Hermeneutik und Erstes Testament: Analysen und Interpretationen*, edited by Hedwig Jahnow, 126–37. Stuttgart: Kohlhammer, 1994.

Jowkar, Forouz. "Honor and Shame: A Feminist View from Within." *Feminist Issues* 6, no. 1 (1986) 45–65.

Kamionkowski, S. Tamar. "Gender Ambiguity and Subversive Metaphor in Ezekiel 16." Ph.D. dissertation, Brandeis University, 2000.

Kandiyoti, Deniz. "Identity and Its Discontents: Women and the Nation." In *Colonial Discourse and Post-Colonial Theory: A Reader*. Edited by Patrick Williams and Laura Chrisman, 376–91. New York: Columbia Univ. Press, 1994.

Kanneh, Kadiatu. "Feminism and the Colonial Body." In *The Post-Colonial Studies Reader*. Edited by Bill Ashcroft, Gareth Griffiths, and Helen Tiffin, 346–48. New York: Routledge, 1995.

Karen, Robert. "Shame." *Atlantic Monthly* (February 1992) 40–70.

Kaufman, Gershen. "The Meaning of Shame: Toward a Self-Affirming Identity." *Journal of Counseling Psychology* 21 (1974) 568–74.

Kee, Howard Clark. "Testaments of the Twelve Patriarchs." In *The Old Testament Pseudepigrapha*. Edited by James H. Charlesworth, 775–828. Garden City, N.Y.: Doubleday, 1983.

Keefe, Alice A. "The Female Body, the Body Politic and the Land: A Sociopolitical Reading of Hosea 1–2." In *A Feminist Companion to the Latter Prophets*. Edited by Athalya Brenner, 70–100. FCB 8. Sheffield: Sheffield Academic, 1995.

———. "Rapes of Women/Wars of Men." *Semeia* 61 (1993) 79–97.

Keesing, Roger M. *Kin Groups and Social Structure*. New York: Holt, Rinehart & Winston, 1975.

Keil, Carl Friedrich. *The Twelve Minor Prophets*. Vol. 1. Translated by James Martin. Edinburgh: T. & T. Clark, 1900.

Kennedy, James M. "Peasants in Revolt: Political Allegory in Genesis 2–3." *JSOT* 47 (1990) 3–14.

Kern, Paul Bentley. *Ancient Siege Warfare*. Bloomington: Indiana Univ. Press, 1999.

Kirmayer, Laurence J. "Landscapes of Memory: Trauma, Narrative, and Dissociation." In *Tense Past: Cultural Essays in Trauma and Memory*. Edited by Paul Antze and Michael Lambek, 173–98. New York: Routledge, 1996.

Klein, Lillian R. "Honor and Shame in Esther." In *A Feminist Companion to Esther, Judith and Susanna*. Edited by Athalya Brenner, 149–75. FCB 7. Sheffield: Sheffield Academic, 1995.

Kressel, Gideon M. "Shame and Gender." *AnthQ* 65 (1992) 34–46.

Krishnaswamy, Revathi. *Effeminism: The Economy of Colonial Desire*. Ann Arbor: Univ. of Michigan Press, 1998.

Kruger, P. A. "Israel, the Harlot (Hos. 2:4-9)." *JNSL* 11 (1983) 107–16.

Kuan, Jeffrey Kah-jin. *Neo-Assyrian Historical Inscriptions and Syria-Palestine*. Jian Dao Dissertation Series 1. Hong Kong: Alliance Bible Seminary, 1995.

Kuhrt, Amélie. "The Cyrus Cylinder and Achaemenid Imperial Policy." *JSOT* 25 (1983) 83–97.

Kuntz, J. Kenneth. *The People of Ancient Israel: An Introduction to Old Testament Literature, History, and Thought*. New York: Harper & Row, 1974.

Lamphere, Louise. "Strategies, Cooperation, and Conflict among Women in Domestic Groups." In *Women, Culture, and Society*. Edited by Michelle Zimbalist Rosaldo and Louise Lamphere, 97–112. Stanford: Stanford Univ. Press, 1974.

Landy, Francis. *Hosea*. RNBC. Sheffield: Sheffield Academic, 1995.

Lang, Bernhard. *Monotheism and the Prophetic Minority: An Essay in Biblical History and Sociology*. SWBA 1. Sheffield: Almond, 1983.

———. *Wisdom and the Book of Proverbs: A Hebrew Goddess Redefined*. New York: Pilgrim, 1986.

Laniak, Timothy S. *Shame and Honor in the Book of Esther*. SBLDS 165. Atlanta: Scholars, 1999.

Lanser, Susan S. "(Feminist) Criticism in the Garden: Inferring Genesis 2–3." *Semeia* 41 (1988) 67–84.

Larner, Christina. *Witchcraft and Religion: The Politics of Popular Belief*. Oxford: Blackwell, 1984.

Laub, Dori. "Bearing Witness or the Vicissitudes of Listening." In *Testimony: Crises of Witnessing in Literature, Psychoanalysis, and History*. Edited by Shoshana Felman and Dori Laub, 57–74. London: Routledge, 1992.

Lawton, Robert B. "Genesis 2:24: Trite or Tragic." *JBL* 105 (1986) 97–98.

Leach, Edmund. *Genesis As Myth and Other Essays*. London: Cape, 1969.

Lederer, Wolfgang. *The Fear of Women*. New York: Harcourt Brace Jovanovich, 1968.

Leick, Gwendolyn. *Sex and Eroticism in Mesopotamian Literature*. London: Routledge, 1994.

Lemche, Niels Peter. *Early Israel: Anthropological and Historical Studies on the Israelite Society before the Monarchy*. VTSup 37. Leiden: Brill, 1985.

———. "Early Israel Revisited." *CRBS* 4 (1996) 9–34.

———. "Israel, History of (Premonarchic Period)." In *ABD* 3:526–45.

Lesko, Barbara S. "Women of Egypt and the Ancient Near East." In *Becoming Visible: Women in European History*. Edited by Renate Bridenthal, Claudia Koontz and Susan Stuard, 41–77. Rev. ed. Boston: Houghton Mifflin, 1987.

Levenson, Jon D. "1 Samuel 25 As Literature and As History." *CBQ* 47 (1985) 617–23.

Levenson, Jon D, and Baruch Halpern. "The Political Import of David's Marriages." *JBL* 99 (1980) 507–18.

Levine, Amy-Jill. "Sacrifice and Salvation: Otherness and Domestication in the Book of Judith." In *"No One Spoke Ill of Her": Essays on Judith*. Edited by James C. VanderKam, 17–30. SBLEJL 2. Atlanta: Scholars, 1992.

Levison, Jack. "Is Eve to Blame? A Contextual Analysis of Sirach 25:24." *CBQ* 47 (1985) 617–23.

Lewes, Darby. *Nudes from Nowhere: Utopian Sexual Landscapes*. Lanham, Md.: Rowman & Littlefield, 2000.

Lindisfarne, Nancy. "Variant Masculinities, Variant Virginities: Rethinking 'Honour and Shame.'" In *Dislocating Masculinity: Comparative Ethnographies*. Edited by Andrea Cornwall and Nancy Lindisfarne, 82–96. London: Routledge, 1994.

Liverani, Mario. "The Ideology of the Assyrian Empire." In *Power and Propaganda: A Symposium on Ancient Empires*. Edited by Mogens Trolle Larsen, 297–317. Copenhagen: Akademisk Forlag, 1979.

Loomba, Ania. *Colonialism/Post-Colonialism*. New York: Routledge, 1998.

Lowery, Richard H. *The Reforming Kings: Cults and Society in First Temple Judah*. JSOTSup 120. Sheffield: JSOT Press, 1991.

Maccoby, Hyam. "Holiness and Purity: The Holy People in Leviticus and Ezra-Nehemiah." In *Reading Leviticus: A Conversation with Mary Douglas*. Edited by John F. A. Sawyer, 153–70. JSOTSup 227. Sheffield: Sheffield Academic, 1996.

Macherey, Pierre. *A Theory of Literary Production*. Translated by Geoffrey Wall. London: Routledge and Kegan Paul, 1978.

MacLachlan, Bonnie. "Sacred Prostitution and Aphrodite." *Studies in Religion* 21 (1991) 145–62.

Magdalene, F. Rachel. "Ancient Near Eastern Treaty-Curses and the Ultimate Texts of Terror: A Study of the Language of Divine Sexual Abuse in the Prophetic Corpus." In *A Feminist Companion to the Latter Prophets*. Edited by Athalya Brenner, 326–52. FCB 8. Sheffield: Sheffield Academic, 1995.

Maier, Christl. "Conflicting Attractions: Parental Wisdom and the 'Strange Woman' in Proverbs 1–9." In *Wisdom and Psalms*. Edited by Athalya Brenner and Carole R. Fontaine, 92–108. FCB 2/2. Sheffield: Sheffield Academic, 1998.

———. "Jerusalem als Ehebrecherin in Ezechiel 16: Zur Verwendung und Funktion einer biblischen Metapher." In *Feministische Hermeneutik und Erstes Testament: Analysen und Interpretationen*, edited by Hedwig Jahnow, 85–105. Stuttgart: Kohlhammer, 1994.

Malina, Bruce J. "Dealing with Biblical (Mediterranean) Characters: A Guide for U.S. Consumers." *BTB* 19 (1989) 127–41.

———. *The New Testament World: Insights from Cultural Anthropology*. 3rd ed. Louisville: Westminster John Knox, 2001.

———. "The Social Sciences and Biblical Interpretation." In *The Bible and Liberation: Political and Social Hermeneutics*. Edited by Norman K. Gottwald, 11–25. Maryknoll, N.Y.: Orbis, 1983.

Marcus, Michelle I. "Art and Ideology in Ancient Western Asia." In *Civilizations of the Ancient Near East*. Edited by Jack M. Sasson, 4:2487–505. New York: Scribner's, 1995.

Martin, James D. "Israel As a Tribal Society." In *The World of Ancient Israel: Sociological, Anthropological and Political Perspectives*. Edited by R. E. Clements, 95–117. New York: Cambridge Univ. Press, 1989.

Marx, Karl, and Frederick Engels. *The German Ideology. Part One, with Selections from Parts Two and Three*. Edited by C. J. Arthur. Reprinted New York: International, 1985.

Matthews, Victor H. "Honor and Shame in Gender-Related Legal Situations in the Hebrew Bible." In *Gender and Law in the Hebrew Bible and the Ancient Near East*. Edited by Victor H. Matthews, Bernard M. Levinson, and Tikva Frymer-Kensky, 97–112. JSOTSup 262. Sheffield: Sheffield Academic, 1998.

———. "Hospitality and Hostility in Genesis 19 and Judges 19." *BTB* 22 (1992) 3–11.

———. "Hospitality and Hostility in Judges 4." *BTB* 21 (1991) 13–21.

———. "Perfumes and Spices." In *ABD* 5:226–28.

Matthews, Victor H., and Don C. Benjamin, eds. *Honor and Shame in the World of the Bible. Semeia* 68 (1994).

———. *Social World of Ancient Israel: 1250–587* B.C.E.. Peabody, Mass.: Hendrickson, 1993.

Mayer, G. "*Kôs.*" In *TDOT* 7 (1995) 101–4.

Mays, James Luther. *Hosea: A Commentary*. OTL. Philadelphia: Westminster, 1969.

McCarter, P. Kyle, Jr. *II Samuel*. AB 9. Garden City, N.Y.: Doubleday, 1984.

McClintock, Anne. *Imperial Leather: Race, Gender, and Sexuality in the Colonial Contest*. New York: Routledge, 1995.

McClintock, Anne, Aamir Mufti, and Ella Shohat, eds. *Dangerous Liaisons: Gender, Nation, and Postcolonial Perspectives*. Minneapolis: Univ. of Minnesota Press, 1997.

McComiskey, Thomas Edward. *The Minor Prophets: An Exegetical and Expository Commentary*. Vol. 1: *Hosea, Joel, and Amos*. Grand Rapids: Baker, 1992.

———. "Prophetic Irony in Hosea 1.4: A Study of the Collocation *Pqd 'L* and Its Implications for the Fall of Jehu's Dynasty." *JSOT* 58 (1993) 93–101.

McCreesh, Thomas P., O.P. "Wisdom As Wife: Proverbs 31:10-31." *RB* 92 (1985) 25–46.

McInlay, Judith. "Bringing the Unspeakable to Speech in Hosea." *Pacifica* 9 (1996) 121–33.

McKane, William. *Proverbs: A New Approach*. OTL. Philadelphia: Westminster, 1970.

McKeating, Henry. *Ezekiel*. OTG. Sheffield: Sheffield Academic, 1995.

———. "Sanctions against Adultery in Ancient Israelite Society, with Some Reflections on Methodology in the Study of Old Testament Ethics." *JSOT* 11 (1979) 52–72.

McKenzie, John L. *Dictionary of the Bible*. New York: Macmillan, 1965.

McNutt, Paula M. *Reconstructing the Society of Ancient Israel*. LAI. Louisville: Westminster John Knox, 1999.

Mendenhall, George E. "The Hebrew Conquest of Palestine." *BA* 25 (1962) 66–87.

———. "The Shady Side of Wisdom: The Date and Purpose of Genesis 3." In *A Light unto My Path: Old Testament Studies in Honor of Jacob M. Myers*. Edited by Howard N. Bream, Ralph D. Heim, and Carey A. Moore, 319–34. Philadelphia: Temple Univ. Press, 1974.

Meshel, Z. "Did Yahweh Have a Consort?" *BAR* 5, no. 2 (1979) 24–35.

Meyers, Carol. *Discovering Eve: Ancient Israelite Women in Context*. New York: Oxford Univ. Press, 1988.

————. "'To Her Mother's House': Considering a Counterpart to the Israelite *Bêt 'Ab*." In *The Bible and the Politics of Exegesis: Essays in Honor of Norman K. Gottwald on His Sixty-Fifth Birthday*. Edited by David Jobling, Peggy L. Day, and Gerald T. Sheppard, 39–51. Cleveland: Pilgrim, 1991.

Michaelson, Evalyn Jacobson, and Walter Goldschmidt. "Females Roles and Male Dominance among Peasants." *SWJA* 27 (1971) 330–52.

Mikaelsson, Lisbeth. "Sexual Polarity: An Aspect of the Ideological Structure in the Paradise Narrative, Gen 2,4—3,24." *Temenos* 16 (1980) 84–91.

Milgrom, Jacob. *Leviticus 17–22*. AB 3A. New York: Doubleday, 2000.

Miller, J. Maxwell, and John H. Hayes. *A History of Ancient Israel and Judah*. Philadelphia: Westminster, 1986.

Miller, Patrick D., Jr. "The Absence of the Goddess in Israelite Religion." *HAR* 10 (1986) 239–48.

Miller, Patrick D., Jr., Paul D. Hanson, and S. Dean McBride, eds. *Ancient Israelite Religion: Essays in Honor of Frank Moore Cross*. Philadelphia: Fortress Press, 1987.

Milne, Pamela J. "Eve and Adam. Is a Feminist Reading Possible?" *BRev* 4, no. 3 (1988) 12–21, 39.

————. "Feminist Interpretations of the Bible: Then and Now." *BRev* 8, no. 5 (1992) 38–43, 52–55.

————. "The Patriarchal Stamp of Scripture: The Implication of Structuralist Analyses for Feminist Hermeneutics." *JFSR* 5 (1989) 17–34.

————. "What Shall We Do with Judith? A Feminist Reassessment of a Biblical 'Heroine.'" *Semeia* 62 (1993) 37–58.

Minkema, Kenneth P. "Witchcraft and Gender Studies in the 1900s." *RSR* 26, no. 1 (2000) 13–19.

Minow, Martha. *Between Vengeance and Forgiveness: Facing History after Genocide and Mass Violence*. Boston: Beacon, 1998.

Mintz, Alan. "The Rhetoric of Lamentations and the Representation of Catastrophe." *Prooftexts* 2 (1982) 1–17.

Moberly, R. Walter. "Did the Serpent Get It Right?" *JTS* 39 (1988) 1–27.

Moore, Carey A. *Judith*. AB 40B. Garden City, N.Y.: Doubleday, 1985.

Moore, Henrietta L. *Feminism and Anthropology*. Minneapolis: Univ. of Minnesota Press, 1989.

Mora, George. "Reification of Evil: Witchcraft, Heresy, and the Scapegoat." In *Evil: Self and Culture*. Edited by M. Nelson and M. Eigen, 36–60. New York: Human Sciences Press, 1984.

Morgen, Sandra, ed. *Gender and Anthropology: Critical Reviews for Research and Teaching*. Washington, D.C.: American Anthropological Association, 1989.

Mosala, Itumeleng J. *Biblical Hermeneutics and Black Theology in South Africa*. Grand Rapids: Eerdmans, 1989.

Mulvey, Laura. "Visual Pleasure and Narrative Cinema." In *Feminisms: An Anthology of Literary Theory and Criticism*. Edited by Robyn R. Warhol and Diane Price Herndl, 432–42. New Brunswick, N.J.: Rutgers Univ. Press, 1991.

Murphy, Robert F. "Social Distance and the Veil." *AmAnth* 66 (1964) 1257–74.

———. "Tuareg Kinship." *AmAnth* 69 (1967) 163–70.

Murphy, Robert F., and Leonard Kasdan. "Agnation and Endogamy: Some Further Considerations." *SWJA* 23 (1967) 1–14.

———. "The Structure of Parallel Cousin Marriage." *AmAnth* 61 (1959) 17–29.

Murphy, Roland E. *The Tree of Life: An Exploration of Biblical Wisdom.* ABRL. New York: Doubleday, 1990.

Myers, Ched. *Binding the Strong Man: A Political Reading of Mark's Story of Jesus.* Maryknoll, N.Y.: Orbis, 1988.

Nakanose, Shigeyuki. *Josiah's Passover: Sociology and the Liberating Bible.* Maryknoll, N.Y.: Orbis, 1993.

Naumann, Thomas. *Hoseas Erben: Strukturen der Nachinterpretation im Buch Hosea.* BWANT 131. Stuttgart: Kohlhammer, 1991.

Nelson, Cynthia. "Public and Private Politics: Women in the Middle Eastern World." *AmEth* 1 (1974) 551–63.

Neu, Rainer. "Patrilokalität und Patrilinearität in Israel. Zur ethnosoziologischen Kritik der These vom Matriarchat." *BZ* 34 (1990) 222–33.

Newsom, Carol A. "Women and the Discourse of Patriarchal Wisdom: A Study of Proverbs 1–9." In *Gender and Difference in Ancient Israel.* Edited by Peggy L. Day, 142–60. Minneapolis: Fortress Press, 1989.

Niditch, Susan. "Eroticism and Death in the Tale of Jael." In *Gender and Difference in Ancient Israel.* Edited by Peggy L. Day, 43–57. Minneapolis: Fortress Press, 1989.

———. "The 'Sodomite' Theme in Judges 19–20: Family, Community, and Social Disintegration." *CBQ* 44 (1982) 365–78.

Nissinen, Martti. *Prophetie, Redaktion und Fortschreibung im Hoseabuch: Studien zum Werdegang eines Prophetenbuches im Lichte von Hos 4 und 11.* AOAT 231. Neukirchen-Vluyn: Neukirchener Verlag, 1991.

Noth, Martin. *Numbers: A Commentary.* Translated by James D. Martin. OTL. Philadelphia: Westminster, 1968.

O'Brien, Joan, and Wilfred Major, eds. *In the Beginning: Creation Myths from Ancient Mesopotamia, Israel, and Greece.* AARASRS 11. Chico, Calif.: Scholars, 1982.

O'Connell, Robert H. "Proverbs VII 6-17: A Case of Fatal Deception in a 'Woman and the Window' Type-Scene." *VT* 41 (1991) 235–41.

O'Connor, Kathleen M. *Lamentations and the Tears of the World.* Maryknoll, N.Y.: Orbis, 2002.

O'Connor, M. "The Pseudo-Sorites in Hebrew Verse." In *Perspectives on Language and Text: Essays and Poems in Honor of F. I. Andersen's Sixtieth Birthday.* Edited by E. W. Conrad and E. W. Newing, 239–53. Winona Lake, Ind.: Eisenbrauns, 1987.

Oded, Bustenay. "Judah and the Exile." In *Israelite and Judean History*. Edited by John H. Hayes and J. Maxwell Miller, 435–88. OTL. Philadelphia: Westminster, 1977.

———. *Mass Deportations and Deportees in the Neo-Assyrian Empire*. Wiesbaden: Reichert, 1979.

———. "Observations on the Israelite/Judean Exiles in Mesopotamia during the Eighth-Sixth Centuries B.C.E." In *Immigration and Emigration within the Ancient Near East*. Edited by K. van Lerberghe and A. Schoors, 205–12. Leuven: Peeters/Departement Orientalistiek, 1995.

Odell, Margaret S. "An Exploratory Study of Shame and Dependence in the Bible and Selected Near Eastern Parallels." In *The Biblical Canon in Comparative Perspective*. Edited by K. Lawson Younger Jr., William W. Hallo, and Bernard F. Batto, 217–33. Lewiston, N.Y.: Mellen, 1991.

———. "The Inversion of Shame and Forgiveness in Ezekiel 16.59-63." *JSOT* 56 (1992) 101–12.

———. "Who Were the Prophets in Hosea?" *HBT* 18 (1996) 78–95.

Oden, Robert A., Jr. "Grace or Status? Yahweh's Clothing of the First Humans." In *The Bible without Theology: The Theological Tradition and Alternatives to It*, 92–105. San Francisco: Harper & Row, 1987.

———. "Religious Identity and the Sacred Prostitution Accusation." In *The Bible without Theology*, 135–53.

Oesterley, W. O. E. *The Book of Proverbs*. Westminster Commentaries 17. London: Methuen, 1929.

Olyan, Saul M. *Asherah and the Cult of Yahweh in Israel*. SBLMS 34. Atlanta: Scholars, 1988.

———. "Honor, Shame, and Covenant Relations in Ancient Israel and Its Environment." *JBL* 115 (1996) 201–18.

———. "'In the Sight of Her Lovers': On the Interpretation of *Nablut* in Hos 2,12." *BZ* 36 (1992) 255–61.

Ortner, Sherry B. "The Virgin and the State." *Feminist Studies* 4 (1978) 19–33.

Osiek, Carolyn. "The New Handmaid: The Bible and the Social Sciences." *TS* 50 (1989) 260–78.

Panofsky, Dora, and Erwin Panofsky. *Pandora's Box: The Changing Aspects of a Mythical Symbol*. New York: Harper & Row, 1965.

Paolucci, Elizabeth Oddone, Mark L. Genuis, and Claudio Violato. "A Meta-Analysis of the Published Research on the Effects of Child Sexual Abuse." *Journal of Psychology* 135, no. 1 (2001) 17–36.

Pardes, Ilana. *Countertraditions in the Bible: A Feminist Approach*. Cambridge: Harvard Univ. Press, 1992.

Pastner, Carroll McC. "Accommodations to Purdah: The Female Perspective." *Journal of Marriage and Family* 36 (1974) 408–14.

———. "A Social Structural and Historical Analysis of Honor, Shame, and Purdah." *AnthQ* 45 (1972) 248–61.

Patai, Raphael. *The Hebrew Goddess*. Philadelphia: Ktav, 1967.

————. "The Structure of Endogamous Unilineal Descent Groups." *SWJA* 21 (1965) 325–50.

Patton, Corrine. "A Dragon in the Seas: Egypt in the Book of Ezekiel." A paper read at the Catholic Biblical Association annual meeting, Scranton, Pa., August 1998.

————. "'I Myself Gave Them Laws That Were Not Good': Ezekiel 20 and the Exodus Traditions." *JSOT* 69 (1996) 73–90.

————. "Priest, Prophet and Exile: Ezekiel As a Literary Construct." *SBLSP* 39 (2000) 700–727.

————. "'Should Our Sister Be Treated like a Whore?' A Response to Feminist Critiques of Ezekiel 23." In *The Book of Ezekiel: Theological and Anthropological Perspectives.* Edited by Margaret S. Odell and John T. Strong, 221–38. SBLSymSer 9. Atlanta: SBL, 2000.

Paul, Shalom M. "Biblical Analogues to Middle Assyrian Law." In *Religion and Law: Biblical-Judaic and Islamic Perspectives.* Edited by Edwin B. Firmage, Bernard G. Weiss, and John W. Welch, 333–50. Winona Lake, Ind.: Eisenbrauns, 1990.

Peckham, Brian. "The Composition of Hosea." *HAR* 11 (1987) 331–53.

————. *History and Prophecy: The Development of Late Judean Literary Tradition. ABRL.* New York: Doubleday, 1993.

Pedersen, Johannes. *Israel: Its Life and Culture.* Vols. 1–2. Translated by Aslaug Møller and A. I. Fausbell. Copenhagen: Branner Og Korch, 1926.

Peña, Manuel. "Class, Gender, and Machismo: The 'Treacherous-Woman' Folklore of Mexican Male Workers." *Gender and Society* 5 (1991) 30–46.

Perdue, Leo G. "Liminality As a Social Setting for Wisdom Instructions." *ZAW* 93 (1981) 114–26.

————. *Proverbs.* IBC. Louisville: Westminster John Knox, 2000.

————. "Wisdom Theology and Social History in Proverbs 1–9." In *Wisdom, You Are My Sister: Studies in Honor of Roland E. Murphy, O.Carm., on the Occasion of His Eightieth Birthday.* Edited by Michael L. Barré, S.S., 78–101. Washington, D.C.: Catholic Biblical Association of America, 1997.

Peristiany, J. G., ed. *Honor and Shame: The Values of Mediterranean Society.* Chicago: Univ. of Chicago Press, 1966.

Peristiany, J. G., and Julian Pitt-Rivers, eds. *Honor and Grace in Anthropology.* Cambridge: Cambridge Univ. Press, 1992.

Perkins, Teresa E. "Rethinking Stereotypes." In *Ideology and Cultural Production.* Edited by Michèle Barrett, 135–59. New York: St. Martin's, 1979.

Petersen, David L. "Israel and Monotheism: The Unfinished Agenda." In *Canon, Theology, and Old Testament Interpretation: Essays in Honor of Brevard S. Childs.* Edited by Gene M. Tucker, David L. Petersen, and Robert R. Wilson, 92–107. Philadelphia: Fortress Press, 1988.

Phillips, Anthony. "Another Look at Adultery." *JSOT* 20 (1981) 3–25.

Pilch, John J. *Introducing the Cultural Context of the Old Testament*. Mahwah, N.J.: Paulist, 1991.

Pippin, Tina. "Eros and the End: Reading for Gender in the Apocalypse of John." *Semeia* 59 (1992) 193–210.

Pitt-Rivers, Julian. *The Fate of Shechem or the Politics of Sex: Essays in the Anthropology of the Mediterranean*. Cambridge: Cambridge Univ. Press, 1977.

———. "Honour and Social Status." In *Honour and Shame: The Values of Mediterranean Society*. Edited by J. G. Peristiany, 19–77. Chicago: Univ. of Chicago Press, 1966.

Pixley, George V. *On Exodus: A Liberation Perspective*. Translated by Robert R. Barr. Maryknoll, N.Y.: Orbis, 1987.

Pleins, J. David. "Poverty in the Social World of the Wise." *JSOT* 37 (1987) 61–78.

Pope, Marvin H. *Song of Songs*. AB 7C. Garden City, N.Y.: Doubleday, 1977.

Postgate, J. N. "The Economic Structure of the Assyrian Empire." In *Power and Propaganda: A Symposium on Ancient Empires*. Edited by Mogens Trolle Larsen, 193–221. Copenhagen: Akademisk Forlag, 1979.

Premnath, D. N. "Latifundialization and Isaiah 5.8-10." *JSOT* 40 (1998) 49–62.

Preuss, H. D. "*Zāra'; Zera'*." In *TDOT* 4 (1980) 143–62.

Propp, William H. "Eden Sketches." In *The Hebrew Bible and Its Interpreters*. Edited by William H. Propp, Baruch Halpern, and David Noel Freedman, 189–203. Winona Lake, Ind.: Eisenbrauns, 1990.

Prouser, O. Horn. "The Truth about Women and Lying." *JSOT* 61 (1994) 15–28.

Purvis, James D., and Eric M. Meyers. "Exile and Return: From the Babylonian Destruction to the Reconstruction of the Jewish State." In *Ancient Israel: From Abraham to the Roman Destruction of the Temple*. Edited by Hershel Shanks, 201–29. Rev. and expanded ed. Washington, D.C.: Biblical Archaeology Society, 1999.

Pury, Albert de. "Yahwist ('J') Source." In *ABD* 6:1012–20.

Rabasa, José. "Allegories of *Atlas*." In *The Post-Colonial Studies Reader*. Edited by Bill Ashcroft, Gareth Griffiths, and Helen Tiffin, 358–64. New York: Routledge, 1995.

Rabichev, Renata. "The Mediterranean Concepts of Honour and Shame As Seen in the Depiction of the Biblical Women." *R&T* 3 (1996) 51–63.

Rad, Gerhard von. *Genesis: A Commentary*. Translated by John H. Marks. Rev. ed. OTL. Philadelphia: Westminster, 1972.

Raitt, Jill. "The *Vagina Dentata* and the *Immaculatus Uterus Divini Fontis*." *JAAR* 48 (1980) 415–31.

Rallis, Irene Kerasote. "Nuptial Imagery in the Book of Hosea: Israel As the Bride of Yahweh." *St. Vladimir's Theological Quarterly* 34 (1990) 197–219.

Reineke, Martha. "'The Devils Are Come Down upon Us': Myth, History and the Witch As Scapegoat." In *The Pleasure of Her Text: Feminist Readings of Biblical and Historical Texts*. Edited by Alice Bach, 117–45. Philadelphia: Trinity Press International, 1990.

Reixach, Joan Frigolé. "Procreation and Its Implications for Gender, Marriage, and Family in European Rural Ethnography." *AnthQ* 71 (1998) 32–40.

Rentería, Tamis Hoover. "The Elijah/Elisha Stories: A Socio-Cultural Analysis of Prophets and People in Ninth-Century B.C.E. Israel." In *Elijah and Elisha in Socioliterary Perspective*. Edited by Robert B. Coote, 75–126. SemeiaSt. Atlanta: Scholars, 1992.

Renz, Thomas. *The Rhetorical Function of the Book of Ezekiel*. VTSup 76. Leiden: Brill, 1999.

Ringgren, Helmer. *Israelite Religion*. Translated by David Green. Philadelphia: Fortress Press, 1966.

Robinson, T. H. *Die zwölf kleinen Propheten*. HAT 14. Tübingen: Mohr/ Siebeck, 1938.

———. *Prophecy and the Prophets in Ancient Israel*. London: Duckworth, 1923.

Rogers, Susan C. "Female Forms of Power and the Myth of Male Dominance: A Model of Female/Male Interaction in Peasant Society." *AmEth* 2 (1975) 727–56.

Rogerson, John W. "Anthropology and the Old Testament." In *The World of Ancient Israel: Sociological, Anthropological and Political Perspectives*. Edited by R. E. Clements, 17–37. Cambridge: Cambridge Univ. Press, 1989.

———. *Anthropology and the Old Testament*. BibSem 1. Sheffield: JSOT Press, 1984.

Rohrlich, Ruby. "State Formation in Sumer and the Subjugation of Women." *Feminist Studies* 6 (1980) 76–102.

Rohrlich-Leavitt, Ruby. "Women in Transition: Crete and Sumer." In *Becoming Visible: Women in European History*. Edited by Renate Bridenthal and Claudia Koonz, 36–59. Boston: Houghton Mifflin, 1977.

Rosaldo, Michelle Zimbalist. "The Use and Abuse of Anthropology": Reflections on Feminism and Cross-Cultural Understanding." *Signs* 5 (1980) 389–417.

———. "Women, Culture, and Society: A Theoretical Overview." In *Women, Culture, and Society*. Edited by Michelle Zimbalist Rosale and Louise Lamphere, 17–42. Stanford: Stanford Univ. Press, 1974.

Rowley, H. H. "The Marriage of Hosea." In *Men of God*, 66–97. London: Nelson, 1963.

Said, Edward W. *Orientalism*. New York: Vintage, 1979.

Sasson, Jack M., ed. *Civilizations of the Ancient Near East*. 4 vols. New York: Scribner's, 1995.

Scarry, Elaine. *The Body in Pain: The Making and Unmaking of the World.* New York: Oxford Univ. Press, 1985.

Schley, Donald G. "The *Shalishim*; Officers or Special Three-Man Squads?" *VT* 40 (1990) 321–26.

Schmidt, Werner H. "A Theologian for the Solomonic Era? A Plea for the Yahwist." In *Studies in the Period of David and Solomon*. Edited by Tomoo Ishida (Winona Lake, Ind.: Eisenbrauns, 1982).

Schmitt, John J. "Like Eve, Like Adam: *mšl* in Gen 3,16." *Bib* 72 (1991) 1–22.

———. "Yahweh's Divorce in Hosea 2—Who Is That Woman?" *SJOT* 9 (1995) 119–32.

Schneider, Jane. "Of Vigilance and Virgins: Honor, Shame and Access to Resources in Mediterranean Societies." *Ethnology* 9 (1971) 1–24.

Schweickart, Patrocinio. "Reading Ourselves: Toward a Feminist Theory of Reading." In *Contemporary Literary Criticism: Literary and Cultural Studies*. Edited by Robert Con Davis and Ronald Schleifer, 118–41. 2nd ed. New York: Longman, 1989.

Scott, James. *Weapons of the Weak: Everyday Forms of Peasant Resistance.* New Haven: Yale Univ. Press, 1985.

Scott, R. B. Y. *Proverbs. Ecclesiastes: Introduction, Translation, and Notes.* I AB 18. Garden City, N.Y.: Doubleday, 1965.

Segal, Lynne. "Competing Masculinities (III): Black Masculinity and the White Man's Black Man." In *Slow Motion: Changing Masculinities, Changing Men*, 168–204. New Brunswick, N.J.: Rutgers Univ. Press, 1990.

Setel, T. Drorah. "Prophets and Pornography: Female Sexual Imagery." In *Feminist Interpretation of the Bible*. Edited by Letty M. Russell, 86–95. Philadelphia: Westminster, 1985.

Sharpe, Jenny. "The Unspeakable Limits of Rape: Colonial Violence and Counter-Insurgency." In *Colonial Discourse and Post-Colonial Theory: A Reader*. Edited by Patrick Williams and Laura Chrisman, 221–43. New York: Columbia Univ. Press, 1994.

Shields, Mary E. "An Abusive God? Identity and Power/Gender and Violence in Ezekiel 23." In *Postmodern Interpretations of the Bible: A Reader*. Edited by A. K. M. Adam, 129–52. St Louis: Chalice, 2001.

———. "Multiple Exposures: Body Rhetoric and Gender Characterization in Ezekiel 16." *JFSR* 14 (1998) 5–18.

Simkins, Ronald A., and Stephen L. Cook, eds. *The Social World of the Hebrew Bible: Twenty-Five Years of the Social Sciences in the Academy.* *Semeia* 87 (1999).

Sivan, Helena Z. "The Rape of Cozbi (Numbers XXV)." *VT* 51 (2001) 69–80.

Skehan, Patrick W., and Alexander A. Di Lella, O.F.M. *The Wisdom of Ben Sira*. AB 39. New York: Doubleday, 1987.

Smith, Daniel L. "The Politics of Ezra: Sociological Indicators of Postexilic Judaean Society." In *Second Temple Studies. Vol. 1: Persian Period*. Edited by Philip R. Davies, 73–97. JSOTSup 117. Sheffield: Sheffield Academic, 1991.

———. *The Religion of the Landless: The Social Context of the Babylonian Exile.* Bloomington, Ind.: Meyer-Stone, 1989.

Smith, Mark S. *The Early History of God: Yahweh and the Other Deities in Ancient Israel.* 2nd ed. Grand Rapids: Eerdmans, 2002.

———. "God Male and Female in the Old Testament: Yahweh and His 'Asherah.'" *TS* 48 (1987) 333–40.

———. "Yahweh and Other Deities in Ancient Israel: Observations on Old Problems and Recent Trends." In *Ein Gott allein? JHWH-Verehrung und biblischer Monotheismus im Kontext der israelitischen und altorientalischen Religionsgeschichte.* Edited by Walter Dietrich and Martin A. Klopfenstein, 197–234. OBO 139. Göttingen: Vandenhoeck & Ruprecht, 1994.

Smith, Morton. *Palestinian Parties and Politics That Shaped the Old Testament.* New York: Columbia Univ. Press, 1971.

Smith-Christopher, Daniel L. "Between Ezra and Isaiah: Exclusion, Transformation, and Inclusion of the 'Foreigner' in Post-Exilic Biblical Theology." In *Ethnicity and the Bible.* Edited by Mark G. Brett, 117–42. BibIntSer 19. Leiden: Brill, 1996.

———. *A Biblical Theology of Exile.* OBT. Minneapolis: Fortress Press, 2002.

———. "Ezekiel on Fanon's Couch: A Postcolonialist Dialogue with David Halperin's *Seeking Ezekiel.*" In *Peace and Justice Shall Embrace: Power and Theopolitics in the Bible: Essays in Honor of Millard Lind.* Edited by Ted Grimsrud and Loren L. Johns, 108–44. Telford, Pa.: Pandora, 1999.

———. "The Mixed Marriage Crisis in Ezra 9–10 and Nehemiah 13: A Study of the Sociology of the Post-Exilic Judean Community." In *Second Temple Studies.* Vol. 2: *Temple and Community in the Persian Period.* Edited by Tamara C. Eskenazi and Kent H. Richards, 243–65. JSOTSup 175. Sheffield: Sheffield Academic, 1994.

———. "Reassessing the Historical and Sociological Impact of the Babylonian Exile (597/587–539 B.C.E.)." In *Exile: Old Testament, Jewish, and Christian Perspectives.* Edited by James M. Scott, 7–32. JSJSup 56. Leiden: Brill, 1997.

Sneed, Mark. "The Class Culture of Proverbs: Eliminating Stereotypes." *SJOT* 10 (1996) 296–308.

Snijders, L. A. "The Meaning of *Zar* in the Old Testament." *OtSt* 10 (1954) 1–154.

Snyman, Gerrie. "Social Reality and Religious Language in the Marriage Metaphor in Hosea 1–3." *OTE* 6 (1993) 90–112.

Soggin, Alberto J. "The Fall of Man in the Third Chapter of Genesis." In *Old Testament and Oriental Studies,* 88–111. BibOr 29. Rome: Biblical Institute Press, 1975.

Stager, Lawrence. "The Archaeology of the Family in Ancient Israel."
    BASOR 260 (1985) 1–36.

———. "The Fury of Babylon; Ashkelon and the Archaeology of Destruc-
    tion." *BAR* 22, no. 1 (1996) 56–69, 76–77.

Stalker, D. M. G. *Ezekiel*. Torch Bible Commentaries. London: SCM, 1968.

Steinberg, Naomi. "Alliance or Descent? The Function of Marriage in Gen-
    esis." *JSOT* 51 (1991) 45–55.

———. "Conflict and Cooperation: Strategies of Domestic Power." Paper
    presented at the SBL annual meeting in New Orleans, November 1990.

———. "The Deuteronomic Law Code and the Politics of State Centraliza-
    tion." In *The Bible and the Politics of Exegesis: Essays in Honor of Norman
    K. Gottwald on His Sixty-Fifth Birthday*. Edited by David Jobling, Peggy L.
    Day, and Gerald T. Sheppard, 161–70. Cleveland: Pilgrim, 1991.

———. "Gender Roles in the Rebekah Cycle." *USQR* 39 (1984) 175–88.

———. *Kinship and Marriage in Genesis: A Household Economics Perspec-
    tive*. Minneapolis: Fortress Press, 1993.

Stephens, Walter. "Witches Who Steal Penises: Impotence and Illusion in
    Malleus Maleficarum." *Journal of Medieval and Early Modern Studies* 28
    (1998) 495–530.

Stiebert, Johanna. *The Construction of Shame in the Hebrew Bible: The
    Prophetic Contribution*. JSOTSup 346. London: Sheffield Academic,
    2002.

Stienstra, Nelly. *YHWH Is the Husband of His People: An Analysis of a Biblical
    Metaphor with a Special Reference to Translation*. Kampen: Kok Pharos,
    1993.

Stocker, Margarita. *Judith: Sexual Warrior Women and Power in Western Cul-
    ture*. New Haven: Yale Univ. Press, 1998.

Stoler, Ann Laura. "Carnal Knowledge and Imperial Power: Gender, Race,
    and Morality in Colonial Asia." In *Gender at the Crossroads of Knowledge:
    Feminist Anthropology in the Postmodern Era*. Edited by Micaela di
    Leonardo, 51–101. Berkeley: Univ. of California Press, 1991.

Stone, Ken. "Gender and Homosexuality in Judges 19: Subject-Honor, Ob-
    ject-Shame?" *JSOT* 67 (1995) 87–107.

———. *Sex, Honor and Power in the Deuteronomistic History: A Narratolog-
    ical and Anthropological Analysis*. JSOTSup 234. Sheffield: Sheffield Aca-
    demic, 1997.

Stordalen, Terje. "Man, Soil, Garden: Basic Plot in Gen 2–3 Reconsidered."
    JSOT 53 (1992) 3–26.

Stratton, Beverly J. *Out of Eden: A Feminist, Theological Study of Reading,
    Rhetoric, and Ideology in Genesis 2–3*. JSOTSup 208. Sheffield: Sheffield
    Academic, 1995.

Streete, Gail P. Corrington. *The Strange Woman: Power and Sex in the Bible*.
    Louisville: Westminster John Knox, 1997.

Stuart, Douglas. *Hosea–Jonah*. WBC 31. Waco: Word, 1987.

Stulman, Louis. "Encroachment in Deuteronomy: Analysis of the Social World of the D Code." *JBL* 109 (1990) 613–32.

———. "Sex and Familial Crimes in the D Code: A Witness to Mores in Transition." *JSOT* 53 (1992) 47–64.

Sweeney, Marvin. "Ezekiel: Zadokite Priest and Visionary Prophet of the Exile." *SBLSP* 39 (2000) 728–51.

Tal, Kalí. *Worlds of Hurt: Reading the Literatures of Trauma*. New York: Cambridge Univ. Press, 1996.

Tarlin, Jan William. "Utopia and Pornography in Ezekiel: Violence, Hope, and the Shattered Male Subject." In *Reading Bibles, Writing Bodies: Identity and the Book*. Edited by Timothy K. Beal and David M. Gunn, 175–83. New York: Routledge, 1997.

Taylor, Gary. *Castration: An Abbreviated History of Western Manhood*. New York: Routledge, 2000.

Thistlethwaite, Susan. "'You May Enjoy the Spoil of Your Enemies': Rape As a Biblical Metaphor for War." *Semeia* 61 (1993) 59–75.

Thompson, J. A. "Israel's 'Lovers.'" *VT* 27 (1977) 475–81.

Throntveit, Mark A. *Ezra–Nehemiah*. IBC. Louisville: Westminster John Knox, 1992.

Timms, Robert J., and Patrick Connors. "Adult Promiscuity following Childhood Sexual Abuse: An Introduction." *Psychotherapy Patient* 8, nos. 1–2 (1992) 19–27.

Todd, Judith A. "The Pre-Deuteronomistic Elijah Cycle." In *Elijah and Elisha in Socioliterary Perspective*. Edited by Robert B. Coote, 1–35. SemeiaSt. Atlanta: Scholars, 1992.

Toews, Wesley I. *Monarchy and Religious Institution in Israel under Jeroboam I*. SBLMS 47. Atlanta: Scholars, 1993.

Tompkins, Jane P. "The Reader in History: The Changing Shape of Literary Response." In *Reader-Response Criticism: From Formalism to Post-Structuralism*. Edited by Jane P. Tompkins, 201–32. Baltimore: Johns Hopkins Univ. Press, 1980.

Tosato, Angelo. "On Genesis 2:24." *CBQ* 52 (1990) 389–409.

Toy, Crawford H. *A Critical and Exegetical Commentary on the Book of Proverbs*. ICC. New York: Scribner's, 1908.

Trible, Phyllis. "Depatriarchalizing in Biblical Interpretation." *JAAR* 41 (1973) 30–48.

———. *God and the Rhetoric of Sexuality*. OBT. Philadelphia: Fortress Press, 1978.

———. "Woman in the OT." In *IDBSup*, 963–66.

Trotter, James M. "Was the Second Jerusalem Temple a Primarily Persian Project?" *SJOT* 15 (2001) 276–94.

Udobata, Onunwa. "The Paradox of Power and 'Submission' of Women in African Traditional Religion and Society." *Journal of Dharma* 13 (1988) 31–38.

Utzschneider, Helmut. *Hosea, Prophet vor dem Ende.* OBO 31. Göttingen: Vandenhoeck & Ruprecht, 1980.

van Alphen, Ernst. "Symptoms of Discursivity. Experience, Memory, and Trauma." In *Acts of Memory: Cultural Recall in the Present.* Edited by Mieke Bal, Jonathan Crewe, and Leo Spitzer, 24–38. Hanover, N.H.: Univ. Press of New England, 1999.

van der Kolk, Bessel A., Alexander C. McFarlane, and Lars Weisaet, eds. *Traumatic Stress: The Effects of Overwhelming Experience on Mind, Body, and Society.* New York: Guilford, 1996.

van der Kolk, Bessel A., and Onno van der Hart. "The Intrusive Past: The Flexibility of Memory and the Engraving of Trauma." In *Trauma: Explorations in Memory.* Edited by Cathy Caruth, 158–82. Baltimore: Johns Hopkins Univ. Press, 1995.

van der Toorn, Karel. "Female Prostitution in Payment of Vows in Ancient Israel." *JBL* 108 (1989) 193–205.

———. "Theology, Priests, and Worship in Canaan and Ancient Israel." In *Civilizations of the Ancient Near East.* Edited by Jack M. Sasson, 4:2043–58. New York: Scribner's, 1995.

van Dijk-Hemmes, Fokkelien. "The Metaphorization of Woman in Prophetic Speech: An Analysis of Ezekiel 23." In *On Gendering Texts: Female and Male Voices in the Hebrew Bible.* Edited by Athalya Brenner and Fokkelien van Dijk-Hemmes, 167–76. BibIntSer 1. Leiden: Brill, 1993.

———. "Traces of Women's Texts in the Hebrew Bible." In *On Gendering Texts: Female and Male Voices in the Hebrew Bible.* Edited by Athalya Brenner and Fokkelien van Dijk-Hemmes, 17–109. BibIntSer 1. Leiden: Brill, 1993.

Van Leeuwen, Raymond C. "The Book of Proverbs. Introduction, Commentary, and Reflections." In *NIB* 5:1–264. Nashville: Abingdon, 1997.

Van Seters, John. "The Creation of Man and the Creation of the King." *ZAW* 101 (1989) 333–42.

Vanderhooft, David Stephen. *The Neo-Babylonian Empire and Babylon in the Latter Prophets.* HSM 59. Atlanta: Scholars, 1999.

Vermeylen, Jacques. "Le Récit du Paradis et la Question des Origines du Pentateuque." *Bijdragen* 41 (1980) 230–50.

Wacker, Marie-Theres. "Traces of the Goddess in the Book of Hosea." In *A Feminist Companion to the Latter Prophets.* Edited by Athalya Brenner, 219–41. FCB 8. Sheffield: Sheffield Academic, 1995.

Waldman, N. M. "The Breaking of the Bow." *JQR* 79 (1978) 82–86.

Wallace, Howard N. *The Eden Narrative.* HSM 32. Atlanta: Scholars, 1985.

Walsh, Carey Ellen. *Exquisite Desire: Religion, the Erotic, and the Song of Songs.* Minneapolis: Fortress Press, 2000.

Wander, Nathaniel. "Structure, Contradiction, and 'Resolution' in Mythology: Father's Brother's Daughter Marriage and the Treatment of Women in Genesis 11–50." *JANESCU* 13 (1981) 75–99.

Washington, Harold C. "The Strange Woman (*'iššh zrh/nkryh*) of Proverbs 1–9 and Post-Exilic Judaean Society." In *Second Temple Studies*. Vol. 2: *Temple and Community in the Persian Period*. Edited by Tamara C. Eskenazi and Kent H. Richards, 217–42. JSOTSup 175. Sheffield: Sheffield Academic, 1994.

————. *Wealth and Poverty in the Instruction of Amenemope and the Hebrew Proverbs*. SBLDS 142. Atlanta: Scholars, 1994.

Webster, Jane S. "Sophia: Engendering Wisdom in Proverbs, Ben Sira and the Wisdom of Solomon." *JSOT* 78 (1998) 63–79.

Weems, Renita J. *Battered Love: Marriage, Sex, and Violence in the Hebrew Prophets*. OBT. Minneapolis: Fortress Press, 1995.

————. "Gomer: Victim of Violence or Victim of Metaphor?" *Semeia* 47 (1989) 87–104.

Wenham, Gordon J. *Genesis 1–15*. WBC 1. Waco: Word, 1987.

Westbrook, Raymond. "Adultery in Ancient Near Eastern Law." *RB* 97 (1990) 542–80.

Westenholz, Joan Goodnick, "Tamar, *Qĕdēšā, Qadištu,* and Sacred Prostitution in Mesopotamia." *HTR* 82 (1989) 245–65.

Westermann, Claus. *Genesis 1–11: A Commentary*. Translated by John J. Scullion, S.J. CC. Minneapolis: Augsburg, 1984.

Wevers, John W. *Ezekiel*. NCBC. Grand Rapids: Eerdmans, 1969.

White, Marsha C. *The Elijah Legends and Jehu's Coup*. BJS 311. Atlanta: Scholars, 1997.

Whitelam, Keith W. "Between History and Literature: The Social Production of Israel's Traditions of Origin." *SJOT* 2 (1991) 60–74.

————. *The Just King: Monarchical Judicial Authority in Ancient Israel*. JSOTSup 12. Sheffield: JSOT Press, 1979.

————. "King and Kingship." In *ABD* 4:40–48.

Whitmeyer, Joseph M. "Endogamy As a Basis for Ethnic Behavior." *Sociological Theory* 15, no. 2 (1997) 162–78.

Whitt, William D. "The Divorce of Yahweh and Asherah in Hos 2.4—7.12ff." *SJOT* 6 (1992) 31–67.

Whybray, R. N. *The Book of Proverbs: A Survey of Modern Study*. History of Biblical Interpretation 1. Leiden: Brill, 1995.

————. "City Life in Proverbs 1–9." In *"Jedes Ding hat seine Zeit . . .": Studien zur israelitischen und altorientalischen Weisheit, Diethelm Michel zum 65. Geburtstag*. Edited by Anja A. Diesel, Reinhard G. Lehmann, Eckart Otto, and Andreas Wagner, 243–50. BZAW 241. Berlin: de Gruyter, 1996.

————. *Wealth and Poverty in the Book of Proverbs*. JSOTSup 99. Sheffield: Sheffield Academic, 1990.

Widom, Cathy Spatz, and Joseph B. Kuhns. "Childhood Victimization and Subsequent Risk for Promiscuity, Prostitution, and Teenage Pregnancy:

A Prospective Study." *American Journal of Public Health* 86, no. 11 (1996) 1607–12.

Wikan, Unni. *Behind the Veil in Arabia. Women in Oman.* Chicago: Univ. of Chicago Press, 1984.

———. "Shame and Honor: A Contestable Pair." *Man* 19 (1984) 635–52.

Wilkie, J. M. "Nabonidus and the Later Jewish Exiles." *JTS* 2 (1951) 36–44.

Williamson, H. G. M. "The Concept of Israel in Transition." In *The World of Ancient Israel: Sociological, Anthropological and Political Perspectives.* Edited by R. E. Clements, 141–61. Cambridge: Cambridge Univ. Press, 1989.

———. *Ezra and Nehemiah.* OTG. Sheffield: Sheffield Academic, 1987.

———. *Ezra, Nehemiah.* WBC 16. Waco: Word, 1985.

———. "Jezreel in the Biblical Texts." *Tel Aviv* 18 (1991) 72–92.

Wilson, Robert R. *Sociological Approaches to the Old Testament.* GBS. Philadelphia: Fortress Press, 1984.

Winter, Urs. *Frau und Göttin: Exegetische und ikonographische Studien zum weiblichen Gottesbild im Alten Israel und in dessen Umwelt.* OBO 53. Göttingen: Vandenhoeck & Ruprecht, 1983.

Wiseman, D. J. "Babylonia 605–539 B.C." In *Cambridge Ancient History.* Vol. 3. Edited by John Boardman, 229–51. 2nd ed. Cambridge: Cambridge Univ. Press, 1991.

Wittenberg, Gunther. H. "Amos and Hosea: A Contribution to the Problem of the 'Prophetenschweigen' in the Deuteronomistic History (Dtr)." *OTE* 6 (1993) 295–311.

———. "The Ideological/Materialist Approach to the Old Testament." *OTE* 7 (1994) 167–72.

———. "King Solomon and the Theologians." *Journal of Theology for Southern Africa* 63 (1988) 16–29.

———. "The Situational Context of Statements concerning Poverty and Wealth in the Book of Proverbs." *Scriptura* 21 (1987) 1–23.

Wolf, Margery. "Chinese Women: Old Skills in a New Context." In *Woman, Culture, and Society.* Edited by Michelle Zimbalist Rosaldo and Louise Lamphere, 157–72. Stanford: Stanford Univ. Press, 1974.

Wolff, Hans Walter. *Hosea.* Trans. Gary Stansell. Hermeneia. Philadelphia: Fortress Press, 1974.

———. "'Wissen um Gott' bei Hosea als Urform von Theologie." In *Gesammelte Studien zum Alten Testament,* 182–205. ThBü 22. Munich: Kaiser, 1964.

Woudstra, Marten. "The Everlasting Covenant in Ezekiel 16:59–63." *Calvin Theological Journal* 6 (1971) 22–48.

Wyatt, Nicholas. "Interpreting the Creation and Fall Story in Genesis 2–3." *ZAW* 93 (1981) 10–21.

————. "When Adam Delved: The Meaning of Genesis iii 23." *VT* 38 (1988) 117–22.

Yadin, Yigael. *The Art of Warfare in Biblical Lands.* Trans. M. Pearlman, 2 vols. New York: McGraw-Hill, 1963.

Yamauchi, Edwin M. "Cultic Prostitution: A Case Study in Cultural Diffusion." In *Orient and Occident: Essays Presented to Cyrus H. Gordon.* Edited by Harry A. Hoffner, 213–22. AOAT 22. Neukirchen-Vluyn: Neukirchener Verlag, 1973.

Yee, Gale A. "An Analysis of Prov 8:22-31 According to Style and Structure." *ZAW* 94 (1982) 58–66.

————. "The Author/Text/Reader and Power: Suggestions for a Critical Framework in Biblical Studies." In *Reading from This Place.* Vol. 1: *Social Location and Biblical Interpretation in the United States.* Edited by Fernando F. Segovia and Mary Ann Tolbert, 109–18. Minneapolis: Fortress Press, 1995.

————. "The Book of Hosea: Introduction, Commentary, and Reflections." In *NIB* 7:195–297. Nashville: Abingdon, 1996.

————. "'By the Hand of a Woman': The Biblical Metaphor of the Woman Warrior." *Semeia* 61 (1993) 99–132.

————. *Composition and Tradition in the Book of Hosea: A Redaction Critical Investigation.* SBLDS 102. Atlanta: Scholars, 1987.

————. "Gender, Class, and the Social-Scientific Study of Genesis 2–3." *Semeia* 87 (1999) 177–92.

————. "Hosea." In *The Women's Bible Commentary.* Edited by Carol A. Newsom and Sharon H. Ringe, 207–15. Rev. ed. Louisville: Westminster John Knox, 1998.

————. "'I Have Perfumed My Bed with Myrrh': The Foreign Woman in Proverbs 1–9." *JSOT* 43 (1989) 53–68.

————. "Ideological Criticism." In *Dictionary of Biblical Interpretation.* Edited by John H. Hayes, 1:534–37. 2 vols. Nashville: Abingdon, 1999.

————. "Ideological Criticism: Judges 17–21 and the Dismembered Body." In *Judges and Method: New Approaches in Biblical Studies.* Edited by Gale A. Yee, 146–70. Minneapolis: Fortress Press, 1995.

————. "'She Is Not My Wife, and I Am Not Her Husband': A Materialist Analysis of Hosea 1–2." *BibInt* 9 (2001) 345–83.

————. "A Socio-Literary Production of the Foreign Woman in Proverbs." In *A Feminist Companion to Wisdom Literature.* Edited by Athalya Brenner, 127–30. FCB 9. Sheffield: Sheffield Academic, 1995.

Yoder, Christine Roy. *Wisdom As a Woman of Substance: A Socioeconomic Reading of Proverbs 1–9 and 31:10-31.* BZAW 304. Berlin: de Gruyter, 2001.

Young, T. Cuyler, Jr. "Cyrus." In *ABD* 1:1231–32.

Yuval-Davis, Nira, and Floya Anthias, eds. *Woman—Nation—State.* New York: St. Martin's, 1989.

Zeid, Abou A. M. "Honour and Shame among the Bedouins of Egypt." In *Honour and Shame: The Values of Mediterranean Society*. Edited by J. G. Peristiany, 243–59. Chicago: Univ. of Chicago Press, 1966.

Zevit, Ziony. "The Khirbet el-Qôm Inscription Mentioning a Goddess." *BASOR* 255 (1984) 39–47.

Zimmerli, Walther. *Ezekiel 1*. Translated by Ronald E. Clements. Hermeneia. Philadelphia: Fortress Press, 1979.

———. *Ezekiel 2*. Translated by James D. Martin. Hermeneia. Philadelphia: Fortress Press, 1983.

Zinner, Ellen S., and Mary Beth Williams, eds. *When a Community Weeps: Case Studies in Group Survivorship*. Series in Trauma and Loss. Philadelphia: Brunner/Mazel, 1999.

Index of Ancient Sources

Index of Authors

Index of Subjects

Abraham, 53–54, 180n. 104
Achsah, 50
Adultery: death penalty laws for, 65–66; and honor and shame value system, 47–48; Oholibah's punishment in Ezekiel, 130–32, 218n. 133; wife's punishment in Hosea, 103–4, 203n. 132, 204n. 133
Ahab, 2, 102
Amalekites, 62
Ammonites, 62
Amos, 85
Artaxerxes I, 140, 142–43, 145, 146
Asherah, 86–87, 96–97, 195n. 41, 196n. 48
Ashurnasirpal, 115, 129–30, 137
Asian American women, 159–60
Assyria, 85, 124–26, 137–38, 217n. 103
Awlad 'Ali bedouin: and honor/shame model, 41, 43–44; patrilineality and family hierarchies of, 37–38, 39–40, 43–44, 54–55, 179n. 95; separate women's community of, 54–55

Baal, 86, 93–94, 97, 107, 196n. 48, 202n. 105
Bedouin, 37, 39–40, 54–55. *See also* Awlad 'Ali bedouin
Ben Sira, 136
bêt 'āb, 35, 56, 174n. 23

Cain, 75
Cambyses, 139
Colonial relations. *See* Ezekiel's revisionist history of Israel and Judah; Israel, colonial; Proverbs and postexilic period intermarriage issues
Cult in eighth-century Israel: Asherah cult, 86–87, 96–97, 195n. 41, 196n. 48; and book of Hosea, 85–89, 95, 96–97; Canaanite deities, 86–87; and conflicts within Israelite polytheism, 85–89; and development of monotheism, 86, 92–95; Hosea and women's popular religion, 96–97; and Hosea's polemical monolatry, 86, 94–95, 96–97, 99, 107–8, 162; interweaving of state and,